MINORITY RELATIONS

MINORITY RELATIONS

Intergroup Conflict and Cooperation

Edited by Greg Robinson and Robert S. Chang

UNIVERSITY PRESS OF MISSISSIPPI / JACKSON

www.upress.state.ms.us

The University Press of Mississippi is a member of the
Association of American University Presses.

First printing 2017

∞

Library of Congress Cataloging-in-Publication Data

Names: Robinson, Greg, 1966– editor, author. | Chang, Robert S., editor,
author.
Title: Minority relations : intergroup conflict and cooperation / edited by
Greg Robinson and Robert S. Chang.
Description: Jackson : University Press of Mississippi, 2017. | Includes
bibliographical references and index.
Identifiers: LCCN 2016029292 (print) | LCCN 2016044219 (ebook) | ISBN
9781496810458 (hardcover : alk. paper) | ISBN 9781496810465 (epub single)
| ISBN 9781496810472 (epub institutional) | ISBN 9781496810489 (pdf
single) | ISBN 9781496810496 (pdf institutional)
Subjects: LCSH: Minorities—United States. | United States—Ethnic relations.
| United States—Race relations. | Minorities—United States—Social
conditions.
Classification: LCC E184.A1 M5448 2016 (print) | LCC E184.A1 (ebook) | DDC
305.800973—dc23
LC record available at https://lccn.loc.gov/2016029292

British Library Cataloging-in-Publication Data available

CONTENTS

ACKNOWLEDGMENTS

The creation of this book has been a long process, and we—Greg Robinson and Robert S. Chang—have received a large amount of help and encouragement along the way. First, we want to recognize the Fred T. Korematsu Center for Law and Equality at Seattle University Law School. The Korematsu Center created the book project, funded the participation of scholars as Korematsu Fellows, and provided for the workshops that brought the contributors together to work on their submissions. We want to single out Lorraine K. Bannai and Margaret Chon for their commitment to the center and our project.

We owe thanks to Craig Gill and the staff of the University Press of Mississippi for agreeing to publish this book and for their patience and flexibility. We also want to thank Ranjit Arab, senior acquisitions editor at the University of Washington Press. Although we did not end up publishing with the University of Washington Press, Ranjit pushed our manuscript and offered useful suggestions on its form. Jean-Francis Clermont-Legros helped prepare the book's index.

Greg Robinson also wants to thank Thanapat Porjit for moral support and research assistance, and family members Ed Robinson, Ellen Fine, Deborah Malamud, Neal Plotkin, Alex Robinson-Gilden, Bob Sandler, and Ann Dwornik for love and encouragement. Heng Wee Tan offered continuing support. Greg also wishes to offer the book in fond memory of a number of late activist friends who provide continuing inspiration: Frank Emi, Ernest Iiyama, Yuri Kochiyama, Setsuko Matsunaga Nishi, Shinkichi Tajiri, Paul Takagi, and Hisaye Yamamoto.

EDITORS' INTRODUCTION

"Can We All Get Along?"

When Koreatown burned in Los Angeles in April 1992, many people puzzled over this eruption of anger and violence directed against Koreans and Korean Americans. After all, the spark was a jury's acquittal of four white police officers for the beating of Rodney King, an African American. How did white-on-black violence, committed by those cloaked with literal badges of power, and made worse when a mostly white jury found it to not be illegal, lead to the burning of Koreatown? Did Korean Americans just get caught in the middle? Or was there more? At the same time, the conflagration was widely characterized in the popular media as a black-Korean conflict, an example of racial hatred.

Symposia and conferences were held; books were written. We learned that, in some ways, Korean Americans did find themselves caught in the middle of the larger, long-standing paradigmatic race conflict, and one that went beyond simple black-white binaries. We also learned, though, that Korean Americans were not simply innocent bystanders in America's complicated story of race and class. Rather, blacks, Asian Americans, and other racialized groups have a long, complex history of interactions, including both alliances against discrimination and conflict. And while our understanding of that particular place and time deepened, we're not sure that anybody really knows how to answer Rodney King's plaintive plea during the LA riots/rebellion/ unrest, "Can we all get along?"

With Rodney King's question operating in the fore- and background, the Intergroup Conflict and Cooperation Project began during the summer of 2010 at the newly launched Fred T. Korematsu Center for Law and Equality at Seattle University School of Law. The project was initiated by the Korematsu Center's director, Robert Chang, who invited the historian Greg Robinson to collaborate on framing the issues. The two agreed on a set of guiding questions regarding past and present connections between and among groups generally considered "minorities," with the goal of stimulating informed debate:

1. What causes individuals to experience conflict or cooperation in group interactions and settings?
2. What are the social considerations underlying group conflict or cooperation?
3. How does law underwrite or disrupt intergroup conflict or cooperation?
4. If group or collective identity is experienced along racial lines, how do other axes such as class, gender, sexuality, and disability impact the dynamics of conflict/cooperation?

Chang and Robinson then brought together a group of scholars from different backgrounds and disciplines as nonresident faculty fellows at the Korematsu Center and asked them to participate in workshops in which they would present papers that would engage with the set of questions we had developed. Half were law school faculty, and half were primarily based in social science disciplines outside legal studies. The choice of these scholars was based on the outstanding nature of their work and their potential for fruitful interaction with the other fellows. (It must be said that the co-conveners had extraordinary good fortune in being able to secure the participation of virtually all the individuals originally marked as first choices for the two workshops—a veritable academic "dream team" of scholars.)

Including the co-conveners, the group of scholars from law schools were:

Taunya Lovell Banks, who writes about the continuing impact of gender, race, racial formation, and racial hierarchies on the quest for social equality;

Devon W. Carbado, who writes in the areas of critical race theory, employment discrimination, criminal procedure, constitutional law, and identity;

Robert Chang, who writes in the areas of race and interethnic relations, including the areas of critical race theory, LatCrit theory, and Asian American legal studies;

Tanya Katerí Hernández, who writes in the areas of comparative civil rights, employment discrimination, critical race theory, Latin American studies, Latino studies, and ethnic studies;

Eric Yamamoto, who works and writes in the areas of civil rights and racial justice, with an emphasis on redress for historic injustice.

The group of social science scholars located outside of law schools included:

Cheryl Greenberg, who writes in the areas of African American history, race and ethnicity in the United States, twentieth-century US history, and civil rights;

Scott Kurashige, who writes in the areas of Asian American history, US urban history, comparative race and ethnicity, African American history, and social movements;

Greg Robinson, who writes primarily in the areas of Asian American history, US political history, and transnational North American studies;

Stephen Steinberg, who writes in the area of sociology of race and ethnicity in the United States;

Clarence Walker, who writes in the areas of black American history: 1450–present; nineteenth-century social and political history of the United States; and history of sexuality, film, and popular culture.

The group of fellows was initially divided into two teams. Each team mixed legal scholars and social scientists, most of whom had never previously met. These teams attended separate two-day workshops at Seattle University in summer 2011, with the co-conveners present at both. Before the workshops began, the participants each wrote a preliminary conference paper–size draft of their papers, which they then circulated. Another participant was then predesignated as discussion leader for that paper. Each paper was then presented during the workshops and was discussed at length by all those present. There was a general consensus among the group that the workshops offered both a fun and productive means of thinking about the different subjects

and obtaining useful feedback. Once the workshops were completed, all
the fellows were invited to expand their drafts into final chapters, with help
from the comments they had received. The expanded drafts then circulated
among the entire group, including members of the other team.

The final result is a collection that sets forth in profound fashion some of
the issues involved in the interplay among members of various racial, ethnic,
and sexual minorities. The essays, all of which (with a single exception)
are original works specifically commissioned for this volume, build on the
particular research and expertise of the legal scholars and social scientists
chosen to participate. The volume is not intended to be comprehensive, nor
could it be, given the enormous size of the field of interminority relations
and the lack of existing literature devoted to it. Rather, the collection is designed as an introduction to stimulate further thinking and writing by social
scientists, legal scholars, and policy makers on the nature of interminority
connections, and more particularly on the nature and limits of intergroup
cooperation and coalition building.

Indeed, the question of how relations between marginalized groups are
inflected by their common (and sometimes competing) search for equal
rights has gained a new importance as demographic projections make it
possible now to imagine a future majority population of color in the United
States.[1] This news has generated mixed reactions. In some communities, the
coming majority of color exists as a specter, the new bogeyman that strikes
fear into the hearts of whites afraid of no longer being the majority.[2] In other
communities, it has engendered new hope that the democratic process that
had allowed white dominance to reign supreme for most of this nation's
history might now be used, not for what might otherwise be regarded as
fair turnabout, but to achieve finally the equality so long promised. The
reason that our discussion of alliances is so vital is that, for marginalized
groups, coalition building seems to offer a privileged pathway to addressing
economic discrimination and reaching some measure of justice with regard
to opportunities and outcomes. The need for coalitions is also an acknowledgment of the limitations of the democratic process, especially given that
racialized groups have faced significant difficulty gaining any real political
power through the ballot box, despite such legislation as the 1965 Voting
Rights Act.[3]

To be sure, racial minorities are not the only groups to seek allies, and
coalition building is more than simply a strategy of access to resources. For
groups as diverse as Americans with disabilities, Jews, and LGBT communities, for example, coalition building has served to overcome social isolation

as well as political powerlessness, and to shift public discourse about their right to equal treatment in order to achieve outcomes that they could not easily accomplish by themselves.

Although the chapters in this volume were not commissioned with any agenda or limitation on subject matter, the final collection divides naturally into three parts, each of which addresses common sets of questions. Part I: The Theoretical Terrain is devoted to exploring how relations among minorities fit into theoretical models of race relations and into the sociology of intergroup relations. In Part II: Episodes, a group of scholars take up particular instances of comparative and interactive history. Their contributions focus on the coalitional politics that arise among different groups, including both their successes and limitations. In Part III: Challenges, the authors move back from distinct incidents or episodes and bring together more long-range and theoretically informed reflections on intergroup connections.

Part I begins with a chapter by Robert Chang, who proposes an analytic model for understanding conflict and coalition on the terrain of race. He then discusses racialization and racial stratification. Chang concludes by discussing the limits of building coalitions in a purely oppositional mode and explores the need for building common cause that extends beyond opposition to white capitalist patriarchy.

Eric Yamamoto and Amanda Jenssen, in "The Power Dynamics of Color on Color: Grappling with Grievances to Forge Alliances," then take a hard look at what the media has characterized as America's "interminority problem." Yamamoto and Jenssen show that the persistent desire for alliance forging often leads theorists and advocates to target what might be characterized as a "common ground" approach that focuses on common issues—"'bread and butter' issues like wages and discrimination while largely avoiding the difficult interrogation of 'the ragged history of power-sharing' and the 'broad ignorance' of one another's culture and social and economic conditions." The common issues are seized upon as opportunities to build bridges and relationships. While such an approach might have some success in the short term, Yamamoto and Jenssen argue that this approach has a tendency to neglect "to deal with [the deeper grievances] honestly and self-critically." They offer a more nuanced approach using the theoretical concepts of *simultaneity* and *differentiation*:

> *Simultaneity* examines the roots of group grievance by interrogating
> historically situated group power arrangements, particularly where a

group now may be simultaneously, in differing ways, oppressed and partial oppressor....

> [D]ifferentiation offers insight into how groups acquire different identities and why differing degrees of political and economic power [and powerlessness] accrue to those identities.

Yamamoto and Jenssen explore these theoretical concepts and suggest concrete ways to apply them.

Part II starts with Cheryl Greenberg's contribution, "Civil Rights, Free Speech, and Group Libel," which examines the contrasting efforts of organizations representing two marginalized groups, blacks and Jews, to counter defamation. In the end, civil rights advocates from both groups came to the conclusion, on a mixture of principled and pragmatic grounds, that it was wiser not to push for adoption of laws against "group libel," such as those that characterize post-Holocaust Europe and Canada. Yet both groups were forced to wrestle with how to organize and justify protest campaigns against bigoted media representations, including threats of economic reprisals, while refuting charges of censorship. Greenberg's essay reminds us that the absolute embrace of free speech in the United States after World War II was far from inevitable.

Taunya Lovell Banks's contribution, "Race, Place, and Historic Moment— Black and Japanese American World War II Veterans: The GI Bill of Rights and the Model Minority Myth," likewise offers a comparative history of minority communities, in this case the impact of the Servicemen's Readjustment Act of 1944 (better known as the GI Bill of Rights). Banks addresses the reasons why Japanese American World War II veterans were able to make greater use of the benefits offered by the law to broker their group's postwar social advancement, while black veterans were restricted in their enjoyment of its advantages. In addition to more potent discrimination against blacks in areas such as housing, one salient distinction between the groups that Banks points to is their differing educational preparation, which led to comparatively greater use by Japanese Americans of the college benefits available under the bill.

Scott Kurashige, in "Re-reading Vincent Chin: Asian Americans and Multiracial Political Analysis," offers a new look at the Vincent Chin case. Chin was a young Chinese American from the Detroit area whose beating death at the hands of two white men in 1982, and the light sentences they received at trial, sparked widespread outrage among Asian Americans and helped catalyze Asian American political organizing. Kurashige pushes readers to move beyond the received ideas in the established narrative about Chin's murder and to understand how the particular spatial, gender, and class dynamics of Detroit influenced the case. In particular, he details the important involvement of African Americans in the case.

Like Kurashige, Greg Robinson, in "The Paradox of Reparations: Japanese Americans and African Americans at the Crossroads of Alliance and Conflict," offers a more complex and multiracial view of history. Robinson revisits the narrative of the Japanese American redress movement and discovers a paradox at its heart: while the campaign by Japanese Americans for reparations for their wartime confinement started at the end of the 1960s as part of a wider antiracist coalition, and received key support in its early stages from African American political leaders, Japanese Americans increasingly distanced themselves from their black allies as the goal of redress grew nearer, even as African Americans became increasingly public in their opposition. Yet the victory of the redress movement in 1988 offered a major precedent, and a model, for reparations efforts by blacks.

Part III opens with a bold revisionist study by Stephen Steinberg. In "The Birth and Death of Affirmative Action: Is Resurrection Possible?" Steinberg argues that the fatal flaw of the discourse on affirmative action is that it treats affirmative action as an ahistorical aberration. By reconstructing the history of efforts to offer compensation for past discrimination to African Americans, Steinberg reveals that the most sustained and formidable opposition did not stem from WASP conservatives. Rather, it was Jewish intellectuals such as Sidney Hook and Nathan Glazer, who were involved as contributors to Commentary magazine, who devised the anti–affirmative action discourse adopted by later neoconservatives. Steinberg offers as well an analysis of the chances for a revival of affirmative action under the current political system in America.

Tanya Katerí Hernández, in her essay "Segregated Together: Latino-Black Interethnic Conflict," discusses the complex and troubled history of interethnic violence between blacks and Latinos. Hernández compares prevailing conditions in areas such as New York's Staten Island, where the chief violence is perpetrated by African Americans on Latinos, and California, where the opposite pattern prevails, and examines the asserted justifications made by the authors of such violence. She concludes that the constant force in reproducing such violent behavior, irrespective of the group responsible, is the surrounding conditions of race-based poverty and residential segregation.

Clarence Walker urges a revision of history. He argues that one of the barriers to coalition building among subordinated groups results from a fragmentation of history. He locates part of this in something that might be described as black exceptionalism, stating: "As it is currently written, the history of black people during this period [1865–1965] of political, social, cultural, and economic change remains largely exceptional, treated as different from the history of Chinese, Mexican, and Japanese Americans during the last third of the nineteenth century and the first six decades of the twentieth century." Walker argues convincingly that to have a more complete and accurate idea of their own history, African Americans must study their connections to other racialized groups.

Devon Carbado, in "Gay Is the New White (Gay Is the New Straight)," issues a challenge to the misappropriation of African American civil rights struggles by white LGBT advocates who present themselves in simple-minded form as the victims of discrimination akin to that (by implication past and resolved) suffered by blacks, and, in the process, continue "to marginalize the experiences of African Americans who are LGBT." In some ways, Carbado takes up the warning issued by scholars such as Trina Grillo and Stephanie Wildman early in the development of critical race theory literature about the seductive dangers of analogies.

While the essays in this volume do not speak with one voice, either in form or point of view, they do point to a common conclusion about the limits of a politics built around minority identity. As the authors of several of the chapters in this book state explicitly or implicitly, identity is both overinclusive and underinclusive as an organizing principle for politics. Despite their common status as minorities, the particular views and priorities of the groups involved can differ widely. For example, in opposing English-only policies or immigration restrictions, Asian Americans and Latinos sometimes find themselves in coalition against whites and blacks. In support of affirmative action, by contrast, Latinos and blacks sometimes find themselves in opposition to whites and Asian Americans. What is more, there may not be a common sense of self-interest even within those considered as the same group. Cuban Americans and Vietnamese Americans have a history of favoring Republicans, while other Hispanic and ethnic Asian populations lean Democrat. The divisions may not even break along subgroup lines. In the affirmative action case before the US Supreme Court during the 2012 October term, *Fisher v. University of Texas at Austin*, we find that Asian American groups submitted amicus (friend of the court) briefs both for and against affirmative action. By speaking as Asian American organizations, each claimed to speak for or represent the particular interests of Asian Americans.

In the end, our authors suggest, such coalitions that exist, whatever their ideological cover, tend to form and dissipate around specific political exigencies and areas of self-interest. Stephen Steinberg reminds us that, even amid a long history of Jewish support for African Americans against Jim Crow, leading Jewish intellectuals quickly turned to attack any form of affirmative action as against their own group interest. A related point, and one that is also touched on by several authors, is that identity politics can be as much a source of contestation as connection among minorities, particularly when access to resources or status is involved. Greg Robinson posits this conflict as stemming from the operation of racial stratification: "[I]n the face of a dominant culture of white supremacy, which generates and reproduces inequality through laws based on racial distinctions, it is tempting and sometimes profitable for members of a racialized group to identify themselves with the white population and to seek equality by distancing themselves from more identifiably nonwhite minorities."[4] Yet as Devon Carbado demonstrates in his discussion of the friction between African American and LGBT activists over their claims to the mantle of civil rights, such competition need not even involve racial identity.

To be sure, even pragmatic coalitions that grow out of minority group self-interest might be understood as an expansive form of identity politics. Still, such coalitions remain strong insofar as those involved are able to discover together a common experience that results in common interests (or common interests that result in a common identity). The most successful cases of such interminority connections, like the postwar alliance for legal equality between blacks and Japanese Americans, seem to have had the extra component of empathy. While during World War II a number of black activists and journalists expressed sympathy for Japanese Americans stripped of their property and herded into government camps on a racial basis, the most durable relationships between individuals and organizations from the two commuties formed in the period after the war, when members of both groups were largely restricted to housing in ghetto areas and faced similar discrimination in employment and public accommodations. Once Japanese Americans were able to overcome the barriers against them, they literally left their old neighbors behind, and their fledgling political alliance began to decay. It is not evident how to foster such empathy or compassion among members of minority groups, especially those who lack effective tools for articulating their experience in the public sphere, but it does seem a vital element in securing durable intergroup understanding, no less among the various minorities than between each group and the dominant society.

Empathy requires both knowledge of the self and the other. Without self- and other-knowledge, we are left with what Clarence Walker describes as fragmented histories that do not support connections between different groups or durable coalitions. We are left with fleeting moments when evanescent multiracial coalitions coalesce around the cause of the day, whether it be Rodney King or, more recently, Trayvon Martin. It is too early to know whether the racially informed police shootings of Michael Brown in Ferguson, Missouri, or of Eric Garner in Staten Island will lead to the kind of deeper intergroup understanding that can develop into positive change. Our hope is that this collection will lead readers to wrestle with the questions posed to the various authors, and that the insights the contributors arrive at through their scholarly discussions will help readers deepen their own self- and other-knowledge.

NOTES

1. *See* PETER BRIMELOW, ALIEN NATION: COMMON SENSE ABOUT AMERICA'S IMMIGRATION DISASTER (1995).

2. *Id.*

3. *See generally* LANI GUINIER, THE TYRANNY OF THE MAJORITY: FUNDAMENTAL FAIRNESS IN REPRESENTATIVE DEMOCRACY (1994).

4. Greg Robinson and Toni Robinson, *The Limits of Interracial Coalition: Mendez v. Westminster Reconsidered, in* RACIAL (TRANS)FORMATIONS: LATINOS AND ASIANS REMAKING THE UNITED STATES 119 (Nicholas De Genova ed., 2006).

Part I

THEORETICAL TERRAIN

1

An Analytic Model of Conflict and Cooperation
on the Terrain of Race

ROBERT S. CHANG

In this chapter, I explore conflict and cooperation between and within minority communities. I begin by offering an analytic model for understanding
conflict and coalition on the terrain of race. I then discuss racialization and
racial stratification. I conclude by discussing the limits of building coalitions
in a purely oppositional mode and explore the need for building common
cause that extends beyond opposition to white capitalist patriarchy.

Against the backdrop of conflict between members of minority communities, white supremacy often gets lost. Despite calls by scholars such as
Charles Lawrence to talk about racism in terms of white supremacy,[1] there is
a tendency in scholarship on race to focus on what I describe as first-order
binary and second-order binary analyses.

In this analytic model of first-, second-, and third-order racial analyses,
the first-order binary model restates the duality of the primary racial opposition in US history—black and white—and recognizes that many analyses
of racial and ethnic conflict follow this basic majority-minority binary opposition. Commentaries and analyses that focus upon majority-minority
relations are first-order binary analyses.

There is nothing wrong with such scholarship unless it purports to constitute the entire analysis of the way racism works to subordinate all groups.
For example, too great a focus on the relationship between whites and blacks
can lead to pushback in the form of a critique of such scholarship. Such a
critique typically includes two components: a critique of the black/white
paradigm as incomplete, which may then provide the space for the analysis
of the relationship between the dominant group and minority B.[2] Though
a second (or third or fourth) minority group has been introduced, I would
still describe this as a first-order binary race analysis, and in the aggregate,
as multiple first-order binary analyses.[3]

Second-order binary analysis stays within a group-to-group binary framework, but looks at the relationship between minority A and minority B. Scholarship using a second-order binary analysis might include rudimentary comparative racialization, a comparison of the similarities and differences between minority A's and minority B's experience with oppression.[4] Sometimes this comparison is characterized as or in fact devolves into a squabble between minority A and minority B over which group is the most oppressed.[5] An example of the former is the one that reportedly took place on President Clinton's national commission on race between John Hope Franklin and Angela Oh over the scope of their investigation. It was reported that Oh commented, "We need to go beyond [black-white relations in America] because the world is about more than that," to which John Hope Franklin responded, "This country cut its eyeteeth on black-white relations."[6]

Mari Matsuda's description of what took place is helpful: "There is a reason why historian John Hope Franklin's admonition that we must learn the history of white over black is seen as oppositional to Angela Oh's admonition that we must remember the unique issues facing a largely immigrant Asian American community. As long as the mainstream press can frame this as an opposition, it can deflect discussion from the core issue of white supremacy."[7] The lesson is that care must be taken when doing second-order binary analysis not to lose sight of the larger political, legal, and social forces that foster conflict between minority groups. In the American context, one must never lose sight of white supremacy.

Another example of second-order binary analysis comes from Tanya Hernandez, commenting on racial violence between Latinas/os and African Americans that is "acrimonious" and "growing hard to ignore."[8] We are told that there is a trend of "Latino ethnic cleansing of African Americans from multiracial neighborhoods."[9] We hear of a "black-versus-Latino race riot at Chino state prison."[10] She appears to engage in second-order binary analysis to try to understand the conflict between Latinas/os and African Americans in Los Angeles. Her title, "Roots of Latino/Black Anger: Longtime Prejudices, Not Economic Rivalry, Fuel Tensions," gives away her punch line. Though mindful of other explanations—labor market competition, tensions arising from changing demographics in neighborhoods, Latinos "learning the U.S. lesson of anti-black racism," or resentment by blacks of "having the benefits of the civil rights movement extended to Latinos"[11]—she locates the roots of anti-black racism among Latinos in Latin America and the Caribbean.[12] While I agree with her conclusion that minority groups must address their own racism, I also agree with Taunya Banks, who in the context of black-Asian relations stated that the "[r]enunciation of simultaneous racism alone, however, will not foster racial coalitions between Asians and Blacks."[13] Further, I worry that the big picture, how the relationship among minority groups is structured by white supremacy, might be lost.

Trying to understand, avoid, exploit, or resolve such conflicts can lead to what I call third-order multigroup analysis. I want to emphasize here that any of these analyses, including third-order multigroup analysis, can serve subordination or antisubordination efforts. I set forth how an understanding of racialization and racial stratification lends itself to third-order multigroup analysis.

With regard to Asian Americans, Yen Le Espiritu offers the notion of panethnicity as a way to theorize an Asian American group that arises out of multiple ethnic or national origin subgroups.[14] She develops this theory of panethnicity against the background of sociological theories of ethnicities.[15] Panethnic Asian Americanness is offered as an oppositional identity that is a product of discrimination but which includes a political aspiration, offering its members some instrumental benefits, including what comes from being part of a larger group. One limitation, though, is that she does not develop themes of black-Asian conflict or coalition in this work. She notes at the beginning a possible comparison of Asian Americans and other groups—Latinas/os, Native Americans, and African Americans—but the comparisons are not developed. Further, comparison is complicated because the relationship between panethnicity and race is not worked out. I would characterize this work as being a first-order binary analysis. As with many first-order binary analyses, it is excellent for what it does, but is limited with regard to what it can tell us about the relationship of multiple groups in racially stratified America.

Neil Gotanda has developed a theory of Asiatic racialization that adapts and modifies ethnic categories and existing understandings of black-white racialization.[16] An examination of the federal and Supreme Court cases in the era of Chinese exclusion reveals that the federal courts modified their understanding of the Chinese category. After initially considering "Chinese" as a term of national origin or national citizenship, Congress definitively adopted a racial understanding—"Chinese" refers to any person of Chinese ancestry—a form of bloodline categorization. To that category, however, foreignness—a permanent condition of inassimilability and disloyalty—becomes the primary racial trait. Foreignness was the assigned racial trait or racial profile rather than any notion of biological or cultural inferiority. The basic method of legal analysis—finding foreignness embedded in judicial decisions and other legal materials—has been developed by other authors writing on Asian Americans and the law.[17]

While this theory of Asiatic racialization by itself is first-order binary, this model is explicitly intended to provide a common language of racialization that permits a comparative analysis around white supremacy. Because the Chinese category is racialized and the primary attribute of foreignness is assigned to the Chinese-Asiatic body, this racialization is similar to historical black-white racialization. The structurally similar bases for racialization offer a theoretical basis for building racial coalitions. As an immediate political platform, such an analysis does not provide immediate common interests as a basis for coalition. But a presentation of foreignness as a racial profile inscribed on Asiatic bodies does provide the beginnings of a common language of racialization that is then available for antiracist politics, something that panethnicity does not do. On the contrary, panethnicity has the danger, like other ethnicity theories, of being organized around a common language of assimilation.[18]

Assimilation is the great promise offered by proponents of the model minority designation for Asian Americans. Thinking through it as a multigroup analysis may offer some theoretical clarity. Here, the idea of racial triangulation holds much promise, especially as advanced by Claire Jean Kim, a political scientist. Her work on black-Korean conflict developed a mapping of blacks, Asian Americans, and whites against two axes—Superior-Inferior and Foreigner-Insider.[19] In this model, whites hold the most privileged position along the Superior-Inferior axis and a coequal position as insiders with blacks on the Foreigner-Insider axis. In contrast, blacks hold the least privileged position along the Superior-Inferior axis, while Asian Americans hold a middle position along the Superior-Inferior axis and the least privileged position as foreigners on the Foreigner-Insider axis. Central to Kim's project is the attention paid to the relationship between blacks and Asian Americans in relation to the white position.

Racial triangulation in the form of inverted triangles can help us to understand the following three examples of third-order multigroup analysis. Depending on the issue, a different group is placed on a horizontal plane of formal equivalence with whites. The triangle is a useful device to emphasize the issues at stake in the coalition and helps to avoid collapsing the politics into a false binary. The triangulation diagram demonstrates the issue-specific way that the invitation to whiteness (actual, honorary, or formal) or Americanness is issued, and highlights the inconsistencies and the hypocrisies.

Example 1—Asian Americans as a Model Minority or "Honorary" Whites

William Petersen, the Berkeley, California, demographer who is credited with coining the phrase "model minority," offered the success of Japanese Americans, who overcame the hurdles of racism through their hard work and culture, as a model for "non-achieving" blacks and Chicanos.[20] Petersen's efforts were directed against Lyndon Johnson's Great Society programs. More recently, Asian Americans were inserted into the debate over affirmative action as a model minority in coalition with whites and therefore in opposition to blacks and Latinas/os.[21]

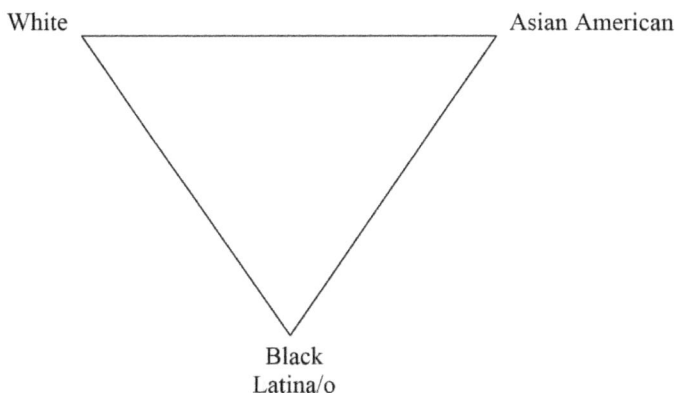

White   Asian American

Black
Latina/o

Figure 1.1. Asian Americans as a model minority.

As discussed earlier, Asian Americans are invited to join whites along a common horizontal plain, in opposition to blacks and Latinas/os at the bottom point of the inverted triangle. Neoconservative politicians and thinkers advocate for the rights of Asian Americans as victims of affirmative action policies, thus insulating themselves from charges of racism for their opposition to affirmative action. Using Sumi Cho's term, Asian Americans become "racial mascots" for whites in this political maneuver.[22]

Some Asian Americans have accepted this invitation, as evidenced by the Asian American groups signing on to amicus briefs opposing affirmative action, failing to recognize that the minority status in "model minority" includes the possibility of negative action, such as the treatment of Asian Americans in admissions to elite institutions of higher education.[23]

ROBERT S. CHANG

Example 2—Blacks as American

In 1986 Congress enacted the Immigration Reform and Control Act, which included sanctions against employers who hired undocumented workers. Althea Simmons, the NAACP's representative in Washington, DC, "testified repeatedly during congressional debates . . . that undocumented immigrants competed with African Americans for jobs and that the NAACP supported strong employer sanctions."[24] Fear about competition from undocumented immigrants is often extended to all immigrants, regardless of legal status.[25] Coalition between whites and blacks was made possible on issues regarding immigration by implicit and explicit appeals to a common Americanness in opposition to the foreignness attributed to Latinas/os and Asian Americans.

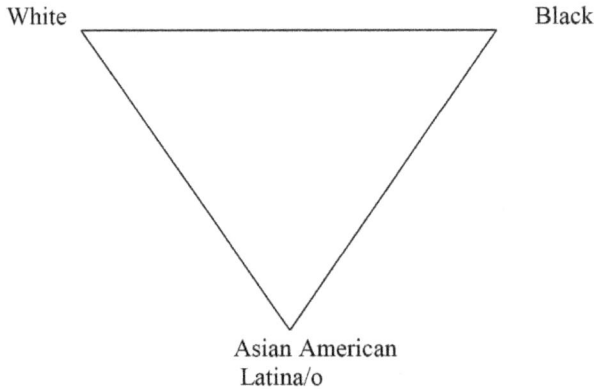

White   Black

Asian American
Latina/o

Figure 1.2. Blacks as American.

Example 3—Latinas/os as White

Early litigation strategy by the League of United Latin American Citizens (LULAC) deployed what has been termed the "other white" strategy to overcome Jim Crow–style segregation deployed against Mexican Americans.[26] Though it had some success in combating discrimination against Mexican Americans,[27] the "other white" strategy ultimately supported white supremacy without actually resulting in equal whiteness for Mexican Americans and other Latinas/os. A startling example of this took place in Texas public schools in the 1960s "when schools began to use Mexicans' 'other white' status cynically to 'desegregate' black schools using Mexicans."[28] In challenging this practice in a case involving Corpus Christi, James DeAnda complained that Corpus Christi Independent School District, like many Texas districts, had turned the "other white" notion to its own illegitimate purposes. In order to delay the court-ordered desegregation, while at the same time obscuring its slow pace, district officials frequently assigned African and Mexican Americans to the same schools, rather than to white schools, a practice often facilitated by the close proximity of the ghettos to the barrios. The administrators maintained that, because Mexican Americans were "white," the barrio-ghetto schools had been desegregated.[29]

The failure to understand this cynical deployment of whiteness in the face of an ideology of white/Anglo supremacy allows for whiteness to reign and complicates coalition between Latinas/os and African Americans and Asian Americans.

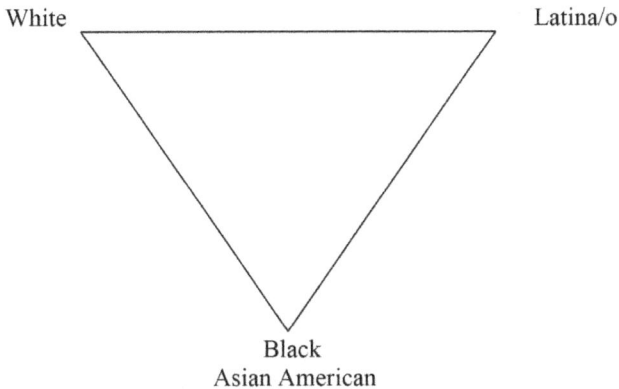

Figure 1.3. Latinas/os as white.

This last example, at least historically, is different from the other two because the horizontal plane of equivalence with whites is claimed by (some) Latinas/os, unlike in the other two examples where the claim of common cause was strategically made by whites seeking to disrupt nonwhite coalitions.

An important aspect of each of these third-order multigroup analyses is the way that the multigroup analysis ends up collapsing into a false binary to create a privileged top and subordinated bottom. There is cynicism and hypocrisy at work because which group is invited to join in coalition with the privileged top may change depending on the particular issue. This political dimension to the multigroup analyses above—the ease with which the dominant group can manipulate coalition politics—reveals the theoretical shortcomings of the minority group politics. In each of the examples, the seduction of being included with the in-group ultimately leads one minority group to lose sight of white supremacy in order to achieve a short-term gain while jeopardizing progress in the long run. Third-order multigroup analysis in the service of subordination makes the following move: within the framework of an established top group and a bottom group, a third group is invited to join the top.[30] The third group is told: "You are like us; you are not like them." This invitation can be seductive. It's easy to say, "Yes, thank you, we are like you and not like them" and to accept the psychological wages that come with whiteness or Americanness, actual or honorary.[31] There are also significant levels of cynicism and denial in accepting such a coalition. Coalitional group politics requires a self-conscious group decision that another minority group will lose important social benefits. And that decision must also include a calculated denial that participation as the junior partner in a racial coalition will eventually mean the enforcement of a "glass ceiling" or even worse in future political developments. Part of the work for critical race theory is to provide the theoretical, moral, and pragmatic grounds for resisting these invitations. There seem to be two imperatives at work here: to get it right as a matter of theory, and to get it right as a matter of politics to foster coalitions.[32]

The cynical deployment of the language of equality, "You are like us and not them," can be seen to be issue-specific. It masks attempts to co-opt without any real granting of equality with whites. It is a way to maintain white dominance.[33]

The use of racial triangulation is not new. Gotanda pointed out in 1985 the rhetorical and structural use of racial triangulation (though not in those words) in Justice John Marshall Harlan's famous dissent in *Plessy v. Ferguson*.[34] In what is taken as Harlan's call for color blindness, which would have invalidated the Louisiana statute requiring that blacks have a separate coach from that of whites, Harlan placed black Americans on a horizontal plane of formal equality with white Americans, but set this up by posing whites and blacks together in juxtaposition to the Chinese:

There is a race so different from our own that we do not permit those belonging to it to become citizens of the United States. Persons belonging to it are, with few exceptions, absolutely excluded from our country. I allude to the Chinese race. But by the [segregation] statute in question, a Chinaman can ride in the same passenger coach with white citizens of the United States, while citizens of the black race in Louisiana . . . who are entitled, by law, to participate in the political control of the State and nation . . . and who have all the legal rights that belong to white citizens, are yet declared to be criminals, liable to imprisonment, if they ride in a public coach occupied by citizens of the white race.[35]

These examples show the way that careful multigroup analysis that keeps an eye on white supremacy can help us see beyond binaries, real and false.

Triangulation can also play a role in fostering a common white identity that elides severe differences based on class and gender. Understanding this requires a closer examination of the way white capitalist patriarchy operates and the way it actively works to foster group enmity to stratify groups to prevent solidarity or coalitions among those who suffer under this regime.

Capital uses various techniques to discipline workers to foster fear and insecurity, which lead to greater investment into holding on to and not sharing what workers already have. Historically, the threat to workers was that they could be replaced. To prevent worker solidarity, one creates and maintains a segmented labor force.

Race has been a very useful tool to segment the labor force. Race enmity is fostered to prevent class unity. As depicted in John Sayles's film *Matewan*, if white workers cause trouble, owners discipline them by bringing in black workers. Or on Hawaiian sugar plantations, Japanese workers are paid more than Chinese workers who are paid more than Korean workers who are in turn paid more than Filipino workers. Some are privileged at the expense of others. Those who are privileged gain something from their racial/ethnic positions. This leads to a positive investment in the category or categories that provide them with privilege.

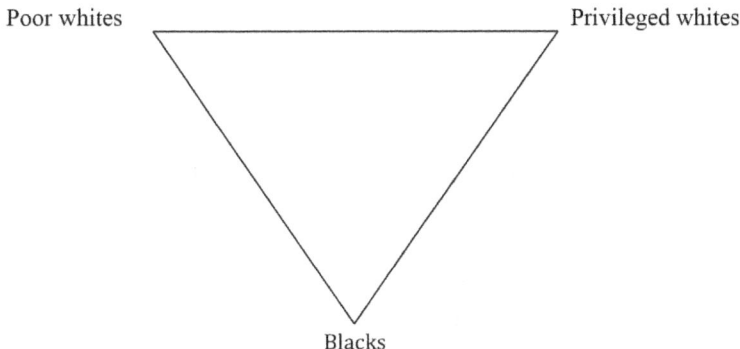

Figure 1.4. Triangulation and the psychological wages of whiteness.

A similar dynamic can be worked with gender, which can be used to segment the labor force to prevent race or class solidarity. Capital disciplines male workers by bringing in female workers. Male workers fear losing their jobs or fear competition with women for jobs and promotions, which leads to a positive investment in maleness and a hostile workplace for women. Capital is satisfied because male workers are distracted and insecure, allowing capital to extract surplus labor power from them.

I want to return to the affirmative action debate that brings together race, gender, sexuality, and economics. I have found it curious that the debate over affirmative action has been racialized in such a way that gender has largely dropped out of the picture. But what about the fact that the primary beneficiaries of affirmative action have been white women? Where are their voices?

It seems that a natural coalition might develop between white women and women of color based on shared gender oppression, or between white women and people of color based on a more broad-based notion of societal oppression. In 1996 an anti–affirmative action initiative was on the ballot, the so-called California Civil Rights Initiative. There were attempts by those opposing the initiative to gain the support of white women. These efforts largely failed. According to polls before the election, approximately 65 percent of white women were in favor of the initiative that would eliminate race and gender affirmative action. At first blush, one might wonder at this position, which seems to go against their self-interest. But this depends on how one characterizes the self. Is the self a racial self? Or a gendered self?

These questions were avoided or masked by the invocation of family. White women have brothers and sons, and making a heterosexist assumption, they have husbands. Insofar as affirmative action is blamed for white men not getting jobs or admission to schools, and insofar as these white men are seen as their husbands, brothers, and sons, this means that affirmative action is hurting the families of white women. Family can be invoked here without explicit reference to race—in 1987, 99 percent of white Americans were married to other whites. Because of statistics such as this, an appeal to family does the work of an explicit call to white racial solidarity. Though interracial unions are on the rise, by 2010, approximately 93 percent of white Americans were married to other whites.

In theory, because white women have been the primary beneficiaries of affirmative action, they should be the primary targets of the anti–affirmative action forces. However, the vote of white women was considered crucial in the states of California and Washington in the 1990s. So how do you avoid gender conflict, especially in light of continued discrimination against women?

The key here is the relationship between family and patriarchy. Because patriarchy operates in such a way that white women earn only 74 cents for every dollar a white man makes, the economic interests of white women may be better served if their husbands, brothers, and sons do well.

In Washington State, there is anecdotal evidence that this was indeed a deciding factor for some of the white women who voted to do away with affirmative action. Some talked about their husbands who had trouble getting jobs. Affirmative action and racial minorities get blamed instead of corporate downsizing, automation, computerization, and capital flight.

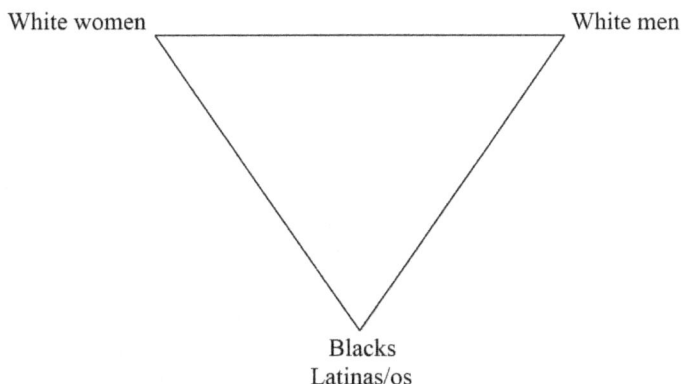

White women   White men

Blacks
Latinas/os

Figure 1.5. Triangulation and gender.

From these examples, we see the intensification of categories. Although categories can provide a useful organizing point in the form of "strategic essentialism," which might be described as the creation, occupation, and maintenance of oppositional identity formations, it is possible that this strategy is ultimately self-defeating. Part of the problem then comes from the identity categories in which we invest and from which we benefit.

Identity is not determinative. One's race, class, and gender identities certainly inform but do not determine one's perspectives or one's commitments. Identity does not prefigure the coalitions in which one participates. However, as discussed above, identity—personal and group—can play a critical role in shaping the development of coalitions.

With regard to the possibility of nonwhite racial coalitions, we cannot presume that a shared history of racial oppression will produce solidarity.

Angela Harris reminds us: "There are no 'people of color' waiting to be found; we must give up our romance with racial community. If any lesson of the politics of difference can yet be identified, it is that solidarity is the product of struggle, not wishful thinking; and struggle means not only political struggle, but moral and ethical struggle as well."[36]

As other chapters in this collection point out, an oppositional stance can be a starting point for coalitions but can also severely limit the ability of a coalition to persist. Coalitions, if they are to persist, cannot just be against something; they must also be for something. Those wishing to develop durable coalitions must decide what it is that they actually favor.

NOTES

This chapter is adapted from Robert S. Chang and Neil Gotanda, *The Race Question in LatCrit Theory and Asian American Jurisprudence*, 7 NEV. L.J. 1012 (2007).

1. *See* Charles R. Lawrence III, *Foreword: Race, Multiculturalism, and the Jurisprudence of Transformation*, 47 STAN. L. REV. 819, 826 (1995).

2. *See* Neil Gotanda, *Other Non-Whites and American Legal History: A Review of Justice at War*, 85 COLUM. L. REV. 1186 (1985); Robert S. Chang, *Toward an Asian American Legal Scholarship*, 81 CAL. L. REV. 1241 (1993), 1 ASIAN L.J. 1 (1994). For a similar move in the LatCrit context, see Juan F. Perea, *The Black/White Binary Paradigm of Race: The "Normal Science" of American Racial Thought*, 85 CAL. L. REV. 1213 (1997), 10 LA RAZA L.J. 127 (1998).

3. Though this chapter focuses on race, there is a necessary further complexity to any analytic race model that includes other identity attributes. *Cf.* Kimberle W. Crenshaw, *Demarginalizing the Intersection of Race and Sex*, 1989 U. CHI. L. FORUM 139; Marlee Kline, *Race, Racism, and Feminist Legal Theory*, 12 HARV. WOMEN'S L.J. 115 (1989); Angela P. Harris, *Race and Essentialism in Feminist Legal Theory*, 42 STAN. L. REV. 581 (1990).

4. This analysis is first order because the binary analysis remains as a comparison of the two groups as a result of minority A's and minority B's separate and independent relationship to the majority.

5. *Cf.* Mary Louise Fellows & Sherene Razack, *The Race to Innocence: Confronting Hierarchical Relations among Women*, 1 J. RACE, GENDER & JUST. 335, 335 (1998) (discussing the problem that they name as "competing marginalities").

6. William Douglas, *Panel Meant to Heal Is Split: Race Relations-Group Divided on History*, NEWSDAY, July 15, 1997, at A15.

7. Mari Matusda, *Planet Asian America*, 8 ASIAN L.J. 169, 179–80 (2001).

8. Tanya Hernandez, *Roots of Latino/Black Anger: Longtime Prejudices, Not Economic Rivalry, Fuel Tensions*, L.A. TIMES, Jan. 7, 2007, at M1.

9. *Id. But see* Jill Leovy, *Are Black-vs.-Brown Racial Tensions Driving Homicide in L.A.?*, *The Homicide Report: Jill Leovy Chronicles L.A. County Homicide Victims*, http://latimes blogs.latimes.com/homicidereport/2007/03/marchers_protes.html (while acknowledging

some cross-racially motivated killings, finding that statistics do not indicate that black versus brown racial tensions are driving up the homicide rate).

10. Hernandez, *supra* note 7, at M1.

11. *Id.*

12. *Id.*

13. Taunya Lovell Banks, *Both Edges of the Margin: Blacks and Asians in Mississippi Masala, Barriers to Coalition Building*, 5 ASIAN L.J. 7, 10 (1998).

14. YEN LE ESPIRITU, ASIAN AMERICAN PANETHNICITY (1992).

15. *Id.* at 3–9 (discussing sociological theories of ethnicity).

16. Neil Gotanda, *Asian American Rights and the "Miss Saigon Syndrome," in* ASIAN AMERICANS AND THE SUPREME COURT: A DOCUMENTARY HISTORY 1087 (Hyung Chan Kim ed., 1982); Neil Gotanda, *Towards Repeal of Asian Exclusion: The Magnuson Act of 1943, the Act of July 2, 1946, the Presidential Proclamation of July 4, 1946, the Act of August 9, 1946, and the Act of August 1, 1950, in* ASIAN AMERICANS AND CONGRESS: A DOCUMENTARY HISTORY 309 (Hyung Chan Kim ed., 1996).

17. *See, e.g.,* Keith Aoki, *"Foreign-ness" & Asian American Identities: Yellowface, World War II Propaganda, and Bifurcated Racial Stereotypes*, 4 ASIAN PAC. AM. L.J. 1, passim (1996); Natsu Taylor Saito, *Alien and Non-Alien Alike: Citizenship, "Foreignness," and Racial Hierarchy in American Law*, 76 OR. L. REV. 261 passim (1997); Robert S. Chang, *Closing Essay: Developing a Collective Memory to Imagine a Better Future*, 49 UCLA L. REV. 1601, 1607 (2002).

18. *See* Stanford L. Lyman, *The Race Relations Cycle of Robert E. Park*, PAC. SOC. REV. 16 (1968); WERNER SOLLORS, BEYOND ETHNICITY: CONSENT AND DISSENT IN AMERICAN CULTURE (1986).

19. Claire Jean Kim, *The Racial Triangulation of Asian Americans, in* ASIAN AMERICANS AND POLITICS: PERSPECTIVES, EXPERIENCES, PROSPECTS, 29, 42 (Gordon H. Chang ed., 2001).

20. ROGER DANIELS, ASIAN AMERICA: CHINESE AND JAPANESE IN THE UNITED STATES SINCE 1850, at 317–18 (1988) (citing William Petersen, *Success Story, Japanese American Style*, N.Y. TIMES MAG., Jan. 6, 1966, at 20).

21. *See, e.g.,* Frank Wu, Neither Black nor White: Asian Americans and Affirmative Action, 15 B.C. THIRD WORLD L.J. 225, 270 (1995).

22. Sumi Cho, "A Theory of Racial Mascotting," Remarks at the First Annual Asian Pacific American Law Professors Conference (Oct. 14, 1994) (discussing how Asian Pacific Americans have been relegated to the role of a "racial mascot" for conservatives in contemporary political battles).

23. DANA Y. TAKAGI, RETREAT FROM RACE: ASIAN-AMERICAN ADMISSIONS AND RACIAL POLITICS (1992); Jerry Kang, *Negative Action against Asian Americans: The Internal Instability of Dworkin's Defense of Affirmative Action*, 31 HARV. C.R.-C.L. L. REV. 1 (1996).

24. William M. Tamayo, *When the "Coloreds" Are Neither Black nor Citizens: The United States Civil Rights Movement and Global Migration*, 2 ASIAN L.J. 1, 18–19 (1995).

25. Bill Ong Hing, *Immigration Policies: Messages of Exclusion to African Americans*, 37 HOW. L.J. 237, 237 (1994) ("Among many African Americans, there is concern that

immigrants are taking away jobs, depressing their wages, or taking away business opportunities in their communities.").

26. *See* Richard Delgado, *Rodrigo's Fifteenth Chronicle: Racial Mixture, Latino-Critical Scholarship, and the Black-White Binary*, 75 TEX. L. REV. 1181, 1189 (1997).

27. *See* George A. Martinez, *Legal Indeterminacy, Judicial Discretion and the Mexican-American Litigation Experience: 1930–1980*, 27 U.C. DAVIS L. REV. 555 (1994).

28. Ariela Gross, *"The Caucasian Cloak": Mexican Americans and the Politics of Whiteness in the Twentieth-Century Southwest*, 95 GEO. L.J. 337, 387 (2007).

29. Steven H. Wilson, *Some Are Born White, Some Achieve Whiteness, and Some Have Whiteness Thrust Upon Them: Mexican Americans and the Politics of Racial Classification in the Federal Judicial Bureaucracy, Twenty-Five Years after* Hernandez v. Texas, 25 CHICANO-LATINO L. REV. 201, 213 (2005).

30. Toni Morrison describes the traditional way that immigrants adopt anti-black racism as a pathway to Americanization. *See* Toni Morrison, *On the Backs of Blacks*, TIME, Dec. 2, 1993, at 57.

31. Whites are also extended this invitation. *Cf.* W.E.B. DUBOIS, BLACK RECONSTRUCTION IN AMERICA, 1860–1880, 701 (1962) (discussing psychological wages of whiteness that promote white solidarity and undercut class solidarity between blacks and working-class whites); DAVID ROEDIGER, WAGES OF WHITENESS (2007) (same); Cheryl I. Harris, *Whiteness as Property*, 106 HARV. L. REV. 1707, 1741–45 (1993) (same).

32. *See, e.g.*, Richard Delgado, *Derrick Bell's Toolkit—Fit to Dismantle That Famous House?* 75 NYU L. REV. 283 306–7 (2000) (discussing the possibility of coordinating anti-discrimination efforts around interest convergence); Kevin Johnson, *The Struggle for Civil Rights: The Need for, and Impediments to, Political Coalitions among and within Minority Groups*, 63 LA. L. REV. 759, 767 (2003) (discussing the need for coalitions to understand and attack racial hierarchy and white supremacy); Catherine Smith, *Queer as Black Folk*, 2007 WIS. L. REV. 329 (using social psychology to provide a framework for building coalitions around superordinate goals).

33. *See* Robert S. Chang, "Racial Triangulation, or Why Multiple Races Are More Effective Than Binary Paradigms in Maintaining White Racial Domination," LatCrit X, San Juan, Puerto Rico, Oct. 7, 2005. Richard Delgado makes a similar point in his discussion of differential racialization. *See* Richard Delgado, *Locating Latinos in the Field of Civil Rights: Assessing the Neoliberal Case for Radical Exclusion*, 83 TEX. L. REV. 489, 513–17 (2004) (reviewing GEORGE YANCY, WHO IS WHITE?: LATINOS, ASIANS, AND THE NEW BLACK/NONBLACK DIVIDE [2003]).

34. Neil Gotanda, *"Other Non-Whites," supra* note 2, at 1189 n.11. This idea was elaborated upon in Gabriel J. Chin, *The Plessy Myth: Justice Harlan and the Chinese Cases*, 82 IOWA L. REV. 151 (1996).

35. Plessy v. Ferguson, 163 U.S. 537, 561 (1896) (Harlan, J., dissenting).

36. Angela Harris, *Foreword: The Jurisprudence of Reconstruction*, 82 CAL. L. REV. 741, 783 (1994).

2

The Power Dynamics of Color on Color
Grappling with Grievances to Forge Alliances

ERIC K. YAMAMOTO AND AMANDA O. JENSSEN

I. OVERVIEW

The media cacophony over immigration at times overwhelms the public imagination about race in America. Should we, dissonant news reports ask, "keep Spanish-speaking illegals out" or "challenge draconian racist anti-immigrant laws"? These disparate sentiments are worthy of close scrutiny. Indeed, the ferocious immigration debate fosters racial characterizations that shape many contemporary conflicts. But that ferocity belies something else significantly at play.

Registering at lower decibels are news stories about America's "interminority problem." Recurring reports about conflicts among communities of color emerge from both small towns and large cities—intergroup violence, local government racial politicking, and color-on-color discrimination in jobs and housing. Consider some headlines: "Deep Divisions, Shared Destiny [Black, Hispanic, and Asian Americans in Workplaces, Schools, Neighborhoods]"; "Latino Gangs . . . Have Targeted Blacks"; "Black Attacks on Asians—Racism or Opportunity?"; "GOP Manufactures Black-Brown Tensions"; "It Goes Back to Minorities Fighting Minorities."[1]

And then ponder accounts of bridge-building struggles: "Black-Asian Unity—Racing to Talk in Tense Times"; "Union Tries to Unite Blacks, Latinos"; and "Thai and Latina Garment Workers Overcoming Suspicion"; culminating in the query: "Natural Allies or Irreconcilable Foes?"[2]

For some observers, these news reports are mainly media sensationalism—local matters blown out of proportion. For others, the reported disputes and efforts at bridge-building reflect something more. They signal attempts to grapple with far-reaching and deeply rooted color-on-color tensions.[3]

Indeed, even though sometimes labeled a black-brown phenomenon, wide-ranging interracial group interactions are at play. Many individuals of color and their organizations regularly interact with one another without conflict, sometimes cooperatively. But African Americans, Latinos, and Asian Americans—citizens and immigrants—do experience face-to-face conflicts. As intimated in the news accounts, the conflicts vary markedly, depending on place (inner cities, barrios, towns, suburbs), setting (neighborhoods, schools, workplaces, city councils, courtrooms), and issue (crime, work, politics, education, health care).[4]

Yet even these accounts, while spotlighting color-on-color interactions, only hint at significant undercurrents. One undercurrent is white facilitation of color-on-color tensions. The US Census Bureau predicts that nonwhites numerically will surpass whites by 2042. This prospect has triggered right-wing strategies for maintaining long-standing racial supremacy. In the words of John Tanton, "Will the present majority peaceably hand over its political power to a group that is simply more fertile? . . . As Whites see their power and control over their lives declining, will they simply go quietly into the night? Or will there be an explosion?" Particularly during rough economic times, the white backlash against mainly Latino immigrants by design draws vocal support from small but noticeable segments of African Americans and Asian Americans.[5]

A second undercurrent runs barely below the surface of these often variegated color-on-color conflicts. It is the volatile mix of poignant historical memories, present-day cultural misunderstandings, and sharp media-generated racial mischaracterizations that coalesce into commonly held group grievances that transcend specific interactions and sometimes transform individual conflicts into race-on-race controversies.[6]

A third and directly related undercurrent is the persistent desire for and struggles with alliance forging. Scholars and justice advocates continue to search for theoretically sound and practical workable approaches for handling specific on-the-ground conflicts and for addressing deeper group grievances—all so that in the long run "groups can work together productively and live together peacefully."[7]

In particular, recent scholarship on interracial group conflicts tends to offer coalition-building approaches primarily focused on locating "common ground" among nonwhite groups—for example, identifying discrimination (mainly by whites) in housing, employment, and education. These general approaches address hard realities and offer a concrete way to handle immediate disputes. For instance, a 2010 coauthored study on African American and

Latino "friction in America" ultimately suggests forming coalitions around common issues to alleviate tensions and create practical opportunities for coordinated action.[8]

Although helpful, this and similar common ground approaches tend to bypass critical assessments of often subsurface color-on-color grievances that impede prospects for longer term alliance forging. By sidestepping close inquiry into historically situated messy power relations that at least partially shape present-day group grievances, these approaches encourage communities and justice advocates to work within an initially useful but ultimately limited framework.[9]

To better conceptualize racial conflict, Robert Chang and Neil Gotanda in 2007 proposed a three-tiered model of intergroup relations. The Chang and Gotanda model is an apt starting point. It provides structural analyses that extend past the search for common ground, and it insightfully accounts for multigroup interactions. The model, by design, points toward, but does not venture in-depth into, the dynamics of grievance and amelioration.[10]

In this chapter, we offer a developing context-sensitive theory of intergroup power dynamics that illuminates key aspects of deeper color-on-color grievances that often undergird face-to-face conflicts. We then illustrate the theory's utility by employing it to partially unravel two varied on-the-ground conflicts with similar underlying grievances.

Our larger goal is to facilitate praxis. We aim to offer justice educators, social justice lawyers, government officials, and community justice advocates the basics of an approach for understanding and grappling with those historically, economically, and culturally situated group grievances so that they might translate theory into ground-level practice for longer term alliance forging and broader social healing. It is our ultimate hope that the approach will prove useful for scholars as well as frontline justice organizations like the Southeast Regional Economic Justice Network (Resisting Rivalry program) and Colorlines (Youth and Race Project) described later.[11]

With this in mind, we refine and deepen the approach first introduced by Eric Yamamoto in *Interracial Justice: Conflict and Reconciliation in Post–Civil Rights America*. The approach acknowledges that immediate conflicts vary widely depending on place, setting, and issue and that no one technique for addressing specific disputes fits all. It also recognizes that historically rooted, culturally constructed images of racial groups often inform collective memories of injustice and resulting grievance. With this backdrop, the approach builds upon social structural analyses, particularly the work of Thomas Wartenberg, and moves the interrogation of the color-on-color grievances into the realm of group power dynamics—all with the larger aim of laying foundations for building more productive and enduring alliances.[12]

Developed in section IV, the approach embraces two central concepts. The first, *simultaneity*, is comprised of three related inquiries into "redeployment of structures and strategies of oppression," "relational positionality," and "social alignment." The second concept, *differentiation*, examines how groups acquire different cultural identities and how differing degrees of power and economic opportunity accrue to those identities. Together, *simultaneity* and *differentiation* provide insight into the power dynamics that contribute to perceived group grievances that often underlie and sometimes exacerbate seemingly individual conflicts. Grappling with these deeper grievances, we submit, is a key predicate to better enabling groups to live together peaceably and work together politically.

Section V illuminates those dynamics by employing the concepts to examine aspects of two controversies: African American and Latino grievances in contested borderlands, and Asian American, African American, and Latino conflicts in the streets and in the halls of academia—both influenced but not controlled by the interests of whites in America. As the concluding part of this chapter, these examinations are incomplete and at points necessarily engage in broad generalizations. The aim is not to offer comprehensive or definitive assessments, but rather to offer situational insights, to demonstrate the practical utility of the analytical concepts, and to facilitate further scholarly inquiry and community action.

II. CONFLICTS AND ALLIANCES: EVENTS AND APPROACHES

We start by describing snapshots of color-on-color conflicts and halting efforts to build alliances.

Rapid demographic changes raise fears about the impact of nonwhite immigration on American society. What, some ask, will happen as Latinos overtake African Americans as the nation's largest nonwhite group and as persons of color collectively surpass whites in number? And how much will economic and political power, still held disproportionately by whites, be shared? One apparent answer to the latter question, at least for some anti-immigrant groups, is "very little."[13]

This often ferocious US immigration debate fosters racial mischaracterizations that are integral to contemporary conflicts among nonwhite racial groups. Indeed, in recent years interracial group tensions are most prominently, and narrowly, telescoped onto immigration controversies. What is often depicted as black-brown conflict over immigration, however, is actually one piece of a larger mosaic of intergroup tensions. Black-brown immigration controversies thus provide an apt starting point—but only a starting point—for the broader inquiry into intergroup grievance and prospects for amelioration.[14]

Some anti-immigration activist groups attempt to drive a wedge between African Americans and Latinos by arguing that African Americans must compete with unworthy and illegal immigrants in a zero-sum game for limited economic opportunities. These groups at times seek to block Latinos—including both documented and undocumented workers—from accessing the American mainstream. And they endeavor to enlist selected spokespersons of color to recast their white supremacist image to help implement their exclusionary political agenda. For instance, the Federation for American Immigration Reform (FAIR)—the nation's largest white-led anti-immigrant group—reportedly sponsors and funds nonwhite-led front groups like Choose Black America (CBA). African American CBA leader Ted Hayes reportedly describes Latino immigration as "the greatest threat to U.S. black citizens since slavery."[15]

The 2010 Arizona immigrant "stop and profile" law mainly pitted white citizens against Latino immigrants. But it also impacted an array of other nonwhites. While many strongly defended targeted Latinos, others, including parts of African American and Asian American communities, appeared divided. As discussed later, beneath the surface of some organizations' positions on the state legislation lay perceived intergroup grievances unconnected to the specific immigration law.[16]

Interracial group tensions that impede prospects for coalition extend well beyond immigration borderlands into the political arena and the everyday workplace. At a large North Carolina meat packing plant, a "common ground" approach to unionizing Latinos and African Americans—in response to across-the-board substandard working conditions and unfair employment practices—contributed to important cross-racial advances. But the approach's limitations also led to an unraveling at crucial junctures. Preexisting racial mistrust, unrelated to activities at the company, emerged as a stumbling block to enduring coalitional action. And that mistrust was in part rooted in the groups' deeper perceived racialized grievances against one another—that is, fears of one group that the other later-arriving group disrespects their history of struggle and is aggressively seeking to climb over them; and fears of the other group that they are being pushed to the bottom of the ladder and excluded from opportunities rightfully theirs by those not willing to work as hard.[17]

In another situation, African American and Latino leaders productively grasped the opportunity to address the deeper grievances—albeit temporarily. The 2005 Los Angeles mayoral election pitted Latino candidate Antonio Villaraigosa against white incumbent James Hahn. Some African American political leaders, who earlier supported Hahn, strongly supported Villaraigosa in the divisive campaign—in part because of Hahn's firing of a popular African American police chief. Lurking beneath the surface of black support lay Villaraigosa's handling of grievances that blamed Latinos for taking African Americans' jobs and countergrievances that accused black leaders of stifling Latino progress. Villaraigosa persuaded a large number of black voters "by focusing on early outreach and mobilization within the Black community and the building of relationships with recognizable Black leaders." In particular, those leaders backed Villaraigosa after he "quell[ed] some of the fears of rising Latino power among Black Angelinos" and promised that Latino officials would be sensitive to African American concerns about "leapfrogging" and "disrespecting our history." In doing so he signaled "the possibility of Black-Brown coalition-building."[18]

Villaraigosa's efforts to address group grievances left unanswered questions: Was this alliance sustainable? Were underlying grievances resolved or merely temporarily salved? At bottom, were the groups' perceptions of one another lastingly transformed? Apparently not. Local black leaders later criticized Villaraigosa for vetoing the $2.7 million lawsuit settlement for an African American firefighter fed dog food by coworkers. This seemingly isolated incident rekindled doubts about Villaraigosa. Is he, along with other Latinos, intent on keeping blacks down? One African American leader noted, "There was always some question on how he was going to deliver on the promises."[19]

In recent years African American and Latino tensions have erupted sporadically in widely reported neighborhood violence beyond gang-on-gang warfare. In the broader Los Angeles area, Latino street gangs reportedly targeted African American neighborhood residents "with the goal of eradicating African Americans from 'Latino' spaces." Interestingly, as Tanya K. Hernandez notes, some among the Latino community tended to place blame less on Latinos and more on African Americans, who are misleadingly portrayed as the aggressors. Something more than simple "turf battles and cultural disputes in changing neighborhoods" is at play.[20]

These often horrible encounters shed some light on the groups' deeper sense of grievance. As discussed later, the "gang crackdowns, sweeps and prosecutions," while appropriate initial responses to ongoing violence, merely scratch the surface at comprehending and addressing the subsurface roots of many of the conflicts.[21]

Although "black and brown" highlights the most visible contemporary color-on-color group interactions, that framing looks past Asian Americans. From a lawsuit by Asian American plaintiffs challenging affirmative action policies benefiting African Americans and Latinos, to violence between African Americans and Korean and Vietnamese small business operators, to the initially suspicious and eventually supportive Latina and Thai garment workers, tensions on the ground tend to surface in group grievances that transform individual conflicts into racial group disputes and sometimes into intergroup conflagrations. Reconsider the Rodney King post-police-trial firestorm.[22]

After a predominantly white jury acquitted Los Angeles police officers for the videotaped beating of Rodney King, long-simmering tensions over police brutality and social inequality in largely African American communities boiled over. White jurors who appeared to wink at white police brutality against African Americans sparked explosive anger against police specifically and whites generally.[23]

That anger over the jury verdict also brought to the surface unresolved grievances that some African Americans in South-Central Los Angeles harbored against Korean immigrant businesses that were perceived as receiving white financial favors. The individual face-to-face conflicts that African American neighborhood residents experienced with Korean shopkeepers, who appeared to them to be rude and unwilling to hire black store clerks, turned into explosive group grievances that far exceeded specific encounters.[24]

The grievances grew in part in the soil of African American perceptions of Korean immigrants as disrespecting them while leapfrogging over them and Korean immigrant characterizations of African Americans as unwilling to work hard and as untrustworthy. Solidified into racial reality by stock stories of past conflicts repeated in the media and by group members themselves, without attention to the history of white exclusionary housing and employment practices, those perceptions morphed into simmering grievances. These substrata grievances, exacerbated by a Korean American neighborhood shopkeeper's widely publicized fatal shooting of African American teen Latasha Harlins over a bottle of orange juice, even though not directly related to Rodney King, almost instantaneously transformed the mainly white jury's "not guilty" police verdict into an inferno of grievances between some Korean American shopkeepers and African Americans in the area.[25]

With intergroup conflicts as backdrop, recent scholarship addressing coalition building tends to focus primarily on African Americans and Latino immigrants and a search for "common ground." An essay in a progressive journal, based on an extensive study, is emblematic. In *Natural Allies or Irreconcilable Foes? Reflections on African-American/Immigrant Relations*, Andrew Grant-Thomas, Yusuf Sarfati, and Cheryl Staats ("Grant-Thomas") posit the importance of building African American and Latino immigrant coalitions. To bridge the sizable social distance between the groups, the authors emphasize targeting the two groups' common issues, including discrimination, low wages, and underresourced education.[26]

Grant-Thomas thoughtfully call attention to some of the likely sources of current black-Latino "friction" in America: "Political, economic and social conflicts of interest, coupled with a ragged history of power-sharing in places where one group has predominated and broad ignorance of each other's historical and current struggles, create a potentially volatile mix." The authors suggest forming African American and Latino alliances through intergroup relationship building around common issue identification and workplace organizing. They propose focusing dialogue on common "bread and butter" issues like wages and discrimination while largely avoiding the difficult interrogation of the "ragged history of power-sharing" and the "broad ignorance" of one another's culture and social and economic conditions.[27]

The search for common ground suggestions is appealing and sensible. *New American Media* polls suggest that African Americans and Latinos overwhelmingly favor "putting aside their differences" and cooperating on issues common to their communities. These polls signal hope that finding common ground and looking beyond past harms might give rise to effective coalition building. Yet Yamamoto and former legal services attorney Julie Su sound a more cautionary note. Based on their scholarly assessments and practical community experiences, they observe that "in neglecting to deal with [the deeper grievances] honestly and self-critically, we miss important opportunities for building real coalitions that are the basis for building a true community of justice." Yamamoto and Su caution that a narrow common ground approach risks missing fundamental predicates for collective action. The deeper group-against-group grievances remain, "creating a volatile mix" that fosters mistrust and mischaracterizations that impede effective and enduring collective action.[28]

Grant-Thomas cite "specialized curriculums and trainings" by community organizations that productively address "the global forces that propel immigration . . . and the relation between racism and the immigration debate" and the "structures that constrain black Americans today." Grant-Thomas's suggestions, however, are generally limited to organizational structure and goals and do not reach beneath the surface to the roots of African American and Latino grievances.[29]

Although useful in developing initial contact and a level of intergroup trust, the suggested "toolkits and curricular materials to dissolve barriers" only indirectly engage the historical and contemporary questions of power that shape the substructure of group grievances. The approach acknowledges but does not engage the reality that genuine coalition building requires addressing "cultural barriers such as the misperceptions that the communities harbor about each other."[30]

At bottom, the proposed Grant-Thomas approach, with supporting materials, marks a significant advance. But its decision not to engage the socioeconomic and political power relationships among white Americans and communities of color that give rise to deep-seated grievances leaves the overall approach helpful but incomplete.

As developed later, justice scholars and advocates interested in building longer term alliances need to venture into the realms of "ragged power sharing" and broad cultural ignorance identified but not fully pursued by Grant-Thomas. To do so, they will need nuanced analytical tools to address underlying intergroup grievances—including past harmful acts and present-day cultural mischaracterizations—and the ways that power alignments and realignments create a persisting underlying substructure for daily conflicts.

As Yamamoto has developed elsewhere, this assessment of buried intergroup grievances, and particularly the power arrangements shaping and sustaining those grievances, is essential to the kind of mutually engaged "social healing through justice" that enables groups over the long haul "to work together productively and live together peacefully."[31]

III. SOME THEORIES OF INTERGROUP POWER

How might we productively comprehend those power arrangements? Generalizing broadly, nonwhite racial groups traditionally have been understood as actors on polar ends of the agency spectrum: either they have unbounded agency, or they are largely powerless to participate affirmatively in the construction of identities and intergroup relations.[32]

At one end of the spectrum, conservative "ethnicity theory" begins with the premise that American society is no longer afflicted with racism. With a level playing field, every racial group is similarly capable of assimilating into the American mainstream. A corollary assumption is that nonwhite groups have unbounded agency to determine their racial identities and are free from institutional and attitudinal barriers. As a result, any group falling short does so because of its own inferior culture. Symptoms of cultural failings— for example, substandard socioeconomic conditions, higher incarceration rates—result directly from volitional actions. Discrimination against those falling short as a group is a *rational* reaction.[33]

In this way, conservative ethnicity theory fails to account for the social structural constraints imposed by an American society that is far from color-blind. It ignores external influences that contribute to the shaping of racial group agency, including housing segregation, limitations on access to credit, racial profiling laws, and poor schools.[34]

At the other end of the spectrum, "nationalism" theories tend to understate nonwhite group agency and responsibility. Intergroup rivalries or conflicts are attributed to a divide-and-conquer mentality by whites in power that pits communities of color against one another as a means of maintaining the racial hierarchy. Accordingly, nonwhite groups' roles as social actors necessarily focus on combating white structures of dominance.[35]

Nationalism theory helps to explain certain structural dimensions to group relations. It does not, however, account for the at least partial capacity of nonwhite groups to participate in shaping their relationships, advancing their interests, and sometimes harming others.

Neither ethnicity nor nationalism theories fully grapple with the kind of racial group agency that is "both enlivened and constrained by multiple shifting contexts"—a concept of agency that recognizes that racial communities simultaneously possess some power in certain situations and little power in others.[36]

In 2000, drawing on the work of many scholars, Yamamoto sought to move beyond the spectral depictions of racial group agency in *Interracial Justice*. As described in the following section, he advanced a theory of situated group power as a way to comprehend and respond to color-on-color grievances that impede alliance forging. He and Julie Su then refined aspects of that theory in *Critical Coalitions*.[37]

In following years an expansive legal scholarship on race noted color-on-color tensions. One work in particular advanced the theorizing on the structure of intergroup conflicts. As mentiond above, in 2007 Robert Chang and Neil Gotanda crafted a broad three-tier model for interminority group conflict. The first tier addressed the traditional black-white paradigm of race relations—"many analyses of racial and ethnic conflict follow this basic majority-minority binary opposition." Disputes between two non-white groups fell within a second-order binary analysis, which includes "a comparison of the similarities and differences between minority A's and minority B's experience with oppression." This analysis was deemed useful if the "larger political, legal, and social forces that foster conflict between nonwhite groups" remain in view.[38]

The third-order multigroup analysis examined the ways in which whites benefit from a temporal relationship with one nonwhite group that alters that group's relationship with another nonwhite group. The aligned nonwhite group achieves a short-term gain at the other nonwhite group's expense. After white interests are furthered, the relationship breaks down, leaving both nonwhite groups disadvantaged and subjugated in the long run.

These three-tier analyses illuminated the basic relational structure among communities of color, while also acknowledging the significant—but not always obvious—role that whites play in fostering tensions. Chang and Gotanda illustrated the third-order multigroup analyses through nuanced depictions of constructed relationships: Asians serving as a "model" for "non-achieving" African Americans and Latinos; African Americans filling a role as fully integrated citizens whose interests will become compromised unless Congress enacts anti-immigration reforms; and Latinos adopting the "white" label for purposes of "desegregating" African American schools. These analyses revealed how whites "can manipulate coalition politics," as "the seduction of being included with the in-group ultimately leads one nonwhite group to lose sight of White supremacy in order to achieve a short-term gain while jeopardizing progress in the long run."[39]

The model offered fresh insight into the structure of intergroup relations and impediments to coalitions. Its conceptual advances, by design, stopped short of offering concepts for grappling with the power dimensions of intergroup tensions that arise from the temporal alignments. Chang and Gotanda recognized the need "to get it right as a matter of theory; and . . . to get it right as a matter of politics to foster coalitions." Beyond this, they pointed toward future exploration of approaches to achieve the desired collective ends.[40]

Several legal scholars responded to the call for approaches to coalition building in specific settings. For instance, Hernandez focused on race discrimination claims in the workplace and insightfully argued that current jurisprudence fails to recognize the dynamics of interethnic civil rights claims, particularly claims involving Latinos and African Americans. Hernandez sought the "development of a conceptual framework for effectively presenting and understanding inter-ethnic discrimination claims with the goal of disrupting the judiciary's singular focus on White/non-White discrimination." Mari Matsuda earlier drew upon feminist theory to envision boundary-crossing coalitions among indigenous and nonnative peoples. And the social scientists Jennifer Gordon and R. A. Lendhardt explored the relationship between African Americans and low-wage Latino immigrants, targeting common goals relating to citizenship and work to foster increased solidarity.[41]

These works mark important if separate steps forward. The time is ripe for further inquiry into the dynamics of color-on-color grievance as a predicate to alliance forging.

IV. THEORY OF COLOR-ON-COLOR POWER DYNAMICS: GRAPPLING WITH GRIEVANCES TO FORGE ALLIANCES

As touched upon in section III, recent years are witness to "intensifying conflict and distrust among communities of color amid shifting racial and class demographics." Understanding interracial tension and its accompanying manifestations—in the context of both daily interactions and the larger-scale conflicts that generate substantial media attention—"requires acknowledging how privilege and oppression are often not absolute categories but, rather, shift in relation to different axes of power and powerlessness." The unique nature of color-on-color relationships thus calls for analytical frameworks that engage the reality that "racial groups may be, in varying ways, simultaneously privileged and oppressed, empowered and disempowered, uplifting and subordinating."[42]

The framework Yamamoto introduced in *Interracial Justice* wrestles with the amorphous and constantly evolving power dimensions to color-on-color relations. This framing of *group agency* and *responsibility* challenges groups to think beyond the black-white paradigm. In doing so, it endeavors to account for the three color-on-color undercurrents described at the outset—the role of whites in color-on-color conflicts; the volatile mix of historical memories and cultural misunderstandings that coalesce into broadly held group grievances that transcend specific disputes; and the recurring desire for and struggles with alliance forging. In "highly fluid, highly contested . . . borderland site[s] of continuing struggles for identity and power," Yamamoto's central concepts of *simultaneity* and *differentiation* aim to "account for both the relational and conflictual nature of power among racial groups." This approach to racial group agency and responsibility explicitly addresses the idea of situated racial group power both enlivened and constrained by multiple, shifting contexts.[43]

Drawing from aspects of postcolonial theory, *simultaneity* addresses a group's shifting power in relation to others amid changing demographics and socioeconomic structures. *Simultaneity* examines the roots of group grievance by interrogating historically situated group power arrangements, particularly where a group now may be simultaneously, in differing ways, oppressed and partial oppressor. It is informed by related inquiries into redeployment, positionality, and alignment.[44]

Redeployment of Structures and Strategies of Oppression

The first *simultaneity* inquiry is into *redeployment*, which addresses a phenomenon observed in a variety of settings where groups struggle against oppression and for liberation. *Redeployment* occurs where an oppressed group with a degree of newly acquired power partially "redeploys structures and strategies of oppression" against those less powerful—for instance, refusing to hire negatively stereotyped members of another disfavored group—even though the emergent group remains largely subjugated in the broader social hierarchy. The concept recognizes two key realities: first, at times a group does unto others that which is done to it; second, despite continuing subjugation by a third and far more dominant group (often but not always whites), the group still possesses some degree of power (and responsibility) to self-define and affirmatively shape interactions with others.[45]

Redeployment recognizes the agency of a group that, despite structural limitations (particularly economic and political), still maintains limited power over other groups in some situations. In this sense, oppressive choices are exercised "not by free agents or autonomous actors, but by people who are compromised and constrained by social context."[46]

Two brief illustrations. The first involves selected African American groups deploying harsh "anti-outsider" language in support of white-led anti-immigrant campaigns targeting Latinos—characterizations of inferiority not unlike those earlier deployed explicitly by whites against African Americans. The second is the Asian American "reverse discrimination" lawsuit that marshals civil rights rhetoric in an effort (initially started and financed mainly by whites) to invalidate affirmative action admissions policies in charter schools and universities—a kind of suit unsupported by most Asian American groups but that, if successful, would eliminate policies that once lifted up Asian Americans and would now significantly diminish admissions of African Americans and Latinos.[47]

In these and myriad other ways, newly empowered groups, struggling to redefine themselves amid a changing environment, at times partially redeploy forms of "rhetorical, institutional, and economic" subjugation, including the reproduction of "essentialist notions of culture and history, conservative notions of territorial and linguistic propriety, and the 'otherness' ensuing from them."[48]

Grappling with redeployment points toward possibilities for new forms of community empowerment. It makes explicit that a central challenge facing any group displacing "a system in which one culture dominates another . . . is to provide for a new order that does not reproduce the social structure of the old system." By first recognizing constrained group agency and a tendency toward redeployment of oppressive structures, a community can acknowledge its responsibility to work to begin to at least partially transform its exercise of power—that is, from exercising "power over" others to employing "power to" coexist and mutually advance. Drawing on feminist theories about transformative power structures, Thomas Wartenberg suggests that "a transformative use of power posits a form of social hierarchy through which dependent beings can be treated in a manner that allows them to achieve independence."[49]

Relational Positionality

The second related inquiry is positionality. It acknowledges that power often runs in multiple directions and explores how a group's power positions are shaped by ongoing interactions. *Relational positionality* reveals how a group can be simultaneously "privileged" in relation to one group and "subordinated" in relation to another; "empowered" compared to some and "disempowered" compared to others. The group's multiple power positions at a given moment depend on the political and economic setting and the tenor of its relations with others.[50]

Immigrant status, employment, race, class, culture, and other distinguishing characteristics influence group relationships, creating multiple systems of possible domination in which power flows in several directions. In addressing women's agency at the juncture of race and gender, feminist legal theorists inquire into how white women, subject to patriarchal oppression, may possess invisible white privilege and sometimes exercise attendant power in ways harmful to women of color. A key to understanding women's agency in this way is the idea of relational positionality. Women engage in many relationships in multiple contexts, with power flowing simultaneously in several directions. In this way, relational positionality significantly complicates fixed categories of victims and victimizers.[51]

Indeed, "victims can also be victimizers; agents of change can also be complicitous, depending on the particular axis of power one considers." A woman's power potential thus depends on her relational position with other social actors. She may be oppressed under one system of domination (patriarchy) and oppressive through others (race and class). In terms of agency, women (like racial groups) can be simultaneously at least partially privileged and subordinated, partially empowered and disempowered.[52]

Social Alignment

Redeployment and positionality delineate the general framework of *simultaneity*, but neither concept examines the microdynamics of intergroup power, or more particularly, the ways in which a social actor, with multiple identities, can be simultaneously subordinated and privileged. The third and final inquiry of *simultaneity*, social alignment, helps deepen this understanding of positional power by asking a question connecting power to oppression: "How does a group generally disempowered in one intergroup relationship acquire and maintain a position of power over another group?"[53]

Social alignment analysis expands traditional power analysis beyond two nonwhite groups located in the primary relationship by taking into account the broader nature of social power. Influenced by the "vicissitudes of politics, the economy, and social demographics," a racial group at times forges alliances with unlikely partners as a means of increasing its respective power over another group. Or sometimes more powerful groups insert themselves into a controversy, uninvited, lending support that furthers their own interests but that also alters the power landscape. *Social alignment* engages these intergroup dynamics, acknowledges their fluidity, and emphasizes how power in a primary relationship can be enhanced or even created by others outside the relationship.[54]

In the race setting, this triangulates the traditional binary group power analysis of, for instance, black and brown. It examines the influence of other groups (for instance, anti-immigrant whites) in shaping the dynamics of the primary relationship, thus taking into account the multidirectional valences of social power.[55]

One example of this phenomenon, discussed earlier, emerges in the immigration realm where certain whites have aligned with selected African Americans and Asian Americans in an effort to subjugate Latino and poor Asian immigrants. Another is the pairing of some whites and a few Asian Americans to challenge affirmative action programs now benefiting both African Americans and Latinos.[56] In each of these instances, one group has gained a comparative power advantage over another group by virtue of its temporal alliance with a third, more dominant group—an alliance that also enhances the power of the dominant group.

The inquiry into social alignments adds depth to the idea of *simultaneity* in three respects. First, it gives concrete meaning to the amorphous idea of "context." Context matters because at least partially powerful outside actors align themselves in varying ways with one central agent rather than the other. Through these alignments "context" empowers one agent over the other in the primary relationship and shapes possible courses of action. Second, it highlights the salience of alliances (general alignments) and coalitions (task-directed groups) to group agency.

Third, social alignment offers a view of intergroup power as fluid and changeable. Because power is an "ongoing social process" rather than a simple static social distribution, the dynamics of these intergroup relationships can change frequently in borderland sites. Since in any single relationship each group may be aligned with several outside agents in the field, one group may have some limited form of power over the other under certain circumstances and may have power over it exercised by the other in other circumstances. This means that power in a given relationship, and certainly in multiple relationships, is shifting and colliding, often operating at cross-purposes. It also means that alignments can at times be strategically harnessed for purposes of addressing group grievances and refashioning relationships.[57]

While the broader concept of *simultaneity* helps explain the multidimensional nature of group power (and power abuses), *differentiation* offers insight into how groups acquire different identities and why differing degrees of political and economic power accrue to those identities. In particular, *differentiation* addresses how "national and localized struggles for identity and power" give rise to "differential racialization"—the divergent culturally generated characteristics attributed, often unfairly, to different groups. It thereby acknowledges that groups have unique cultures, distinct histories of oppression and liberation, and varying present-day social and economic challenges—and therefore differing levels and types of power (and powerlessness).[58]

These differences bear not only on group identities but also on political organization and the range of available responses. For example, African American groups, whose predecessors spearheaded the modern civil rights movement, may organize around different issues than recent Latino or Asian immigrants or Native Americans, whose group histories are vastly different. Divergent goals, as well as perceptions of power or lack of power, often underlie group conflicts. Thus "localized analysis of differential power among communities of color" is often a necessary predicate to addressing the roots of those conflicts.[59]

Differentiation analyses are important for two reasons. First, acknowledging differential power between nonwhite groups is a tacit recognition that a group possesses some degree of economic or political power in certain settings and is consequently responsible when exercises of even limited power harm other groups. Second, differential racial group power analyses set the stage for intergroup empathy, which is a precursor to building coalitions and developing ways of living together peaceably and working together productively. These analyses encourage both groups to ask: "To what extent are this other group's formative experiences (and culture) similar to and different from ours? What marks the human dimensions to their struggles for survival and advancement? And by viewing this other group through the lens of our experience, in what ways have we overlooked or misunderstood their racial wounds and justice grievances as well as their cultural vibrancy?"[60]

To better demonstrate the analytical utility of *simultaneity* and *differentiation* in helping unravel the often hidden power dynamics of underlying face-to-face conflicts, we highlight two recent controversies among nonwhite racial groups whose long-standing and often overlooked grievances tend to undercut promising alliances and impede broader social healing.

V. DEPLOYING THEORY ABOUT INTERGROUP POWER ARRANGEMENTS IN ADDRESSING GROUP GRIEVANCES AS A PREDICATE TO ALLIANCE FORGING

As discussed, theories of color-on-color conflicts have not fully integrated analyses of the power dimensions of underlying grievances. They have yet to thoroughly coalesce insights into redeployed oppressive structures, the positional flow of power, the impact of shifting alignments, and the significance of differing group histories and cultures into an analytical framework for grappling with hidden substructures of grievances that at times impede the formation of enduring alliances. The preceding section, building on prior work, endeavored to point coalitional scholarship and action in that direction.

This section aims to partially illuminate the utility of a developing framework that moves beyond common interests and embraces nuanced concepts of *simultaneity* and *differentiation*. It does so by examining aspects of two realms of color-on-color conflicts and underlying grievances: racialized anti-immigrant controversies, and disputes, including violence, in neighborhoods and schools with an overlap of challenges to affirmative action programs.

In particular, the examination embraces two thematic aims—to reveal how perceived group-on-group grievances sometimes underlie and exacerbate specific face-to-face conflicts, and to deploy analytical tools for grappling with the substructure of those grievances as a predicate for forging productive and lasting alliances. Especially for an essay, the examination is necessarily preliminary. It at times engages in broad generalizations and does not fully interrogate the conflicts or grievances or employ all concepts to provide comprehensive assessments. Its aim is to offer a glimpse into theory and ground-level realities that lay a foundation for further scholarly inquiry and community action.

The immigration debate, fueled by stock stories of illegal immigrant job takeovers and "anchor babies," has demeaned and divided communities of color and sparked unlikely alliances. An aggressive white nativist movement with racist roots has garnered a good deal of public support while promoting exclusionary initiatives designed in part to polarize nonwhite communities.[61]

In early 2011 white anti-immigrant Republicans attempted to fuel black and brown tensions to facilitate passage of anti-immigrant bills. On a public panel called "Making Immigration Work for American Minorities," Republican representatives Elton Gallegly, Steve King, and Lamar Smith argued not that immigration could "work" to benefit "American minorities" but rather that many new immigrants should, in effect, be excluded from the American polity. They aimed their pitch at African Americans, indicating that Latino "immigrants drove down wages and were primarily responsible for the unemployment crisis in black communities."[62]

The Congressional Black Caucus criticized the Republicans' tactics. Representative Emanuel Cleaver called out "the majority's attempt to manufacture tension between African Americans and immigrant communities. . . . They would like for our communities to think about immigration in terms of 'us versus them,' and I reject that notion." He identified the real roots of African American grievances—an economic system that sends good high-paying jobs overseas and a "broken immigration system [that] creates a race to the bottom for the worst paying and most difficult jobs." Playing racial "politics with immigration," he concluded, "only reinforces the status quo."[63]

Frank Sherry, head of the immigration reform advocacy group America's Voice, echoed that message: "Another day, another hypocritical attempt by Republican immigration hardliners to disguise their mass deportation agenda in more popular terms. But these politicians have been voting against the rights of workers for years. This hearing is a transparent attempt to rebrand their extreme, anti-immigration agenda, and it won't work."[64]

Immigrant and civil rights advocates also cited Immigration Policy Center research showing that "immigration does not cause black unemployment, and that there was no strong correlation between the two." The president of the Leadership Conference on Civil and Human Rights testified that "high unemployment rates in black communities was a persistent trend spanning decades and was due more to the war on drugs and mass incarceration policies, as well as black folks' restricted access to high quality public education and decent housing and jobs."[65]

According to these civil rights and immigrant advocacy organizations, many white anti-immigration advocates are aiming to divide African American and Latino communities under the guise of immigration reform. FAIR, for example, is the best-known anti-immigration organization in the United States. With direct past ties to white supremacist groups, FAIR is viewed by some as an extremist organization that scapegoats immigrants for the country's ills, including crime, poverty, and racial tensions.[66]

In an attempt to generate an appearance of a broad-based nativist movement, FAIR reportedly launched other anti-immigrant groups that claimed to represent African Americans and Latino Americans. For instance, one FAIR front group, the CBA—a self-professed nationwide coalition of black business, academic, and community leaders—spread the alarmist message that "mass illegal immigration has been the single greatest impediment to black advancement in this country over the past 25 years." In creating and supporting the CBA and thereby aiming to align whites and African Americans against Latino immigrants, FAIR rhetorically framed the controversy as illegal Latino immigrants taking African Americans' jobs and depressing African Americans' wages. CBA spokespersons, claiming to represent the "vast majority" of African Americans, reportedly declared, "You got silly naïve black leadership who don't understand that those people [Latinos] are not coming here to get along with black folks. They are coming here to compete with black folks."[67]

By offering a "black face" to its movement, some predominantly white anti-immigrant groups like FAIR attempt to strategically align African Americans with the anti-immigrant cause while shielding themselves from accusations of racism. In response to this seemingly unlikely black and white alliance, Earl Ofari Hutchinson, an African American columnist, criticized FAIR for exploiting genuine concerns about immigration. "We haven't seen them involved in any issues beyond immigration that impact the black community. Why all of a sudden would [African Americans] align ... with groups who have murky ties with other groups that are racist?" Similarly, African American leaders Rev. Jesse Jackson and Rev. Al Sharpton characterized the anti-immigrant movement as antithetical to the broader ideals of the African American–led civil rights movement.[68]

FAIR also reportedly sponsored the launch of You Don't Speak for Me, a Latino American group that describes itself as "a group of concerned Americans of Hispanic/Latino heritage, some first or second generation, others recent legal immigrants, who believe undocumented immigration harms America and a guest worker amnesty will do the same." According to FAIR, group members comprise a cross section of the Latino American community.[69]

Political leaders and scholars wonder why some nonwhite spokespersons for racially identified organizations are redeploying oppressive rhetoric and providing "window dressing" for an overwhelmingly white movement. Shayla Nunnally observes that "[i]t goes back to minorities fighting minorities, while fighting the overall oppression isn't being addressed." Taking perhaps the broadest view, Sheila Jackson Lee, an African American congresswoman from Texas, calls the calculated efforts to divide African Americans and Latinos over immigration "the civil rights issue of our time."[70]

While spotlighting color-on-color conflicts, narrow accounts and sweeping generalizations about black and brown tensions tend to overlook significant undercurrents. How do communities make clearer sense out what some describe as a simple white "divide and conquer" maneuver or what others characterize as "minorities fighting minorities"? More specifically, how can scholars, advocates, and policy makers more productively grapple with the underpinnings of some of the intergroup tensions between African Americans and Latinos (both immigrants and citizens)—as Cleaver, Sherry, and Lee began to do—as well as the unaddressed "overall oppression" identified by Nunnally?

The *simultaneity* inquiry into "redeployment of structures and strategies of oppression" offers insight. The inquiry begins with these questions: First, in what ways have the economic, political, and legal systems, coupled with social practices, historically structured overall an exclusionary or oppressive setting in the area? Second, to what extent is a historically subordinated group that has attained some degree of newly acquired power situationally redeploying dominant structures and strategies to undercut a more vulnerable group even while itself remaining partially oppressed?[71]

In the context of immigration in border states, for instance, African American members of the CBA appear to perceive Latino immigrants as a threat to their political, economic, and social well-being. White nativist leaders are playing upon this perceived threat to put nonwhite faces on the broader anti-immigrant movement to enhance the power of that movement.

Through alignment with anti-immigrant conservatives, a limited segment of African Americans becomes partially empowered by (and empowers) the white-driven nativist movement. It redeploys oppressive strategies by stereotyping Latino immigrants as inferior and undeserving intruders in justifying support for draconian anti-Latino immigrant laws like Arizona's. Those laws harshly impact documented as well as undocumented Latinos in workplaces, schools, buses, and health clinics. And this exclusionary and harassing impact resembles the oppression historically visited by many whites upon African Americans.[72]

Prominent African American leaders criticize the Arizona law and endeavor to build bridges around a common interest in civil rights. A noticeable number of African Americans, however, find little traction on the issue. Wilbert Nelson, president of the NAACP in Arizona, characterizes the sentiment of a segment of African Americans there as indifference. "We don't see it as an issue for us. . . . We see it as an issue of [Latino] folks crossing the border." For this reason, a social justice advocate observes that "it appears that African-Americans on the ground approve of or are ambivalent about the law" and that "[t]hese attitudes not only compound [Latinos'] isolation,

they also undermine social justice more generally." And the advocate might
have added, "and increase tensions between the two groups."[73]

This redeployment of exclusionary forms of oppression by selective yet
visible Arizona African Americans occurs even as African Americans as a
group are simultaneously the continuing targets of negative racial stereotyping and exclusion. The concept of redeployment reveals that some African
Americans (here, some political leaders and supporters of the nativist movement) may be reemploying a strategy (with different targets) long deployed
by mainly white businesses and law enforcement to cleave apart white and
black workers in order to diminish wages and social opportunities and mobility for the latter.[74]

Simultaneity's inquiry into social alignment further illuminates this
dynamic. It explores, in a two-party relationship, how one party's alliance
with a third party enables it to exert "power over" the other party. For instance, alignment with dominant white-led anti-immigrant groups enhances
the power of white nativists while seemingly empowering some African
Americans—and some Asian Americans—by enabling the nativist groups
collectively to target Latinos for exclusion. Greatly influenced by political,
economic, and social forces within a specific setting, the alignment inquiry
recognizes that a splinter group, which does not represent the majority, sometimes forges unlikely alliances in order to increase its power over others in
ways that reflect back onto the larger group. When CBA leader Ted Hayes
describes Latino immigration as "the greatest threat to U.S. black citizens
since slavery," he attempts to pit African Americans generally against nonwhite counterparts and simultaneously forge a closer alliance with dominant
whites—for the benefit of African Americans and white nativists at the expense of Latino immigrants.[75]

Moreover, as mentioned, some African American political leaders appear
reluctant to directly engage the positional dynamics of white anti-immigrant
advocates' impact on black and Latino grievances. While perhaps under-
standable as a political matter—the engagement would be energy consuming
and messy, would generate backlash, and would likely not yield immediate benefits—political inaction exacerbates black and brown tensions and
impedes short-term coalition building and long-term alliance forging over
immigration and other related challenges.

Viewed through the prism of *simultaneity*, the redeployment of structures
of oppression and positional alignments contributes to apparent Latino
community grievances against not only African Americans with expressed
anti-immigrant sentiments but also more broadly against those African

Americans who are seen generally as standing by in tacit approval. We are, of course, speaking of broad perceptions, not specific realities. Yet perceptions of events and interactions, conveyed through media and culture, are key shapers and drivers of grievance—hence the need for incisive inquiry and in-depth understanding.

Some African Americans, too, harbor group grievances against Latinos. And Asian Americans are a part of the complex positional flow of power and grievance that at least partially informs specific conflicts.

Latinos and African Americans

As discussed, simmering tensions between Latinos and African Americans, with sporadic outbursts of violence, continue to mark borderland sites. In particular, in a struggling working-class area near Los Angeles, a Latino gang actively sought to rid neighborhoods of longtime African American residents. In direct response, Latino and African American communities, city politicians, and police tried, with some, though limited, success, both to stem the violence and to repair frayed relations.

Just outside of Los Angeles, the Azusa community struggled to understand the roots of Latino gang violence against and harassment of African American residents. In June 2011 a federal grand jury indicted fifty-one Latinos for conspiring to seriously injure or kill African Americans in Azusa. The indictment followed a three-year investigation of a prominent Latino gang charged with "attempting to racially cleanse Azusa of African Americans during two decades of intimidation and attacks." According to Azusa police, the gang members "violated the civil rights of African Americans in the city from 1992 to May 2010."[76]

Implicating racial dynamics, the Latino defendants were accused of aiming their attacks not at rival gangs but rather at African American neighborhood residents whom they "wished to push out of the city or prevent from moving there." According to observers, Latino gang violence "rang[ed] from racist graffiti to murder" and was fueled in part by a perception of African Americans encroaching on expanding Latino territory.[77]

In another publicized instance of Latino violence against African American residents, in 2006 two reputed Latino gang members fired shots into a group of African Americans, killing a fourteen-year-old girl. The sporadic violence between the groups culminating in the murder of Cheryl Green triggered wide-ranging reactions that, for the most part, however, had limited long-term effect. Government officials responded to the murder of Green and other violence by implementing a militarily framed "'surge' on [area Latino] gangs."[78]

Others, including both Latino and African American neighborhood residents and community activists, jointly mobilized to protest the violence that devastated many and to build bridges among the seemingly divided groups. Following Green's murder, over 100 community members—many African Americans and some Latinos—rallied together and walked down 204th Street to the nearby liquor store. Explaining the significance of the rally, participant and community activist Najee Ali said, "It was an act of defiance.... Anyone from the community should have the right to walk and shop wherever they please."[79]

Ali's call for the march and joint resistance was a good practical start. But, as a strategy, it was limited. It focused on finding immediate common interests between African American and Latino communities: stopping the violence and attendant fear—a worthy goal. But by focusing on a short-term common interest without also attending to the deeper underlying grievances harbored by groups, it was an approach likely to, as it eventually did, stall. While gang members declined in numbers after the community's powerful demonstration and police surge, deeper community understandings of the roots of the violence, it appears, still awaited. Some area residents who were aware of the tensions nevertheless "den[ied] there is a racial problem and refuse[d] to talk about it." And some feared that when increased policing (with its own problems) waned, the Latino gang that "has shown a tremendous hatred toward blacks in that community" would regroup.[80]

The attacks by Latino gangs on African American neighborhood residents were tragic events, specific in time and place. Yet with at times intense local and national media coverage, the reverberations were far-reaching. As alluded to in the foregoing truncated account of the controversy, the violence and strong but limited resistance can only be fully understood and proactively addressed in building future relations by first unraveling the broader and deeper group grievances—both grounded and imagined.

Why have a few visible African Americans, with what some organizations claim to be far broader silent support, expressed varying degrees of resentment toward perceived intruding "illegal hordes" of non-English-speaking Latinos who displace struggling African Americans in the workplace and neighborhoods? And why have some Latinos characterized African Americans as unwilling to work hard and as using local political muscle to attempt to block Latino advancement? And why have members of each group at times accused the other of standing by in tacit approval of continued harsh economic and social discrimination by businesses, politicians, and government institutions, particularly those with a strong white or Asian American presence?

What, if anything, is grounded in real experiences, and what is imagined and passed on as implicit biases through collective memories and present-day cultural practices? How much is simply attitude and perception, and how much is hard action driven by attitude and perception? And, perhaps most important for alliance-forging prospects, what group grievances are generated and sustained by these largely stereotypic group characterizations and outside alignments, shaping and often exacerbating face-to-face conflicts and thereby morphing individual disputes into group-on-group controversies?

The complex backstory to these stereotypes and underlying sense of grievance, and the likely backlash and counterstereotyping, may or may not have fueled the just-described neighborhood cleansing drives by the Latino gang. Nevertheless, the face-to-face on-the-street conflicts were likely undergirded at least in part by broader color-on-color grievances—whether real, imagined, or constructed largely by others. And it was attention to these deeper grievances that was missing from Ali's common interest ("stop the attacks") approach to building more enduring collaborative Latino and African American actions. The void may have been a heat-of-the-moment necessity—a needed practical first step. A group's agency in the moment is constrained by many contextual factors—the extent of media attention; the availability of resources; the alignment with politicians, government officials, and social justice groups; the area's history of economic and social exclusion. But without ensuing steps—penetrating inquiry into and new group understandings of self and others (including ways that the two groups, both facing hard discrimination, are nevertheless differentially racialized)—the journey toward rapprochement and enduring collective action halts.

Searching for concepts and language to explain what was missing from the limited "crackdown on violence" and "surge" approach to the controversies, highly regarded Los Angeles civil rights attorney Constance Rice highlighted the need for simultaneous prevention and intervention strategies. She emphasized crucial next steps: mutual, difficult, and complex inquiries that are "learned" from the "right experts" and community members to get at underlying factors fueling what appear to be grievances toward a group rather than individuals. Those factors, she implied, are linked in part to differing cultures and values, to the differing impacts of the disappearance of jobs overseas, and to the similar yet differing citywide histories of discrimination in jobs, housing, and business financing. Rice explained that "[s]trategic suppression is essential, a strong response to violent gangs . . . is necessary, as a first step, and the effort will need more resources. But it is unclear whether the city has learned that suppression must be *coordinated with comprehensive prevention and intervention strategies.*"[81]

Rice then insightfully linked the next step, "comprehensive prevention and intervention strategies," with cool-headed interrogation of the historical and cultural roots of underlying group grievances. She advocated, in essence, *simultaneity* and *differentiation* analyses because communities and "politicians must connect with the right experts, who can diagnose the unique neighborhood factors" and the underlying broader economic forces and cultural misunderstandings that "fuel the gang's dominance." She concluded that Los Angeles "must launch a [comparative] 'cultures and values' campaign to end the violence and killing of *la vida loca.*"[82]

With this in mind, the public fears aroused by reports of Latino gangs attempting to "ethnically cleanse" some Los Angeles neighborhoods raise a pressing realpolitik question: to what extent are the Latino and African American communities, government officials, and the populace willing and able not only to address the specific events with boots on the ground policing but also to tackle long-standing and in some respects intensifying mutual group grievances—both to deter immediate violence and to generate more lasting and far-reaching approaches to collaborative community action?

We can better understand the underpinnings of the intergroup tensions between Latinos and African Americans, just described, through the *simultaneity* inquiry into the "redeployment of structures and strategies of oppression." In Los Angeles, for instance, some believe Latinos have gained an economic advantage over African Americans mainly through rapid demographic growth and its impact on the election of Latino politicians as well as through many small-scale economic opportunities bolstering an emerging Latino middle class.

Latinos, a historically subordinated group in the United States, continue to face violence in borderlands areas and discrimination in jobs, schools, and housing. And they face harsh stereotyping by segments of the public fearful of overwhelming numbers of "illegal" immigrants destroying jobs for citizens and diluting mainstream culture. A recent poll found that mainly because of their perceived immigrant status, Latinos face significant discrimination in America.[83]

Yet some Latinos, through demographic shifts, their own efforts, or alignments with others, have become at least partially empowered in certain communities and have uplifted themselves and others. But in some situations, with that constrained power, they are seen as partially deploying oppressive social structures and power strategies. For instance, behind the scenes, some Latino politicians and community advocates are charged with standing by "in silence" as African Americans are threatened, or worse, by Latinos. Without attention to the current effects of the economic system's history of racially discriminatory practices, some characterize socioeconomic advancement as zero-sum urban competition between less-deserving African Americans and more worthy Latinos. Certain Latino gangs, it appears, draw a sense of enhanced power from this stereotypic form of racialization, and African American residents with no gang affiliations thereby become easier targets for neighborhood harassment and violence. As mentioned, this redeployment of forms of oppression by certain Latinos occurs even as Latinos as a group are simultaneously the targets of ill will, discrimination, and even violence.[84]

These insights also implicate *simultaneity*'s inquiry into relational positionality. Positionality acknowledges that power runs in multiple directions simultaneously and explores how a group's power positions are shaped by ongoing interactions. It reveals that sometimes behind the group's grievances lie maneuverings by more powerful, usually white, employers, andlords, and financiers. Just as African American anger toward Korean shopkeepers was fueled in part by the disappearance on inner-city jobs and by perceptions of special favors from white landlords and banks, so too have been some Latinos' perceptions of special government treatment of African Americans who are seen as now trying to shut the door on hardworking Latinos.[85]

Simultaneity's inquiry also sheds light on the question of social alignment by exploring, in a two-party relationship, how one party's alliance with a third party sometimes enables the first party to exert "power over" the second party. For instance, local Los Angeles Latino political leaders were accused of idly standing by despite heavy publicity about Latino gang killings of African American neighborhood residents. Kerman Maddox of the African American Summit on Violence Prevention therefore asked, "Why are Latinos committing violent crimes targeted against African Americans . . . and why aren't Latino leaders speaking out against them?" Former mayor Villaraigosa visited an area of Latino–on–African American violence to encourage residents "to get along" and to offer assistance "to help solve some of the socioeconomic problems." But, as one observer pointed out, "other Latino political leaders have been silent." And the mayor's exhortation to get along without real efforts to deal with the social structural problems or the mutually held group grievances was easily taken as all words and no action, an approach that, for some, portends the risk of an eventual Los Angeles "racial meltdown."[86]

Villaraigosa's public response initially provided cover for local Latino politicians who appeared to take a largely hands-off approach to the controversy. The tepid Latino political criticism and relative inaction enabled Latino gangs to maintain some degree of power over fearful African Americans. As a possible result, and generalizing broadly, African American residents were left to their own resources or to align either with the outsider police for protection, despite their historically difficult and distrusting relationship with the police, or with white anti-immigrant groups who claimed to be protective of African Americans.[87]

All of this—despite an expressed desire by both sides of the divide to build bridges—appears to have deepened area tensions and reinforced group grievances. The perceived apathy of partially empowered Latino political leaders heightened ongoing mistrust, further dampening prospects for significant collective action.

While the broader concept of *simultaneity* helps explain the multidimensional nature of group power and the ways constrained exercises of power inform grievances, the *differentiation* inquiry reveals how Latino and African American group grievances are partly rooted in misunderstood histories and differing present-day economic and political situations.[88]

Differentiation acknowledges that different groups tend to have unique cultures (including family orientations, religions, practices, and languages), distinct histories of oppression and liberation (whether persisting challenges of slavery and segregation or anti-immigrant vilifications), and varying present-day social and economic challenges (in terms of prior economic discrimination and limited access to education, health care, housing, and jobs), as well as differing group levels and types of power (politics, business, and media) and powerlessness. In the right settings, discussed later, this inquiry enables Latinos and African Americans to better empathize with, and accept partial responsibility for, the multifaceted struggles of the other group. The exploration also helps groups grasp sources of mutual misunderstandings and stereotyping and sets the stage for realistically assessing the possibilities and limitations of "common ground" as a basis for collective action. This kind of messy, slow yet more fully informed assessment is a critical step toward intergroup understanding and, ultimately, alliance forging.

As suggested, and as implied by civil rights leader Rice, a predicate to forging those alliances are the redeployment, alignment, and differentiation inquiries that enable groups to acknowledge each other's history and present situations, assess the roots of their mutual grievances, and move toward not only deeper understanding but also ameliorative action (where reparative steps are appropriate). *Simultaneity* and *differentiation* thus are integral dimensions of a framework for nuanced assessment of the power dynamics often underlying group grievances. Properly translated and employed, they may prove to be useful tools for communities and advocates from all sides to investigate and grasp the dynamics shaping the underlying group-on-group grievances that transcend (and often exacerbate) specific on-the-ground conflict.

African American and Asian American Grievances

In another illustration of how face-to-face surface conflicts are at least partially undergirded by long-standing grievances among communities of color, recent street violence between Asian American and African American individuals reignited debate about simmering group-on-group tensions.

In April 2010 Chinese immigrants Tian Sheng Yu, fifty-nine, and son Jin Cheng Yu, twenty-seven, traveled from their San Francisco home to an up-and-coming neighborhood in Oakland for daytime shopping. In what African American mayor Ron Dellums then described as "a brutal and random attack," two African American teenagers, Lavonte Drummer and Dominic Davis, approached the younger Yu while the elder Yu searched for parking. Without apparent provocation, one of the teens struck the son in the face. A second altercation ensued during which Jin Cheng Yu was punched multiple times and his father once. Tian Sheng Yu fell from the single blow. His head hit the ground, and he died a few days later. In weeks following, the communities, police, media, and the Yu family struggled to understand the tragedy.[89]

Might the attack best be viewed as an isolated street corner conflict, as badly misguided youthful aggression—as some contended? Or, as others wondered, did it reflect something far more that needed addressing on a much larger scale? Was it at least partially rooted in a sometimes supportive and sometimes turbulent history of group relations, with group grievances shaping perceptions (and misperceptions) of the "other"? How connected, if at all, was a history of similar conflicts in the region and sporadic albeit highly publicized violence in Southern California, including the 1991 Asian American shop owner's fatal shooting of African American teen Latasha Harlins and the civil unrest in Koreatown following the Rodney King police brutality verdict?

One local newspaper reported four Bay Area "high-profile attacks involving blacks and Asians" in the first three months of 2010. One month prior to the Tian Sheng Yu incident, a fifteen-year-old African American teenager threw an elderly Asian American woman off a bus platform after an attempted robbery. The fall left her unconscious in the bus's path. Earlier in the year five African American youths reportedly beat an eighty-three-year-old Bay Area Asian American man into a coma at a bus station. He eventually died. And in fall 2009 two African American youth beat and robbed an Asian American senior citizen who suffered a broken collarbone.[90]

Were these incidents personally tragic but unexceptional instances of random violence in a large multicity region? The depth of the reactions indicated that much more was at play. While spotlighting the specific violence, the initial accounts hinted at significant color-on-color undercurrents. As discussed earlier, running barely below the surface of these often variegated conflicts sometimes is a volatile mix of poignant historical memories, current cultural misunderstandings, and sharp media-generated racial mischaracterizations of African Americans and Asians (both immigrants and American citizens) that coalesce into commonly held group grievances. With a history of white discrimination and present-day economic struggles as backdrop, these grievances transcend specific interactions and sometimes transform individual conflicts into group-on-group disputes. In this way a youth's attack on an elder can morph quickly into a community-wide race controversy.

Community controversies then become a nationwide challenge when media reporting and word of mouth accounts characterize the violence, even if sporadic, as part of a larger pattern. This dynamic explains in part why observers began to link the Yu killing to events unconnected in time, space, and participants. In early 2010 fifty Asian American high school students were attacked by African American classmates in Philadelphia, prompting the Asian American Legal Defense and Education Fund to file a civil rights complaint with the Department of Justice. In April of the same year a group of African American teenagers serially attacked five elderly Asian American women on the Lower East Side of New York City. Some perceived a linkage between the Bay Area, Philadelphia, and New York violence: African American youths' group-derived grievances toward perceived "weak foreign yet successful" Asians. Others even saw ironic parallels in the Latino gang attacks on African American neighborhood residents in Los Angeles—with Latinos as aggressors acting in part on perceived group-derived grievances against vulnerable neighborhood African Americans as victims.[91]

But still others cautioned against easily characterizing Yu's killing as a racial attack. A lawyer for one of the teens adamantly asserted that the crime was not motivated by race. Prosecutors ultimately agreed, charging Drummer and Davis with murder but not hate crimes.[92]

Community bitterness remained. In a meeting organized by the police, Asian American residents recounted stories of muggings by African American youths. Yu's death and the limited criminal prosecution exposed an underside of black and Asian distrust, even though violence and fear are common facts of life in struggling Asian American and African American communities. At a rally outside San Francisco's city hall, Tammy Tan of the Asian Pacific American Community Center commented, "We don't want to escalate with African-Americans, so we don't say it.... But it is racial."[93]

Yet despite the apprehensions, a salutary undercurrent emerged in the rough movement toward building bridges. In the weeks following Yu's death, hundreds of Asian American community members packed the Oakland Asian Cultural Center for two news conferences and participated in other rallies. "This just sent them over the top," said an organizer. "This is an activist city, but this isn't an activist population at all." At the rallies, African Americans supported Asian Americans.[94]

In some respects, the community outpouring and cross-racial outreach resembled the passionate public response of African Americans and Latinos to the killing of Cheryl Green in Los Angeles that aimed to stop the violence through joint police and community action. Yet both efforts to build bridges around common interests in halting the violence were limited in terms of prospects for long-term social healing. Although meaningful symbolically and in taking initial steps, these joint community efforts largely bypassed the deeper roots of the street conflicts.

African American leader Rev. Cecil Williams identified an underlying sense of group grievance grounded not in racial antipathy but in power dynamics—that is, in feelings of displacement from "power shifts." "At one point, one group may emerge because they've got greater population and another group feels pushed out—feels like they don't have any voice anymore.... It involves a kind of power shift. That, of course, creates some of the tension."[95]

Bay Area columnist Sam Cacas offered poignant commentary. On the one hand, he observed that without public outcry against violence and legal "sanction from the community, government and law enforcement, perpetrators feel encouraged, and in some instances are incited, to inflict hate crimes like the killing of Tian Sheng Yu." On the other hand, Cacas also noted, an outcry against violence and legal sanctions are not enough. If they do not address the "racism" by both sides that underlies the altercations, the authorities, communities, and media may be exacerbating an already volatile situation. In other words, by sidestepping close inquiry into historically situated messy power dynamics that at least partially shape present-day group grievances—what Rev. Williams calls "power shifts" and Cacas characterizes as "racism"—the responses encourage communities and justice advocates to work within an initially useful but ultimately limited bridge-building framework.[96]

Given the complex practical realities of the moment, the immediate responses may be the best possible first steps. But as recognized by Williams, Cacas, and Rice, they are still limited in terms of long-range salutary color-on-color impact.

The broader Oakland community's proactive yet halting efforts to grasp and characterize the conflict in order to deal with at least momentarily frayed Asian American and African American relations underscore how genuine alliance forging is a multifaceted, messy, and time-consuming process that extends well beyond community meetings and the criminal justice system. The prosecution of Drummer and Davis for murder (but not hate crimes) did little to quell the outpouring of emotions attributable to largely unaddressed racial tensions. Assurances by the San Francisco deputy police chief that "[i]t's very rare for hate crimes to take place in Oakland" and that Asian Americans comprise a small proportional percentage of victims in aggravated assaults did little to assuage Asian American community concerns or further a process of addressing deeper grievances.[97]

According to community advocates, Asian Americans (and especially Asian immigrants) tend to refrain from reporting incidents because of language and cultural barriers, an unfamiliarity with and fear of law enforcement, a fear that reporting attacks will draw attention to their vulnerability and provoke further violence, and a belief that their complaints will be disregarded by the government. These generalized fears fall prey to racialized stereotypes about dangerous African American males. And those stereotypes—even without firsthand negative interpersonal interactions—give rise to implicit biases that are bolstered by reports of sporadic black-on-Asian violence that, for some, translate into a generalized sense of group grievance.[98]

At the same time, some African Americans hold group-based grievances against Asian Americans. As are all group grievances, they emerge out of a mélange of historical memories (real and imagined), stock stories, and culturally communicated stereotypes as well as daily economic constraints and actual face-to-face interactions. Publicized African American complaints about disrespectful inner-city Asian merchants leapfrogging Asian immigrant workers and "economically privileged" Asian Americans, discussed earlier, contribute to a sense of socioeconomic grievance.[99]

Another related source of grievance are the few yet highly publicized legal attacks by some Asian Americans on affirmative action primarily benefiting African Americans and Latinos. Whether a reflection of those Asian Americans' ambitions or an effort by aligned whites to deploy Asian Americans to legitimate the partial exclusion African Americans and Latinos from desired schools and jobs for the benefit of whites—or something else—is an open question.[100]

Consider a 1996 lawsuit with far-reaching impacts. The parents of a group of Chinese American students filed suit to invalidate a largely African American–procured judicial consent decree desegregating the public schools in San Francisco. The plaintiffs argued that the enrollment cap that prevented any single racial group from having a disproportionate number of its students at a charter school violated civil rights laws. They blamed what they considered to be "underperforming" African Americans for taking spots that otherwise would have gone to "more qualified" Asian American students.[101]

In a pattern similar to certain African Americans' alignment with white nativists to exclude Latino immigrants, those Asian Americans appeared to align with anti–affirmative action whites in an effort that could set back African American advancement. Without attention to *differential racialization*, the Asian American plaintiffs and their lawyers adopted ideas refined by conservative scholars and advanced by mainly white anti–affirmative action advocacy organizations and commentators. Using the language of "meritocracy," "individual rights," and "color blindness," the Asian American plaintiffs and their supporters aligned themselves with the anti–affirmative action advocates who expressed sympathy for the plight of Asian Americans facing discrimination as part of their larger plan to dismantle affirmative action largely benefiting African Americans and Latinos.[102]

This triangulated positioning of the Asian American plaintiffs with the mainly anti–affirmative action forces and against African Americans and Latinos, and the plaintiffs' apparent lack of self-awareness of their ironic use of civil rights laws and rhetoric, likely exacerbated some African Americans' sense of grievance. Noticeably absent from the plaintiff's litigation strategy was an expressed awareness of how the "suit's harsh rhetoric and claims—in essence accusing African Americans of benefitting from discrimination against Asian Americans—were generating backlash against Asian Americans generally for 'barring the door' and squandering moral capital, on the one hand, and misappropriating civil rights strategies, leapfrogging, and complicity, on the other."[103]

In the high-profile 2003 challenge to the Michigan Law School's affirmative action admissions policy, nearly all Asian American groups strongly defended the policy. But the few that did not received seemingly disproportionate attention—cast by the challengers and media as Asian Americans aligning with whites against affirmative action.

In 2006 Jian Li, a Chinese American with immigrant roots, filed a civil rights complaint against Princeton University, alleging that the school's admissions policies discriminated against Asian Americans. The complaint cited a 2005 Princeton study showing that the abolition of affirmative action in admissions would benefit Asian Americans denied admissions but who had higher test scores than some admitted African Americans, Latinos, and whites. Largely white anti–affirmative action advocates aligned in support.[104]

The challenge was characterized in some circles as another Asian American attack mainly on African Americans through the co-optation of civil rights laws and language. That characterization, however, missed underlying relational dynamics. It overlooked what Li actually argued and his acknowledgment and partial rejection of an alignment with white anti–affirmative action advocates. He fashioned his claim not as Asian Americans paying the price for admission of lesser qualified African Americans and Latinos. Rather, he asserted that Princeton effectively forced applicants of color to fight for a limited number of "nonwhite" seats while largely maintaining the number of spaces for white students. Drawing implicitly on positionality and alignment power analyses, he framed his claim as a charge against a triangulated and "calculated move by a historically white institution to protect its racial identity while at the same time maintaining a facade of progressivism."[105]

In that respect, Li sought admission to the school not by expressly aligning himself with white anti–affirmative action advocates but by challenging Princeton's alleged effort to maintain itself as a predominantly white institution. But despite rhetorical framing that differed from the characterization of the challenge to the San Francisco charter school admission caps, the legal result would have been the same—markedly fewer African American students enrolled in a highly desired school. And in that fashion Li did align with anti–affirmative action scholars and advocates. Did Li anticipate the ways in which his legal challenge on the East Coast (with national news headlines and editorials) might perpetuate racialized stereotypes and deepen a sense of African American grievance against Asian Americans generally? Might his actions, despite the rhetoric, in a broad indirect yet important way have contributed to a milieu of heightened group grievances?

The two Asian American lawsuits challenging affirmative action programs just described differ in important respects. The *simultaneity* and *differential racialization* power analyses nevertheless reveal related ways that the two suits, and the underlying programs themselves, may be have contributed to deeper African American and Asian American grievances that shape a broader array of specific conflicts and prospects for handling them.

For groups struggling to build bridges, after grappling with and gaining a stronger, more nuanced understanding of underlying grievances, the question arises: What's next? It is beyond the scope of this chapter to offer a comprehensive response. As mentioned, Eric Yamamoto in other works is developing a multidisciplinary approach to social healing—that is, healing the wounds of injustice of those suffering and of communities and possibly the larger society. The aim here is to offer insights into what appear to be deep underlying group grievances that shape or exacerbate seemingly individual conflicts and that, unaddressed, impede long-term alliance forging. The aim also is to encourage further development of a power analysis framework to foster that kind of threshold inquiry and understanding, however messy and difficult, that is a predicate to building enduring alliances.[106]

VI. CONCLUSION

Some existing programs appear positioned to grapple with the theoretical insights into the dynamics of color-on-color grievances developed here. In differing ways, and with varying goals, the programs mentioned below endeavor to engage community advocates, neighborhood residents, teachers, government officials, policy makers, and scholars in the struggle to understand and act upon group-on-group conflicts. At the threshold of efforts to heal wounds and build bridges, these education-into-action programs inevitably face the dynamics of intergroup power and grievance. That is precisely why, for purposes of explanation and guidance, they need something more developed than rudimentary ideas of "common interest" coalitions.

For instance, the Crossing Borders program, developed jointly by the Center for Community Change, Fair Immigration Reform Movement, and CASA de Maryland, focuses on "activities that inform African Americans about the global forces that propel immigration to the United States and the relation between racism and the immigration debate, the history of the Civil Rights struggle in the U.S., the centrality of African Americans in the struggle, and the structures that constrain black American communities today." The program's thoughtful and detailed training curriculum targets "organizers and leaders" from groups desirous of building "power and community among people who are different—people who don't look alike, talk alike and haven't lived alike," with an emphasis on differences marked by "race, ethnicity, language, class, power and economics . . . that prevent meaningful and healthy [group] relationships." Its four educational modules productively encompass "Demographic Shifts," the "History of Domination and Pursuit of Work and Opportunity," "Five Dimensions of the African American and Immigrant Tension," and "Jobs, Race and Immigration."[107]

The curriculum makes clear from the outset that central to the Crossing Borders program is a collaborative analysis of power relations and their role in creating and dismantling social hierarchies. Specifically, the program is for "those interested in *power and community*" who are willing to take risks "for the sake of building *new power configurations* that bring diverse people into relationship with one another in order to win on issues of common interest." While "win[ning] on issues of common interest" is an eventual desired outcome, searching for common immediate ground is not the focus of the program's education and action approach. Rather, the focus is on "power and community" as the route toward "new power configurations" among groups in conflict, particularly around axes of race and immigration.[108]

The curriculum does an impressive job overall in developing its training modules. It is noticeably thin, however, in its articulation of the key cross-cutting issue it identifies: the dynamics of group-related power. It succinctly describes "two kinds of power—Power over (someone or group of people) AND power with (someone or group of people)," noting that "Love by itself = sentimental mush. Power by itself = domination." but "Power + Love = Justice." It then observes that tensions between African American and immigrant communities are largely about *power over*, and that these "tensions exist because there are no healthy and meaningful mechanisms for us to build *power with*."[109]

What the curriculum does not do—and would benefit significantly by doing—is articulate and build into its training more rigorously developed concepts and language about intergroup power dynamics in order to help communities generate the "mechanisms" for transforming "power over" into "power to" (or "power with"). Described and partially illuminated by case studies in this chapter, the multifaceted dynamics of *underlying grievance* (that explode individual conflicts into group controversies), informed by the multilayered analytical concepts of *simultaneity* and *differentiation* developed here, aim to provide needed praxis tools to help foster collaborative community generation of the mechanisms for these transformations. Infusing these concepts and language may deepen and further enliven important efforts like the Crossing Borders program to collectively generate and sustain peaceable *and* just relationships among groups with a history of conflict.

Crossing Borders is but one program that aims to grapple with the many dimensions of intergroup power, integrating theory and practice, in order to address ground-level conflicts. Here is a glimpse of a few others. The Building a Race and Immigration Dialogue in the Global Era program, created by the National Network for Immigrant and Refugee Rights and the Highlander Research Center, includes "a set of popular educational tools and exercises designed to engage the immigrant and refugee community members in a dialogue about racism, migration and global economic structures in relation to migration." The Southeast Regional Economic Justice Network's Resisting Rivalry program employs direct interaction methods, including focus groups and workshops, "in an effort to build intentional relationships among youth, women and low-wage workers of African-American and Latino communities." The South by Southwest program, launched through the partnership of Southern Echo, Southwest Organizing Project, and the Southwest Workers Union, aims to "build bridges to empower a true majority" by addressing "historical narratives and art as a way to transform the identities of their constituents and create cultural bridges." And there are many others, like the Colorlines Youth and Race Project, sponsored by the Applied Research Center ("innovators helping young people organize around structural racism") and the Leadership Development in Interethnic Relations Program (community-based training to help educate and strengthen community leaders and members on how to facilitate change and build more effective intergroup relations).[110]

Each of these programs has distinct aims, practices, limitations, and constituencies. Despite many differences, one key commonality among them is the salutary effort to identify and then move well beyond a generic "common ground" approach toward mutual understanding and collective action. Contributing to that effort is the aim of the approach offered here for assessing the power dynamics of color-on-color grievances as a predicate to forging alliances.

NOTES

1. Brentin Mock, *What's Behind a "Black" Anti-Immigration Group*, Southern Poverty Law Center, Intelligence Report, Fall 2006, No. 123, http://www.splcenter.org/get-informed /intelligence-report/browse-all-issues/2006/fall/smokescreen?page=0,0; Andrew Grant-Thomas, Yusuf Sarfati, & Cheryl Staats, *Natural Allies or Irreconcilable Foes? Reflections on African-American/Immigrant Relations*, Poverty & Race Research Action Council, Mar./ Apr. 2010, 19:2; NewAmericaMedia.org, *Deep Divisions, Shared Destiny—A Poll of Black, Hispanic, and Asian Americans on Race Relations*, Dec. 12, 2007, http://news.newameri camedia.org/news/view_article.html?article_id=28501933d0e5c5344b21f9640dc13754; Greg Risling, *Feds Accuse Gang of Targeting Blacks in Calif City*, ABC NEWS, June 7, 2011, http://abcnews.go.com/US/wireStory?id=13783898#.T4orq1GXRsI; Nanette Asimov, *Black Attacks on Asians: Racism or Opportunity?*, S.F. CHRON., May 2, 2010, http://www .sfgate.com/cgi-bin/article.cgi?f=/c/a/2010/05/02/MNF31D6V5F.DTL&feed=rss .news; Julianne Hing, *Rep. Cleaver: GOP Manufactures Black-Brown Tensions*, COLORLINES, Mar. 2, 2011, http://colorlines.com/archives/2011/03/rep_cleaver_gop_manufacturing _black-brown_tension_for_anti-immigrant_policies.html.

2. Sam Cacas, *Black-Asian Unity: Racing to Talk in Tense Times*, OAKLANDSEEN, May 6, 2010, http://www.oaklandseen.com/2010/05/06/black-asian-unity-racing-to-talk-in -tense-times/; Darryl Frears, *Union Tries to Unite Blacks, Latinos*, WASH. POST, July 24, 2006, http://www.washingtonpost.com/wp-dyn/content/article/2006/07/23/AR2006072300698 .html; Grant-Thomas, *supra* note 1.

3. *See* Mark Q. Sawyer, *Racial Politics in Multi-Ethnic America: Black and Latino Identities and Coalitions, in* NEITHER ENEMIES NOR FRIENDS: LATINO/AS, BLACKS, AFRO LATINOS (Anani Dzidzienyo & Suzanne Oboler eds., 2005); ERIC K. YAMAMOTO, INTERRACIAL JUSTICE: CONFLICT & RECONCILIATION IN POST–CIVIL RIGHTS AMERICA (2000).

4. *See* Grant-Thomas, *supra* note 1; YAMAMOTO, *supra* note 3. Native Americans too are at times implicated in these controversies, although with seemingly lesser frequency.

5. *See generally* Sumi Cho, *Redeeming Whiteness in the Shadow of the Internment: Earl Warren, Brown, and a Theory of Racial Redemption*, 60 B.C. L. REV. 73, 75 (1998) (in addition to material aspects, describing "racial redemption" as a "psycho-social and ideological process through which whiteness retains its fullest reputational value"); Mock, *supra* note 1 (quoting Tanton).

6. See Tanya K. Hernandez, *Roots of Latino/Black Anger; Longtime Prejudices, Not Economic Rivalry, Fuel Tensions*, L.A. TIMES, Jan. 7, 2007, at M1; YAMAMOTO, *supra* note 3.

7. Sawyer, *supra* note 3; Julie A. Su & Eric K. Yamamoto, *Critical Coalitions: Theory and Practice, in* CROSSROADS, DIRECTIONS AND A NEW CRITICAL RACE THEORY 379–92 (Francisco Valdes et al. eds., 1999); YAMAMOTO, *supra* note 3.

8. *See, e.g.*, Grant-Thomas, *supra* note 1; Sawyer, *supra* note 3.

9. Earlier works in differing ways insightfully engage the historically situated messy power interactions among communities of color in specific settings. *See* Taunya Lovell Banks, *Both Edges of the Margin: Blacks and Asians in Mississippi Masala, Barriers to Coalition-Building*, 5 ASIAN L.J. 7 (1998); William M. Tamayo, *When the "Coloreds" Are*

Neither Black Nor Citizens: The United States Civil Rights Movement and Global Migration, 2 ASIAN L.J. 1 (1995); Kevin Johnson, *The Struggle for Civil Rights: The Need for, and Impediments to, Political Coalitions among and within Minority Groups,* 63 LA. L. REV. 759 (2003); DANA TAKAGI, RETREAT FROM RACE: ASIAN-AMERICAN ADMISSIONS AND RACIAL POLITICS (1992); Natsu Taylor Saito, *Alien and Non-Alien Alike: Citizenship, "Foreignness," and Racial Hierarchy in American Law,* 76 OR. L. REV. 261 (1997); Lisa C. Ikemoto, *Traces of the Master Narrative in the Story of African American/Korean American Conflict: How We Constructed "Los Angeles,"* 66 S. CAL. L. REV. 1581 (1993).

10. Robert S. Chang & Neil Gotanda, *The Race Question in LatCrit Theory and Asian American Jurisprudence,* 7 NEV. L.J. 1012 (2007).

11. Eric K. Yamamoto, *Critical Race Praxis: Race Theory and Political Lawyering in Post–Civil Rights America,* 95 MICH. L. REV. 821 (1997) (calling for development and translation of theory for frontline justice practice). In other works Yamamoto addresses the follow-up question about how to move from knowledge about the complex dynamics of grievances to dealing constructively with those grievances to "heal" and build bridges. That question is beyond the scope of this chapter. In those earlier works, Yamamoto has addressed that question, developing and employing a multidisciplinary approach to healing the wounds of injustice and thereby to facilitate building relational bridges. That approach is rooted in expanded notions of reconciliation and is termed "social healing through justice." *See* Eric K. Yamamoto & Ashley Kaiao Obrey, *Reframing Redress: A "Social Healing through Justice" Approach to United States–Native Hawaiian and Japan-Ainu Reconciliation Initiatives,* 16 Asian Am. L.J. 5 (2009); Eric K. Yamamoto & Sara Lee, *Korean "Comfort Women" Redress 2012: Through the Lens of U.S. Civil and Human Rights Reparatory Justice Experiences,* 11 J. Korean L.J. 123–49 (2012); Eric K. Yamamoto, Miyoko Pettit, & Sara Lee, *A Joint South Korea and United States "Jeju 4.3 Tragedy" Task Force to Further Implement Recommendations and Foster Comprehensive and Enduring Social Healing through Justice,* 15 Asian-Pac. L. & Pol'y J. 1 (2013); Eric K. Yamamoto & Susan K. Serrano, *Reparations Theory and Practice Then and Now: Mau Mau Redress Litigation and the British High Court,* 18 UCLA Asian-Pac. Am. L.J. 71 (2013).

12. Hernandez, *supra* note 6; Tanya K. Hernandez, *Latino Inter-ethnic Employment Discrimination and the "Diversity" Defense,* 42 HARV. C.R.-C.L. L. REV. 259 (2007); Sharon K. Hom & Eric K. Yamamoto, *Collective Memory, History and Social Justice,* 47 UCLA L. REV. (2000); THOMAS WARTENBERG, FORMS OF POWER: FROM DOMINATION TO TRANSFORMATION (1990); YAMAMOTO, *supra* note 3.

13. Lynette Clemetson, *Hispanics Now Largest Minority, Census Shows,* N.Y. TIMES, Jan. 22, 2003, http://www.nytimes.com/2003/01/22/us/hispanics-now-largest-minority-census -shows.html; William Booth, *One Nation, Indivisible: Is It History?,* WASH. POST, Feb. 22, 1998, at A-1.

14. Randal C. Archibold, *Arizona Enacts Stringent Law on Immigration,* N.Y. TIMES, Apr. 23, 2010, http://www.nytimes.com/2010/04/24/us/politics/24immig.html.

15. Mock, *supra* note 1; Anthony Asadullah Samad, *Is Ted Hayes the New Ward Connerly?,* NEW AM. MEDIA, July 15, 2007, http://news.newamericamedia.org/news/view_article .html?article_id=3570784ee74258efd5613d69c5719e1f (former homeless advocate in the

1990s and now a prominent "Black Republican," Ted Hayes is described by some as the "black face" of the anti-immigration movement).

16. Arian Campo-Flores, *Will Arizona's New Immigration Law Lead to Racial Profiling?*, NEWSWEEK, Apr. 27, 2010, http://www.newsweek.com/2010/04/26/will-arizona-s-new-immigration-law-lead-to-racial-profiling.html; L.A. Focus, *Blacks Split Over Arizona's Immigration Bill SB 1070*, CAL. BLACK MEDIA, June 14, 2010, http://calblackmedia.com/news/la-focus/314-blacks-split-over-arizona-immigration-bill-sb-1070.html; Kevin R. Johnson, *Case against Race Profiling in Immigration Enforcement*, 21 IMMIGR. & NAT'LITY L. REV. 531 (2000).

17. Frears, *supra* note 2 (union officials allege that Smithfield collaborated with authorities in a 2007 federal immigration raid on the plant in order to discourage Latino employees from voting); Julia Preston, *Immigration Raid Draws Protest from Labor Officials*, N.Y. TIMES, Jan. 26, 2007, http://www.nytimes.com/2007/01/26/us/26immig.html; Charlie Leduff, *At a Slaughterhouse, Some Things Never Die; Who Kills, Who Cuts, Who Bosses Can Depend on Race*, N.Y. TIMES, June 16, 2000, http://www.nytimes.com/2000/06/16/us/slaughterhouse-some-things-never-die-who-kills-who-cuts-who-bosses-can-depend.html?pagewanted=all.

18. Regina Freer & Melina Abdullah, *Pushing and Pulling Towards Coalition: African American Voters and the 2005 Los Angeles Mayoral Election* (2006), http://www.allacademic.com/meta/p152087_index.html.

19. Phil Willon, *Wooing Latinos for Obama: The Pitchman Role for Villaraigosa, Who Backed Clinton, Stands to Benefit Both Men*, L.A. TIMES, July 24, 2008, http://articles.latimes.com/2008/jul/24/local/me-coalition24.

20. Tanya K. Hernandez, "Latino-Black Inter-Ethnic Violence: The Untold Tale of Bias Turf Defense," Draft for the Intergroup Conflict and Cooperation Project at the Fred T. Korematsu Center for Law and Equality, July 14, 2011, at 5, 6, 8 (manuscript on file with author).

21. Earl Ofari Hutchinson, *Will Latino Gang Arrests Deepen Black-Brown Divide?*, TheGrio.com, June 8, 2011, http://www.thegrio.com/opinion/will-latino-gang-arrests-deepen-black-brown-divide.php.

22. Yamamoto, *supra* note 11 (challenge to affirmative action in desegregation consent decree); Rachel Gordon et al., *Son Describes Oakland Assault That Left Father Near Death*, S.F. CHRON., Apr. 18, 2010, http://articles.sfgate.com/2010-04-18/bay-area/20854594_1_punched-father-son; Su & Yamamoto, *supra* note 7, at 387 (addressing obstacles and foundations for significant coalitional action by harshly treated Thai and Latina garment workers in the Los Angeles area); YAMAMOTO, *supra* note 3, at 35; Jeff Chang, *Race, Class, Conflict and Empowerment: On Ice Cube's "Black Korea,"* 19 AMERASIA J. 87 (1993).

23. YAMAMOTO, *supra* note 3, at 35.

24. *Id.*; Ikemoto, *supra* note 9; Chang, *supra* note 22.

25. Ikemoto, *supra* note 9; YAMAMOTO, *supra* note 3, at 35.

26. *See, e.g.*, Grant-Thomas, *supra* note 1. This essay is an edited version of the authors' 2009 research report, *African American–Immigrant Alliance Building*, which presents five case studies highlighting "the challenges and opportunities that characterize collaborative efforts between immigrant and African American communities in the United States."

27. *Id.*

28. NewAmericaMedia.org, *supra* note 1; Su & Yamamoto, *supra* note 7, at 386, 387.

29. Grant-Thomas, *supra* note 1.

30. *Id.*

31. This groundwork for group reconciliation encompasses Yamamoto's "Four Rs" approach to genuine social healing—in particular, the recognition and responsibility steps entail a sophisticated inquiry into existing power relationships and the damage inflicted by power alignments. YAMAMOTO, *supra* note 3.

32. *Id.* at 101.

33. We use "ethnicity theory" as a shorthand description of a variety of perspectives that tend to posit largely unfettered ethnic group agency and therefore unrestrained responsibility for their socioeconomic conditions. Similarly, we use "nationalism" theory as a shorthand for the converse. In doing so, for purposes of this section's description of polar ends of a spectrum, we are not attending to the many nuanced differences among the views. *See generally* Ian Haney-Lopez, *The Social Construction of Race: Some Observations on Illusion, Fabrication, and Choice,* 29 HARV. C.R.-C.L. L. REV. 1, 47 (1994); YAMAMOTO, *supra* note 3, at 102; DINESH D'SOUZA, THE END OF RACISM: PRINCIPLES FOR A MULTIRACIAL AMERICA (1995) (ethnicity theorist who expounds on the concept of "rational discrimination").

34. Rutgers University-Center for Race and Ethnicity, "Race, Ethnicity, and the Subprime Mortgage Crisis," Mar. 2008, 1:7, http://raceethnicity.rutgers.edu/ SubprimeMortgageCrisisSummary.html (noting that "blacks have been a major target of predatory lending since Reconstruction"); Archibold, *supra* note 34 (discussing bill signed in April 2010 by Arizona governor granting police broad powers to detain anyone suspected of being in the country illegally); Stephanie McCrummen, *In N.C., a New Battle on School Integration,* WASH. POST, Jan. 12, 2011 (in 2010, the Tea Party–backed school board in Raleigh, North Carolina, abolished the district's diversity policies in favor of a new policy that critics claim will result in poor minority students being grouped together in underfunded schools), http://www.washingtonpost.com/wp-dyn/content /article/2011/01/11/AR2011011107423.html.

35. YAMAMOTO, *supra* note 3, at 104–5.

36. *Id.* at 109.

37. *Id.*; Su & Yamamoto, *supra* note 21.

38. Chang & Gotanda, *supra* note 10, at 1018–19.

39. *Id.* at 1020–21.

40. *See generally id.*

41. Hernandez, *supra* note 12, at 264; Mari J. Matsuda, *Beside My Sister, Facing the Enemy: Legal Theory Out of Coalition,* 43 STAN. L. REV. 1183 (1991); Jennifer Gordon & R. A. Lenhardt, *Rethinking Work and Citizenship,* 55 UCLA L. REV. 1161 (2008).

42. YAMAMOTO, *supra* note 3, at 8, 16; Eric K. Yamamoto, *Rethinking Alliances: Agency, Responsibility and Interracial Justice,* 3 UCLA ASIAN PAC. AM. L.J. 33 (1995) (*citing* John A. Powell "The Multiple Self: Exploring Between and Beyond Modernity and Postmodernity").

43. YAMAMOTO, *supra* note 3, at 98, 101, 109; Jeff Chang, "Lessons of Tolerance: Rethinking Race Relations, Ethnicity and the Local through Affirmative Action in Hawaii" (1994), at 12, paper presented at the annual meeting of the Association for Asian American Studies, (manuscript on file with author).

44. YAMAMOTO, *supra* note 3, at 110.

45. *Id.* at 110–11.

46. Haney-Lopez, *supra* note 33, at 47.

47. Mock, *supra* note 1; Yamamoto, *supra* note 11.

48. YAMAMOTO, *supra* note 3, at 111; REY CHOW, WRITING DIASPORA: TACTICS OF INTERVENTION IN CONTEMPORARY CULTURAL STUDIES 16–17 (1993).

49. CHOW, *supra* note 48, at 16–17; WARTENBERG, *supra* note 12, at 195.

50. Susan Stanford Friedman, *Beyond White and Other: Relationality and Narratives of Race in Feminist Discourse*, 21 SIGNS 1, 35 (1995); see YAMAMOTO, *supra* note 3, at 114.

51. STEPHANIE M. WILDMAN, PRIVILEGE REVEALED: HOW INVISIBLE PREFERENCE UNDERMINES AMERICA (1996); Angela P. Harris, *Race and Essentialism in Feminist Legal Theory*, 42 STAN. L. REV. 581 (1990); *see also* Friedman, *supra* note 50.

52. WILDMAN, *supra* note 51; Friedman, *supra* note 50.

53. YAMAMOTO, *supra* note 3, at 114; *see* WARTENBERG, *supra* note 12, at 74, 76, 141–45, 148.

54. WARTENBERG, *supra* note 12; YAMAMOTO, *supra* note 3, at 115–16.

55. Claire Jean Kim, *The Racial Triangulation of Asian Americans, in* ASIAN AMERICANS AND POLITICS: PERSPECTIVES, EXPERIENCES, PROSPECTS (Gordon H. Chang ed., 2001); Chang & Gotanda, *supra* note 10, at 1012.

56. Yamamoto, *supra* note 27 (*citing* Ho v. San Francisco Unified Sch. Dist., 965 F. Supp. 1316 [N.D. Cal. 1997]).

57. *See* WARTENBERG, *supra* note 12, at 164.

58. MICHAEL OMI & HOWARD WINANT, RACIAL FORMATION IN THE UNITED STATES: FROM THE 1960S TO THE 1990S (2d ed. 1994); Yamamoto, *supra* note 3, at 122.

59. OMI & WINANT, *supra* note 58, at 118.

60. Chang, *supra* note 22, at 102–3; YAMAMOTO, *supra* note 3.

61. Nathan O'Neal, *"Anchor Baby" Phrase Has Controversial History: Examining the Nickname the Media Uses to Describe a Proposed Law in Arizona*, ABC NEWS, July 3, 2010, http://abcnews.go.com/Politics/anchor-baby-phrase-controversial-history/story?id =11066543&page=1.

62. Hing, *supra* note 1.

63. *Id.*

64. *Id.*

65. *Id.*

66. *Id.*

67. *Id.*

68. *Id.*; Grant-Thomas, *supra* note 1.

69. Mock, *supra* note 1; The Dan Stein Report: A Project of FAIR, *American Hispanics Tell Illegal Marchers "You Don't Speak for Me,"* May 01, 2006, http://www.steinreport.com /archives/009158.html.

70. Duke Falconer, *Anti-Immigration Groups and the Masks of False Diversity*, Epluribusmedia.org, Feb. 5, 2007, http://www.epluribusmedia.org/features/2007/20070205_immigration_p1.html; Mock, *supra* note 1.

71. YAMAMOTO, *supra* note 3, at 110.

72. Campo-Flores, *supra* note 16; L.A. Focus, *supra* note 16.

73. Dawinder Sidhu, *Why Arizona's Immigration Law Should Concern All Minorities*, Salon.com, May 12, 2010, http://www.salon.com/2010/05/12/minority_solidarity_arizona_immigration_law/; Todd Johnson, *Black Arizonans on the Fence about Immigration Law*, TheGrio.com, Apr. 26, 2010, http://www.thegrio.com/news/black-arizonians-on-the-fence-about-immigration-law.php.

74. STEPHEN STEINBERG, THE ETHNIC MYTH: RACE, ETHNICITY, AND CLASS IN AMERICA (2001); JUAN F. PEREA ET AL., RACE AND RACES: CASES AND RESOURCES FOR A DIVERSE AMERICA (2007).

75. YAMAMOTO, *supra* note 3, at 116; Falconer, *supra* note 70.

76. Hernandez, *supra* note 20, at 6; Christina Ng, *Latino Gang Charged with Racial Cleansing Attacks in California Town*, ABC NEWS, June 9, 2011, http://abcnews.go.com/US/latino-gang-charged-racial-cleansing-california-town/story?id=13794815.

77. Hernandez, *supra* note 20, at 6; Hutchinson, *supra* note 21; Sam Quinones, *Two Reputed Latino Gang Members Are Charged in Fatal Shooting of Black Girl*, L.A. TIMES, Dec. 27, 2006, http://articles.latimes.com/2006/dec/27/local/me-charged27.

78. Constance L. Rice, *A "Surge" on Gangs Alone Won't Help: Violence-Plagued Neighborhoods Need Real Reform, Not Just More Cops Walking the Streets*, L.A. TIMES, Feb. 8, 2007, http://www.latimes.com/news/la-oe-rice8feb08,0,7775435.story.

79. Quinones, *supra* note 77.

80. *Id.*; Hernandez, *supra* note 20, at 6

81. Rice, *supra* note 78.

82. *Id.*

83. Julia Preston, *Hispanics Cite Bias in Survey*, N.Y. TIMES, Oct. 28, 2010, http://www.nytimes.com/2010/10/29/us/29pew.html; Alan Fram, *Poll: Hispanic Discrimination High*, MSNBC, May 20, 2010, http://www.msnbc.msn.com/id/37263388/ns/us_news-life/t/poll-hispanic-discrimination-high/#.TonVn4cgdsI.

84. *See* Kerman Maddox, *Latino Leaders' Silence Is Killing Blacks: L.A. Is Headed for a Racial Meltdown Unless the Two Groups Form a Coalition*, L.A. TIMES, Mar. 21, 2007, http://www.latimes.com/news/opinion/commentary/la-oe-maddox21mar21,0,6579264.story.

85. YAMAMOTO, *supra* note 11, at 114.

86. Maddox, *supra* note 84.

87. *Id.*; Will Beall, *Street Gang Realpolitik: Black and Latino Gangsters Aren't at War with Each Other. They're Business Partners*, L.A. Times, Mar. 25, 2007, http://www.latimes.com/news/opinion/commentary/la-op-beall25mar25,0,6374583.story (noting that Latino and African American gangs in certain areas exist in a hierarchical social and economic relationship. The city's Latino gangs, which outnumber African American gangs, can be "deferential, even cordial to their cross-racial counterparts.").

88. OMI & WINANT, *supra* note 58.

89. Gordon et al., *supra* note 22; Bay City News, *Prosecutors Weigh if Oakland Murder of SF Man Was Hate Crime*, Apr. 20, 2010, http://sfappeal.com/alley/2010/04/prosecutors-weigh-if-oakland-murder-of-sf-man-was-hate-crime.php.

90. Asimov, *supra* note 1; C.W. Nevius, *Asian American Attacks Focus at City Hall*, S.F. CHRON., Apr. 29, 2010, http://articles.sfgate.com/2010–04–29/bay-area/20878116_1_city-hall-african-americans-asian-americans; Juliana Barbassa, *Attacks Fuel Racial Tensions in San Francisco*, ASSOCIATED PRESS, May 16, 2010, http://www.chron.com/disp/story.mpl/nation/7007174.html.

91. Patrick Walters, *Racial Bullying Roils a Philadelphia High School*, ASSOCIATED PRESS, Jan. 21, 2010, http://abcnews.go.com/US/wireStory?id=9628752; Pablo Guzman, *Teen Suspects to Appear in Family Court Saturday*, CBS NEW YORK, Apr. 10, 2010, http://wcbstv.com/local/asian.women.attacked.2.1621825.html.

92. Henry K. Lee, *Lawyer: Punching-Death Defendant "Not Evil,"* S.F. CHRON., Apr. 24, 2010, http://www.sfgate.com/cgi-bin/article.cgi?f=/c/a/2010/04/24/BA7D1D42N4.DTL&feed=rss.news.

93. Asimov, *supra* note 1; Gerry Shih, *Attacks on Asians Highlight New Racial Tensions*, N.Y. TIMES, May 2, 2010, http://www.nytimes.com/2010/05/02/us/02sfcrime.html?pagewanted=all.

94. *See* Sawyer, *supra* note 3; William Wong, *Oakland Street Killing: Shocking*, S.F. CHRON., Apr. 23, 2010, http://www.sfgate.com/cgi-bin/blogs/wwong/detail??blogid=156&entry_id=62052; Barbassa, *supra* note 90.

95. Barbassa, *supra* note 90.

96. Cacas, *supra* note 2.

97. Asimov, *supra* note 1; *Town Hall Meeting Over Oakland Beating Death*, CBS S.F., Apr. 29, 2010, http://cbs5.com/local/oakland.beating.death.2.1663241.html.

98. Japanese American Citizens League, *When Hate Hits You: An Asian Pacific American Hate Crime Response Guide* (2003), http://www.jacl.org/public_policy/documents/WhenHateHits.pdf.

99. HARLON DALTON, RACIAL HEALING (1998).

100. YAMAMOTO, *supra* note 3, at 29.

101. Yamamoto, *supra* note 11, at 822 (*citing* Ho v. San Francisco Unified Sch. Dist. [N.D. Cal. 1994]).

102. *Id.*

103. YAMAMOTO, *supra* note 3, at 31.

104. Timothy Egan, *Little Asia on the Hill*, N.Y. TIMES, Jan. 7, 2007, http://www.nytimes.com/2007/01/07/education/edlife/07asian.html?_r=1&pagewanted=1&oref=slogin.

105. *Id.*

106. *See supra* note 11.

107. CROSSING BORDERS: RELATIONSHIPS ACROSS LINES OF DIFFERENCE (2007) (detailed educational training curriculum), http://intergroupresources.com/rc/CROSSING%20BORDERS%20toolkit.pdf.

108. *Id.* at 5.

109. *Id.* at 16.

110. The National Network for Immigrant and Refugee Rights, www.wkkf.org/racial-eq uity/data/2010National-Network-For-Immigrant-And-Refugee-Rights.org; intergroupre sources.com/rc/Glue%20elements.pdf; Leroy Johnson et al., Building Bridges to Empower a True Majority: The South by Southwest Experiment, www.racialequality.org/docs /CIF4BuildingBridges.pdf; www.arc.org/content/view/2266/132/; www.ldir.org/?pageid=8.

Part II

EPISODES

3

Civil Rights, Free Speech, and Group Libel

CHERYL GREENBERG

Picture this study scenario: after passing through the secret attic rooms in which Anne Frank and her family hid in Amsterdam until their betrayal and capture by the Nazis, and another long room filled with Holocaust pictures and ephemera, visitors enter a final room with a video screen. There, playing in a continuous loop, are "point-of-view" vignettes—a video of Nazis marching in Skokie, Illinois, cutting to fearful Holocaust survivors with their tattoos, then to homophobic protesters surrounding a gay pride march. After each set of scenes, carefully balanced to present arguments for both free speech and protection of minorities, viewers are asked to vote on the same question: should the bigots be allowed to speak or should they be prevented from speaking in order to protect the targeted, and vulnerable, minority group? Each vote came out the same way—the Americans in the audience came down on the side of free speech, while the Europeans prioritized the protection of minority groups. I know this because each vote was 15 or 16 to 1, and I was the only American in the room. Still, without overgeneralizing, I suspect that most Americans see things the same way.

I found this divergence in perspectives interesting but not surprising. Europeans, after having just seen what their own parents or grandparents had proven capable of, could not trust unfettered free speech. Most European countries, and Canada too, have group antidefamation laws (sometimes called group libel laws) that restrict speech designed to demean or marginalize minority groups. Only Americans, with their very different history, have the luxury of faith in human decency triumphing in the marketplace of ideas. But if the United States never conducted a systematic genocide, it did collaborate in appalling acts of systematic racism and discrimination against Native peoples and minority groups, including those who had also been persecuted by the Nazis. How would those Americans view this choice between free speech and security?

Indeed, well before the civil rights movement, ethnic, religious, and racial civil rights agencies had debated these questions both publicly and privately. How should they respond organizationally to racism, anti-Semitism, or similar prejudicial expressions in books, radio and television shows, or motion pictures? How should they balance civic protection and civil liberties? The embrace of free speech in the United States after World War II was far from inevitable. Many state-imposed restrictions already qualified free speech in American jurisprudence. Why shouldn't similar legal restrictions also protect those who had already experienced violence at the hand of mobs? By the end of the 1950s virtually the entire civil rights community had come down on the side of free speech. But the civil rights community did not all start there.

This essay explores the history of these deliberations among African American and Jewish American civil rights groups, because they have been historically the most active and visible in their engagement with defamation in the public sphere. Put in simple terms, this essay asks: what led them to the eventual decision to follow a more libertarian than protectionist model? In the process, the essay explores two corollary issues as well. First, in lieu of calls for legal or legislative action, what alternative strategies did they pursue? Second, to what extent did these strategies themselves effectively act to censor speech? These organizations may have decided in the end not to pursue group libel laws, but they, and often other groups as well, employed their own free speech rights to challenge media representations they considered malicious and dangerous to minority communities—challenges that included pressuring creators, editors, or distributors to themselves remove the problematic representation.

The United States, founded on the race-based enslavement of people of African ancestry and the marginalization or relocation of Native Americans, long enshrined racial, ethnic, and religious discrimination in both law and social practice. Laws were slow to change; social attitudes, especially when informed by law, were slower still. Not surprisingly, then, into the twentieth century every form of American media featured stereotyped images of Jews, African Americans, and other ethnic and racial groups. Some long-standing forms of entertainment, such as vaudeville and minstrelsy, based their attraction on precisely these distortions—the bumbling, "happy-go-lucky" but phlegmatic black man; the greedy, scheming Jew; the devious Asian (first Chinese and later Japanese); and a host of others. But no form of communication or entertainment was immune. Books, photographs, advertisements, and even the newer motion picture and radio industries broadcast stereotypical and demeaning depictions of groups outside the Protestant

Anglo-Saxon norm. At the same time, many southerners considered any positive depictions of black people or interracial harmony as dangerous and called for the suppression of such "anti-American" materials.

While these depictions had been common for some time, systematic protest against them came only after the emergence of civil rights organizations formed by oppressed minority groups for their own protection. The American Jewish Committee (1906), the American Jewish Congress (1916), the Anti-Defamation League (ADL) (1913), the National Council of Jewish Women (NCJW) (1893), the National Association for the Advancement of Colored People (NAACP) (1910), the National Association of Colored Women (1896), and the National Urban League (1911) were all organized within approximately a decade and a half of each other. Mary McLeod Bethune created a political umbrella for African American women's groups, the National Council of Negro Women (NCNW), in 1935. Each of these groups called for the integration and acceptance of its members into the broader society with the full rights and privileges of citizenship. While most of these agencies' civil rights efforts focused on legal challenges to equality—from segregation to immigration restrictions, from employment discrimination to restrictive housing covenants—and crusaded for legal protection against lynching and other forms of discriminatory violence, they also understood that demeaning stereotypes about their group legitimated and perpetuated the poor treatment they received.[1]

Perhaps the best-known example of a protest against racial stereotyping is that of the NAACP against the film *Birth of a Nation*. The 1915 motion picture celebrated the founding of the Ku Klux Klan by alleging the horrors of southern life after the Civil War. The movie presented African Americans (actually white actors in blackface) as uncivilized, dangerous, lecherous, ignorant, newly freed slaves who took over southern legislatures only to corrupt them, and who tried to rape virtuous white virgins. Only brave white Ku Kluxers could defend white womanhood and the white way of life. President Woodrow Wilson, who screened it in the White House, was reportedly deeply moved by the film.

The NAACP took a rather more jaundiced view. Despite vigorous internal debates over free speech, NAACP leaders fought hard to prevent the movie from being shown.[2] First, they urged local officials and motion picture censorship boards in major cities like Boston, Los Angeles, and New York to ban the movie altogether or, when that failed, to require the filmmaker to eliminate the worst scenes. Until this point, censorship boards considered only sex or violence as grounds for rejecting a film, although some also did so if the film's contents posed an apparent threat to public order. Racist portrayals of African Americans, however, rarely rose to the level of threat as far as most of these film boards were concerned. The NAACP launched a lawsuit in New York, and chapters in several states and cities including Boston, Pittsburgh, and Chicago explored adding to existing censorship laws bans on "any show or entertainment which tends to excite racial or religious prejudice."[3]

Meanwhile, protest delegations of black religious, women's, and civil rights groups in dozens of cities, including New York, Boston, Oakland, Des Moines, Gary, New Haven, Minneapolis, Pittsburgh, Los Angeles, and Chicago, met with mayors and local law enforcement personnel and demanded a ban on film screenings. Here the arguments about public safety occasionally proved more persuasive, and several towns, cities, and even states issued temporary injunctions against showing the film. But these did not last. The NAACP's New York lawsuit was dismissed. Despite the few and fleeting political victories, the film eventually played to delighted audiences across the nation. Only Ohio's ban on the film, and those of a few small cities, held for any length of time.

Early on in the *Birth of a Nation* fight, then, the NAACP and other groups concerned with the image of African Americans concluded that calling for censorship—the outright suppression of public forms of expression—could not succeed. They lacked both public sympathy and the political clout to achieve it. Internal debates over the wisdom of limiting free speech also helped curtail such efforts.

Instead, local chapters of the NAACP, the NCNW, and a number of other black civic groups sought to use their own free speech to counter the film. They appealed to distributors' fairness and civic virtue and pressed individual theater owners not to screen the film. Combining both public protest and economic pressure, they mounted picket lines to publicize their concerns and called on patrons to boycott the film and theaters that showed it. The NAACP collected dozens of protests into a forty-seven-page pamphlet called *Fighting a Vicious Film*.[4] Two thousand men and women demonstrated in Boston, and groups of 500 or more picketed several Philadelphia theaters. Dozens of cities experienced some form of public picketing and private pressure, emphasizing patriotic themes of national unity, pluralism, and civil peace. Those protests, along with the diminished interest in silent films, proved effective enough that by the 1940s the film was rarely shown in public theaters.

While legal and political challenges to Jim Crow and other forms of discrimination obviously remained the primary focus for civil rights agencies, the NAACP and its sister organizations continued to fight racial stereotypes in the public media. To remove offensive images in advertisements and plays, they moved away from the legal and political strategies that had proven ineffective and turned instead to more targeted and individual actions like those they had used to challenge *Birth of a Nation*.

One way to fight offensive stereotypes was to put factual counterinformation before the public. NAACP secretary Walter White, for example, pleaded with scholar Norman Hesseltine in 1937 to "analyze the misinformation and historical inaccuracies—to put it as mildly as possible—of GONE WITH THE WIND." The tremendous popularity of the novel and the forthcoming movie "make it imperative that everything possible be done to offset the grievous harm done by this book and others of its sort." Although he acknowledged that "the harm has been done. . . . an expose . . . can be of great value when done by a distinguished authority like yourself in opening the eyes of those who are educable and also in preventing the repetition of future books of this character."[5]

More often, however, these efforts took place behind the scenes and in direct contact with the offenders. Not only had black activists learned the limits of public appeals for racial unity in a still deeply racist nation, but they also hoped publishers or owners might be more amenable to making changes if objections were raised in private (with the polite threat of boycotts, which in the era of widespread don't-buy-where-you-can't-work protests had some credibility).

In the case of textbooks, for example, in 1936 the NAACP's Lawrence Reddick examined the most commonly used American history texts in New York for racial bias or historical inaccuracies. His detailed and careful investigation took more than a year. Not surprisingly, he found that many of the books ignored black contributions to American history, depicted black people as happy under slavery, and distorted the post–Civil War South. Mary White Ovington, the longtime activist and cofounder of the NAACP, concluded optimistically that if the association contacted the publishers with its analysis, "slight changes might be quite possible."[6] In 1939 the NAACP drew up a list of books that "fall within the category of distorting the role of the Negro citizen in American life" to be used as a "point of attack in the solution of the problem." The list included not only American history textbooks but two encyclopedias, a book of zoology, and *Biology for Beginners*.[7]

While the main NAACP files contain nothing further regarding these two specific matters, correspondence from the NAACP to a school superintendent in Pennsylvania in 1933 suggests the form the association's protests took. The letter opened by explaining that "certain colored citizens of your community have voiced an objection" to the use of a particular text, and "we heartily agree with the objections which have been made." While the NAACP assured the superintendent it believed the authors "are not hostile, nor are they vicious," they were nonetheless "hopelessly misinformed and lacking information which was available to them." Readers of this textbook "would never learn . . . that the Negro had been anything but an inferior and, on the whole, useless encumbrance on American life." Yet these readers would become future leaders, shaping public policy and public opinion.

> As an educator we feel certain that you would not wish to be a party, however innocently, to the creation of dangerous and distorted opinions. We very much hope, therefore, that you will use your influence and that the other responsible authorities will take action to remove this book from the curriculum . . . and substitute for it one which gives a more adequate picture of a race which forms one-tenth of the population of the United States.[8]

What the letter did not mention was that the parent who had written the original complaint letter to the NAACP had first gone to the superintendent to complain, but reported to the association that "he was a little sarcastic."[9] Instead, the NAACP's appeal took the moral high ground. It pointed out that this concern was voiced by constituents who were both citizens and a significant portion of the population. It resisted any presumption of evil intent. It praised the superintendent as undoubtedly a decent person with an intelligent grasp of history and a commitment to the truth. Although the contact was not made public, a copy of the letter also went to the book's publisher.

The NAACP used similar politely barbed language to challenge offensive word choices. A 1930 letter to Harper and Brothers, the publisher of *New York World Today*, complained about the use of the word "darkey" in an advertisement. "We are sure you would wish to be informed," the ostensibly helpful letter began, that this word was "intensely offensive to colored people." After proposing a few less offensive alternatives, the NAACP noted that "it might interest you to know that" it had succeeded in convincing Andrew Mellon, treasury secretary, not to use the word either. Its political reach thus established, the association shifted back toward collegiality.

In calling this to your attention, we have no desire to be captious and we have no doubt that the person responsible for the use of the word "darkey"... was ignorant of the resentment it arouses among Negroes, but we cannot forbear to point out to you that you would probably hesitate before using ... any words offensive to other groups of the population, such as "wop," "dago," or "kike."[10]

There were occasional successes. The association, presumably using less abrasive language, asked Irving Berlin in 1942 to reconsider the lyrics of his song "Abraham," part of the forthcoming film *Holiday Inn*. The Jewish songwriter, who had also written a number of antiracist songs for other productions, agreed to change "darkey" to "Negroes," winning a banner headline in the black press: "Berlin Says He'll Change Slur in Song."[11]

More often, however, the battle seemed an uphill one. Walter White had tried the same polite tactic with Dodd, Mead and Company in 1932 regarding a book it published called *Ten Little Nigger Boys*. After noting that the term "is most objectionable to colored people and to a great many white people," expressing certainty that the publishers "would not wish to give offense to any considerable group of American citizens," and assuring them, "We feel also equally certain that use of this objectionable phrase was an unwitting one," the letter concluded, "We take the liberty of urging that some other title be found for the book." The publishers were unmoved. "We quite appreciate the fact that the term 'nigger' is objectionable to colored people, but this little book is so amusing, and innocuous in every respect, that it never occurred to us that there would be any criticism."[12] How White managed to keep his temper was not noted in the NAACP's files.

By the late 1940s few protests pretended any longer, even for the purposes of diplomacy, that such publicly expressed racism occurred inadvertently. In a 1946 talk on the radio industry, the National Urban League's executive secretary, Lester Granger, observed: "Radio has consciously or unconsciously—and I would be naive indeed to believe that the 'error' has been unconscious—continued the great mistake which other areas of business and industry are just beginning to correct."[13] Rarely after this point did black groups use mitigating language about unintentional harm in their communications.

Not surprisingly, black organizations like the NCNW and NAACP continued to find examples of racism well after this point and continued to challenge their producers directly. The June 1952 report of the NAACP secretary, for example, reported

Protests filed: The Aughinbaugh Canning Company of Biloxi, Mississippi, was sent a letter of protest concerning the distribution of oysters and shrimps bearing the offensive ["Niggerhead Brand"] label. …A change of policy was requested. The Southern Finance Company of Anniston, Alabama, was asked to change its policy of using sign-boards bearing a caricature of a Negro picking cotton with the word "Easy Pickins for a Loan." The Governor of the State of Alabama and the State Board of Education were asked to reconsider their requests for revision of the textbook "The Challenge of Democracy." This pro-test came about as a result of the Governor's calling for a complete elimination of Chapter 28 which dealt with the question "Minority Groups Should Share Equally with All Others in the American Way of Life."[14]

Although this last was an example of dealing with a public official rather than a corporation, the NAACP maintained the same tactics of personal contact, explanation of the problem, and a request for a change.

In the same era, Jewish groups also divided over the question of limit-ing free speech, and they too concluded, for their own reasons, that moral suasion was preferable to legal calls for censorship. "We ask … that all that holds the Jew up to ridicule and discrimination be eliminated," urged Mrs. Charles Long, chairwoman of the Educational Department of the NCJW in 1918. Yet, perhaps mindful of the many historical examples of Christians burning Jewish books, the council opposed outright censorship of books and movies.[15] Instead, most Jewish agencies used the same techniques black groups did, including careful examination, factual clarification, and appeals to patriotic values of equality and tolerance. ADL staff routinely reviewed books and movies with Jewish characters. The main character of *Broad Is the Way* "is a disgrace to Jewry," Benjamin Epstein complained to his ADL colleagues in 1939 after a careful reading of the book, and the portrayal could well lead "the general public to condemn the Jews as a group."[16]

Yet they, even more than African American groups, believed success more likely if done quietly. So, for example, the American Jewish Committee ap-pealed privately to George Putnam in 1920 not to publish the anti-Semitic *The Cause of World Unrest* or the *Protocols of the Elders of Zion*.[17] Many feared that public accusations of anti-Semitism would bring greater attention to the very statements or ideas they were protesting. ADL's policy "is … not to intervene in any situation unless some advantage can be gained … and only when they can achieve their goal without creating further animosity for the Jewish people," explained Leonard Finder, secretary of its New York regional office, to a member who had complained about a German movie. "We do not believe in meddling from mere officiousness or so as to gain a false appearance of activity."[18] To call attention to oneself not only invited the scrutiny of anti-Semites but also, by highlighting Jews' still-marginal status, made it more difficult to assimilate into the mainstream. Such "sha sha" techniques, as critics labeled them, reflected American Jewish fears of ubiquitous, latent anti-Semitism waiting to be ignited by rabble-rousers.[19]

Nor did Jews feel any more confident in their relationship to power than did African Americans. Public appeals seemed to have little chance of success. In a 1940 discussion about whether to challenge *Native Son* by the African American novelist Richard Wright for identifying many foreign and Communist characters as Jews, Philip Chasin complained to Finder, "In every one of these cases the word 'foreigner' could be substituted for 'Jew' without any loss of the sense or meaning of the various phrases." Finder agreed that the "implied relationship of Jews and Communists is invidious" but observed that several ADL leaders "expressed strong disapproval of any representations, because they feared that it would be the type of complaint which would make us unpopular, which would make us seem to be guilty of censoring the press, and which would not accomplish the desired result anyhow."[20]

Although Jewish stereotypes differed from black stereotypes, the danger was similar. A 1939 Warner Brothers documentary on colonial hero Haym Solomon "may prove injurious . . . principally because the picture leaves the impression that the money requested to be raised by Washington was contributed solely by Jews." This impression was factually false, the ADL insisted, as well as dangerous in that it would reinforce existing canards about Jews and money. The league suggested the addition of a scene of Christian donations to the republican cause.[21]

In *Fun with Figures* a brainteaser challenged readers: "Out-Jewing the Jew (It Can't Be Done)." The publisher responded to the ADL's complaint: "We regret exceedingly to learn from your letter . . . that . . . FUN WITH FIGURES is giving offense to anyone." Although the book had been published thirteen years earlier, "until the last year or so no criticism whatever came to us. We are sorry indeed that offense has now been taken; we can assure you none was intended."[22] More satisfying was the response of the distributor of *Mystery Dream Book*, which had explained that "to see Jews in your dream . . . indicates that you will be deceived." E. T. Browne thanked the ADL for calling the issue to his attention. "It is needless for us to mention that we have stopped all shipments of these books, regardless as to the cost to ourselves, and, furthermore, you can imagine our feelings at having this appear in a book put out by our house, where 75% of the distributors are Jewish folks."[23]

The situation became more delicate when the offending material appeared in religious Christian movies or tracts. These routinely portrayed Jews as Christ-killers. Fearful of stepping on Christian sensibilities, but mindful of the risks raised by perpetrating these images, the ADL and others tiptoed carefully. *Golgotha,* "probably one of the worst pictures ever made" artistically, according to one ADL reviewer, would please any "German storm trooper. . . . In it the Jew is painted throughout as crafty and cruel, a grubber after money and power, a coward and a bloodthirsty maniac. This is not an exaggeration." Rather, "It almost looks like purposeful anti-Semitic propaganda."[24] The ADL did not use such sharp rhetoric in its actual challenge to the film, however. In response to the film owners' attempts to book the film in theaters, the ADL's director instructed the league's "Friends" (presumably members or contacts of its local branches) to "tactfully present to your local theatre owners the facts concerning this picture, so that through lack of information they make no mistakes with regard to bookings." Sensitive especially at a time of rising Nazi anti-Jewish actions, the letter concluded, "Because of present restlessness particularly and the unhappy aspects of world conditions, it is imperative that we give particular attention to any agency which might add to current disquietude."[25]

The campaign apparently failed; the next year the ADL main office explained that "we looked into this matter before and . . . some little furor was caused on account of this picture," so any further action "would probably be fruitless."[26] The oblique reference to "some little furor" is illuminated in a later letter. There, Horace Marston of the ADL's Eastern Regional Office explained that the year prior he had met with a representative of the film owners "who told us, in unveiled language, that Father Coughlin was to be interested in this controversy." Leonard Finder elaborated. "There were certain charges against the ADL relative to this picture which were voiced . . . by Father Coughlin in 'Social Justice,'" he reported.[27] Coughlin, the popular political commentator and (anti-Semitic) "radio priest," was heard on stations around the country. If Jewish groups needed more evidence of the importance of expressing their concerns privately, this episode provided it.

Marston also related his more recent attempt to discuss the matter with a representative of Films, Inc. Although he was "a very pleasant man to talk to and tried very hard to reconcile his business interest with fairness and decency . . . [h]e told me that there was nothing he can do, because he is under contract with the owners of the picture." Although he claimed he would have avoided taking on the film had he known there would be a controversy, his boss "thought there was nothing wrong with the picture," and "the owners, who are interested in protecting their investment, stubbornly insist upon at least getting their money back."[28]

Between Father Coughlin and Christian sensibilities, the ADL's subsequent discussions reflected the matter's delicacy. "We have to be most careful about this film for the reason that its exploiters have not always been over-scrupulous," Finder explained. "If they could find any evidence of Jewish 'interference' as already has been charged, they probably would be willing to make capital of it. . . . Therefore any representations made by us must be done most diplomatically." This was particularly true when church groups screened the film, in which case

> protests by us will be most difficult. Yet, even there, if the minister is known to be friendly and a true liberal, that person acquainted with him can point out that this picture is detrimental to good will and better understanding. In other words, if there should be any such discussion, the minister should be assured that there is no desire to interfere in the showing of a picture which tells of a sacred incident, but at the same time even such films can do more harm than good when they distort the actual facts or are based upon historical inaccuracies.[29]

These strategies of reframing the offensive stereotype as simply a historical inaccuracy any responsible author or artist would wish to correct, emphasizing respect for religious conviction, and appealing to patriotic values of democracy and tolerance in light of current world events were evident also when the ADL discovered a problematic *Watch Tower* pamphlet put out by the Jehovah's Witnesses. *Cure* apparently claimed that "the Jews' religion" led to the crucifixion and the later persecution of Christians. Finder first tried to set the historical record straight:

> Christian historians have long since disproven these charges. Without going into all of the reasons, suffice it to say that crucifixion was not a Jewish form of punishment but Roman, that it was impossible for the Sanhedrin to have tried Christ as is commonly maintained, etc.
>
> The issue was not merely historical accuracy, however. While I am fully appreciative of the principles which inspire your society . . . I

wish to suggest to you some of the consequences of such statements. These are not normal times; there are many groups and even nations, which are trying to arouse hatred among men. Inadvertently, declarations such as that in "cure" [sic] aid the cause of those bodies who would fan the fires of religious and racial intolerance in order to destroy democracy itself.

The ADL insisted its concern was not that the pamphlet criticized Jews but rather, it asserted disingenuously, "because the article contains a possible misunderstanding injurious to good will." The league urged "greater caution" for future publications "so as to prevent . . . allegations which could breed only bigotry and tend to destroy our internal peace."[30]

The American Jewish Congress also attended to Christian expressions of anti-Semitism. "A thorough examination of textbooks used in Christian religious schools is being made," the *American Jewish Congress Courier* reported, in order "to ask Christian authors to remove from books placed in the hands of children those elements which tend to create ill-feeling between Jew and Christian."[31]

Even if these Jewish defense organizations insisted on discretion for pragmatic reasons, however, their goal was far larger than correcting a single example of injustice. "Please be sure to have those boys who write to the management of the Astor Theatre to do so very tactfully," Leonard Finder instructed a New York member. "While we do wish to have the management made aware that we realize and resent the undesirable message of pictures such as 'The Wandering Jew' we do not wish to make enemies. The object of the letters is, not to antagonize, but to prevent a repetition of this incident, and therefore these letters should be very diplomatically worded."

In the case of *The Wandering Jew*, the ADL sought a private meeting with the movie house and one of the film's sponsors, primarily to persuade them not to invest in future films with offensive content. "The gradual building up of cooperating agents in various fields of public education may prove to be an essential and important part of the work which you do in the New York area," ADL director Richard Gutstadt explained. "Through one exhibitor, you may be able to reach another; through other motion picture contacts high in the industry we may be able to reach additional people so that we are constantly building up a body of support upon which we may at some time want to rely. It is not, after all, the specific instance of the Wandering Jew that concerns us primarily. It is the achievement of a congenial relationship."[32]

Such efforts often paid off. In 1938 Finder reported that after the ADL previewed the British film *Dead Men Tell No Tales* and alerted promoters that it contained offensive Jewish stereotypes, the problematic scenes were removed before any American distribution.[33]

More committed to free speech from the start than the NAACP and other Jewish organizations, the ADL did nonetheless flirt with legal censorship, as the NAACP had done in response to *Birth of a Nation*. World War II, not surprisingly, heightened Jews' conviction that anti-Semitism threatened domestic peace. *The Octopus*, produced by a known fascist and anti-Semitic organization, prompted a letter from ADL counsel Arnold Forster to Chief Inspector Aldrich of the Post Office in 1941: "We are convinced that wise discretion would rule that the book is an unmailable piece of literature under the postal law and regulations." In fact, as Forster wrote to a colleague,

Nothing in the book . . . , so far as I can find, comes within the prohibition of any of the statutes. However, a reading of the statutes leaves the reader with the impression that books of a certain "odor" cannot go through the mails. In view of the fact that Aldrich is supposed to be an understanding person, and because he probably realizes the real need for unity at this time, I can see where he might stretch a point and rule as I have requested.

Although the Post Office concluded that the book was not "unmailable under the Postal Laws and Regulations," Aldrich did instruct postmasters to refuse to permit the book to be mailed at the reduced book rate, "[i]n view of the character of the publication," and urged Forster to bring the book to the attention of the FBI. Even in this case, the ADL maintained its strategy of quiet intervention rather than instigating public or legal action.[34]

When private contacts and moral suasion failed to work, however, civil rights organizations did move to more public or more economic pressure tactics. Even groups like the ADL that tried to avoid public campaigns nonetheless used economic pressure when diplomacy failed. The February 1, 1938, issue of *Vogue* contained an illustration by famed British fashion photographer Cecil Beaton. Small but visible letters in the drawing read: "M. R. Andrews Ball at the El Morocco Brought out All the Dirty Kikes in Town."[35] Walter Winchell called attention to it in a column, and the ADL followed up with *Vogue*'s publisher, Condé Nast. As Finder commented in a letter to Richard Gutstadt, although "the art editor of the magazine should have caught these words (because small as they are, they are legible to the

naked eye) . . . we are aware of Conde Nast's very fair attitude and certainly do
not intend to hold the firm accountable. Yet, some responsibility is involved,
since the thing appeared in 'Vogue.'" He also reported that several clothing
manufacturers had already expressed their concern. His telephone call to
Condé Nast was cordial but pointed. A follow-up letter explained the call
was intended

> not so much to complain, for we know that the sketches were not
> indicative of the Conde Nast Publications viewpoint, but to consider
> the whole problem. . . . [Y]our own prompt and extremely fair rem-
> edy in [issuing a statement of apology and] recalling the copies about
> to be distributed makes unnecessary any meeting between us. . . . I
> wish you to know that we are appreciative of your conduct in this
> incident.

New York newspapers covered the event, including a strong statement from
Nast explaining that he had fired Beaton, and the ADL pronounced itself
satisfied. Almost certainly Nast's action was based on more than his sense
of morality or social responsibility (and all evidence suggests he was in fact
deeply offended). One version of the events explained it as the result of
"pressure from advertisers and the reading public." Nast himself told Beaton
he had found himself in the midst of a firestorm.

Not everyone at the ADL was delighted with the outcome. Its Chicago office, still advocating a low public profile for league campaigns, expressed relief
that no Chicago papers mentioned the story. "I believe few people would
have noticed anything wrong with the sketch if the attention of the public
had not been called to these drawings by the New York papers and Walter
Winchell. Unquestionably, there will be a great demand for the 'forbidden'
edition of 'Vogue.'"

The story did not end there. At the end of that year, *U.S. Camera Magazine*
announced its intention to publish more of Beaton's work, the first "since the
affair of the *Vogue* Americana number." The Photo League quickly informed
a New York camera group of this fact and urged it to protest. "We of the
Photo League feel that if *U.S. Camera* wishes to be the record of American
photography today, Cecil Beaton has no place within its covers." The Manhattan Camera Club contacted the magazine immediately. After expressing
its "complete disapproval of your intentions" because Beaton's work "is an
insult to all those in this country who have fought against all 'isms' and all
manifestations of racial intolerance," it threatened: "Our readers enjoyed the

first issue of U.S. Camera Magazine and we hoped that we could continue to support this publication, but we regret exceedingly that such support will be impossible if you persist in your sponsorship of Mr. Beaton."[36]

A decade later, Jewish groups were still pursuing similar pressure tactics. The Atlanta Jewish Community Council reported its successes in preventing

> [e]xpressions of discrimination or anti-Semitism on the radio: . . . After Atlanta A.D.L. secured information about the concerned individual, the facts were made known to the station or program manager. Where religious preaching was involved, a rabbi, priest, and minister monitored the programs at the request of the station manager and gave their recommendations. In other cases, the station manager monitored future scheduled broadcasts in connection with the facts presented. In almost all cases, the offending programs were dropped by decision of the station manager.[37]

A few groups went even further. The American Jewish Congress, which often took more public action than did the ADL, testified against the *New York Daily News*'s petition for an FM license in 1948, using the new legal technique of content analysis to demonstrate that some of the *Daily News* stories had been anti-Semitic.[38]

The more reticent ADL disapproved of the congress's actions. Despite its own abortive attempt at censorship during the war (or perhaps because of its failure), the ADL opposed such drastic legal measures. A 1946 article in the *Jewish Post* critical of the ADL made exactly that point. When notorious anti-Semite Gerald L. K. Smith was hauled into court,

> the American Jewish Congress was a prominent member of the group which supported court action. The Anti-Defamation League refused to participate.
>
> The argument of the ADL was along the line that hauling Smith into court was playing directly into the hands of this enemy of democracy. The Congress, on the other hand, believes . . . that to allow Mr. Smith to continue his attacks on democracy unmolested by laws already on the statute books is to repeat the same error made by the Jews of Germany, who felt the best and wisest procedure was to carry on a long range fight while doing everything to stop anti-Jewish activities quietly and without publicity.[39]

Although civil rights groups had not yet fully resolved the question of legal restrictions on free speech, by the mid to late 1940s all of them, including the ADL, had become more public in their critiques of offensive portrayals of any minority group. The war had brought heightened scrutiny of racism and discrimination, thanks to the need for black labor in the war effort, a certain amount of regret over the incarceration of Japanese Americans among those who knew of it, and the images of emaciated bodies and mass graves from European concentration camps. Pluralist celebrations of diversity moved from minority view to majority conviction, at least as it pertained to white ethnic groups, and Cold War pressures to woo nonaligned, nonwhite nations prompted government action to ease the harshest facets of Jim Crow. Civil rights successes mounted, as enforcement of restrictive housing covenants, segregated travel on interstate transit, all-white primaries, and finally segregated public schools were struck down as affronts to the Constitution.

In such a heady if still contested moment, minority groups grew increasingly active on all fronts, including public struggles against defamation, almost always expressed as a political matter of fostering the broader social good. Even communities whose agencies had not become involved earlier launched such efforts after World War II. Although the tiny Japanese American Citizens League (JACL) had focused primarily on legal and political challenges to anti-Japanese restrictions before the war, for example, it engaged more actively thereafter. Perhaps internment had brought home the importance of challenging racial stereotypes, as it had dramatized the serious consequences and potential costs of such stereotyping. Perhaps the antagonism that met those returning from incarceration called for a more open fight against bigotry. Whatever the reason, the JACL, through its organ the *Pacific Citizen*, began challenging the use of the term "Jap" in newspapers by the 1940s, and by the early 1950s the JACL had begun contacting television stations broadcasting old movies "requesting that they be more careful in their selection of films, etc., which might in any way reflect upon the loyalty and the character of the Japanese Americans and, to some extent, the Japanese people." If offensive movies were shown nonetheless, local Japanese Americans occasionally even staged public protests. When the film *Beast of the East* was shown in Salt Lake City, for example, they organized a protest, and "official apologies were made, not only by the television stations [*sic*] managers, but also by the Mayor of Salt Lake City, and the newspapers."[40]

Perhaps the most publicly visible action of the period was the NAACP's full-bore campaign to persuade advertisers to withdraw their sponsorship of the show *Amos 'n' Andy*. The *Pittsburgh Courier* and several black churches had protested the show for its racist portrayal of black people in the 1930s, but the NAACP chose not to join in. After the show moved to television in 1951, however—this time with black actors rather than whites portraying the characters—it became a major focus of NAACP action. Using the same forceful approach as it had against *Birth of a Nation* in 1915, but this time focusing on economic rather than legal threats, the NAACP sent this 1951 telegram to the Blatz Brewing Company:

> National Association for the Advancement of Colored People vigorously requests you withdraw your sponsorship of television show Amos 'n' Andy as a gross libel on the Negro and distortion of the truth. . . . We could not conceive of your sponsoring a similar distortion of Jewish, Catholic, Irish, or other minorities. No one of the fifteen million American Negroes who spend annually today in excess of twelve billion dollars which includes Blatz Beer . . . can fail to resent such libel nor can fair minded white citizens similarly fail to do so by purchasing products of other manufacturers who do not gratuitously insult their customers. . . . [We] request that you transfer your sponsorship to a television program which is in consonance with contemporary concepts of racial democracy at this period of world peril.[41]

The NAACP asked its branches and other organizations with which it had cooperated in the past to join the effort "using every means at their disposal either through individual action or collectively through their respective members to discourage the sponsorship and presentation of such a program." A number of black newspapers and local branches took up the fight, and the Milwaukee CBS affiliate agreed to stop showing it.[42] In 1953 the Blatz Brewing Company agreed to stop sponsoring the show, although CBS continued to air reruns until 1966. At the same time, the association held meetings with representatives from television networks and unions. Together they issued a statement promising to press for greater and more accurate "representation of Negroes on television programs, matching their role in everyday life and providing opportunities for the employment of the many qualified Negro artists."[43] This last promise was honored by television executives only in the breach.

One might expect groups as exquisitely tuned to bigotry to see it when directed at groups other than their own. This was not always the case. While sensitive to troubling Jewish images in a Warner Brothers' Merry Melodies cartoon in 1944 called *Sweet Sioux*, the ADL did not appear to be concerned with the troubling Native American images much more prevalent in the cartoon.[44]

In general, however, civil rights agencies often cooperated on these issues, both directly and in broader, coordinated programs organized by the American Civil Liberties Union (ACLU), since they shared a broader concern about offensive stereotyping. The Associated Film Audiences (AFA), an organization founded in 1937 that gave "active encouragement" to producers to make films "that support democracy, civil liberties and peace," sought to "promote better understanding and improve neighborly relations between racial and religious groups" by previewing movies and communicating their views to movie houses and the broader public. The AFA, which came under the scrutiny of the House Un-American Activities Committee (HUAC) in later years as a possible Communist front, counted among its members the American Jewish Congress, American League for Peace and Democracy, Central Conference of American Rabbis, Federal Council of Churches of Christ, NCJW, Fellowship of Reconciliation, International Brotherhood of Sleeping Car Porters, Methodist Episcopal Church, NAACP, National Negro Congress, National Urban League, Women's International League for Peace and Freedom, and International Ladies Garment Workers Union.[45]

Even as public protests grew more visible, direct collaborations increased steadily. The ADL turned to A. Philip Randolph, who it referred to as "an outstanding Negro labor leader in the United States," in 1944 for help in challenging *The Whole Truth*, a film produced by the Church of God and Christ in Memphis.[46] A 1951 ADL memo discussed joint efforts with the Los Angeles office of the JACL to address "a number of problems pertaining to Japanese-Americans, the film, television and radio industries." The ADL agreed to restart its Los Angeles Mass Media Committee "to call together representatives of the seven local TV stations and to discuss with them ... the problems presented by the showing of old movies in which various members of minority groups are usually depicted in an unfavorable light, e.g. the Negro, the Mexican-Americans, the Japanese, the Chinese, and sometimes, the Jew." The national JACL would contact television stations across the country and urge them to be mindful of anti-Japanese stereotypes.

Perhaps, mused the ADL staffer who wrote the memo, the ADL might propose a gathering of Jewish organizations and others "like the NAACP, the Urban League, the JACL, the American Council of Spanish-Speaking People, some kind of topside committee which could work out similar arrangements on a national scale. . . . We are not suggesting censorship, but rather more careful selection, particularly is this true of films which portray Negro characters and Japanese characters."[47]

The ADL also began to take on the performance of fund-raising minstrel shows by nonprofit organizations—including Jewish ones. As it wrote in 1948 to a Pennsylvania B'nai Brith lodge planning such a show, "It has been our practice to advise . . . against such performances. We feel that the Negroes have a perfect right to object to the stereotyping of their words and actions. . . . We ourselves have frequently objected to the stereotyping of the Jew in alleged humorous skits." In 1954 an ADL staffer engaged in halting these performances suggested the ADL consider "consulting with leading Negro organizations regarding an attack on the whole minstrel show proposition."[48]

African Americans took similar positions on behalf of other groups. "The best way to further interracial goodwill is for members of various races to work together for community well-being," one black minister insisted. "The use of terms which discount minority groups should be discouraged. . . . Stories disparaging Negroes, Jews, Irish, and other minorities ought to be stopped."[49]

Meanwhile, black activists, perhaps ignorant of the NAACP's activities, also urged their leadership to follow Jews' lead against media bias. "A new children's edition of 'Arabian Nights' . . . has been withdrawn from sale because of its anti-Semitic reference," read a *Chicago Defender* editorial in 1948.

> The book has been under fire from the American Jewish Congress which protested to the publishers that it would poison the minds of young people against Jews. The Jewish leaders know how subtly racism operates and they are alert to those forces which shape the minds and opinions of the American people. . . .
>
> Our schools and colleges are full of text books which contain a definite bias against Negroes. Over the air and through the newspapers, the flow of racial poison . . . is powerful and dangerous.
>
> The propaganda against racial and religious minorities must be challenged by our leadership if we hope to change the hostile public opinion which thwarts our progress.[50]

For all these civil rights groups, protesting stereotypes of all kinds was framed as a matter of national rather than parochial importance. Beyond the evident similarity between black and Jewish groups' approaches, whether working alone or in concert, these examples also highlight how fine the line remained between protest and censorship. Regardless of whether they acted privately or publicly, virtually all of these protests combined reassurance with threat. They couched the problem in terms of American democratic values or intergroup harmony, but behind the polite words lay heavy economic pressure. If the group in question did not disassociate itself from the offensive material, the economic consequences could be severe.

This use of economic and public pressure prompted many internal debates about censorship. While few objected to a person or group raising concerns about particular words or images deemed offensive, calling on distributors or sponsors to withdraw their support seemed more like trying to prohibit something from being viewed at all. Was that in fact akin to violating free speech? After many such discussions, the ADL finally concluded in 1949 that the issues related to protest and free speech were too complex for a single policy to cover. Instead, its civil rights committee provided the league several specific guidelines.

1. The ADL should continue to exercise its right to express adverse opinion about motion pictures even though one natural consequence would be refusal of distributors and sponsors to handle them.
2. While we acknowledge the right to picket the exhibition of motion pictures we believe harmful, [the ADL] nevertheless looks with disfavor upon such picketings. However, when special circumstances seem to indicate the propriety of picketing, [they should be decided case by case].
3. The ADL may advocate that the public refrain from attending showings of motion pictures which it believes prejudicial to good human relations.[51]

One of the most controversial antidefamation campaigns in the Jewish community raised all these questions at once. In 1948 Alec Guinness played Fagan in a new, British-made version of the Dickens classic *Oliver Twist*. True to the original, and convincingly portrayed by Guinness, the evil Fagan was a stereotypically greedy, plotting, evil Jew, complete with hooked nose. The film was screened on army bases in Germany and Austria and provoked some protest. When the producers began to promote the film in Canada and the United States at the end of 1948, Jewish groups in both countries swung into action.[52]

Unable to convince the filmmakers to delete the problematic scenes, the ADL requested theater owners and bookers not to show the film. A number of groups published editorials in newspapers calling the portrayal anti-Semitic and urging the public to avoid the film. Some urged formal action, like pushing the Motion Picture Association or the Production Code board to refuse its endorsement of the movie; others advocated taking no action unless anti-Semitic incidents actually occurred at or after a screening. The NCJW called for calm, insisting that Fagan's caricature was so far from modern Jews that anti-Semitism was unlikely to result from viewing the movie. Other groups like the left-leaning Civil Rights Congress called for boycotts and organized picket lines. The Board of Rabbis condemned the picture. The conservative Council for Judaism insisted that any interference at all with the showing of the film would violate free speech rights.

The National Jewish Community Relations Advisory Council (NCRAC), the umbrella association of Jewish agencies, debated whether and when to issue a statement criticizing the movie but maintaining the producers' right to make it. Even that view, precisely that of the ADL and the Jewish War Veterans, did not succeed in staving off public accusations that Jewish groups were trying to limit free speech, especially after theaters in a number of cities either refused to screen the movie or cut its run short.

None of these actions came without intense internal debate. And those debates continued even after the *Oliver Twist* controversy ran its course. Was protest action indeed a form of censorship? And if so, did that make it inappropriate?

As part of an effort to address this question, the NCRAC invited the sociologist David Riesman to speak to Jewish leaders about civil liberties and responding to anti-Semitism. Speaking at a time of McCarthyism and right-wing pressure against "subversive" individuals and materials, he took a fairly strong libertarian line, even as Shad Polier, leader of the American Jewish Congress, defended his group's more direct engagement. As Polier argued, "Does the concept of censorship properly apply . . . to actions taken by groups, rather than by government? If an individual Jew is justified in withholding his advertising from a newspaper according to his own choice, does it become wrong for a group of Jews to band together to withhold advertising from a newspaper which is anti-Semitic or which has an anti-Semitic columnist? Does that become a boycott, and if so, is it illegal? Are the same criteria to be used . . . in judging the legality of such a boycott, directed at the preservation of the right of existence of a people, as are applied in labor disputes?"[53]

Arnold Forster of the ADL responded that protesting was not the same thing as a boycott. "I don't want to deny freedom of speech. . . . I want the

equal right to stand up and call a man a liar . . . and if, as a result of calling
him those names, there are those in the market place of listeners who refuse
further to listen to him, I am not engaging in boycott, I am not denying him
his freedom of speech, I am simply exercising my own constitutional right
to speak as I please."[54]

Regarding *Oliver Twist*, Forster explained, the ADL had never denied the
producers' right to show the film. Rather, the league "had insisted upon its
right to criticize the motion picture in newspapers, in magazines, and over
the radio, and to declare through all those media that the movie was potentially dangerous and harmful. As a result . . . many persons had decided that
they did not wish to view the picture and some exhibitors had decided that
they did not wish to exhibit it. This . . . was no denial of freedom of speech
but rather insistence upon the right to stand up and criticize."[55] Maurice
Fagan, however, countered by asking whether such actions could "in any
circumstances constitute an abridgment of freedom of speech . . . [since] the
purpose of such picketing and advertising . . . [was] to discourage a producer
from producing a similar film in the future."[56] Because outsiders understood
Jewish protests as demands for censorship, David Sher of the American
Jewish Committee added, there was also a practical reason to resist taking
such actions: they might also spur resentment of Jews, which would increase
rather than decrease anti-Semitism.[57]

Ironically, despite Polier's distinction between "actions by groups," which
he suggested were acceptable, and those "by governments," which, by implication, were not, the American Jewish Congress had always been more
sympathetic to developing legal grounds for censorship. When it proposed
the passage of what it called group libel legislation, laws barring defamatory
expressions, these issues about the nature of censorship sharpened further.
Discussions within Jewish organizations on the wisdom of group libel laws illustrate the challenge minority groups found in balancing protection and free
speech rights, a challenge that implicitly engaged the growing debate over
free speech for alleged Communists. A 1945 column produced by American
Press Associates laid out the dilemma everyone felt.

American Press Associates, the brainchild of the ADL and Workers' Defense League, which produced and distributed weekly columns on race and
trade unions, published *The New Negro* by Rev. John Haynes Holmes, a board
member of the ACLU. He described recent efforts in Connecticut to prevent
the performance of *Uncle Tom's Cabin*. "A plain violation of civil liberties, it
was an unfortunate episode, and happily unsuccessful," he wrote. "But there
was a conviction behind this attempt at censorship which is important." The

glorification of the "subservient, submissive, obsequious, obedient Negro who is always ready to kow-tow to the whites" outraged the "'new Negro' ... who walks straight and tall, an equal among equals. . . . He is conscious of his rights as a citizen under the law and as a human being under God, and is quick to defend and vindicate these rights." In other words, the situation involved two competing rights: free speech and the right to live securely and speak freely as an equal citizen.[58]

For the American Jewish Congress, the question was slightly different. Shad Polier was not persuaded that "a strict regard for civil liberties would assure a better world to live in, a world that 'will let us live in it as Jews.' ... How far must we attempt to depart from the pure civil libertarian approach . . . in order to achieve" that minimum goal "in a world where terror against people has become such a fine art that it threatens their very existence?"[59]

The congress had been exploring the possibility of legislation to ban defamatory speech at least since 1945. At its final plenary session, the 1948 Biennial National Convention of the American Jewish Congress passed a resolution on group libel:

> WHEREAS, the American Jewish Congress recognizes that under present Federal Law there is no adequate recourse by minority or ethnic groups, to slanderous untruths or printed statements directed against such groups; and
>
> WHEREAS, it further recognizes that the average individual, susceptible to appeals of race prejudice, is not inclined to carefully sift and consider the derogatory statements made against such groups, and is therefore subject to emotional and prejudicial influences without the requirement of proven evidence
>
> NOW, THEREFORE, BE IT RESOLVED: that the National Commission on Law and Social Action of the American Jewish Congress . . . explore avenues for drafting a bill, that will have as its objective, the punishment of individuals and/or groups found guilty of the insidious crime of "mass or group libel."

The conference chairman acknowledged that "it is a pretty difficult thing to find the kind of a bill that will prove to be constitutional."[60]

In 1949 a group libel bill drafted by the American Jewish Congress with advice from a number of constitutional lawyers was introduced in the House of Representatives. The bill, H.R. 2270, argued that "false and defamatory statements designed to arouse intergroup conflict" posed a danger to the nation and did not serve the public interest. Therefore such statements should be prohibited. No materials "with intent to create ill will against a racial or religious group" could be sent through the mails or travel via interstate or foreign commerce.[61]

The American Jewish Congress argued that freedom of speech or the press did not extend to "offensive language which is not part of an exposition of ideas." Racist and anti-Semitic publications threatened minority groups and reinforced latent prejudices, but there was as yet no legal remedy available to protect such libeled groups. A few states had such laws, but because the material came from many places, only a federal law could succeed in limiting that flow. Because group hatred was so invidious, supporters claimed, the usual techniques of positive propaganda were insufficient. When reason and prejudice compete, the congress argued, reason could not always be relied upon to triumph. The truth did not emerge from lies and denials, but rather from suppressing the spread of those lies to begin with. Bigotry constituted a clear and present danger to the well-being of minority groups and was an evil that government can and must combat.[62]

The congress's position by no means reflected a consensus in the civil rights community. By this point anti-Communism had begun to chill public discussion of any progressive views, including those regarding civil rights. Many Jewish leaders argued, as did David Sher of the American Jewish Committee, that given such a climate, "civil liberties are basic to Jewish security. ... [I]t is the premise of much of what we do, whether it is in the American Jewish Congress or in the American Jewish Committee or in the ADL, that the civil rights of all groups and all peoples is [sic] a necessary prerequisite to Jewish security and to healthy Jewish living." Therefore "it is much more important to maintain inviolate civil liberties" than to prevent the showing of a particular movie or book. Free speech guarantees, after all, protected minority voices.[63]

Others agreed this legislation was too dangerous, as likely to work against minorities as for them. Because the legislation included the stipulation that an honest belief in the claim was a defense against libel, many also insisted that any trial could become simply another forum for bigotry. Furthermore, any minority criticism against an oppressive majority could face a libel charge, one far more likely to succeed than the reverse because the jury would inevitably come primarily from the majority's ranks. The NAACP, possibly the most active of civil rights groups in seeking to prevent offensive materials from reaching the public, made precisely this argument. In 1945, when first considering its position on group libel laws, the American Jewish

Congress contacted the NAACP to learn its view. "We have consistently adopted a stand against this type of legislation," the association responded. "There is grave danger that these bills when enacted will serve to throttle the Negro and any other press which seeks to champion the cause of minority groups." The bill's wording "might be used to apply to almost any critical statement."[64] The NCNW agreed.[65] It was one thing to agitate for censorship in earlier years, when speech was generally far more limited. By midcentury, writers and artists, newspapers and booksellers were beginning to chip away at such restrictions, while McCarthyism showed up the dangers censorship posed for anyone whose views differed from the mainstream.

The American Jewish Committee also opposed the legislation unequivocally. Most fundamentally, as S. Andhil Fineberg pointed out in a memo regarding his own views, free speech permitted citizens to criticize government, a vital protection against totalitarianism. "To permit any religious or racial group immunity from criticism, however well justified, would make it possible for such a group to pursue hurtful policies without granting anyone the right to conduct a successful opposition through public discussion.... In such a situation one may be sure that it would be the minority groups which would suffer most." Furthermore, libel was difficult to prove, especially to a jury, and the publicity given the charge often cemented the charge in the public mind, even if legally found to be false and defamatory. Furthermore, a bigot could confirm his or her libelous claim simply by citing a few examples of individuals who had the particular trait that the bigot asserted for the group. "Group libel laws are *impractical, umworkable* and *unwise* and *dangerous,*" he concluded.[66]

The committee agreed and issued a memorandum summarizing its position:

Since such legislation seeks to limit, rather than protect constitutional rights, its validity must be determined on the basis of the traditional American approach to civil liberties. In this context, despite arguments to the effect that these laws reinforce civil liberties by withdrawing defamatory, obscene and blasphemous utterances from the market of free ideas, there is no doubt that the practical effect of such legislation is to deprive certain individuals of their right to speak. Accordingly, the legislation violates the traditional American approach to civil liberties. For this reason, such legislation, if passed, may boomerang against the very minority groups for whose protection it is invoked. Since minority rights are bound up with the protection of civil liberties, just as they are bound up with the protection of other constitutionally guaranteed rights, any inroads on civil liberties will create a potential threat to minority groups. Moreover, this legislation, essentially punitive in character, in no sense educational in function, and designed essentially to outlaw attitudes of prejudice rather than to regulate the manifestations of prejudice, would appear to be totally foreign to a reasoned and consistent socio-legal approach.[67]

Although the ADL had originally supported the idea of group libel legislation, arguing before the President's Committee on Civil Rights, for example, that it believed the danger of anti-Semitic material was significant and imminent enough to justify taking some sort of governmental action, it took no formal position on the congress's call for legislation. It did warn, however, that such legislation would be difficult to draft. H.R. 2270 forced the question, and after long discussion and debate the ADL concluded that the legislation as written might well be unconstitutional. The Supreme Court, however, upheld Illinois's group libel law in *Beauharnais v. Illinois* (1952), which removed that particular objection.[68]

Now using its universalist argument of the broader social good in defense of civil liberties, the league argued further that

> [i]n a democratic regime men must be free to criticize the opinions and activities of all groups which, in their judgment, are detrimental to the public welfare, even though such criticism may create hostility to or prejudice against groups criticized. There is serious question as to whether this right of free criticism is not substantially destroyed if attached to it is a condition that the person criticizing must be in a position to substantiate the truth of his criticisms or to show that they arise out of an honest belief based on reasonable grounds.[69]

The ADL's civil rights committee appreciated that the victims of vicious propaganda were entitled to redress, and that in theory group libel was "no more an infringement of free speech than to punish individual libels." The group, then, did not oppose group libel legislation as such. Nevertheless, the committee feared that "in this critical day . . . advocacy of a group libel statute would play into the hands of those who seek to repress and curtail individual freedoms" and concluded after long deliberation that

it is opposed to the proposed federal group libel bill, H.R. 2270, because the bill would not achieve the elimination of anti-Semitic literature and might do more harm than good to the Jewish community.
. . . After careful consideration, . . . [we find we have] not yet seen an
effective proposed group libel law which both contains all the necessary constitutional safeguards, and at the same time does not dan-
gerously circumscribe the full freedom of speech essential to a true
democracy.[70]

The NCJW positioned itself firmly against any form of legal censorship.[71] The
Jewish Labor Committee also opposed the bill, arguing almost the reverse
position: the proposed legislation was not strong enough and was too protective of civil liberties to effectively muzzle the worst offenders.[72]

It was not fear of publicity that held these other organizations back. The
agencies that refused to endorse the group libel bill, like the ADL and NC-
RAC, had already demonstrated their willingness to engage on the public
and legal levels. In 1949 the NCRAC opposed group libel legislation but
declared that it "was the consensus. . . . that action should be taken against
radio broadcasters and stations which show bias," including protesting their
broadcasting license, as the American Jewish Congress had done the year
previous. The NCRAC's Motion Picture Committee "recommended study of
community relations principles for a general code of ethics for the television
industry."[73] Although opposing group libel legislation in 1949 and again in
1955, the ADL, in a move reminiscent of its wartime efforts, "approve[d] in
principle legislation extending the present postal provisions to make non-
mailable cards or envelopes which bear on their face libels of racial and
religious groups." It also advocated legislation against the public use of masks
in order to weaken the Klan.[74]

Yet by the end of the 1950s most Jewish groups had come down solidly on
the side of civil liberties and free speech. Each now belonged to the umbrella
organization the National Clearinghouse on Civil Liberties (and the NCJW
had also chartered the National Organization on Civil Liberties for women's
groups), which opposed virtually every government attempt to restrict the
free expression rights of individuals or organizations in the name of anti-
Communism. Thus, when group libel legislation was proposed again in 1959,
the NCRAC executive committee, made up of its member agencies, voted to
oppose it. Certainly mindful of the McCarthy-era civil liberties violations, the
NCRAC laid out its concerns: "Such legislation threatens to curtail freedom

of speech and expression in a way that might readily be turned against free public debate on issues of grave concern. These freedoms cannot be applied selectively; no law yet drawn has applied only to hate peddlers without . . . applying to the authors of any views that may be unpopular or deemed dangerous at some particular time. We cannot seek to silence our detractors at the cost of impairment of our liberties."

NCRAC members rethought even their earlier support for postal restrictions. "Postal censorship would pose an even greater threat to freedom of speech than group libel legislation, for it would place discretion in the hands of non-elected administrative officials," the executive committee concluded.[75] By 1960, then, Jewish groups had joined their black colleagues definitively on the side of free speech, which they now argued was in the best interest of all minority groups. They had little choice. Their investment in liberalism, which relied on public discourse that challenged the racist status quo to move civil rights forward, and their recognition that anti-Communist limitations on speech had limited civil rights speech as well, required the formal protections of free expression. In an ironic twist, it may well be the case that, absent McCarthyism, civil rights agencies might have come out in support of greater restrictions on free speech.

Throughout the twentieth century, every civil rights organization has agreed it had the right to protest offensive caricatures. There has been far less agreement on how public the protest should be or what to demand. A few called for outright censorship or the barring of certain materials from the mails. Some called for boycotts or threw up picket lines to deter viewers or sponsors. Several groups called for the passage of legislation criminalizing what they called group libel. Others issued public statements criticizing the offending material, or tried to persuade distributors not to send it out.

The NAACP, often the most aggressive of the black civil rights agencies in the early twentieth century, understood that legislation might never pass and particular protests might not succeed, but public expressions of outrage, especially couched as appeals to civic ideals, would serve to educate the public about the dangers of such stereotypes. That organization's members therefore supplemented direct contacts with publishers or manufacturers with pickets and other public protests to call attention to their cause. And they used the purchasing power of the black community to back up their demands for change.

Jewish groups had begun more quietly, hoping discreet appeals to producers might prevent stereotyping without a public outcry, which they believed would only stir up hatred. Facing the horrific threat of Nazism, however, these agencies reevaluated their tactics. They too began to use economic pressure as well as appeals to American values as leverage. Some, like the American Jewish Congress, became far more public and outspoken, and argued that the protection of vulnerable minorities was of paramount importance. It argued that since free speech ended at libel, the rule could properly apply as well to the libel of entire groups. Other Jewish groups flirted with such views as well, especially during World War II when the crisis seemed most imminent.

In the end, however, each civil rights agency in the black and Jewish communities came down on the side of free speech. Jews insisted that free speech kept the United States from going the way of Nazism, and both communities recognized the dangers posed by the limits on free speech during the McCarthy era. Speech—even unpleasant, bigoted, or offensive speech—must be protected. Their joint struggle to extend the protection of the Bill of Rights to all Americans required a defense of freedom from censorship. But they had also become more outspoken, insisting that public protest, private pressure, and economic threats were all legitimate means of exerting their own free speech rights.

No matter what tactics any of these groups decided to pursue, many in the larger public considered all of them to be efforts at censorship. Even without calls for governmental action, opponents insisted that these groups were trying to suppress the offending material, and were therefore preventing free speech. And, in the end, although no one wanted to set legal limits around free expression, it was in fact extremely difficult to distinguish between protest and censorship since the goal of these protests was in fact to persuade others not to read, watch, produce, or distribute the material.

No single strategy proved reliably successful, and none escaped the accusation of censorship. Each group struck its own balance between free speech and suppression of offensive materials, between public expression of discontent and demands for censorship, between security for vulnerable populations and the limiting of the free exchange of ideas.

In the end, I would argue, the question of censorship cannot be reduced to a simple legal or constitutional question. Rather, calls for censorship operate on a continuum between more and less coercive. These questions remain relevant today. A number of American scholars and activists have renewed the call for group libel laws like those enacted in Europe and elsewhere on behalf of specific populations. Such arguments have emerged largely (but not exclusively) from critical race theory and other contemporary challenges to seemingly settled legal and social assumptions regarding free speech.[76] Here, history may prove instructive. Perhaps, in our current political terrain, civil rights agencies will rethink their earlier positions, rooted as they were in a different social context. Or perhaps their alternative approaches to fighting defamation can offer a different set of strategies for contemporary activists. In every age and for every minority group, the challenge of navigating these waters remains.

NOTES

1. Other groups, like the Chinese and Japanese, also used the law for redress of racial grievances, but organized less often to fight media stereotypes in these years. *See, e.g.*, JEAN PFAELZER, DRIVEN OUT: THE FORGOTTEN WAR AGAINST CHINESE AMERICANS, especially chs. 6 & 8 (2007). Greg Robinson cited several films receiving complaints by Japanese and Japanese Americans, including Cecil B. DeMille's 1915 *The Cheat*. Correspondence with author, Mar. 6, 2012.

2. For the best overview of black protests against the film, see MELVYN STOKES, D. W. GRIFFITH'S "THE BIRTH OF A NATION": A HISTORY OF THE MOST CONTROVERSIAL MOTION PICTURE OF ALL TIME 129–70 (2007).

3. Text of the Massachusetts bill, *quoted in* STOKES, *supra* note 2, at 147. An amended bill did pass in Massachusetts, but it failed to stop theaters from showing the film. For more on censorship in film, see LEE GRIEVESON, POLICING CINEMA: MOVIES AND CENSORSHIP IN THE EARLY TWENTIETH CENTURY (2004); CHARLES LYONS, THE NEW CENSORS: MOVIES AND THE CULTURE WARS (1997).

4. STOKES, *supra* note 2, at 323; city and state protests, *id.* at 129–70.

5. Letter from Walter White to Norman Hesseltine, Harvard University (Sept. 27, 1937) (on file with the Library of Congress Manuscript Division, NAACP papers box I C 217 [hereafter cited as NAACP]).

6. Report of Miss Ovington on Textbook Investigation by Mr. Reddick at 2, 3 (Apr. 11, 1938) (on file with the Library of Congress Manuscript Division, NAACP I A 18).

7. Untitled list of books with explanation (1939) (on file with the Library of Congress Manuscript Division, NAACP I C 217, Quotation: 1).

8. Letter from Walter White to Prof. R. K. Smith, Superintendent, Dunbar Township High School, Dawson, PA (Sept. 16, 1933) (on file with the Library of Congress Manuscript Division, NAACP I C 220).

9. Letter from Mrs. Callie Browne to James Weldon Johnson (Sept. 13, 1933) (on file with the Library of Congress Manuscript Division, NAACP I C 220).

10. Letter from RWB [Robert Wellington Bagnall], NAACP Director of Branches, to Harper and Brothers (Mar. 7, 1930) (on file with the Library of Congress Manuscript Division, NAACP I C 219).

11. *Berlin Says He'll "Change Slur in Song,"* and *Irving Berlin Orders Song Word Change*, BALT. AFRO-AM., n.d. [clipping] (on file with ADL Library, Anti-Defamation League microfilms, "Yellows 1942: Negro Race Problems"). Ironically, the Abraham song—with the

changed lyrics—was a minstrel number done by Bing Crosby in blackface. Some theaters refused to show it for that reason.

12. Letter from Walter White to Dodd, Mead and Company, New York (Oct. 18, 1932); Reply (Nov. 1, 1932) (on file with the Library of Congress Manuscript Division, NAACP I C 219). Ironically, White himself had faced the question in 1926 when his friend Carl van Vechten published a novel entitled *Nigger Heaven*. On grounds of authenticity, White concurred with van Vechten's public use of the term.

13. Lester Granger, "Participation of Negroes in Radio," at "Radio and Inter-group Understanding: A Progress Report," n.d. [Oct. 1946] (on file with ADL Library, Anti-Defamation League microfilms, "Yellows 1946: Negro Race Problems").

14. Report of the Secretary of the NAACP (June 9, 1952) (on file with the Library of Congress Manuscript Division, 8, NAACP II A 145); JOYCE ANN HANSON, MARY MCLEOD BETHUNE AND BLACK WOMEN'S POLITICAL ACTIVISM 98 (2003).

15. Mrs. Charles Long, *in* Addresses and Proceedings of the Fifty-Sixth Annual Meeting of the National Education Association 426 Washington, DC (July 2, 1918).

16. Letter from Benjamin Epstein to Leonard Finder (Nov. 27, 1939) (on file with ADL Library, Anti-Defamation League microfilms, "Yellows 1939: Motion Pictures" [hereafter cited as MP]).

17. STEVEN CARR, HOLLYWOOD AND ANTI-SEMITISM 58 (2001). The ADL files, curiously, do not contain material about the notorious publication during the same era of the *Protocols* in Henry Ford's newspaper, the *Dearborn Independent*.

18. Letter from Finder to Leon Bloom [? illegible] (Apr. 27, 1937) (on file with ADL Library, Anti-Defamation League microfilms, "Yellows 1937: MP"). While both black and Jewish groups generally chose to proceed out of the public eye in the first half of the twentieth century, this decision was not made by every community wishing to challenge offensive presentations. The Catholic Legion of Decency, which had organized in 1933, for example, had no hesitations about launching public demands to ban films and books it found offensive. It also published lists of such items and forbade Catholics to watch or read them.

19. For more on the "sha sha" approach and its critics, see CHERYL GREENBERG, TROUBLING THE WATERS (2006).

20. Letter from Chasin to Finder (Mar. 8, 1940); Letter from Finder to Gutstadt (Mar. 15 1940) (on file with ADL Library, Anti-Defamation League microfilms, "Yellows 1940: Native Son"). No letter to the publisher appears in the ADL files, suggesting the ADL in fact declined to make any protest.

21. Letter from Epstein to Joseph [illegible], Warner Bros. (June 3, 1939) (on file with ADL Library, Anti-Defamation League microfilms, "Yellows 1939: MP"). Carr asserts that from Warner Brothers' point of view, the challenge of the movie was to not make it appear so philosemitic that it would appear to the public to be pro-Jewish propaganda. *See* CARR, *supra* note 17, at 210.

22. To "Jew someone down" was, in the slang of the day, to be cheap or haggle. Letter from Frank Dunetz to D. Appleton-Century Co., Inc. (Mar. 4, 1941); Letter from Epstein to D. Appleton-Century Co., Inc. (Mar. 29, 1941); Letter from John Williams, D. Appleton-Century Co., Inc. to Epstein (Mar. 31 1941) ("regret"). Equally unsatisfactory was an inquiry regarding *The Doctor and His Patient*, Letter from Epstein to Arthur Hertzler (the author)

(Jan. 2, 1941); Reply (Jan. 6, 1941) (who claimed the reference was "facetious" and insisted, "Many of my best friens [*sic*] are jews [*sic*]. One of them knows more jokes on the jews than will ind [sic] in the books. Whenever he visits me he has a new 'Jew joke.'" He concluded, "I believe you people make it hard for yourselves as well as your friends by being so sensative [*sic*]" (on file with ADL Library, Anti-Defamation League microfilms, "Yellows 1941: Books, undesirable").

23. Letter from Gutstadt to Finder (Aug. 16, 1937) ("to see"); Letter from E. T. Browne to "Sir," n.d. ("needless") (on file with ADL Library, Anti-Defamation League microfilms, "Yellows 1937: Investigations"). For similar protests, see, for example, Letter from Epstein to McLaughlin Bros., Inc. (Jan. 4, 1940) (*The Big Book of Nursery Rhymes*); Letter from Max Kroloff to David Coleman, (Nov. 3, 1941) (John Reeves's *The Rothschilds—the Financial Rulers of Nations*) (on file with ADL Library, Anti-Defamation League microfilms, "Yellows 1941: Books, undesirable"); Letter from Les Forrest [?] to National Broadcasting Co. (July 29, 1941) (Jim Flynn's radio show); Letter from Epstein to National Broadcasting Co. (Aug. 27, 1941) (*The Abbots* radio show) (on file with ADL Library, Anti-Defamation League microfilms, "Yellows 1941: National Broadcasters"); Letter from Epstein to Arthur Israel (Apr. 16, 1940) (*La Cancion del Milagro*, a film in Mexico City) (on file with ADL Library, Anti-Defamation League microfilms, "Yellows 1940: MP"). These did not receive answers that appear in the files. However, a similar attempt by the American Jewish Committee succeeded: Letter from Frank Trager to Mr. Depinet [? illegible] (Nov. 12, 1942) (the film *Once Upon a Honeymoon* received a cordial reply on November 16 that all the offending scenes had been removed) (on file with ADL Library, Anti-Defamation League microfilms, "Yellows 1942: MP").

24. "Golgotha," n.d. (on file with ADL Library, Anti-Defamation League microfilms, "Yellows 1938: MP").

25. Letter from Gutstadt to "Friends" (Mar. 10, 1938) (on file with ADL Library, Anti-Defamation League microfilms, "Yellows 1938: MP").

26. Letter from Finder to David Robinson, Oregon ADL (July 11, 1939) (on file with ADL Library, Anti-Defamation League microfilms, "Yellows 1939: MP").

27. Letter from Finder to I. A. Davis (Nov. 10, 1939) (on file with ADL Library, Anti-Defamation League microfilms, "Yellows 1939: MP").

28. Letter from Marston to Robinson (Sept. 25, 1939) (on file with ADL Library, Anti-Defamation League microfilms, "Yellows 1939: MP").

29. Letter Finder to Davis, *supra* note 27.

30. Letter from Finder to Watch Tower Bible and Tract Society (June 18, 1938) (on file with ADL Library, Anti-Defamation League microfilms, "Yellows 1938: Magazines and Pamphlets").

31. "Anti-Jewish Materials in Christian Text Books," AM. JEWISH CONGRESS COURIER, n.d. (1933?), at 16 (on file with American Jewish Committee Library).

32. Letter from Finder to William Grunsner [? illegible] (Aug. 11, 1937) ("tactfully"); Letter from Gutstadt to Finder (Aug. 27, 1937) (meeting); Letter from Gutstadt to Finder (Nov. 19, 1937) ("cooperating agents") (on file with ADL Library, Anti-Defamation League microfilms, "Yellows 1937: MP").

33. Letter from Finder to Gutstadt (Oct. 10, 1938); Letter from Finder to Mr. Kaufman [?];Letter from Finder to Mr. Rogers (Oct. 13, 1938); Letter from Gutstadt to Finder (Oct. 17, 1938); Letter from Finder to Mr. Moss (Oct. 21, 1938); Letter from Finder to Mr. Kaufmann (Nov. 7, 1938) (film will be changed) (on file with ADL Library, Anti-Defamation League microfilms, "Yellows 1938: MP"). *See also* ADL, "Minutes of National Executive Committee Meeting," June 24–25, 1955 (regarding the National Motion Picture Committee) (on file with ADL Library, ADL warehouse box 178: 1955–56 NEC meeting).

34. Letter from Forster to K. P. Aldrich (June 19, 1941); Letter from Forster to Max Kroloff, ADL (June 27, 1941); Letter from Third Assistant Postmaster General to Postmaster, Wichita, KS (June 27, 1941); Letter from Aldrich to Forster (July 9, 1941) (on file with ADL Library, Anti-Defamation League microfilms, "Yellows 1941: Books, undesirable"). The ADL also turned information about groups creating defamatory materials over to the FBI when there seemed to be "possible subversive and seditious connections of one of the parties concerned." The FBI proved "very much interested in this matter." Letter from Gutstadt to Nissen Gross, ADL (Apr. 14, 1944); Reply (Apr. 21, 1944) (FBI) (on file with ADL Library, Anti-Defamation League microfilms, "Yellows 1944: MP"). Following the entry of the United States into World War II, under quiet pressure from the Roosevelt administration, the Catholic Church ordered Father Coughlin to cease his radio talks and shut down his *Social Justice* newspaper.

35. The story that follows, including quotations, is told in a series of letters: Letter from Alvin Gardner, B'nai Brith Bergen County Lodge, to Finder (Jan. 24, 1938); Letter from Finder to Gutstadt (Jan. 24, 1938); Letter from Finder to F. L. Wurzburg, Conde Nast (Jan. 25, 1938); Letter from Wurzburg to Finder (Jan. 26, 1938); Letter from Finder to Wurzburg (Jan. 27, 1938); Letter from Miles [? illegible], Chicago ADL, to Finder (Jan. 27, 1938) (on file with ADL Library, Anti-Defamation League microfilms, "Yellows 1938: Magazines"). *See also* CAROLINE SEEBOHM, THE MAN WHO WAS VOGUE: THE LIFE AND TIMES OF CONDE NAST 209–15 (1982).

36. Letter from Max Yavno, Photo League to Manhattan Camera Club (Nov. 30, 1938); Letter from Manhattan Camera Club to Thomas Maloney, *U.S. Camera* (Dec. 3, 1938) (on file with ADL Library, Anti-Defamation League microfilms, "Yellows 1938: Magazines").

37. Atlanta Jewish Community Council, "Review of Minutes, Decisions and Policies 1946–1953," at 7, American Jewish Committee Vertical Files, "Community Files: Atlanta." *See also* Letter from Charles Schlaifer [? illegible], Twentieth Century Fox, to Finder (Sept. 27, 1943) (regarding Budd Schulberg's *What Makes Sammy Run*) (on file with ADL Library, Anti-Defamation League microfilms, "Yellows 1943: MP").

38. *Dean Katz Argues Two Cases*, CHI. TRIB., Sept. 13, 1948 (clipping on file with American Jewish Congress Library "CLSA Binder").

39. *The Difference Between the Congress and the A.D.L.*, JEWISH POST, May 10, 1946 (on file with American Jewish Congress Library, "Clippings on Racism and Anti-Semitism").

40. Described in Letter from Philip Lerman to Oscar Cohen, ADL (Aug. 31, 1951), 1–2 (quotation from 2) (on file with ADL Library, Anti-Defamation League microfilms, "Yellows 1949–52: Pro-org JACL"). *See, e.g.*, Gordon H. Chang, *"Superman Is About to Visit the Relocation Centers" and the Limits of Wartime Liberalism*, 19 AMERASIA J. 37–60 (1993); Larry Tajiri, *Race Hatred Is a Business*, CROSSROADS, Jan. 25, 1951, *reprinted in* PACIFIC

Citizens: Larry and Guyo Tajiri and Japanese American Journalism in the World War II Era 224 (Greg Robinson, ed., 2012).

41. NAACP, Secretary's Report for July and August 1951, at 3 (on file with the Library of Congress Manuscript Division, NAACP II A 145). The company agreed to discuss the situation with the NAACP.

42. *Id.* at 4–5. While the National Urban League could not legally take action, its leadership reported their "personal antipathy towards the program." *Id.* at 5.

43. The NAACP also protested racial slurs in an army radio program and was promised it would not happen again. *Id.*

44. Mr. Kantor to "Sir" (ADL) (Aug. 15, 1944); Harry Goldberg, ADL, to Herbert Lizt, ADL (Aug. 23, 1944); Lizt to Kantor (Aug. 28, 1944) (on file with ADL Library, Anti-Defamation League microfilms, "Yellows 1944: Misc. News MP").

45. Despite the membership of those allies and the ACLU, the ADL refused to join, citing "its attack upon the Legion of Decency." That "bitter attack" worried the ADL "because we were fearful that possibly this [was] a Jewish-promoted organization, and therefore, that attack could be made the source of further friction between the Catholic and Jewish groups." Leonard Finder to Henry Monsky, ADL (Sept. 29, 1938) (Finder assured Monsky that the AFA was not Jewish-sponsored); "Plan and Purpose of Associated Film Audiences," n.d. (includes member organizations) (on file with ADL Library, Anti-Defamation League microfilms, "Yellows 1938: Magazines and Pamphlets").

46. Letter from Charles Sherman to K. B. Weissman (Dec. 27, 1944) (concerned about film) (on file with ADL Library, Anti-Defamation League microfilms, "Yellows 1944: Negro Race Problems").

47. Letter from Lerman to Cohen, *supra* note 40, at 1–2.

48. Memorandum from Bill Pinsley to Harold Braverman, ADL at 2 (Feb. 5, 1954) (on file with ADL Library, Anti-Defamation League microfilms, "Yellows 1953–58: Discrimination general race"). This memo chronicled the ADL's intervention with a proposed minstrel show to be put on by the Boy Scouts and the encouragement of such activities by the Lions Club International. Pinsley's suggestion was unnecessary; the ADL had already been following NAACP protests of such shows and supporting them where appropriate. *See, e.g.,* Letter from Monroe Steinberg, ADL, to Max Heller, B'nai Brith (Nov. 15, 1948) (our practice) (on file with ADL Library, Anti-Defamation League microfilms, "Yellows 1948: Negro Race Problems"); Letter from Braverman to Elsie Elfenbein, NCJW (June 16, 1950); Letter from Alexander Miller to Elfenbein (June 27, 1950) (regarding a planned NCJW minstrel show "with a mixed Negro and white cast") (on file with ADL Library, Anti-Defamation League microfilms, "Yellows 1949–52: Negro Race Problems"); Letter from Edward Zeizler (ADL?) to L. Zachs, Beth Israel Men's Club, Vancouver, BC (Jan. 16, 1950) (the Men's Club canceled the planned show after learning of the ADL's objections); Letter from P. Allen Rickles, ADL, to Leonard Krivends [? illegible], Jewish Community Council of Stockton, CA (Oct. 20, 1949) (regarding planned minstrel show in the Jewish Community Center) (on file with ADL Library, Anti-Defamation League microfilms, "Yellows 1949–52: Negro Race Problems"); Letter from Harvey Schechter to Braverman (Nov. 25, 1953) (which described a Lions Club brochure, "Everything for Your Minstrel Show," as "without a doubt

the filthiest thing I have ever seen") (on file with ADL Library, Anti-Defamation League microfilms, "Yellows 1953–58: Discrimination general race").

49. "Negro Churchmen Speak to White Churchmen," Pamphlet at 11 (1944) (on file with the Library of Congress Manuscript Division, National Urban League papers, box A70).

50. *Roots of Prejudice*, CHI. DEFENDER Jan. 24, 1948 (on file with the American Jewish Congress Library, "Clippings on racism and anti-Semitism").

51. ADL Minutes of Commission Meeting at 19 (May 14–15, 1949) (on file with ADL Library, ADL warehouse box 176); ADL Civil Rights Committee memo, "Free Speech," May 20, 1949, at 2 (on file with ADL Library, Anti-Defamation League microfilms, "Chicago reel 12, Civil Rights Division Policies 1948–52"). The ADL reaffirmed its policies in 1949, stating that it "looks with disfavor upon picketing of motion pictures as an expression of disapproval except when special circumstances indicate the propriety of such action. The ADL may [however] advocate that the public refrain from attending motion pictures considered prejudicial." ADL, "Freedom of Speech: Censorship," n.d. (1949) (on file with ADL Library, ADL warehouse box 42 "ADL positions").

52. *Oliver Twist* was only Guinness's second movie appearance. The following narrative comes from the many dozens of documents on the *Oliver Twist* controversy in Jewish agency files. *See,e.g.*, ADL, "Yellows 49–52: MP Oliver Twist" (containing ADL position papers, deliberations, letters to film producers and reports) (on file with ADL Library, Anti-Defamation League microfilms); Domestic Affairs Committee binder 1947–1953 (on file with the American Jewish Committee Library) (see particularly Oct. 19, 1948, 1–2; Nov. 16, 1948, 3–4; May 3, 1949, 3–6); and periodical files of the American Council on Judaism's COUNCIL NEWS, which discusses the film in its January 1951 issue at 21–22. For a discussion of Canadian Jewish protests, see, for example, Abraham Feinberg, "'Time-Life' and 'Oliver Twist' (A New Twist in News Control)," January 1949 (on file with ADL Library, Anti-Defamation League microfilms, "Yellows 1949–52 MP").

53. Shad Polier, Remarks at NCRAC panel by David Reisman on responses to anti-Semitism, n.d., 6, American Jewish Historical Society. These words are the note taker's report of Polier's remarks rather than a verbatim quotation.

54. *Id.* at 7.

55. Forster, remarks at NCRAC presentation by Reisman, at 7. Quotation is note taker's paraphrase.

56. *Id.* at 7–8.

57. *Id.* at 8.

58. John Haynes Holmes, *The New Negro*, AM. PRESS ASSOC., Dec. 11, 1945 [possibly 1944], at 1 (on file with ADL Library, Anti-Defamation League microfilms, "Yellows 1945: Negro Race Problems"). The column concluded with praise for the mental emancipation of black people that allowed them to protest, even if he believed their political position on free speech to be incorrect.

59. Polier, *supra* note 53, at 6.

60. Transcript, American Jewish Congress Final Plenary Session of its Biennial National Convention, Apr. 4, 1948, 445–46 (motion), 447 (constitutional) (on file with the American Jewish Congress Library, "American Jewish Congress conferences and conventions").

61. *See* American Jewish Congress Minutes of Executive Committee, Dec. 19, 1948, at 9; Sol Rabkin (ADL), "Group Libel Legislation," Report, n.d. [1949?] (on file with ADL Library, Anti-Defamation League microfilms, "Chicago Microfilms 12: Chisub: Civil rights division, policies, minutes"). A group libel law crafted by the Jewish Labor Council had been introduced in 1946 but was opposed by other Jewish groups and failed to pass the House.

62. Rabkin, *supra* note 61, at 3–4; Rabkin, "Addendum," May 5, 1949, at 1 ("offensive language").

63. David Sher, remarks at presentation by Reisman, *supra* note 53, at 8.

64. *Id.* at 9; Rabkin, *supra* note 61, at 6–7; NAACP: Letter from Edward Dudley, NAACP, to Alexander Pekelis, American Jewish Congress (June 18, 1945) (on file with the Library of Congress Manuscript Division, NAACP I A 360).

65. Kathleen Laughlin, *Our Defense against Despair: The Progressive Policy of the National Council of Jewish Women after WWII, in* A JEWISH FEMININE MYSTIQUE? JEWISH WOMEN IN POSTWAR AMERICA 58–59 (Hasia Diner, Shira Kohn, & Rachel Kranson, eds., 2010).

66. S. Andhil Fineberg, "Group Libel," Apr. 14, 1947, at 1–3 (on file with the American Jewish Committee papers, Proskauer files box 7). Ironically, the president of the American Jewish Committee pointed out that Fineberg's reference to an organization as a "communist front" could be considered a libelous epithet according to recent court decisions. Letter from Judge Proskauer to Dr. Slawson, Apr. 15, 1947. *See also* American Jewish Committee Domestic Affairs Committee minutes, 1–2. Interestingly, the committee suspected that if the legislation were introduced again, the NAACP would support it, although the association opposed the 1949 bill. *Id.* at 2.

67. Edward Newman, AJC, "Philosophy Underlying the Socio-Legal Approach as a Technique in Dealing with Problems of Group Adjustment," Mar. 25, 1947 (on file with the American Jewish Committee Library, "Civil Rights files").

68. *Beauharnais*: American Jewish Committee, Minutes of the Domestic Affairs Committee, June 8, 1953, at 1. The law prohibited the publication or exhibition of anything that portrayed the "depravity, criminality, unchastity, or lack of virtue of a class of citizens of any race, color, creed or religion." Beauharnais v. Illinois, 343 U.S. 250 (1952).

69. Rabkin, *supra* note 61, at 3.

70. ADL Civil Rights Committee Memorandum, "Free Speech," *supra* note 51, at 3. *See also* Minutes of the ADL National Commission, April 1955, at 1–2 (committee reported on its reconsideration of the question "critical day"). It repeated its support in principle for a group libel bill but found no existing proposals acceptable, "particularly in view of the danger of aggravating the current climate of repression." *Id.* at 2. It did approve, again in principle, legislation to ban offensive cards or envelopes from the mail. Decision affirmed by ADL, Apr. 29, 1955.

71. Laughlin, *supra* note 65, at 59.

72. Rabkin, "Addendum," *supra* note 62, at 3.

73. "Summary of Decisions by NCRAC Bodies," 3 (oppose group libel legislation), 4 (radio and television) (on file with ADL Library, Anti-Defamation League microfilms, "Yellows 1949–52: Pro-org NCRAC Assignments Committee").

74. Minutes of the ADL National Commission, 1955, at 2; Masks: Minutes of ADL National Executive Committee meeting, May 14–15, 1949, at 9 (on file with ADL Library, ADL warehouse box 176).

75. NCRAC, "Positions on Congressional Investigation of Hate Mongers, Group Libel Legislation, Postal Censorship, White House Conference on Compliance with Law, Adopted by the Executive Committee, Jan. 11, 1959," at 2–3 (on file with the American Jewish Historical Society archives, NCRAC papers). According to the report, only two groups did not support the position. The Jewish War Veterans decided to reconsider the question before taking a position, and the Jewish Labor Committee asked that its vote be recorded later. That the minutes lacked any mention of dissenting votes suggests that even the American Jewish Congress had backed away from support of a group libel bill.

76. *See, e.g.,* Mari Matsuda, *Public Response to Racist Speech: Considering the Victim's Story,* 87 MICH. L. REV. 2320 (1989); MARI MATSUDA ET AL., EDS., WORDS THAT WOUND: CRITICAL RACE THEORY, ASSAULTIVE SPEECH, AND THE FIRST AMENDMENT (1993); MONROE H. FREEDMAN & ERIC M. FREEDMAN, EDS., GROUP DEFAMATION AND FREEDOM OF SPEECH: THE RELATIONSHIP BETWEEN LANGUAGE AND VIOLENCE (1995); Michael Polelle, *Racial and Ethnic Group Defamation: A Speech-Friendly Proposal,* 23 B.C. THIRD WORLD L.J. 213 (2003). Current efforts focus more on hate speech than on media stereotypes, but not all; Polelle's article challenges the portrayals of Italians in *The Sopranos.* For a good overview of the debates within civil rights groups and the prioritizing of free speech rights, see SAMUEL WALKER, HATE SPEECH: THE HISTORY OF AN AMERICAN CONTROVERSY (1994).

4

Race, Place, and Historic Moment

Black and Japanese American World War II Veterans:
The GI Bill of Rights and the Model Minority Myth

TAUNYA LOVELL BANKS

The most commonly touted social change in the United States following the end of World War II is the expansion of the American middle class. Prior to the war, homeownership was unattainable for the vast majority of Americans, especially nonwhites, and few Americans were college educated or middle class. The availability of benefits through the Servicemen's Readjustment Act of 1944 (aka the GI Bill of Rights) is one commonly cited trigger for this change. Under the GI Bill, eligible veterans qualified for a series of major benefits: job placement; unemployment compensation; low-interest home, farm, and business loans; and mortgage insurance. The most notable benefit, however, was up to four years of paid education or vocational training. The common narrative holds that the GI Bill, by providing veterans previously unavailable educational opportunities, elevated the socioeconomic status of a substantial segment of the American population as they entered their most productive working years. Increased educational, employment, and housing opportunities, in particular, gave rise to a new middle class able to accumulate wealth and attain economic security for their children and grandchildren.[1]

The end of World War II also marked a second equally significant change. Both black and Japanese American soldiers who fought abroad in racially segregated units returned to a country that continued to treat them in varying degrees as second-class citizens based on their race. Later, these veterans, along with others, fought for full citizenship rights at home in the civil rights movements of the mid-twentieth century.[2]

Over the next twenty years, America made significant strides toward remedying institutionalized racial inequality. During this period second-generation Japanese Americans (Nisei), but not blacks, achieved near economic parity with whites. Although most first-generation Japanese Americans (Issei) never fully recovered from the setbacks occasioned by World War II, the Nisei's relative postwar success later caused some to label them as a "model minority." This stereotype, criticized by scholars, appeared in the mid-1960s and has been imposed on all Asian Americans.[3]

However, the historian Roger Daniels questioned this characterization, writing that "the transformation [of Japanese Americans] from 'pariah to paragon' [was not] merely a mechanical adjustment of market forces." Rather, he writes, this "model minority status, real or imagined, [if such a transformation ever occurred] . . . did not take place right after the war but sometime later." Daniels urged historians to more closely examine the factors contributing to the relative postwar economic success of Japanese Americans.[4]

This chapter takes on an aspect of Daniels's challenge, questioning claims that Japanese Americans achieved postwar success, despite structural discrimination, because of some inherent "goodness" or cultural values not possessed by black Americans. It asks whether the advantages allegedly conferred on World War II veterans who received GI Bill benefits explain the current socioeconomic status of Japanese Americans, or whether other factors better explain their relative postwar success. By exploring the impact of racial subordination situated in both geographic location as well as historic moment, this chapter compares and contrasts black and Japanese American veterans' abilities to use GI Bill benefits in their quest for racial equality. This examination illustrates how universal social uplift legislation seldom results in equal outcomes for whites and racial minorities. It concludes that a variety of factors explain the different socioeconomic outcomes for blacks and Japanese Americans in the twenty years following the end of World War II.

BLACK VETERANS AND THE GI BILL OF RIGHTS

The historian Ira Katznelson argues that the GI Bill created an expanded postwar middle-class American society "almost exclusively for whites." This statement is correct as applied to black GIs. From the beginning, black Americans were poorly positioned to take advantage of GI Bill benefits, and in some cases were deliberately excluded. Initially, the military actively discouraged the enlistment and induction of blacks, even in the all-segregated units that then composed the army, resulting in proportionately more white men being inducted. "Complaints from whites who had been drafted while eligible blacks remained at home, pressure from the Selective Service System, and the recommendations of Paul V. McNutt, chairman of the War Manpower Commission, finally forced the army to reverse its policy of limiting the number of all-black units." Beginning in 1943 the induction of blacks into the army increased rapidly because so many eligible white men were already fighting or employed in essential occupations. Other branches resisted enlisting large numbers of black draftees and volunteers.[5]

In addition, many military-age black men were ineligible for military service, even during wartime, due to crippling disadvantages resulting from growing up in the segregated South. For instance, a disproportionate number of southern rural blacks could not meet the minimum educational requirements due to woefully inadequate schooling, while others were ineligible for health reasons as a result of extreme impoverishment and endemic disease. Thus, relative to their demographic numbers, blacks remained underrepresented in the US military during this time period.[6]

Entry into the military, moreover, did not guarantee black men access to veterans' benefits. To qualify for GI Bill benefits, a veteran must have an honorable discharge, which proved difficult for black veterans who "were disproportionally, and often unfairly, given dishonorable discharges at dismissal." Moreover, even an honorable discharge was no guarantee; geographical location, as well as the effects of past discrimination, hampered access to GI Bill benefits.[7]

This outcome was by design. Congressman John Rankin (D-Mississippi), a hard-core segregationist, was the mastermind of the facially neutral law that consciously prevented black veterans' access to benefits. Rankin, a sponsor of the bill and chair of the Committee on World War Veteran's Legislation, feared that if black veterans returned to the South, with the aid of the GI Bill, they could "shift the balance against segregation." Under the guise of states' rights, Rankin effectively tailored the GI Bill to rely on local, decentralized administration of unemployment and loan benefits, thus creating a structural framework giving local authorities wide discretion in the distribution of benefits.[8]

The law provided that veterans had to apply for extended job placement, unemployment compensation, and loan approval benefits at their local Veterans Administration (VA) and United States Employment Service (USES) office. These local offices in the South employed few or no black counselors, leaving black veterans open to discriminatory treatment. Commonly, white counselors placed black veterans in low-skill jobs, even when they qualified for skilled or semiprofessional employment. Refusing to accept a menial labor position foreclosed the possibility of unemployment compensation.[9]

Black veterans also faced difficulty obtaining the generous low-interest home, business, and farm loans offered under the GI Bill because private lenders controlled loan awards. The VA only guaranteed up to 50 percent of the loan, and this guarantee was contingent on the veteran securing a loan from a bank or other type of lending agency. Further, many black veterans lacked the collateral demanded by lending agencies, or were subject to discriminatory lending practices. Free to make loans as they pleased, private lenders either openly refused to lend to blacks or redlined areas occupied by blacks, effectively denying loans to black veterans unable or unwilling to purchase property in white neighborhoods.[10]

Similarly, structural impediments hindered black veterans' access to educational benefits. Most southern black veterans, even those with a high school education, were products of underfunded and inadequate racially segregated black public schools. Thus they were unprepared, academically, for college, even outside the South. But even if academically prepared for college, once again, the structure of the GI Bill posed yet another impediment for black veterans. Public and private institutions of higher education maintained complete control over admissions criteria. Title II of the GI Bill allowed colleges and educational institutions to continue existing patterns of racial exclusion, allowing racial segregation in the South and racial quotas in the North. In the postwar South, de jure segregation was the rule; the "separate but equal" doctrine was still a reality. Black veterans in the South, therefore, had little choice but to pursue college degrees at black institutions.[11]

But here, too, they faced numerous obstacles. In 1947 white colleges outnumbered black colleges in the South by more than five to one, even though blacks constituted a quarter of the population of the South. Black colleges also lacked the funds for the kind of temporary expansion (students in trailers and part-time faculty teaching) that white institutions underwent to welcome returning GIs. Thus southern black colleges had limited seats available for returning black veterans. They also were inferior to white colleges in terms of library size, student-faculty ratio, quality of laboratories, and professors. With limited access to higher education, many black veterans chose to pursue vocational training, but segregation laws or racial quotas limited their admission to many trade schools. Here again, the lack of meaningful federal oversight enabled such discriminatory abuse. As a result, most of the postwar black educational gains are attributed to the small number of black veterans in northern states, who had access to integrated colleges and meaningful vocational training. But even in the North, black GIs often were impeded because "quotas at many institutions limited enrollment (as they did for Jews and other minorities)."[12]

Lack of access to educational benefits, however, was not limited to black veterans. Class as well as race complicated access to GI benefits, even for white veterans. More than half of all veterans had less than a high school education when discharged from the service. These veterans, without regard to race, were less likely to attend college. Still, black veterans comprised a much larger proportion of this group. According to the historian Lizabeth Cohen, "the G.I. Bill targeted those citizens defined as *deserving* according to the narrow tests and prejudices of a traditionally defined military." The veterans who gained the most from the bill's educational benefits were those already on the "college track," most of whom were white.[13]

The overall structure and application of the GI Bill thus effectively reinforced existing racially based labor divisions. Especially in the South, educational advancement and acquisition of better jobs and home mortgages, factors that contribute to the accumulation of wealth, were difficult for black veterans to obtain. As a result of the legal and structural impediments faced by black GIs, "[t]he gap in educational attainment between blacks and whites widened rather than closed."[14]

The persistent education (and homeownership) gap between white and black Americans from 1940 to 1960 is the cumulative consequence of the prewar and wartime discrimination that targeted black Americans. These difficulties disproportionately impacted the large number of postwar black veterans living in southern and border states, who were subject to an ensemble of racially discriminatory laws and practices that governed almost every aspect of life. Fifteen years after the war ended, the median educational level of blacks had only risen from 5.7 to 8.2 years, less than the median level of whites in 1940. Similarly, while homeownership for whites increased from 43 percent in 1940 to 77 percent by 1980, with most of the increase occurring before 1960 (the GI benefit years), black homeownership only increased from 29 percent in 1940 to 49 percent in 1980, with much of the increase in the post–civil rights period.[15]

The socioeconomic progress of black American World War II veterans illustrates the impact of long-term race discrimination, prewar socioeconomic status, and geographical location on the ability of individuals to benefit from the GI Bill. These same factors, in turn, help explain the dramatically different outcomes for another group of nonwhite veterans, Japanese Americans.

Despite severe race-based discrimination, especially during the internment era when the vast majority of mainland Japanese Americans had their lives and careers interrupted, second-generation Japanese Americans, including veterans, advanced significantly in the postwar years. As the following sections illustrate, they were better positioned prewar to take advantage of postwar opportunities.

JAPANESE AMERICANS AND THE GI BILL

At the time that Japan bombed Pearl Harbor, Japanese Americans constituted the largest group of ethnic Asians in the United States. Thousands were in the US Army. Two months after Pearl Harbor, President Franklin D. Roosevelt issued Executive Order 9066, authorizing the forcible removal of some 112,000 citizens and noncitizens of Japanese ancestry living on the West Coast to "relocation" camps. Ultimately, 120,313 people were interned. Second-generation Japanese Americans from California, Oregon, and Washington, who, unlike most black Americans, could vote freely, were treated not as second-class citizens but as noncitizens—aliens—solely because of ancestry. Ironically, the slightly larger and more concentrated Japanese American population living in the American-controlled territory of Hawaii—some in the shadow of Pearl Harbor—was not interned.[16]

In June 1942 the War Department formally stopped accepting Japanese Americans into the military (making official a policy largely in place since Pearl Harbor), but that order was quickly modified, and by 1943 the army, though not the navy, was recruiting volunteers from both Hawaii and the US mainland. By January 1944 Nisei men, including those in internment camps, were subject to the draft. As with black military recruits, the demand for more soldiers trumped racial antagonism and suspicion toward Japanese American recruits, though both groups remained relegated to segregated units. "Between November 1940 and December 1945, approximately 25,778 Japanese Americans, almost 10 percent of the total ethnic population, volunteered or were drafted into the armed forces."[17]

There is virtually no analysis of the GI Bill's impact on Japanese American World War II veterans and whether the bill's benefits contributed to the postwar prosperity of Japanese Americans. In this section I provide evidence for the argument that the relatively high socioeconomic status of contemporary Japanese Americans has little relationship to World War II veterans' access to GI Bill benefits. Rather, the socioeconomic success of the

Nisei more likely reflects the geographic, demographic, and socioeconomic position of Japanese Americans immediately prior to and following World War II. The success of second-generation, but not first-generation, Japanese Americans in improving their socioeconomic status resulted from a variety of factors. These factors include the pre- and postwar settlement patterns of Japanese Americans, their prewar educational levels, group civil rights advocacy, citizenship status, and birth cohort, as well as the postwar racial attitudes of other Americans toward them.

Some scholars invoke the model minority stereotype when explaining the socioeconomic progress of the Nisei and their children and the relative lack of progress for black Americans during the last half of the twentieth century. These scholars, however, fail to take into account the average age cohort and educational levels of Japanese Americans at the war's beginning. Unlike black Americans, virtually all immigrants from Japan—including the women, on whose educational access the next generation built—were literate, "reflecting the minimum sixth-grade educational standard" set by their home country. In the prewar period, a majority (approximately 70,000) of mainland Japanese Americans lived in California, where quality education, including a free public university system, was readily available. As a result, the Nisei, who attended college in disproportionate numbers, were generally more educated than their white counterparts. Despite their high prewar education levels, Japanese Americans still ranked lower than whites in terms of income and occupation. The disparity between education level and occupation reflected in the 1940 census is best explained by race-based discrimination in employment, including near exclusion from public sector jobs, and restrictions on access to property. Although most West Coast Japanese Americans remained heavily concentrated in agricultural, wholesale, or retail trade jobs, state alien land laws enacted by California, Washington, and Oregon in the early 1900s prohibited individuals "ineligible for citizenship" (Asian American immigrants) from owning agricultural land or leasing the land for more than three years. Thus economic opportunities for the Issei were artificially restricted. In addition, racially restrictive covenants hampered all Japanese Americans, and other Asian Americans, in the western states from buying or leasing all forms of property. Thus restrictions on employment opportunities and the ability to own property artificially suppressed the traditional pathway to the accumulation of wealth in America.[18]

By the early 1940s the Nisei, whose median age was seventeen, outnumbered their Issei parents. Thus, numerically speaking, there was a large number of well-educated Japanese Americans about to enter college or the workforce. The internment interrupted their education, although approximately 200 students transferred to colleges outside the Western Defense Command before the evacuation order. The rest were incarcerated in the camps.[19]

During the internment years, approximately 4,000 students were allowed to leave the camps to study at colleges outside the restricted areas of the Western Defense Command. Students were recruited by the National Japanese American Student Relocation Council (NJASRC), which also raised funds for scholarships (along with Japanese American communities in the camps) and helped students secure admission into colleges willing to accept them. Though two historically black colleges, Howard and Fisk University, offered to accept these students, the council resisted forwarding them student names. One NJASRC member expressed the fear that any Nisei willing to attend these institutions might "collaborate with negro student agitators in causing a troubled situation." As a result, none of the students were encouraged to attend historically black colleges. Instead, many Nisei, often isolated in small, all-white denominational colleges in the middle of nowhere, were able to continue their education, leaving them well positioned for employment and other opportunities for advancement in postwar America.[20]

The experiences of West Coast interned Japanese Americans before and during the war stands in sharp contrast to their counterparts in Hawaii. From the beginning, their circumstances differed in many significant ways. Formerly a sovereign nation, Hawaii was seized and annexed as an organized incorporated American territory in 1898. Prior to annexation, "the white elites of Honolulu formulated crude strategies for keeping the [largely Asian American] immigrant community in its place ... [as] they imported workers by the tens of thousands." Thus, when Hawaii was annexed, there already were ethnic Japanese in the Islands.[21]

After 1907 the Issei in Hawaii were consigned to the Islands. In that year Congress, in an immigration act, gave the president authority to deny entry to people holding Japanese passports on certain technical grounds. The idea was "to reduce immigration without public embarrassment to the Japanese." Almost immediately "Roosevelt ... issued an executive order stopping the movement of Japanese residents of the U.S. Territory of Hawaii to the U.S. mainland." As a result, Japanese immigrant noncitizens and their underage American-born children remained concentrated on the Islands.[22]

As "thousands ... drift[ed] from the plantations, and thousands more [were] born to the original immigrants, [Japanese Americans] gradually took over much of the smaller island trades." According to ethnic studies scholar Ronald Takaki, there was no large white working-class population in the Hawaiian Islands, thus "Japanese were needed as laborers, and . . . had been incorporated by the planters into a paternalistic racial hierarchy. . . . [Their] problems and difficulties were primarily related to their condition as [plantation] workers. . . . On the mainland, however, the Japanese faced a fundamentally different situation: they were a racial minority . . . [d]enied access to employment in the industrial labor market." By 1940 roughly 65 percent of the 157,905 Japanese Americans living in Hawaii were under the age of twenty-five, and fully a third were between ten and twenty-four. Like their mainland counterparts, a significant number of Hawaii Japanese were primed to enter college and the workforce as the war broke out.[23]

Unlike California, which initially tried to thwart the education of Japanese American children (like their Chinese American counterparts) through de jure segregation, which in the end it carried through on a limited basis, Hawaii did not, and the Nisei in Hawaii never experienced de jure racial discrimination in primary and secondary public education. Rather, anti-Japanese bias in education was more subtle. Public schools in Hawaii tended, especially in the early years, to be segregated along racial lines. Most white students attended one of the ten English Standard schools, created to mollify white parents who resisted sending their children to schools where students, and many teachers, spoke Hawaiian Creole (pidgin). Although these schools never denied admission to nonwhite students on the basis of race, "Hawaiian Creole remained the primary dialect of most Nisei," and entrance to English Standard schools was determined by an applicant's proficiency in Standard English. As a result of the merger of "racist sentiments . . . with concerns over class and language," a majority of Asian Americans in Hawaii who spoke pidgin were relegated to racially segregated public schools.[24]

Opportunities for advanced education were limited as well. Despite open access for the Nisei at the University of Hawaii, before World War II the university had no graduate programs and minimal facilities. Upon graduation from high school or college, Japanese Americans in Hawaii also found opportunities to enter most white-collar professions very limited. As a result, many college-educated Nisei in Hawaii were encouraged by their families to become public school teachers or other civil servants, an option unavailable to virtually all educated mainland Japanese Americans. Many of the most talented Nisei, however, migrated to the mainland.[25]

Despite these informal restrictions on employment, according to the 1940 census, "nearly fifteen percent of gainfully employed Japanese Americans were in preferred professional occupations." More important, by 1940 approximately 40,000 Japanese Americans in Hawaii were registered to vote and constituted "nearly half of the [territory's] registered voters." Thus, because of their numbers, Hawaiian Nisei had unrealized political power, a potential tool not enjoyed by their mainland counterparts.[26]

Although military restrictions disrupted the community following the attack on Pearl Harbor, unlike on the mainland there was no mass evacuation of Japanese Americans in Hawaii during the war. Despite continuing anti-Japanese bias and occasional violence during the war, the military government of Hawaii operated on a formally race-neutral basis. Nevertheless, military authorities often imposed searches, confinement, and other forms of intimidation on Hawaiian Japanese Americans. Arguably during the war Japanese Americans in Hawaii were better positioned than their mainland counterparts to continue their education and benefit from the economic opportunities World War II presented for advancement and the accumulation of wealth. They also adopted a slightly different approach to their quest for equality after the war.[27]

Today, Japanese American World War II veterans are widely touted outside their community as superpatriots who willingly sacrificed their lives while their families were interned at home. The historian Scott Kurashige writes that this change in attitude started shortly after the war ended when government officials such as General Joseph W. Stilwell and others promoted the "Nisei as model American citizens" during the war. After the war "[h]ighly publicized accounts of Nisei heroism . . . offered white Americans a positive image of Japanese Americans," an image not widely shared about black GIs until very recently.[28]

Kurashige speculates that the image of Japanese American GIs fighting in racially segregated units developing "[a] sense of brotherhood-in-arms especially registered with some white soldiers," especially after Nisei soldiers, at great personal loss, came to the aid of the all-white Texas "Lost Battalion." This positive image, he argues, resulted in faster postwar acceptance of Japanese Americans by white veterans. He cites as an example the resolution passed in October 1945 by the 500-member Los Angeles Area Council of the American Veterans Committee (AVC) "calling for a halt to anti-Japanese hate crimes and advocating legislation to 'stop such un-American persecution.'" But the AVC was not a conventional veterans group. Rather, the organization was a progressive multiracial veterans group that quickly picked up membership in the late 1940s before declining in membership after infighting and claims of Communist associations. The AVC also supported black civil rights efforts, joining with the American Veterans of World War II in 1946 to openly support federal antilynching measures following the lynching of several black veterans returning home to the South. Nisei veterans also were not exempt from racial hatred.[29]

After the war, anti-Japanese animus continued, especially on the West Coast. In his memoir, the famous World War II cartoonist Bill Mauldin describes his shock when living in California at the postwar treatment of Japanese Americans. Decorated and permanently wounded Nisei veterans "found themselves getting kicked out of Arizona barbershops and San Francisco restaurants just as if they had never left home." Like black veterans, Nisei veterans remained second-class citizens at home. But shortly "[a] new image of the Nikkei [Japanese Americans] began to emerge, [as] patriotic, hardworking people who had served their country well despite great adversity." Americans were somewhat embarrassed and apologetic about the wartime internment of Japanese Americans. This embarrassment, however, did not stem the continuing employment discrimination experienced by Issei and Nisei throughout the nation.[30]

In many other respects, the postwar lives of Nisei veterans were similar to those of other able-bodied and honorably discharged veterans of all races. Veterans who entered the military before age twenty-one were able to "maximize [their] chances for a redirection of the life course through developmental growth, a delayed entry into family roles, and greater opportunity to get ahead." Older veterans, however, did not fare as well because military service disrupted their families and careers. Likewise, younger school- or college-age Japanese Americans had better outcomes after the war than older Japanese Americans who suffered because their careers were interrupted by their forced withdrawal from the American labor market and the despoiling of their property. Working-age internees who remained economically disadvantaged into the 1970s were likely to be older or individuals whose socioeconomic status before the war was low.[31]

According to the sociologist Setsuko Matsunaga Nishi, five years after their release from the internment camps, most mainland Japanese Americans were in the process of recovering from the "severe economic shock" of their forced dislocation and job and property losses. Although more recent empirical studies, including Nishi's own ongoing work, contest this rosy narrative of Japanese American success and deal with a different population demographic, these studies do not specifically factor in the impact of racial discrimination, especially on the West Coast, which continued to artificially suppress job and business opportunities during the early postwar years, impacting the ability of working-age Nisei to move to the next economic level.[32]

Despite these initial barriers, Japanese American veterans in California had greater educational opportunities than veterans in other states because "the state of California increased the ... availability of higher education by offering all residents with a high school diploma a tuition-free path to a college degree." A large percentage of Japanese Americans, though not as high as prewar, returned to or settled in California after the war ended and the camps closed. According to one study, two-thirds of veterans in the state completed college, and by 1970 (twenty-five years after the war ended) this high completion rate is reflected in their occupational standing. Thus, for Japanese American veterans in California, the availability of GI Bill benefits for veterans may not have been as crucial for their upward mobility as the state's own policy, although the bill did provide additional financial support.[33]

Moreover, the state of California enjoyed a decades-long postwar economic boom. In sum, California's strong system of public education, coupled with its comparative postwar economic prosperity, benefited all state residents, including the small number of black Californians. But most black Americans remained concentrated in the South and had to compete and succeed in an economy that was relatively poor compared to the rest of the country, and especially California. The South did not begin to experience its own less dramatic boom until the 1970s, when World War II veterans would have been too old to reap the benefits.[34]

By virtue of the GI Bill's educational benefits, returning Nisei veterans, especially outside California, could begin, or continue, their advanced education. According to Nishi, a preliminary analysis of a subset of Japanese American veterans interviewed for a study on wartime incarceration and the long-term life course of Japanese Americans indicates that they used the educational and housing benefits at about the same rates as other veterans. Unsurprisingly, fifteen years after the war ended, as before the war, Japanese Americans appear better situated educationally than even most white Americans.[35]

In sum, the existence of real differences in the postwar socioeconomic well-being of mainland blacks, Japanese Americans, and whites do not necessarily support the model minority theory or any conclusions about whether it was the GI Bill benefits that most contributed to the change. According to the Survey of Income and Education (SEI) for each group, average levels of income and education for whites, Japanese Americans, and blacks increased from 1940 to 1970. While Japanese Americans in some respects surpassed whites, the gap between blacks and whites remained vast.

A closer examination of these statistics, however, is telling. Even though Japanese Americans on the West Coast were better educated than their white counterparts, thus explaining at least in part their high socioeconomic indicators, in 1960 (fifteen years after the war ended) their occupational standing as a group still lagged behind whites. This difference reflects lingering employment discrimination, higher family labor force participation by Japanese Americans, and the concentration of minorities in urban areas. The population included in these statistics also includes some Issei.[36]

Some researchers still conclude that despite their "occupational underattainment," Japanese Americans' "above-average educational achievements" explain their economic success. These researchers also found that residence was not a statistically significant factor in explaining Japanese Americans' educational achievements, but concede that geographical location posed a slight obstacle for ethnic Japanese men. This finding seems counterintuitive. Undoubtedly the researchers are referring to the interruption in schooling caused by the internment that artificially suppressed educational advancement for some mainland Japanese Americans or perhaps the concentration of Japanese Americans on the West Coast where barriers of discrimination were highest. Nevertheless, place of residence contributed to the disparities in socioeconomic well-being between black and Japanese Americans before and after the war. As the next section spells out, location also explains the slightly different postwar experiences of Nisei veterans in Hawaii.[37]

Like their mainland counterparts, many Nisei veterans experienced discrimination when they returned to Hawaii. However, unlike mainland Japanese Americans, their numbers in Hawaii gave them political power after the war, especially after Hawaiian statehood in 1959. Nisei veterans were unwilling to return to the island plantations, even as Hawaii had started to change during the war. Under martial law, "the influence of the oligarchy's paternal system" diminished, though that is hardly the dominant reason for Hawaii's changing society. After the war, Japanese American veterans were instrumental in changing the political and social discourse in the territory. Although postwar political involvement by Nisei, including veterans, was bipartisan, Nisei veterans were notably essential in "revitalizing and redirecting the Democratic Party in Hawaii towards goals of economic reform[,] . . . social justice and equality."[38]

Veterans' benefits allowed some GIs, like Daniel Inouye, later a US senator from Hawaii, to attend college and professional school at prestigious mainland universities, an opportunity not widely available for many Island Japanese Americans before the war. Although the number of Japanese American males in professional occupations had increased only slightly over the prewar years by 1950, by 1970 (twenty-five years after the war's end) Japanese

Americans, despite their stunted occupational mobility in Hawaii, shared economic and political power with whites and Chinese Americans. Nevertheless, while Japanese Americans have achieved relative economic parity with whites in Hawaii, there has been no collective upward mobility for most of Hawaii's nonwhite populations. Today whites, Chinese Americans, and Japanese Americans are the dominant socioeconomic groups in the Islands, while Native Hawaiians, Filipino Americans, Samoans, other Pacific Islanders, Puerto Ricans, and Southeast Asians are the socioeconomically subordinate groups, and the small black population occupies a somewhat liminal status.[39]

A word of caution is warranted about comparisons of Japanese Americans in Hawaii and on the mainland. "While occasionally the economic trends of Hawaii and [mainland] America converged, . . . Hawaii has been consistently different." As Hawaii became the engine of the wartime thrust in the Pacific theater, real personal income in the Islands rose 36 percent between 1940 and 1944, almost three times the rate on the mainland. This number includes the incomes of Japanese American workers, most of whom were not interned or in the military. Unlike the mainland's, Hawaii's economy faltered immediately after the war, but was revived and prospered by the late 1950s due to an increase in mass tourism prompted by jet airplane development and by Cold War military expansion and Asian wars. "School budgets . . . increased significantly. Huge sums went to creating infra-structure. . . . The expanded budget also financed more generous welfare payments for the needy."[40]

Today, the Islands' dependence on tourism and the military for employment limits the socioeconomic mobility of subordinated ethnic minority groups. So too does "ongoing institutional discrimination, together with the non-implementation of equal opportunity and affirmative action policies that restrict access . . . to higher education and . . . employment status." While Japanese Americans in Hawaii have prospered since the war, due in part to the fact that their numbers gave them considerable political power, inequality persists for other ethnic groups.[41]

POST–WORLD WAR II LITIGATION ATTACKING RACIAL BARRIERS

As a plurality ethnic population in Hawaii, Japanese Americans were able to use their collective political power to improve their socioeconomic status via electoral politics. Conversely, mainland Japanese Americans, like black and other nonwhite veterans, because of their minority status and, in the case of blacks, institutionalized limitations on voting, relied more on the courts in their fight for first-class citizenship. Not hampered by an extensive de jure racial segregation system, mainland Japanese Americans focused their initial efforts on laws that restricted their ability to acquire property and on legal discrimination against the Issei.[42]

In 1945, immediately after the war ended, anti-Japanese forces in California attempted to reinforce the Alien Land Law by targeting Nisei veterans who helped their Issei parents evade the law. During the war, the state legislature appropriated a considerable sum to support the initiation of escheat litigation against violators and placed a proposed constitutional amendment on the 1946 ballot that would incorporate the Alien Land Law into the state constitution. This measure was defeated after an opposition campaign led by the Japanese American Citizenship League (JACL) and the American Civil Liberties Union (ACLU). Nisei veteran Mike Masaoka "spearheaded a statewide campaign against Proposition 15." Nevertheless, prosecutions of Nisei, including veterans, continued until the US Supreme Court in 1948 declared the state Alien Land Laws unconstitutional as applied to US citizens. The Court's decision in the *Oyama* case rendered the law ineffectual even aganst Japanse aliens. Japanese Americans were supported in this cause by the distinguished statesman and Washington lawyer Dean Acheson, later secretary of state under President Truman. Acheson served pro bono as chief counsel during the oral argument in that case. His participation reflected the extent to which attitudes toward Japanese Americans, at the top of government, had changed due, no doubt, to the increasing importance of Japan in America's postwar foreign policy. The ACLU, National Lawyers Guild, and American Jewish Congress filed amicus briefs in the *Oyama* case, but not the NAACP, whose aid was not solicited.[43]

That same year the Court accepted certiorari in four restrictive covenants cases involving real estate transactions with black purchasers in Missouri, Michigan, and Washington, DC. A few months later, Yin Kim, a Korean American, and Tom Amer, a Chinese American, both decorated World War II veterans and American citizens, filed a consolidated petition for certiorari with the Court challenging California decisions permitting judicial enforcement of racially restrictive covenants. Loren Miller, a black California lawyer, represented both Yin Kim, a Bronze Star recipient, and Orsel McGhee, the black petitioner in the Michigan case. Miller had hoped that the *Kim* and *Amer* cases would be consolidated with the black petitioners' case. For reasons that have not survived, the JACL filed an amicus brief with the Court in *Hurd v. Hodge*, where the plaintiff claimed he was an American Indian, and not in the other cases that involved black plaintiffs arguing that restrictive covenants applied to other nonwhites should be included with the cases the Court agreed to hear. The JACL also sponsored the appeal in *Kim* and *Amer*, but, once again, the NAACP did not file an amicus on behalf of Kim and Amer.[44]

Logically, the cases of the black and Asian American petitioners seemed the same, in that race was used to restrict nonwhites' access to property. That was the JACL's main reason for pushing *Kim* and *Amer*. But the Court decided the black restrictive covenant cases without ruling on the petition, declaring that under the Equal Protection Clause, restrictive covenants were not enforceable in a court of law. A week later the Court issued a per curiam opinion in the *Amer* and *Kim* cases granting the petition for writs of certiorari and remanding the cases to the California Supreme Court for reconsideration "in the light of *Shelley* and *McGhee*."[45]

The Court's refusal to join the Asian restrictive covenant cases with the black cases may simply reflect the timing of the *Amer* and *Kim* petition. Oral argument in *Shelley* was heard in January 18, 1948, two months after the *Amer* and *Kim* petition was filed. It is unlikely that the Court's action reflects a reluctance to concede any similarity in the mistreatment of Asian and black Americans since the *Shelley* decision was cited in *Oyama*, as well as in *Korematsu*.

Following resolution of *Shelley* and of the *Amer* and *Kim* cases, Asian Americans had less and less difficulty acquiring property. In contrast, black Americans needed federal legislation, enacted almost twenty years later, to gain greater access to property, and housing discrimination against them still persists into the twenty-first century. Thus it took at least a generation longer for black Americans to gain greater access to property, and this delay constituted a significant barrier to the acquisition of wealth.[46]

The failure of the NAACP to file amicus briefs in *Oyama* and the Asian American restrictive covenant cases is subject to multiple explanations. Two scholars suggest that the NAACP's failure to file amicus briefs might be attributed to its small staff, limited financial resources, and heavy workload rather than any anti-Japanese or anti-Asian animus. However, the historian Mark Brilliant argues that the NAACP had made a tactical decision to only focus on litigation "where race could be isolated as a doctrinal variable." This explanation makes sense since the petitioner's alienage linked to race was a factor in the *Oyama* case. Nevertheless, the NAACP did file an amicus brief in *Takahashi v. Fish & Game Commission*, which successfully challenged a California law prohibiting "aliens ineligible for citizenship" from obtaining commercial fishing licenses. Brilliant's reasoning, however, does not explain the NAACP's failure to file an amicus in the *Kim* and *Amer* cases, where the issue was squarely race.[47]

An insight might be obtained from a 1947 exchange between Abraham Lincoln Wirin, the chief legal strategist in the Japanese Alien Land Act cases, and NAACP legal counsel Thurgood Marshall, following oral argument in the *Oyama* case. Marshall, in explaining his presence at the oral argument, reportedly said: "This case . . . will tell the Negroes what we're going to get out of this court." According to Brilliant, Wirin interpreted this statement to mean that "'[t]he Japanese cases' . . . had to be decided favorably before the Supreme Court was ready to decide 'the Negro cases.' . . . *Oyama* involved a variation on the same legalized segregation theme that the NAACP was attacking in its cases that culminated with *Brown*. The former simply involved 'small[er] segregation' than the latter." Thus tactical differences about how to attack race-based exclusionary laws in the courts may have divided rather than unified blacks and Japanese Americans on the mainland.[48]

This difference is even clearer in the legal attack on state antimiscegenation laws. The historian Peggy Pascoe writes that the JACL, bolstered by the 1948 the California Supreme Court's decision in *Perez v. Sharp* striking down that state's antimiscegenation law, joined with the ACLU and other civil rights organizations for a full-scale challenge to other state laws restricting intermarriage between Asians and whites during the 1950s. The JACL got involved in the issue because "Japanese war brides (i.e., Occupation brides) had been deliberately excluded from the war brides programs that provided immigration assistance to European and even Chinese women married to American soldiers." The JACL opposed antimiscegenation laws by "presenting their clients as innocent young couples eager to enter the respectable state of marriage," what Pascoe calls the "politics of respectability."[49]

Notably, the NAACP did not participate in these early efforts, which ended in 1955 when a challenge to Virginia's miscegenation law was rebuffed by the US Supreme Court, which refused certiorari in *Naim v. Naim*. Pascoe argues that the NAACP failed to join with the coalition (the JACL, ACLU, Chinese-American Citizens' Alliance, Filipino Federation of American, and Korean National Association) in *Naim* because it feared challenging miscegenation laws would undermine its goal of racially integrated public schools. During this period the threat of racially integrated schools triggered fears in white minds, especially in the South, of intermarriage between whites and blacks. Thus any association with an effort to challenge antimiscegenation laws in the 1950s would have undoubtedly played into the fears of these white Americans, thwarting desegregation efforts.[50]

After the *Brown* decision in 1954, conversely, the NAACP focused on adultery and fornication laws used by states to punish interracial couples, not antimiscegenation laws. Japanese Americans, concerned with preserving their carefully crafted postwar image as superpatriots and "respectable" citizens, were reluctant to be seen as promoting illicit sex. An attack on adultery and fornication laws would undercut their carefully crafted image of respectability and their embrace of model minority status. Thus the JACL refused to join in the NAACP's effort to challenge these laws. In 1967, however, both the JACL and NAACP, neither of which had brought the case, filed amicus briefs in the ACLU's successful challenge to Virginia's antimiscegenation law. The differences in approach to antimiscegenation laws reflects how postwar stereotypes—Japanese Americans as model citizens and black Americans as the ultimate social pariah—influenced legal strategies in attacking de jure segregation laws.[51]

Sociologists have long acknowledged that "[i]nequalities in the distribution of social assets, opportunities and values are . . . central to stratification" between racial and ethnic groups. This brief examination of the different outcomes of black and Japanese American World War II GIs and their communities post–World War II illustrates this point. For example, parents' educational attainment is the most important explanation for educational variables in a child's educational attainment. Black and Japanese Americans differed significantly in this regard. In addition, "the intergenerational transfer of racial education gaps was significant, and the cumulative impact of racial discrimination in southern education . . . was far-reaching."[52]

Despite being entitled to generous benefits on paper under the GI Bill that might have jump-started and narrowed the socioeconomic gap between blacks and whites, black advancement was further dampened until the mid-1960s, thereby giving whites, and Japanese Americans, a generation's head start. Second-generation Japanese Americans, despite racial discrimination, were better positioned after World War II than black Americans to take advantage of the limited opportunities afforded them. They had a generation head start over blacks in advancing socioeconomically. This advantage, rather than notions of group exceptionalism, goodness, or cultural values, better explains the difference between the socioeconomic status of Japanese Americans and blacks in the 1960s. Thus the slower postwar socioeconomic advancement of black Americans, including World War II veterans, illustrates how universal social legislation can fail in providing equal opportunity in a highly racialized society.

NOTES

1. Servicemen's Readjustment Act of 1944, Pub. L. No. 78–346, 58 Stat. 284. For a discussion of the impact of this bill and other GI bills, see generally EDWARD HUMES, OVER HERE: HOW THE G.I. BILL TRANSFORMED THE AMERICAN DREAM (2006); IRA KATZNELSON, WHEN AFFIRMATIVE ACTION WAS WHITE: AN UNTOLD HISTORY OF RACIAL INEQUALITY IN MODERN AMERICA (2005); MICHAEL J. BENNETT, WHEN DREAMS CAME TRUE: THE GI BILL AND THE MAKING OF MODERN AMERICA (1996); GLENN C. ALTSCHULER & STUART M. BLUMIN, THE GI BILL : A NEW DEAL FOR VETERANS (2009); SUZANNE METTLER, SOLDIERS TO CITIZENS : THE G.I. BILL AND THE MAKING OF THE GREATEST GENERATION (2005); KEITH W. OLSON, THE G.I. BILL, THE VETERANS, AND THE COLLEGES (1974); LIZABETH COHEN, A CONSUMERS' REPUBLIC: THE POLITICS OF MASS CONSUMPTION IN POSTWAR AMERICA (2003); Melissa Murray, *When War Is Work: The G.I. Bill, Citizenship, and the Civic Generation*, 96 CAL. L. REV. 967 (2008); Marcus Stanley, *College Education and the Midcentury G.I. Bills*, 118 Q.J. ECON. 671, 701 (2003); John Bound & Sarah Turner, *Going to War and Going to College: Did World War II and the G.I. Bill Increase Educational Attainment for Returning Veterans?*, 20 J. LABOR ECON. 784, 790 (2002).

2. *E.g.*, METTLER, *supra* note 1, at 129 (noting that Latino veterans denied membership in local chapters of the Veterans of Foreign Wars "formed their own vibrant organization known as G.I. Forum, and also participated . . . in the federated League of United Latin American Citizens [LULAC], Community Service Organization [CSO], and others that flourished in the postwar era"). It is also important to mention that while Japanese Americans constituted the largest group of Asian American World War II veterans, approximately 250,000 Filipino nationals volunteered or were inducted into the US military during the war. As nonresident foreign nationals, they were largely excluded from benefits under the GI Bill. *See* Michael A. Cabotaje, Comment, *Equity Denied: Historical and Legal Analyses in Support of the Extension of U.S. Veterans' Benefits to Filipino World War II Veterans*, 6 ASIAN L.J. 67 (1999).

3. *See, e.g.*, Neil Gotanda, *New Directions in Asian American Jurisprudence*, 7 ASIAN AM. L.J. 5, 8 (2010); Harvey Gee, *Asian Americans, Critical Race Theory, and the End of the Model Minority Myth*, 19 TEMP. POL. & CIV. RTS. L. REV. 149 (2009); Nancy Chung Allred, *Asian Americans and Affirmative Action: From Yellow Peril to Model Minority and Back Again*, 14 ASIAN AM. L.J. 57 (2007); Pat K. Chew, *Asian Americans: The "Reticent" Minority and Their Paradoxes*, 36 WM. & MARY L. REV. 1 (1994); Robert S. Chang, *Toward an Asian American Legal Scholarship: Critical Race Theory, Post-Structuralism, and Narrative Space*, 81 CAL. L. REV. 1243, 1258–65 (1993).

4. Roger Daniels, *The Exile and Return of Seattle's Japanese*, 88 PAC. N.W.Q., 166, 171 (1997).

5. Benefits were impacted by race and gender. *See* KATZNELSON, *supra* note 1, at 114; METTLER, *supra* note 1, at 158; Murray, *supra* note 1, at 987. Benefits for blacks were impacted by discrimination in certain military service branches as well as by the way selective service was conducted. *See* Paul T. Murray, *Blacks and the Draft: A History of Institutional Racism*, 2

J. BLACK STUD. 57, 62 (1971); George Q. Flynn, *Selective Service and American Blacks during World War II*, 69 J. NEGRO HIST. 14, 20 (1984) (the marines "refused all Negro applications" and the navy "limited blacks to messmen duty"). *See also* Selective Service System, Special Monograph No. 12, 2 *Quotas, Calls, and Inductions* 72, 90 (GPO 1947) (Table 126. Monthly Calls and Inductions, July 1941–December 1945, by State, White, and Table 127. Monthly Calls and Inductions, July 1941–December 1945, by State, Negro).

6. COHEN, *supra* note 1, at 167; *Selective Service and Victory 4th Report* 187–96 (1948).

7. COHEN, *supra* note 1, at 167 ("[b]etween August and November 1946, 39 percent of black soldiers and only 21 percent of white soldiers were dishonorably discharged from the service"); David H. Onkst, *"First a Negro . . . Incidentally a Veteran": Black World War Two Veterans and the G.I. Bill of Rights in the Deep South*, 31 J. SOC. HIST. 517, 524 (1998).

8. KATZNELSON, *supra* note 1, at 126; HUMES, *supra* note 1, at 95; Murray, *supra* note 1, at 980 (local control of the distribution of employment and loan benefits was prone to "parochialism and racism").

9. ALSCHULER & BLUMIN, *supra* note 1, at 518–23.

10. *Id.*; *G.I. Loans: Colored Vets Who Borrow Cash Prove Sound Business Investments*, EBONY 2, no. 10, at 23 (August 1947) (in the summer of 1947, the VA guaranteed 3,229 veterans loans in thirteen Mississippi cities, but only two loans went to black veterans). Further, a black veteran lucky enough to receive a home or business loan under the GI Bill had more limited home options because of redlining practices. *See, e.g.,* DOUGLAS MASSEY & NANCY DENTON, AMERICAN APARTHEID: SEGREGATION AND THE MAKING OF THE UNDERCLASS (1993). Black veterans who moved into a white neighborhood, for example, might find their homes vandalized or set ablaze. Edward Humes, *How the GI Bill Shunted Blacks into Vocational Training*, 53 J. BLACKS IN HIGHER EDUC. 92, 96 (2006).

11. Humes, *supra* note 10, at 97; ALSCHULER & BLUMIN, *supra* note 1, at 132; KATZNELSON, *supra* note 2, at 131.

12. Humes, *supra* note 10, at 97; Onkst, *supra* note 7, at 530 (increased funding insufficient to accommodate most black veterans); ALSCHULER & BLUMIN, *supra* note 5, at 132, 135 (black colleges turned 55 percent of black veterans away due to overcrowding, whereas white colleges turned away 28 percent of veterans due to overcrowding); KATZNELSON, *supra* note 2, at 133 (less than 5 percent of black colleges were accredited by the Association of American Universities).

13. COHEN, *supra* note 1, at 143, 156–57, 159.

14. ALTSCHULER & BLUMIN, *supra* note 1, at 134; Onkst, *supra* note 7, at 519–20; KATZNELSON, *supra* note 1, at 139.

15. U.S. Dep't Ed., Nat. Center for Ed. Stat., *120 Years of American Education: A Statistical Portrait* 21 (Tom Snyder, ed., 1993) (median educational level in 1940 for males twenty-five years and over was 8.7 years for whites and 5.4 years for blacks and "other" races; by 1950 the median years of education for males twenty-five years and over had risen slightly to 9.3 years for whites and 6.4 for blacks and "other" races; by 1960 the median educational level for males twenty-five years and over was 10.6 years for whites and 7.9 years for blacks and "other" races); William J. Collins & Robert A. Margo, *Race and Home Ownership from the End of the Civil War to the Present*, 101 AM. ECON. REV. 355, 356 (2011).

16. U.S. Dep't of the Interior, War Relocation Authority, *The Changing Character of Japanese Population in the Continental United States, Hawaii and Alaska, 1900–1940, According to United States Census Returns*, WAR TIME EXILE: THE EXCLUSION OF THE JAPANESE AMERICANS FROM THE WEST COAST 25 (1946), http://www.internmentarchives .com/showdoc.php?docid=00174&search_id=22759&pagenum=25; U.S. Dep't of the Interior, War Relocation Authority, THE EVACUATED PEOPLE: A QUANTITATIVE DESCRIPTION 125–26 (1946), http://www.internmentarchives.com/showdoc.php?docid=00002&search _id=45001&pagenum=142; Exec. Order No. 9066, 7 Fed. Reg. 1407 (Feb. 19, 1942); ERIC K. YAMAMOTO ET AL., RACE, RIGHTS AND REPARATIONS: LAW AND THE JAPANESE AMERICAN INTERNMENT 194 (2001).

17. THE EVACUATED PEOPLE, *supra* note 16, at 25–26; GREG ROBINSON, A TRAGEDY OF DEMOCRACY 208–9 (2009).

18. ROBINSON, *supra* note 17, at 27 ("Although the majority of the native-born were under eighteen throughout the prewar years, a group of young adult Nisei established a set of fledgling organizations to defend the interests of the new generation."); TOM COFFMAN, THE ISLAND EDGE OF AMERICA 16 (2003). In contrast, 44 percent of black Americans were classified as illiterate in 1900, and although the black-white illiteracy gap narrowed, the gap remained until 1979. U.S. Dep't Ed., Nat. Center for Ed. Stat., *supra* note 15, at 9, 21; Setsuko Matsunaga Nishi, *Japanese American Achievement in Chicago: A Cultural Response to Degradation*, dissertation, Dep't of Soc. U. Chicago, 1963, at 29–30, 32–33; Keith Aoki, *No Right to Own?: The Early Twentieth-Century "Alien Land Laws" as a Prelude to Internment*, 40 B.C. L. REV. 37, 57–62 (1998); Robert Higgs, *Landless by Law: Japanese Immigrants in California Agriculture to 1941*, 38 J. ECON. HIST. 205 (1978); Michael Jones-Correa, *The Origins and Diffusion of Racial Restrictive Covenants*, 115 POL. SCI. Q. 541 (2000–2001).

19. Thomas James, *"Life Begins with Freedom": The College Nisei, 1942–1945*, 25 HIST. EDUC. Q. 155, 156–57 (1985).

20. *Id.* at 156 ("The effort . . . became known as an 'Underground Railroad.' . . . The metaphor suggested a transit not merely from camp to college, but from slavery to freedom."); ALLAN W. AUSTIN, FROM CONCENTRATION CAMP TO CAMPUS: JAPANESE AMERICAN STUDENTS AND WORLD WAR II 84 (2005) (discussing the role of the NJASRC in directing students to universities, including away from historically black colleges); SCOTT KURASHIGE, THE SHIFTING GROUNDS OF RACE: BLACK AND JAPANESE AMERICANS IN THE MAKING OF MULTIETHNIC LOS ANGELES 189 (2008).

21. EVELYN NAKANO GLENN, UNEQUAL FREEDOM: HOW RACE AND GENDER SHAPED AMERICAN CITIZENSHIP AND LABOR 192–93 (2002); COFFMAN, *supra* note 61, at 20; RONALD TAKAKI, A DIFFERENT MIRROR: A HISTORY OF MULTICULTURAL AMERICA 247 (1993) (between 1886 and 1924 Japanese came to the Hawaii as contract laborers on the islands' plantations).

22. Act to Regulate the Immigration of Aliens into the United States, 34 Statutes-at-Large 898 (Feb. 20, 1907); Katherine Benton-Cohen, *The Rude Birth of Immigration Reform*, 34 WILSON Q. 16, 18 (2010) (discussing early attempts to control which immigrants entered the United States).

23. COFFMAN, *supra* note 18, at 178; TAKAKI, *supra* note 21, at 265–67 (planters who "saw Japanese Americans as a colonized labor force" feared that making educational

opportunities available to the Nisei meant fewer second-generation plantation workers, and this was correct); Table 2: Age, by Race and Sex, for the Territory and for Honolulu City: 1940 and 1930, SIXTEENTH CENSUS OF THE UNITED STATES: 1940, TERRITORIES AND POSSESSIONS: POPULATION, HOUSING BUSINESS AND MANUFACTURERS; POPULATION, 2ND SERIES, CHARACTERISTICS OF THE POPULATION: HAWAII 6 (1943).

24. Aoki, *supra* note 67, at 48–50 (discussing San Francisco's unsuccessful effort to segregate Japanese American children in public schools); Eileen H. Tamura, *The English-Only Effort, the Anti-Japanese Campaign, and Language Acquisition in the Education of Japanese Americans in Hawaii, 1915–40*, 33 HIST. EDUC. Q. 37, 56 (1993).

25. HARRY H. L. KITANO, JAPANESE AMERICANS: THE EVOLUTION OF A SUBCULTURE 173 (2d ed. 1976) (noting that prior to World War II, Japanese Americans constituted "a large majority in every class" at the University of Hawaii); ALEXANDER MACDONALD, REVOLT IN PARADISE: THE SOCIAL REVOLUTION IN HAWAII AFTER PEARL HARBOR 184 (1944) ("Many of the newspaper advertisements . . . for business office employment carried the qualification, 'Japanese need not apply.' [As a result, m]any university graduates went to work as clerks in the tiny shops their parents had started."); Roger Daniels, *Educating Youth in America's Wartime Detention Camps*, 43 HIST. EDUC. Q. 91, 97 (2003).

26. MACDONALD, *supra* note 25, at 184–85.

27. *Id.* at 190–98 (discussing restrictions, searches, violence, and other discriminatory treatment); YAMAMOTO ET AL., *supra* note 16, at 39 (discussing mass evacuation on the mainland and lack thereof in Hawaii); COFFMAN, *supra* note 18, at 66–72 (describing the strength of the Japanese American community in Hawaii as compared to the mainland).

28. COFFMAN, *supra* note 18, at 98; KURASHIGE, *supra* note 20, at 187, 191; Wil Haygood, *"Miracle" Adds Black Soldiers to WWII Films' Iconography*, SEATTLE TIMES, Sept. 22, 2008, http://seattletimes.nwsource.com/html/movies/2008192272_blackwwiifilms22.html ("[N]o black soldiers received the Medal of Honor during World War II. . . . In 1993, the Army employed historically black Shaw University in Raleigh, N.C., to look into medal disparities during World War II. Eventually, President Bill Clinton presented the Medal of Honor to seven black Army veterans in a White House ceremony in 1997.").

29. KURASHIGE, *supra* note 20, at 190; Steve Schmadeke, *American Veterans Committee to Close Last Chapter, Based in Forrest Park*, CHI. TRIB., Feb. 7, 2008, http://articles.chicagotribune.com/2008-02-07/news/0802061200_1_avc-american-veterans-committee-veterans-group; *AVC, Amvets Urge Action to Prevent Lynchings*, AFRO-AMERICAN, Aug. 10, 1946, at 5; Fred Jerome, *Einstein, Race, and the Myth of the Cultural Icon*, 95 ISIS 627, 628–29 (2004) ("In the first fifteen months after Hitler's defeat, a wave of anti-black terror, mostly but not only in the southern states, killed fifty-six African Americans, with returning veterans the most frequent victims.").

30. BILL MAULDIN, BACK HOME 162, 168 (1947); ROBERT ASAHINA, JUST AMERICANS, HOW JAPANESE AMERICANS WON A WAR AT HOME AND ABROAD: THE STORY OF THE 100TH BATTALION/442D REGIMENTAL COMBAT TEAM IN WORLD WAR II 218, 227–32, 237 (2006) (discussing examples of violence or racial hostility directed toward veterans); Sandra Taylor, *Leaving the Concentration Camps: Japanese American Resettlement in Utah and the Intermountain West*, 60 PAC. HIST. REV. 169, 191 (1991); Kurashige, *supra* note 20, at 190; GREG ROBINSON, AFTER CAMP: PORTRAITS IN MIDCENTURY JAPANESE AMERICAN LIFE AND POLITICS 60–66 (2012).

31. Glen H. Elder Jr., *War Mobilization and the Life Course: A Cohort of World War II Veterans*, 2 Soc. F. 449, 450 (1987); Aimee Chin, *Long Run Labor Market Effects of Japanese American Internment during World War II on Working Age Male Internees*, 23 J. LABOR ECON. 491 (2005) (some economists have estimated that the forced internment reduced the average income of interned males 9–13 percent in the following twenty-five years).

32. Nishi, *supra* note 18, at 31; Chin, *supra* note 31, at 521 ("earnings loss for working-age male internees as a whole likely exceed 9%–13%" twenty-five years afterward); KURASHIGE, *supra* note 20, at 195–97 (Japanese Americans on the West Coast were not as successful as Japanese Americans who resettled in the Midwest and on the East Coast because of the high level of anti-Japanese bias on the West Coast).

33. Elder, *supra* note 31, at 460 ("At least in education, the G.I. Bill became a primary source of greater life opportunity for the California veterans in this study.").

34. Gerald D. Nash, *Stages of California's Economic Growth, 1870–1970: An Interpretation*, 51 CAL. HIST. Q. 315, 324–25 (1972); Gavin Wright, *The Economic Revolution in the American South*, 1 J. ECON. PERSP. 161, 173 (1987).

35. E-mail from Setsuko Nishi, Principal Investigator, Japanese American Life Course Project, to author (Sept. 4, 2010) (on file with author); Charles Hirschman & Morrison G. Wong, *Socioeconomic Gains of Asian Americans, Blacks and Hispanics: 1960–1976*, 90 AMER. J. SOC. 584, 594 (1984) (Table 2 source: 1960 Population Census, .01PUS; 1970 Population Census, .01 PUS).

36. *Id.* at 598 ("Education or years of schooling plays the major intervening role in the production of ethnic differentials in occupational standing."). The researchers also note that "all minorities (except Chinese in 1960) are below the white level in terms of occupational attainment." They provide no explanation for this difference.

37. *Id.* at 599–600; Charles Hirschman & Morrison G. Wong, *The Extraordinary Educational Attainment of Asian-Americans: A Search for Historical Evidence and Explanations*, 65 SOC. F. 1 (1986–87).

38. Hirschman & Wong, *supra* note 35, at 599; DANIEL K. INOUYE, JOURNEY TO WASHINGTON 189–91 (1967); COFFMAN, *supra* note 18, at 100, 105–6; Jonathan Y. Okamura, *Race Relations in Hawai'i during World War II: The Non-internment of Japanese Americans*, 26 AMERASIA J. 128–29 (2000).

39. FRANKLIN ODO, NO SWORD TO BURY: JAPANESE AMERICANS IN HAWAI'I DURING WORLD WAR II 253–59 (2004); JONATHAN Y. OKAMURA, ETHNICITY AND INEQUALITY IN HAWAI'I 42, 49, 57 (2008).

40. COFFMAN, *supra* note 18, at 167–70.

41. OKAMURA, *supra* note 39, at 57–58, 132.

42. *See, e.g.*, Oyama v. California, 332 U.S. 633 (1948) (alien land laws); the JACL sponsored the appeal in Amer v. Superior Court, 334 U.S. 813 (1948) and Yin Kim v. Superior Court, 334 U.S. 813 (1948) (restrictive covenants applied to Asian Americans); Takahashi v. Fish & Game Com., 334 U.S. 410 (1948) (restriction on commercial fishing licenses by aliens).

43. RONALD TAKAKI, STRANGERS FROM A DIFFERENT SHORE: A HISTORY OF ASIAN AMERICANS, 411 (updated and revised 1998); Kevin Allen Leonard, *"Is That What We Fought For?" Japanese Americans and Racism in California, The Impact of World War II*, 21

W. HIST. Q. 463, 469–71, 477–81 (1990); MARK BRILLIANT, THE COLOR OF AMERICA HAS CHANGED: HOW RACIAL DIVERSITY SHAPED CIVIL RIGHTS REFORM IN CALIFORNIA, 1941– 1978, 42, 44, 45 (2010); Greg Robinson & Toni Robinson, *Korematsu and Beyond: Japanese Americans and the Origins of Strict Scrutiny*, 68 L. & CONTEMP. PROB. 29, 36 (2005); Oyama v. California, 332 U.S. 633 (1948).

44. Shelley v. Kraemer and McGhee v. Sipes, 334 U.S. 1 (1948) (Missouri and Michigan); Hurd v. Hodge and Urciolo v. Hodge, 334 U.S. 24 (1948) (District of Columbia). Although the lower federal court determined that Hurd, like Urciolo, was black, the Court noted: "James M. Hurd maintained that he is not a Negro, but a Mohawk Indian." Hurd, *supra* 334 U.S. at 27 n.2. The petitioners Amer and Kim were "decorated overseas veterans of the Armed forces." Gabriel J. Chin, *Segregation's Last Stronghold: Race Discrimination and the Constitutional Law of Immigration*, 46 UCLA L. REV. 1, 44 n.215 (2008); Consolidated Petitions for Writs of Certiorari at 4, Amer v. Superior Court, 334 U.S. 813 (1948) (No. 47–429), and Yin Kim v. Superior Court, 334 U.S. 813 (1948) (No. 47–430) (on file with author); BRILLIANT, *supra* note 43, at 103; Robinson & Robinson, *supra* note 43, at 42; Brief of the Japanese American Citizens League, Amicus Curiae, on Petitions for Writs of Certiorari at 2 (Frank Chuman was Of Counsel on this brief).

45. Shelley v. Kramer, 334 U.S. 1, 22 (1948) ("[e]qual protection of the laws is not achieved through indiscriminate imposition of inequalities"); Amer v. Superior Ct., 334 U.S. 813, 814 (1948).

46. *See* Fair Housing Act of 1968, codified at 42 U.S.C. 3601–19. For a discussion of the persistent problem of housing discrimination, see Michelle Ghaznavi Collins, Note, *Opening Doors to Fair Housing: Enforcing the Affirmatively Further Provision of the Fair Housing Act through 42 USC § 1983*, 110 COL. L. REV. 2135 (2010) (public housing receiving federal funds); John P. Relman, *Foreclosures, Integration, and the Future of the Fair Housing Act*, 41 IND. L. REV. 629 (2008) (subprime mortgage foreclosure problem as evidence of the Fair Housing Act's failure).

47. Robinson & Robinson, *supra* note 43, at 42; BRILLIANT, *supra* note 43, at 51; Takahashi v. Fish & Game Comm'n, 334 U.S. 410 (1948).

48. BRILLIANT, *supra* note 43, at 54.

49. Perez v. Sharp, 32 Cal. 2d 711 (1948); PEGGY PASCOE, WHAT COMES NATURALLY: MISCEGENATION LAW AND THE MAKING OF RACE IN AMERICA 199, 206, 249 (2009).

50. PASCOE, *supra* note 49, at 206, 228–30. Naim v. Naim, 197 Va. 80; 87 S.E.2d 749 (1955), *vacated*, 350 U.S. 891 (1955); ALAN SCOT WILLIS, ALL ACCORDING TO GOD'S PLAN: SOUTHERN BAPTIST MISSIONS AND RACE, 1945–1970, 20 (2005) ("Ultimately, the greatest fear in the South concerning integration and 'social equality' was the 'amalgamation of the races.' The possibility of interracial marriage terrified southern whites who believed in the 'purity' of the white race.").

51. Brown v. Board of Education, 347 U.S. 483 (1954); McLaughlin v. Florida, 379 U.S. 184 (1964) (striking down a Florida law prohibiting interracial cohabitation); Loving v. Virginia, 388 U.S. 1 (1967); PASCOE, *supra* note 49, at 249.

52. MICHAEL GARFIELD SMITH, CORPORATIONS AND SOCIETY: THE SOCIAL ANTHROPOLOGY OF COLLECTIVE ACTION 272 (1975) (discussing racial stratification in the Caribbean); Ashenfelter & Blumin, *supra* note 1, at 225–27.

5

Re-reading Vincent Chin
Asian Americans and Multiracial Political Analysis

SCOTT KURASHIGE

Coming to terms with the complexity of multiracial diversity and interethnic relations necessarily means working to see things from new vantage points. Scholars in Asian American studies and activists working in Asian American communities should thus seek to maximize opportunities to learn from and about academic and organizing work being done with relation to other racial and ethnic groups.

At the same time, we need to recognize the challenges and opportunities to rethink issues we have long studied and addressed in order to develop analyses that are more responsive to the increasingly diverse society we seek to understand. For instance, in previous work, I have tried to draw new insights from the study of Japanese American internment and the rise of the African American civil rights movement by bringing the two topics into a common frame of analysis. I have particularly focused on Los Angeles as a crucial site to study because its twentieth-century transformation from a self-consciously white-dominant city into a multicultural "world city" anticipated many of the demographic, cultural, and political changes that are remaking the United States in the twenty-first century.[1]

While Los Angeles has garnered significant attention from Asian American scholars and activists, it is ironically Detroit—my primary personal and political home from 2001 to 2014—that gave birth to one of the most pivotal narratives of Asian American history since the 1970s. I am referring, of course, to the story of Vincent Chin, the twenty-seven-year-old Chinese American man beaten to death by two white men following an altercation in the Fancy Pants bar and strip club in June 1982. It is a story that has traveled extensively because of the way it brings into focus several core concerns.

For starters, Chin's killing and the circumstances under which it occurred draw attention to the transnational dynamics that have shaped the experience of Asians in America. As Don Nakanishi pointed out four decades ago, transnational concerns have always been central to Asian American politics broadly considered. In particular, the "race war" character of World War II particularly heightened the stereotype of the Japanese enemy as a "yellow peril" in ways that have continued to haunt Japanese Americans decades after their wartime incarceration.[2]

The Chin case highlights the recurring notion of Asia as a threat, foregrounding the representation of Asians in America as perpetually foreign and alien in the conflated scapegoating of Asia and Asian Americans for the economic woes of the United States. Chin's killers, Ronald Ebens and his stepson, Michael Nitz, had strong connections to the auto industry during a time of intense animosity directed at purportedly unfair Japanese competition. During the fight, witnesses heard Ebens at one point yell to Chin, "It's because of you motherfuckers that we're all out of work." It mattered not that Chin was ethnically Chinese and a US citizen, the adopted son of a Chinese American veteran of World War II. Thus Chin's case was properly seen not as a Japanese American or Chinese American issue but rather as a panethnic Asian American concern.

Chin's killing further represents a racist hate crime against an innocent Asian American victim, such that it is easy for other Asian Americans to see themselves or their loved ones in Chin's shoes. It was also a brutal and wanton act, given that Chin was beaten repeatedly with a baseball bat on a busy public thoroughfare in view of two police officers.

Just as important, the Chin narrative foregrounds the significance of political protest and activism in response to the failures of our justice system. The prosecution allowed Ebens and Nitz to avoid standing trial for murder by pleading guilty to manslaughter. They next received sentences of three years' probation and a small fine. Outrage at the leniency of these sentences—seen by Asian American activists as a heinous crime on top of another heinous crime—prompted rise of the national "Justice for Vincent Chin" movement. The movement helped push the federal government to try the defendants for civil rights violations, and a jury in Detroit found Ebens guilty of violating Chin's civil rights and sentenced him to twenty-five years in prison. However, after the defense successfully appealed on procedural grounds for a new trial and change of venue, Ebens was cleared of all charges by a Cincinnati jury.

While the Chin case has been widely studied and discussed, it is worth revisiting and re-reading.[3] In this essay, I highlight three factors that should complicate our understanding of the Chin case. The first matter is geography. Named as the setting for the events, Detroit is too often viewed monolithically as an economically depressed and racially hostile automotive capital. In fact, the principals in the story came from two different suburbs outside of Detroit and clashed in the municipality of Highland Park. When we avoid flattening out the geography of the Chin case, we can develop a more nuanced understanding of how the politics of race and class played out and how both in turn were informed by the history of African American segregation and civil rights.

Second, I argue that much more can be done to promote an intersectional analysis of the Chin case that further incorporates discourses of gender and sexuality into the analysis of race, class, and nation. Here I am particularly concerned to demonstrate how recent inquiries into transnational Asian American studies can open new lines of thought about the multiracial construction of national identity and political consciousness in the shift from industrial to postindustrial society.

Finally, I offer some thoughts on how Asian American studies can provide a critical intervention into key debates at the center of recent political history by situating the Chin case with relation to the discourse on Asian Americans and civil rights during the Reagan era. On the one hand, Asian American activists sought to advance the Justice for Vincent Chin campaign by building ties to African American civil rights leaders and situating the case within a conceptual framework emerging from the black freedom struggle. In turn, the defense of Chin's killers drew upon an anti-black backlash against civil rights discourse while simultaneously distancing Asian Americans from African American claims to justice.

THE CHIN CASE AND THE POLITICS OF URBAN SPACE

Undoubtedly, the story of Vincent Chin represents a defining moment in Asian American history and arguably the closest thing to a foundational text to be produced by the field of Asian American studies. While other historical events (for example, Chinese Americans building the transcontinental railroad or the Japanese American internment) continue to occupy a more prominent place in the general consciousness of both the American public and professional historians, the Chin narrative more profoundly embodies the panethnic notion of "Asian American" identity and activism as first conceived by youthful social movement organizers in the late 1960s. Today, professors of Asian American studies almost universally know and teach the history of the Chin case. In death, Chin has achieved iconic status. A slew of T-shirts can be found emblazoned with Chin's image, while memorials are regularly held across the nation exhorting us to never forget his tragic demise. This is not to say that there is not a particular resonance for Chinese Americans, but that the activism and the historical commemoration have been panethnic.

For the sake of this essay, my discussion of the Chin case will largely reference the (version of the) narrative presented in Renee Tajima and Christine Choy's Academy Award–nominated documentary *Who Killed Vincent Chin?* (1988). While I draw on court records, demographic data, and a contemporary newspaper story of particular salience, there are substantive reasons to focus on the film, which most likely appears on more syllabi than any other written or multimedia text in all of Asian American studies. Masterfully constructed by Tajima and Choy, *Who Killed Vincent Chin?* presents a Rashomon-style narrative cutting back and forth between the voices of Chin's mother and his friends; Chin's assailant, Ronald Ebens, and his family and friends; and third-party witnesses to the attack. We see the shock on the face of the witnesses, while the despair of Chin's mother contrasts with the alternately stoic and indignant faces of Ebens, his wife, and his stepson, Michael Nitz. Undoubtedly, the emotionally powerful film has now reached exponentially more people than did the original Justice for Vincent Chin movement that it chronicles. In other words, it is largely the film's narrative that has become ingrained in Asian American public consciousness and sustained the legacy of Vincent Chin.

For most Asian Americans watching the film, Detroit, at best, tends to function as metaphor—a symbol of American (especially white working-class) economic woes that provides the context for a narrative built around racial scapegoating. As Yen Le Espiritu has argued, the Chin case represents a prime example of "racial lumping"—that is, the racist notion that all Asians look alike to non-Asians and are thus subject to being attacked on the basis of any Orientalist stereotype. Frequently the product of "racial lumping," anti-Asian violence and hate crimes generated an outpouring of what Espiritu terms "reactive solidarity" during the 1980s. In another well-publicized incident, a Chinese American college student named Jim Loo was killed in 1989 by two white men, brothers Lloyd and Robert Piche, who had called Loo and a group of his Asian American friends "stupid gooks" and claimed that their "brothers . . . didn't make it back from Vietnam."[4]

For many Asian Americans of the post-1960s generation, Vincent Chin is the martyr par excellence (à la Emmett Till) who sparked the awakening of Asian American civil rights activism. Author Helen Zia was one of the founding members of the Detroit-based Asian American collective—known as American Citizens for Justice (ACJ)—that launched the Justice for Vincent Chin campaign. In her now standard interpretation of the case, Zia writes, "American Citizens for Justice showed the ways in which Asian Americans had been made scapegoats for the ills of the modern American economy, naming anti-Asian violence as a present-day phenomenon that should concern all people." This was a critical moment when Asian Americans "chose to step out of the 'safe' shadows of the white establishment . . . and cast their lot with the more vulnerable position of minorities seeking civil rights."[5]

It is thus possible to sum up the key traits that have rendered the Chin narrative so enduring. First, it is a narrative of the pervasiveness of anti-Asian stereotypes, one that seeks to negate the "model minority" ideology according to which Asian Americans have achieved a level of acceptance that transcends serious problems with racism and discrimination. Second, the narrative highlights the ever-present danger of violence and hatred that can accompany such racial prejudice, and suggests that any Asian American, regardless of ethnicity or class, can become the target of anti-Asian violence as part of a phenomenon like "Japan-bashing." Third, it draws attention to the institutionalization of racial bias, as particularly represented by the judicial system but also more broadly reflected by popular media and political representation. And lastly, it celebrates the power and ability of activists to build a grassroots coalition of diverse Asian ethnicities and a multiracial coalition linking Asian American concerns to the broader cause of civil rights and social justice. These are, in brief, the lessons likely to be drawn from the narrative via the film in an introductory Asian American studies course.

While certain elements of this narrative do ring true, what is glaringly absent from this narrative is a discussion of locality and the politics of urban space and place. Scenes of Detroit and depictions of a specific urban geography are readily evident in *Who Killed Vincent Chin?* but they are generally overlooked by audiences (at least those situated outside Detroit) seeking a more simplified analysis of hate crimes and racial justice. One of the key questions I am thus posing to Asian Americanists with this project is "how does the Chin narrative change if we put Detroit at the center of it?"

Detroit has remained largely invisible to Asian Americanists, whose work has tended to neglect the "flyover" regions between the coasts. For instance, Thomas Sugrue's seminal book on postwar Detroit, *The Origins of the Urban Crisis,* has profoundly shaped the historical analysis of race and class segregation in urban America.[6] However, this work is generally not well known by the nonhistorians in the field of Asian American studies. The Motor City was overlooked both by the first wave of new social histories of Asian America examining the origins of immigrant communities on the West Coast as well as the next wave of discursive studies following the cultural turn. In one sense, this is hardly surprising, given the relative invisibility of Asians in Detroit. In the early 1980s the city was on its way to becoming over 80 percent black while remaining barely 1 percent Asian. Yet the long-standing role of Asians in the city's cultural and political landscape makes such oblivion regrettable.

Detroit's landscape is represented in *Who Killed Vincent Chin?* by repeated scenes of urban industrial and residential abandonment. These scenes, paired with news reports about the extent of layoffs and unemployment, paint a picture of a city in deep crisis. During an era of soaring gas prices and recession, Detroit's Big Three automakers are floundering in the face of foreign, especially Japanese, competition. This is the critical backdrop to the master theme of "Japan-bashing" and anti-Asian violence as a form of scapegoating. The voices of Detroit-area politicians and white workers speak directly to the threat posed by "the Japanese" while imploring consumers to "buy American." The filmmakers then employ dramatic music to accompany public displays of metro Detroit residents emphatically smashing Japanese import cars with a sledgehammer.

Detroit, however, is obviously far from a monolithic space when considered on a metropolitan scale. The city proper was once over 90 percent white before World War II and home to a total population of roughly two million as late as the 1950s. Prompted by the migration of southern blacks seeking employment in the industrial city, racial integration within the factories, schools, and neighborhoods was staunchly opposed by most whites, who actively fought to exclude blacks while passively fleeing to the suburbs. Entrenched and systemic racism stalled the pursuit of black advancement and led to the uprising of 1967, an event that accelerated (but did not initiate) a corporate disinvestment and white flight from the city already in motion. By 1982 Detroit's mass depopulation and the region's stark black/white segregation were dramatic: nearly 90 percent of blacks in the metropolitan area lived in the city of Detroit, whereas nearly 90 percent of whites lived in the suburbs.[7]

Where do Asian Americans fit into the multiracial production of metropolitan space? This in my view is a pertinent question to which the film offers but a few intriguing glimpses. Here, then, is another instance where we must go beyond the standard narrative of the Chin case. I would argue that Asian Americans occupied an interstitial position between white and black in both the physical and cultural geography of postwar metro Detroit. On the one hand, Asian Americans were more likely than blacks to be accepted in suburban neighborhoods and less concentrated within the central city. On the other hand, their dispersal throughout the region was uneven; anecdotal evidence suggests that Asian Americans felt more welcome in some areas than others. Moreover, the general dispersal of Asian American residents to the suburbs was not entirely voluntary and also served to fragment and dilute the presence of Asians within metro Detroit.

The most dramatic example of Asian American urban dislocation was the demolition of Detroit's "old" Chinatown, settled by immigrant pioneers in the early twentieth century on the western edge of downtown (following a pattern in many other North American cities, including Boston, Philadelphia, Montreal, and Los Angeles). From the 1950s to the early 1960s, Chinatown properties were either privately purchased or seized through eminent domain to make way for the Lodge Freeway and similar slum removal projects. This followed on the heels of the bulldozing of black Detroit's most predominant small business district (Hastings Street), historic entertainment district (Paradise Valley), and residential district (Black Bottom) at the eastern edge of downtown. As Chinatown redevelopment projects proposed by city planners near the old site failed to materialize, some businesses and residences relocated to a "new" Chinatown district just north of downtown in the lower Cass Corridor district. But the "new" Chinatown would never become as firmly established as the original. Admittedly, attempts to relocate entire communities are always complex, particularly when the opening of the suburbs offers alternative resettlement options. However, what arguably most sealed the fate of the "new" Chinatown was the simultaneous decision by city authorities to mark the lower Cass Corridor as the concentrated site for all of the city's marginal populations. Homeless shelters, soup kitchens, and substance abuse treatment centers from around the city moved to the district during the postwar era in which the "new" Chinatown was attempting to take hold. Moreover, as nearby areas were cleared for urban renewal and gentrification, this had the effect of pushing the illicit trade in drugs and prostitution into the lower Cass Corridor. The neighborhood would become known as the birthplace of Detroit's counterculture, but it repelled the sort of consumers and residents the "new" Chinatown sought to attract.[8]

One such group was the Chin family. Although the Chin family had many personal connections to Detroit Chinatown's merchants and associations (Vincent had been a service worker in a "new" Chinatown restaurant), they had long lived in Highland Park, which Vincent's mother, Lily Chin, remarks (speaking in Chinese with English subtitles in the film) was "high-class back then" in the 1950s. However, the Chins witnessed their own municipality undergo a similar process of racial transition and deindustrialization during those years. Surrounded on all sides by Detroit, Highland Park saw its fortunes rise and fall with the vagaries of the auto industry, even more so than Detroit. The city was essentially the creation of Henry Ford, who gave birth to the modern factory when he constructed his "crystal palace" in 1913 and Model T's began rolling off the assembly line. The municipality became the site of stately homes, mostly residences of Ford management, and more modest single-family residences for its "five-dollar-day" workers. But Highland Park's population peaked during the Great Depression, just as Ford was shifting production to the massive state-of-the-art River Rouge plant in Dearborn. After the war, there was a new wave of black population growth. Some of the city's dwellings aged gracefully as they were adopted by aspiring black homeowners; others aged ungracefully as they sat abandoned or were demolished. By 1980 the city's industrial job base had all but disappeared. Its population was half its peak size and only 14 percent white. Meanwhile, its median income stood at only $13,180 (or about 25 percent less than Detroit's). Like many other Chinese American families during the 1960s and 1970s, the Chins relocated from Highland Park to the outer suburb of Oak Park, near Detroit's northwestern flank.[9]

Still, if both Chin and Ebens were suburban residents, their respective municipalities garnered notice for vastly different reasons during the long recession of the 1970s to the 1990s. In 1982 Vincent Chin lived with his mother in Oak Park. His father had just passed away the year before. Interviewed in the film, Lily Chin (who passed away in 2002, only days before the twenty-year anniversary of her son's beating) gives no particular indication as to why they chose to move to Oak Park, which like most of suburban Detroit sprouted up during the postwar era as an almost exclusively white bedroom community. What we do know is that to a greater degree than just about any other suburb in the area, Oak Park's civic leaders came to embrace the concept of racial integration, working cooperatively with civil rights leaders on several occasions beginning in the 1960s. By 1980 Oak Park's demographic profile—71 percent white (heavily Jewish), 14 percent non-white (mostly black), and about 15 percent Iraqi Chaldean—was the closest thing in metro Detroit to what social scientists generally deem integrated. In the 1980s the city launched a series of cultural and educational initiatives promoting diversity. These were intended at least in part as "neighborhood stabilization" measures, the contradictory politics of which are beyond the scope of this essay. The point is that this middle-class suburb with a large Jewish presence would have been viewed by Asian Americans as a relatively welcoming place.[10]

East Detroit, Ronald Ebens's 1982 place of residence, presents a striking contrast. Whereas Oak Park sat in relatively white-collar Oakland County, East Detroit lay in relatively blue-collar Macomb County. (This juxtaposition mirrored an earlier east–west class divide that once existed within Detroit.) East Detroit, it must be pointed out, was an independent municipality connected to Detroit by name only (a point to which I will return). Located on Detroit's northeastern flank, East Detroit (though its origins date back to the rural nineteenth century) was also largely the product of postwar white flight from the central city. Relatively undeveloped before World War II, its population shot up to 21,000 in 1950 and to 46,000 by 1960. The filmed depictions of Ebens's neighborhood in East Detroit are of modest ranch homes on quiet tree-lined streets, that is, not significantly a visual departure from the Chins' neighborhood. However, unlike the Oakland County suburbs to the west, East Detroit's demographic profile was heavily white ethnic (non-Jewish) and working class. These were the type of folks who during the postwar era fought to keep their unionized jobs in the auto industry but were confronted with the "fight" or "flight" dilemma over housing as the percentage of blacks within Detroit's population steadily rose. Sugrue's evidence suggests that those who abandoned their Detroit homes for places like East Detroit and Macomb County were more likely to have first fought to keep blacks away, using both grassroots agitation and outright violence.[11]

East Detroit was the type of place that overtly resisted racial integration. However, by the 1980s its ability to attract white residents had diminished severely. With new factory jobs drying up, East Detroit's population was in steep decline. Residential growth had stagnated between 1960 and 1970 and had fallen nearly 20 percent by 1980. Between 1970 and 1980, the city's black population actually doubled, although that statistic is highly deceptive. What that meant in practice is that the total black population rose from thirteen people to twenty-six living within the municipality. Inhabiting an inner-ring suburb, many of East Detroit's residents became particularly defensive because they were living adjacent to Detroit. These anxieties notably surfaced in 1983, when a group of homeowners organized to change the name of East Detroit. After persistent efforts, the campaign eventually succeeded in renaming it Eastpointe (by majority vote in 1992). The move was an attempt (unsuccessful for the most part) to link themselves to the wealthy Grosse Pointe cities. "We need to rid ourselves of being associated with the crime and slum image of Detroit," its leader, George Lawroski, told the *Detroit Free Press*. "I don't care what the name is, as long as it's not Detroit," he added. "If my name were Hitler, I'd want to change that."[12]

East Detroit fit into a broader pattern of white, blue-collar suburbanization in Macomb County. Between 1940 and 1970, the county's population soared from 107,638 to 625,309, while remaining nearly all white. These were not all bedroom communities. Scores of factories—large Big Three plants accompanied by smaller parts suppliers—set up shop in Macomb County, as did a navy manufacturing plant and an army tank factory. By 1976 the county was home to over 100,000 manufacturing jobs. Macomb's gains in population and jobs came in many ways at Detroit's expense. This fact was not lost on the average white resident of Macomb, who often felt he or she was forced to flee Detroit.[13]

An immediate neighbor to the west of East Detroit, the city of Warren likewise sits on the proverbial city/suburb border known as "8 Mile" (and made famous to those outside of the region by Eminem). Many residents of this southern portion of Macomb County had probably moved first from areas near downtown to the outer edges of Detroit. By the 1980s those who could do so were moving to more distant suburbs. During this process, Macomb County became the site of new battles once situated within Detroit. In 1970 a no-longer-silent majority arose in response to the Nixon administration's effort to cram what some residents viewed as a liberal Washington agenda down the throats of an unsuspecting local populace. George Romney, the former Republican governor of Michigan and then secretary of Housing and Urban Development (HUD), told the residents of Warren, the county's largest city, that HUD had approved its request for a multimillion dollar grant to support housing and economic development. All the municipal government of Warren had to do to receive the money was agree not to discriminate against minorities in any development the city built using federal funds. In response, a crowd of angry Warren-ites said "hell no!" to such "forced integration," chasing Romney out of town and rejecting outright the federal aid.[14]

By the 1980s flare-ups of this sort had become less common, and the public discourse had shifted away from racial hatred. Still, the negative sentiments about Detroit and the threat posed by "outsiders" were in many ways just as pronounced, as expressed in surveys conducted by the political scientist Stanley Greenberg during the mid-1980s. "For these white suburban residents," Greenberg found, "the terms *blacks* and *Detroit* were interchangeable. The city was a place to be avoided—where the kids could not go, where the car got stolen, and where vacant lots and dissolution have replaced their old neighborhoods." In an interview published in 1990, Richard Sabaugh, a Macomb County commissioner and public relations executive, remarked: "The attitude [of whites in Macomb] isn't as much racist as one of fear. People don't see every black as bad. But the image of Detroit is of a decaying, crime-ridden city headed by a mayor who makes racist remarks. We view the values of people in Detroit as completely foreign. To us it's like a foreign country and culture. The language is different and the way people think there is different. We just want to live in peace. And we feel that anybody coming from Detroit is going to cause problems." Sabaugh concluded, "It's all one complex—blacks, Coleman Young, crime, drugs, Detroit. People feel they've been driven out once, and it could occur again."[15]

If these were the carefully chosen words of a public relations expert and elected official speaking on the record, one can only imagine what kind of white racist populism Macomb residents espoused behind closed doors. Indeed, a friend and supporter of Ronald Ebens invites us to do just that when he appears in *Who Killed Vincent Chin?* "Ron's not that way," says Ebens's friend, Rich Wagner. "He's not the type of person that's outward [*sic*] prejudiced. You always might have some little comments or something when you're alone, but he wouldn't go into a bar or public place and really make the kinds of gestures and things that were said during that time."

This abbreviated tour of metro Detroit provides a context for reevaluating the altercation between Chin and Ebens. Detroit (and, by extension, Highland Park) was not just a city facing economic woes. It was a place that had become a "foreign country" to residents of Macomb County. Meanwhile, Macomb County was a home to people who had learned not to appear "outward prejudiced" in public but only to express their "little comments" among themselves.

The white suburban denigration of inner-city Detroit and Highland Park must not be overlooked when assessing Ebens's wanton acts. Vincent Chin (born 1955) and at least one of his white associates, Gary Koivu, had grown up together as best friends in Highland Park during its relatively prosperous postwar period. While both had since moved to the suburbs, they had on occasion returned to old haunts like the Fancy Pants. By contrast, Ebens (born circa 1940) had lived most of his first three decades of life in small midwestern towns before Chrysler relocated him to metro Detroit. He then apparently lived only in suburban bedroom communities. Detroit—more specifically the ironically named Lynch Road plant—was just a place to earn a paycheck and not a place to make a home. While Chin and Koivu can be viewed as engaging in a nostalgic act of slumming, Ebens's behavior is, by contrast, not tempered by any sentimental attachment to Detroit or Highland Park. It is not coincidental that self-identifying "married, family-orientated people" from the suburbs would go to a "foreign country" like Detroit to blow off steam at a strip club (and bring their sons along with them). Suburbs often adopt a NIMBY attitude toward such "nuisances," while inner-city communities tend either to be less discerning of any taxable property/business or possessing of less clout to restrict them. Thus, in the eyes of many suburbanites, Detroit becomes a space marked by license (that is, like American youths taking spring break in tropical destinations or Californians making night jaunts to Tijuana). Moreover, Ebens exhibits the behavior of a person who felt he possessed a form of extraterritorial privilege, as if he were free of the cultural restraints he would observe in his own suburban municipality and immune from formal laws operating in Detroit/Highland Park.

From here, I next want to push toward a deeper analysis that is intersectional, multiracial, and transnational in scope.

RACE, CLASS, GENDER, AND TRANSNATIONALISM

In *Who Killed Vincent Chin?* Ronald Ebens is quoted describing his altercation with Vincent Chin as something that "was preordained to be." His attitude is that of someone nonplussed: he stresses that the beating death was an accident that he cannot explain. It was as if an "audible click" went off in his head just before he administered the blows. This was his testimony before a federal district court in 1984.

How did Ebens end up in federal court? Recognizing that Ebens and Nitz could not be resentenced or retried for killing Chin following the light sentence imposed in state court, ACJ and supporting activists shifted tack. Through a protracted local and nation campaign, they convinced the federal Department of Justice to charge Ebens and Nitz with violating Vincent Chin's civil rights (ironically, a tactic notably developed during the civil rights movement in the case of the murder of a Detroit white woman, Viola Liuzzo, by Ku Klux Klan members). In response, Ebens claims he was flabbergasted. "I'm no racist!" he can be heard saying in the film. "I've never been a racist. I've never had anything against anybody in this whole world. And with God as my witness, that's the truth."

During his federal court trial, a jury of whites and blacks from the Detroit region nonetheless rejected the central claim of Ebens's defense—the notion that racial or ethnic prejudice played no role in the beating. Ebens was found guilty and sentenced to twenty-five years in federal prison. (The jury acquitted Michael Nitz, reasoning that while he was an accomplice to the beating, the prosecution lacked evidence that he committed specific civil rights violations.) Two years later, however, Ebens won an appeal to overturn the conviction on a legal technicality and to move his retrial to a new venue. In 1987 a federal jury in Cincinnati found Ebens not guilty on all counts. *Who Killed Vincent Chin?* captures the drama of these twists and turns.

For five years, from the incident at the Fancy Pants bar through the end of his trials, Ebens had often refused (presumably on advice from his lawyers) to give extended interviews to the press. He had already turned away scores of other media types, deeming them "a bunch of jerks" and saying "to hell with them." (In the documentary, in fact, Ebens is seen berating a group of Japanese reporters for trying to "put words in [his] mouth.") In 1987 he finally opened up in an interview, after weeks of phone requests to him and his lawyers, with a thirty-three-year-old writer for the *Detroit Free Press*. "This is your chance to tell your side of the story," the reporter impressed upon Ebens.[16]

So who was this young, persistent writer who scored the first interview with Ebens? It was none other than Michael Moore.

Moore was not a household name yet, and there is no mention of him in *Who Killed Vincent Chin?* (*Roger and Me*, the documentary that first brought Moore Hollywood fame, would not come out until the year after *Who Killed Vincent Chin?*) But his long overlooked role in the narrative of Vincent Chin may have been quite critical.

One can just picture Michael Moore in his frumpy shirt and Olde English "D" Detroit Tigers baseball cap egging on Ebens with an early test run of his regular-Joe brand of interviewing. And his piece conveys this in words. "If he [Ebens] got through all of this without a scratch," Moore writes in reference to the mass protests and serial trials, "what harm can an interview do?"

Moore presents this as a rhetorical question. Whether or not he posed it directly to Ebens, he certainly convinced him that he has nothing to fear. Apparently pleased with the interview, Ebens says good-bye to Moore by shaking his hand firmly with one hand and giving him "a big, friendly squeeze" with the other hand. "Now, I don't look like some killer, do I?" he says.

August 30, 1987: "THE MAN WHO KILLED VINCENT CHIN: By Michael Moore" blares the cover of the Sunday magazine of the *Detroit Free Press*, the region's largest circulating newspaper. Flanked by pictures of Ebens and Chin, the cover quotes Ebens as saying Chin "was looking for trouble and got it."

Ebens would eventually find company among legions of regretful Moore interviewees. The image of the white male victim of "reverse racism" that he willingly allowed Moore to publish is one that would ultimately lend crucial and visceral power to the narrative presented in *Who Killed Vincent Chin?* Feeling comfortable, justified, and empowered to reveal both his prejudices and his sense of self-righteousness to Moore, Ebens effectively incriminated himself in the court of public opinion. As he repeated similar sentiments for local TV news reporters, these recordings became crucial and foundational sources for the filmmakers Tajima and Choy. The upshot was that Ebens evaded conviction of federal civil rights charges but ensured that his name, face, and words would live on in infamy. For as much as Lily Chin's uncontrollable sobbing and steadfast determination to fight to avenge her son's death, as much as Helen Zia's strident arguments against racism and calls to organize, it is Ronald Ebens's utter remorselessness and brazen claims to victimhood that prove most memorable and lend power to the Rashomon-style fractured narrative presented in *Who Killed Vincent Chin?*

Inside, Moore's story bears a new headline, "THE WAGES OF DEATH." It opens with his characterization of Ebens as "elated" that the "system has worked to his advantage."

"That's it, it's over!" declares Ebens in the aftermath of his federal acquittal. "Done. Finished. Over! Yeah!"

Moore intercedes, "He can barely contain his excitement, sounding like a fan whose baseball team has just won the pennant."

Later, Moore produces from Ebens the exact sort of self-contradictory statements that thousands of viewers of *Who Killed Vincent Chin?* would come to see as thinly veiled racism. "Everybody has some racist feelings," Ebens states, "you, the Chinese, everyone. I can't honestly say I harbor any feelings against any ethnic group, OK? That doesn't mean I want to live with them, OK?"

Indeed, Moore writes that Ebens "wants it known that East Detroit is not the east side of Detroit." "No way," says Ebens. "We're like Roseville," referring to a nearby suburb in Macomb County that was then predominantly white (though roughly 20 percent nonwhite now).

In one sense, Ebens's quotes suggest that his "racist feelings" are not restricted to one "ethnic group." The "them" that he does not want to live with seems just as likely if not more so to refer to black Detroiters than it does to Asian Americans, as do the "little comments" that he makes among friends.

In another sense, however, we might read this situation differently considering more recent scholarship that has focused on "differential" and "relational" forms of racialization. I want to draw particular attention to transnational Asian American studies that have highlighted the gendered nature of Orientalist discourse. As I wrote in my book *The Shifting Grounds of Race: Black and Japanese Americans in the Making of Multiethnic Los Angeles*, the dominant ideology regarding Japanese Americans (and, more generally, Asian Americans) shifted from a pre–World War II regime of exclusion toward a postwar regime of integration.[17]

This shift derived from two sources. First, as Christina Klein, Mary Dudziak, Penny Von Eschen, and others have argued in various ways, the United States, in response to Cold War foreign policy imperatives, developed a "global imaginary of integration" (complementing the more recognized discourse of "containment"), one that Klein labels "Cold War Orientalism." This was expressed both at the level of politics and at the level of "middle-brow" culture, where periodicals, stage productions, and films generated a "sentimental discourse" that worked to sustain popular support for US intervention in Asia by creating affinities between American citizens and Asian subjects.[18]

Meanwhile, in her book *America's Geisha Ally: Reimagining the Japanese Enemy*, Naoko Shibusawa especially highlights the role that gender played in the shift away from exclusionist discourses of "yellow peril" toward the integrationist discourses of the Cold War. To accept the reformist goals of the American occupation of Japan and to more broadly accept Japan as a "special ally" and "bulwark" against Communism, the US public (and the military and civilian occupiers themselves) would need to move beyond depictions of the Japanese as an immutably savage race, to transcend the very widespread stereotypes that had animated the Pacific war as a "race war" and a "war without mercy." Thus the official postwar American discourse on Japan stressed the subservient geisha as a model over and against the bucktoothed kamikaze of wartime or the Japanese soldier as gorilla or vermin lacking civilization and marked for extermination. Japan was also viewed as childlike, thus situating two ostensibly "natural" hierarchies—"man over woman and adult over child"—at the cultural and ideological core of the relationship between the United States as a "white" nation and Japan as a "nonwhite" nation. "The ideologies of gender and maturity helped to minimize racial hostility," Shibusawa writes. "Feminizing the hated enemy or regarding them as immature youths made it easier to humanize the Japanese and to recast them as an American responsibility."[19]

Second, just as Japan became relatively humanized in the eyes of Americans in response to the threat of Soviet and Asian Communism, so was the "model minority" image of Asian Americans propagated in response to the perceived threat of black political challenges to the nation. In Detroit, the "model minority" image of Japanese Americans began to take root during the wartime resettlement of Nisei (second-generation, American-born) from state-sponsored internment camps to the Midwest. Both the War Relocation Authority and nongovernmental sponsors of resettlement insisted that the Japanese American subjects assimilate into white mainstream society. While making public appeals for racial tolerance, the federal government sought to release from the internment camps (from 1942 to the rescinding of the exclusion order in 1944) primarily those Nisei deemed most "loyal" citizens and most fit to be incorporated back into society. The Nisei resettled to the Midwest were a selective group heavily comprised of college students seeking an education (many of whom were women). Thus a certain domestic feminization of the midwestern Japanese American subject occurred as well. (By contrast, Japanese Americans continued to be viewed through the lens of the "yellow peril" in the West Coast areas still governed by the exclusion order. There, the US government sought to ensure the public that all suspected spies, saboteurs, or otherwise "disloyal" figures would continue to be held in camps or sent back to Japan.) As oral histories I have conducted have largely confirmed, Nisei who resettled to Detroit generally abided by the bargain with the government—that is, you will be treated like a full citizen if you disperse and assimilate within mainstream society. But what clearly also shaped this process was the reality that the small Japanese American presence, when compared to that of the large and rapidly growing population of blacks, did not pose a significant threat of encroachment on white neighborhoods in metro Detroit as the postwar era progressed. Consequently, it was largely the specter of black integration that would provoke a racist reaction articulated through masculinist tropes of invasion, violence, and criminality.

Yet, as Robert G. Lee has pointed out, the "model minority" must be seen as dialectally connected to rather than binarily opposed to the production of the "gook" discourse. Indeed, as the "model minority" became a means to incorporate Asians into American culture, it also set the terms and boundaries by which Asians must be held in place and contained. If the original goal of "model minority" discourse was to discredit the demands that black (and Latino) protest placed upon the state and white society, the implicit assumption was that Asian American beneficiaries of this "positive" form of stereotyping would passively play along. When they refuse to stay in their place, Asian subjects become a problem rather than the solution. In other words, when the notion of Asian or Asian American "success" threatens hegemonic notions of whiteness or upsets normative constructions of American culture and nationhood, the "model minority" can transform into the "gook." John Dower has further suggested that "war hates" tied to the "yellow peril" never disappeared; they were simply transferred to other politically useful outlets like Korea and Vietnam. During the 1980s, they rebounded back upon Japan. Between 1978 and 1981, American auto employment plummeted from 760,000 to 490,000 jobs industry-wide. This quick unraveling caught the United Auto Workers (UAW) with its guard down, increasing the sense that American workers were vulnerable and that established structures and institutions could no longer guarantee their economic security. Japan's export-driven economic growth threatened to upend the hierarchical order established during the American occupation of Japan. Now the specter of "unfair" Japanese competition prompted a backlash from Americans whose long memories of the "sneak attack" on Pearl Harbor would shape the new discourse of a transpacific "trade war."[20]

Let us now return to the altercation between Ebens and Chin. What was the "audible click" that caused Ebens to snap? The argument in the now standard narrative of the Chin case is that a latent racial prejudice was the catalyst. Ebens's response, of course, is that he is neither racist nor violent by nature. He tells Moore that he is not the type of person who "just goes down clearing the streets of Asians." Ebens adds, "I'm a macho, and it's hard for me to admit that I'm really just a pussycat."

The gendered language that Ebens employs is particularly telling. It is worth noting that his defense lawyer, Frank Eamon (as quoted in the film), deploys a similar discourse of gender. But the lawyer does so to dispute the notion that his client committed a civil rights violation: "Ron Ebens is guilty of having too much to drink, being a macho man who wouldn't back down from a fight and wanted to avenge ... his stepson. He's guilty of letting himself go too far and killing somebody with a baseball bat—a serious crime, no doubt. He's not guilty of doing this because of racial animus or racial feelings or racial bias or racial prejudice. It so happens the person he was involved with was Chinese."

What seems most evident is that both race and gender were operating in an intersecting rather than mutually exclusive fashion. Some additional details must now be provided. The conflict began, of course, at a strip club. Vincent told his mother he was going out with his buddies for a "bachelor party" days before his wedding. Meanwhile, Ebens's friend Wagner said it was normal for guys like them—"married, family orientated people"—to go to a strip club and blow off steam after a day at the factory. The setting was gendered, as was the interaction. Ebens and Chin exchanged words after competing for the attention of an African American stripper, Starlene. Ebens first angered Chin by calling him "boy" and "little fucker."

"This black girl dancing was a knockout, OK?" Ebens told Moore. "Now if you think Mike and I are going to be sitting there making comments about the car industry with her dancing there, well, you got to be some kind of wimp. I mean, get serious." Ebens deliberately invoked the image of Starlene to stress that his commitment to a heteronormative model of masculinity overshadowed any sentiment he would have had about Asians or the state of the economy.[21]

I would argue, however, that it is only Ebens's naturalization of whiteness that allows him to pit his performance of gender and sexuality against his racial consciousness. Indeed, there's nothing contradictory about Ebens simultaneously asserting his white masculine dominance over Starlene, as an African American woman performer, and Chin, whom he saw as a nuisance impeding his sexual pleasure. Both to Moore and in interviews presented in the film, Ebens admitted that he had rarely interacted with Asian Americans. "Do you see any Asian-Americans around here?" he told Moore. (According to the US Census, Asians comprised about 0.5 percent of East Detroit's 1990 population.) "I don't even know them. I don't know what their plight is. I've never been around them. The only ones I had ever met are the ones in the Chinese restaurants, and they were always nice and I was always nice to them." Thus his limited recollection of real-life Asians is of "nice" restaurant workers in a subservient position. This would clearly have conformed to the construction of the "Oriental" as "model minority" that millions of Americans internalized by imbibing the popular stereotypes of the Cold War era and beyond.

Ebens's initial attempts to belittle Chin as a "boy" and "little" evince an air of subordination and recall the gendered hierarchy that has typified relations between whites/Americans and Asians. (He later characterized Chin's friend Jimmy Choi as a "little pest" to Moore.) Chin's open defiance of such terms of relation clearly upset Ebens. It seems unlikely that a similar encounter with white or black patrons would have provoked Ebens to respond in the specifically aggressive and hostile way that he did. When his friend said Ebens would usually not get into public altercations but would instead keep his "little comments" private, he was probably being somewhat truthful with regard to his previous interactions with whites and blacks.

My argument here builds on Robert Chang's call to see how Ebens's sense of "double displacement ... marks the killing of Vincent Chin as an episode of racial-sexual policing." Chang challenges us to see beyond the "standard account" of the Chin case as "one of anti-Asian violence and the conflation of all Asian groups by the mainstream American public, a flattened story of race and/or ethnicity which ignores the dimensions of class, gender, nation, and sexuality." In Ebens's eyes, Chin symbolized the economic displacement of American autoworkers and was sexually out of place by disrupting his heteropatriarchal gratification.[22] The "audible click" that triggered his violent act could very well have been a response to this sense of double displacement.

Even after his acquittal, Ebens continued to play out his lawyer's characterization of him as a "macho man who wouldn't back down from a fight." But in doing so, Ebens added two new contradictions to his story that could only be resolved using contorted, racist logic. First, consistent with his legal defense, Ebens portrayed Chin both as the initial aggressor in their altercation and the one who persisted as an antagonist. After both parties were thrown out of the bar by security, Ebens reports that Chin said, "Come on you chicken shits, let's fight some more." Through interview footage in the film, he further insists that he did nothing to provoke Chin. Although it seems plausible that he did not expect a physical altercation to erupt, his claim that he never said a word to Chin before Chin came over and struck him is clearly and directly repudiated by multiple witnesses.

Therefore, if Ebens was in fact surprised that Chin confronted him, what also seems plausible and likely is that Ebens was verbally taunting Chin—to the point of using racist "fighting words"—and felt license to do so without fear of repercussion, all the while seeing Chin as an inferior who would passively accept his belittling or at most verbally retort. In this case, what Chin most threatened was not Ebens's physical safety but his ego. Ebens describes what finally pushed him completely over the edge: "We seen Vincent and Jimmy [Choi] standing in front of McDonald's. They were sitting there laughing. All I could think was 'They're laughing. They really put one over on us.'"

Second, Ebens sought to account for his losing the initial fight with Chin by insisting that that Chin "sucker punched" him. As reported in the film, Chin's friends were unable to intervene immediately, so Chin fought Ebens and Nitz one-against-two. The odds were seemingly stacked against the Chinese American whom Ebens viewed as "little" and a "boy." Hence, Ebens's rationalization is that Chin would not fight fair and square—that is, he would not "fight like a man." Such characterizations befit the "Japan-bashing" discourse underlying Ebens's taunting of Chin. Japan was not merely viewed as an economic competitor but more notoriously as an unfair competitor. As

Michigan's US senator Carl Levin remarks in the film, "We are being shot at and shot up by the Japanese, who have the most protectionist economy in the world. But some of those who hold up the specter of a trade war ignore that we are already in the middle of such a war, but only the Japanese are shooting."

The "sucker punch" discourse was also invoked by Ebens to help ratio-nalize a quest for vengeance that led him to use a car and a bat to hunt down Chin, who was both on foot and completely unarmed. Chin's supposed transgression of the rules of manly combat—initiating a fight with a "sucker punch"—seems to have generated for Ebens a license to retaliate with dis-proportionate and ultimately deadly force. In this regard, the "sucker punch" can be seen as a variation or continuation of the characterization of Pearl Harbor as a "sneak attack."[23] The notion that Japan was not just as an enemy but namely a savage, evil, and racialized enemy that would not abide by Western standards of warfare facilitated the American targeting and murder of Japanese civilians on a mass scale through the use of atomic bombs and firebombing during World War II. During the wars in Korea and Southeast Asia, Asian enemies of the United States were similarly racialized as faceless "gooks" who did not understand "civilized" methods of war and by definition did not value life in the same manner as Americans. Hence, in the face of deceptive and evasive maneuvers, American forces often turned to superior technology and more powerful weaponry to eliminate the "gooks" en masse. Such instances are testimony to how a long history of racist dehumaniza-tion has allowed crimes against humanity to be committed in the name of upholding civilization and democracy.

Moving beyond the standard narrative, the idea that Chin confronted Ebens rather than turn the other cheek denies him status as a passive victim of Ebens's hate in ways that may trouble some Asian Americans seeking to elicit sympathy for him. However, one could counter that viewing Chin as an innocent murder victim does not necessitate seeing him as passive or completely nonviolent. Indeed, Asian American audience members are likely to sympathize with Chin for beating up Ebens, given that the film provides ample evidence Ebens is a foul-mouthed racist who initiated the argument. Seen in this light, Chin could be held up as an antiracist warrior who defeated Ebens and Nitz in hand-to-hand combat before his ultimate martyrdom. One must be careful, however, not to frame political resistance in ways that reify the patriarchal trope of the heroic male figure. If we are correct to recognize Ebens's hate crime as intersectionally driven by race, gender, and sexuality, it is necessary to recognize the largely gendered manner by which Chin has been put on a pedestal as a martyr for Asian Americans for defying the image of the so-called emasculated Asian male. Though a full analysis is beyond the scope of this essay, we must be mindful of how "model minority" discourse is designed to set up a series of traps, including some that seek to ensnare those fighting to overturn it. The following section seeks to identify some of the pitfalls of "model minority" politics in the midst of the neoconservative turn that defined Reaganism.

ASIAN AMERICANS AND RACIAL POLITICS IN THE REAGAN ERA

In his efforts to explain white ethnic and blue-collar support for Republicans, the pollster and subsequent Bill Clinton adviser Stanley Greenberg focused his research on Macomb County, Michigan, beginning in the 1980s. Greenberg argued that a backlash against civil rights combined with economic insecurity to mark the suburban region as fertile ground for Reagan's "morning in America" message of a "prouder, stronger, and better" nation. The ideological assault on "welfare queens" and other symbols of so-called liberal excess fanned the flames of white working-class sentiments of victimization. In the early 1960s Macomb was "the most Democratic suburban county in the country." But the development of factories in Macomb peaked by 1967. Between 1979 and 1982, the county lost 21 percent of its manufacturing jobs, and unemployment rose to 15.3 percent by March 1981. During this period, beginning in 1972 and extending to 1992, Macomb became a reliable source of Republican support. Greenberg concluded: "These white defectors from the Democratic Party expressed a profound distaste for black Americans, a sentiment that pervaded almost everything they thought about government and politics. Blacks constituted the explanation for their vulnerability and for almost everything that had gone wrong in their lives; not being black was what constituted middle class; not living with blacks was what made a neighborhood a decent place to live."[24]

Greenberg's research helped influence the shift toward "moderate" or "centrist" policies adopted by Clinton and other Democrats in the aftermath of the Reagan landslide. While a full analysis of this shift is beyond the scope of this essay, what is most pertinent has been the drive to win back white voters by downplaying policies that explicitly address matters of race to center "middle-class" interests. Such a strategy seemed to pay off in electoral success for Clinton—although the actual impact of this strategy is still hotly debate. Indeed, it might even be viewed as more central to Barack

Obama's attempts to satisfy the desire of white voters for a postracial order. Nevertheless, a simplistic formula for elevating "economics" above race and "cultural issues" fails to grapple with the growing diversity and complexity defining twenty-first-century politics as the nation moves toward becoming majority nonwhite.

In this final section, I return to the Chin case to discuss some of the ways that Asian American history complicates our interpretation of recent political history, especially our understanding of the "Reagan Democrats." I focus particularly on the contested discourses of civil rights and nationalism during this period. Until we fully comprehend the ways in which race, class, nation, and politics have shifted and are continuing to shift under the weight of globalization and multiethnic diversity, our sense of the "middle class" and the "majority," as well as "racial and economic justice," will be impoverished.

With the Justice for Vincent Chin campaign ultimately hinging on the cause of civil rights, it forced Ebens and his defense team to confront a very specific predicament. Given the slap on the wrist he received in response to his original manslaughter plea, Ebens had effectively gotten away with murdering Chin. But it also laid the groundwork for him to be vilified in the court of public opinion. Marshaling a groundswell of outrage at the beating and the light sentence, ACJ activists pushed the federal government to try Ebens (and Nitz) on civil rights charges. The ACJ campaign necessitated a deft negotiation of a multiracial discourse of civil rights that was particularly notable for its engagement with black history and consciousness. In turn, Ebens's lawyers were required by the terms of the trial to focus on defending their client against the specific charge of racial/ethnic motivation. In a different manner, they too would deploy a multiracial strategy.

In the city of Detroit, Asians have historically been tiny in numbers and politically marginal. Thus ACJ's ability to organize a mass demonstration (600 to 700 persons) in front of Detroit city hall to protest the lenient sentencing of Chin's assailants in March 1983 projected what must surely have been a surprising visibility to non-Asians and Asians alike. Key to the strategy of ACJ—activists who had come of age within the Asian American movement and "Third World" liberation struggles of the early 1970s—was to make the Chin case comprehensible to those whose civil rights consciousness had been framed in terms of black and white. This was both a popular strategy to drum up support for ACJ's cause within a majority black city and a necessary legal strategy as ACJ sought the federal civil rights charges against Ebens and Nitz. Indeed, ACJ attorneys initially had to convince representatives of the Justice Department that Asian Americans were a protected group under civil rights law.[25]

In the course of developing its argument, ACJ brought forward a considerable number of African American witnesses who figuratively testified to the injustice committed against Chin on camera for the documentary and in some cases literally testified in federal court, largely in support of the prosecution of Chin's assailants. The African Americans directly witnessing aspects of the altercation included Jim Perry, a young man outside the club who said Ebens offered him $20 to help "catch these Chinese guys," and the two police officers who testified both to the ferocity with which Ebens struck Chin and the cavalier nature with which the plea bargaining and sentencing were handled by the municipal court. (These witnesses remark in *Who Killed Vincent Chin?* that they were never asked to testify before the county prosecutor or before the judge who settled the plea and handed down the prison-free sentence to Ebens and Nitz.) A broader validation of the Chin case as a civil rights case is offered in the film by prominent black Detroiter Horace Sheffield Jr., who connects the Chin case to the history of racism African Americans have experienced while commenting that "freedom is indivisible." As a longtime activist and former director of the NAACP, Sheffield can be symbolically seen to be putting the clout of Detroit's civil rights community behind ACJ. This leads to a later scene in the film of Jesse Jackson speaking before another well-attended Justice for Vincent Chin event, as the campaign built nationwide momentum with the support of the Rainbow Coalition.

Through presentation of these black voices, *Who Killed Vincent Chin?* effectively frames Chin as a victim who had suffered a modern-day form of lynching, while exposing the inability of persons of color to receive a fair hearing before the court. The film misses, however, a deeper connection between race and class that must have resonated with some working-class African Americans. While Jackson's view of a Rainbow Coalition significantly advanced the idea of America as a multicultural nation, it also explicitly sought to build unity (or at least to a significant degree bridge the divide) between civil rights supporters and organized labor. Although the long-term impact of the Rainbow Coalition and Jackson's presidential campaigns is still being debated, both clearly achieved some breakthrough successes. In 1988, most notably, Jackson won the Michigan Democratic caucus with 55 percent of the vote over Michael Dukakis. The success of his campaign relied in substantive measure on his ability to offer besieged autoworkers a different path forward. Meanwhile, Horace Sheffield's intervention in the Chin case also carried a deeper meaning eluded by the film in which he comes across as a somewhat generic black activist voice. Helen Zia's written account does go further, recognizing Sheffield as "a dependable supporter at ACJ events" and president of the Detroit-Area Black Organizations. What still unfortunately goes unstated is Sheffield's long-standing connection to the auto industry. Thus his reading of the Chin case should properly be viewed as having been informed by a lifetime of witnessing and fighting racism within the plant (and the union) while advancing working-class solidarity as a critical vehicle for black and multiracial advancement.[26]

Federal prosecutors in the 1984 trial of Ebens seized upon the themes advanced by the Justice for Vincent Chin campaign. They deployed African American witnesses in order to validate the claim that Ebens was a racist, as they sought to portray the beating of Chin as a racially motivated act in violation of civil rights law. They further called at least one witness forward to demonstrate that Ebens had a history of anti-black prejudice predating the altercation with Chin. "This was more than some barroom fight," argued federal attorney Theodore Merritt. "This was violent hatred turned [loose]. This was years of pent-up racial hostilities and rage unleashed. This was a modern-day lynching, but there was a bat instead of a rope." Placing such a frame on top of the evidence of Ebens's statements about "you motherfuck-ers" inflicting job losses on American workers proved effective before the Detroit jury of whites and blacks, who convicted Ebens on one count of violating Chin's civil rights.[27]

In their defense at the 1984 trial and their subsequent appeal to overturn the conviction, Ebens's lawyers constructed a multilayered argument. First, at the most general level, they appealed to the sensibilities of Reagan Demo-crats disinclined to believe that the forcible hand of the federal government should be imposed upon respectable northern whites who were not Klan-style racists. "These suburban [Macomb] voters felt nothing in common with Detroit and its people and rejected out of hand the social-justice claims of black Americans," surmised Stanley Greenberg. "They felt no sense of personal or collective responsibility that would support government anti-discrimination and civil rights policies." Ebens expressed such sentiments in his interview with Michael Moore. He stated his belief that affirmative action was only necessary in "some place like down in Alabama where they have been passed over just because they were black. But then it is taken to the other extreme where they are promoted over the white guy who has a higher score and stuff, and I don't think that's right at all." Ebens's comment on affirmative action bears the mark of southern exceptionalism—that is, the idea of white northerners that historical and contemporary racism in America has generally been caused by "bad" whites in the South—and individual rights ideology. It was intended to refute a recent accusation that the East Detroit police department was guilty of discrimination owing to its dearth of blacks on the force.[28]

Furthermore, the defense consistently argued that ACJ fabricated the entire notion of racial motivation. In court, the defense lawyers insisted that a volunteer ACJ attorney, Liza Chan, had coached witnesses (Chin's three friends who accompanied him to the Fancy Pants) to stick to a common narrative that explicitly identified racial speech by Ebens. The defense's contention was substantially acknowledged by the federal appeals court, which ruled that the trial judge had erred when she disallowed the defense to present the full transcript of Chan's meeting with the witnesses. The appeals court overturned the conviction against Ebens in part because it opined that the defense was denied a full opportunity to make its case that ACJ fabricated evidence of racial motivation. The question of whether Chan had in fact improperly coached the witnesses, rather than simply prepared them in typical lawyer fashion, seems debatable; in any case, it may not have been decisive in the Detroit trial. Rather, according to a juror interviewed in *Who Killed Vincent Chin?*, Chin's friends did not come across as the most credible witnesses anyhow. The key witness for the prosecution in the eyes of the jury was Racine Colwell, a white dancer who had no connection to ACJ and no apparent motive to take sides in the case. Colwell testified that she was situated closest to Ebens and clearly heard him say, "It's because of you motherfuckers that we're all out of work."[29]

Two other aspects of the defense's successful appeal proved especially pertinent. First, the defense argued that the trial judge erred in denying its request for a change of venue. The Detroit jury pool, Ebens claimed, had been tainted by ACJ's advocacy and saturated media coverage. In other words, the defense deployed ACJ's effective mobilization strategy—without which there would never have been a federal civil rights trial—against ACJ. Though the appellate court noted that this adverse publicity was so extensive that "it probably would have been advisable for the trial judge to have ordered a change of venue," it found that this was not reversible error. However, on remand, when defense counsel renewed their motion for a change of venue, the judge followed the advice of the appellate court and moved the retrial to Cincinnati. Moving the 1987 retrial of Ebens to Cincinnati, where no comparable alliance between Asian American and African American civil rights advocates had been established and where little of the national awareness-raising about the case had taken hold, was a major victory for the defense.[30]

Second, the defense went to great lengths to divorce the Chin-Ebens case from any notion of anti-black racism and African American civil rights. This was a rather sophisticated tactic. On the one hand, it offered a general appeal to those buying into the white "backlash" against civil rights. On the other hand, it recognized that it would need a different tack in the federal trials to address African American jurors and white liberals. The frame the defendants used tended to discredit the general idea that Asian Americans were an oppressed or aggrieved societal group. The defense's most far-reaching claim was that the case should be dismissed because "Orientals" were not a protected class under federal civil rights statutes. While the legal basis of this petition was rejected in both the district and appeals courts, the thrust of the argument pervaded the defense's account. As Ebens declared to Moore, he was exploited by activist groups like ACJ "to show the plight of the Asian-American in America." When Moore asked what that plight was, Ebens answered, "Hey, I didn't even know there was one, that's how dumb I am. I still don't know what their plight is." In the film, Ebens refers to the "alleged plight" of Asian Americans. But even without explicit references, most of the American public (circa 1987) would have been conditioned by cultural norms to accept the "model minority" image of Asian Americans and set Asians apart from a concept of civil rights associated (positively or negatively) with blacks. Here again, the change of venue was critical because the general public in Cincinnati had little immediate grasp of the Japan-bashing controversies that erupted in Detroit in the early 1980s. It is dubious to conclude that the most "impartial" jury is one bathed in relative ignorance of such social, cultural, and political context. Such a jury as found in Cincinnati was relatively inclined to believe that ACJ fabricated the idea of racial motivation.[31]

At the same time, the defense sought to obscure the nature of Ebens's relationship to African Americans. Thus his lawyers took both reactive and proactive measures. Reactively, the defense barred on appeal the testimony of a black Detroiter named Willie Davis. The prosecution had sought to make Davis a key witness to prove that Ebens had a long history of anti-black racist behavior. Going into the trial, it believed it had secured clear testimony from Davis identifying Ebens as someone who had once called him "nigger" and forced him out of a dive bar under threat of violence. Somewhere between meeting with the prosecution and testifying in the 1984 trial, Davis changed his story. The court transcript suggests that it was possible that Davis was coaxed or intimidated by the defense team. In any event, Davis became a hostile prosecution witness and would only state that the person who threatened him in the bar was a "man named Ron" who matched the general physical profile of Ebens (but whom he was not sure was Ebens). Given the vagueness of the testimony and its prejudicial content, the appeals court ruled that the trial judge erred in denying the defense request to bar Davis's testimony. Hence, the prosecution was denied a pillar of its strategy to mark Ebens as a man who had exhibited smoking gun evidence of racism.[32]

Proactively, the defense argued that what made Ebens initially upset with Chin was his defamation of the character of the African American exotic dancer, Starlene. It stressed that the conflict between Ebens and Chin was strictly tied to Ebens's lambasting of Chin and his friends for not giving Starlene a proper tip. What are we to make of this? While such behavior would in no way justify Ebens's deadly actions, there is nothing in *Who Killed Vincent Chin?* refuting the notion that Chin or his friends may have chided or belittled Starlene. What we do know is that there is more to the story than the film lets on. In fact, Angela Rudolph, who is only identified by her stage name Starlene on camera, played a more complicated role in the case than one would be led to believe from watching the film. The filmmakers situate her opposite Ebens and use her interview to challenge his credibility. Specifically refuting two of Ebens's claims, Starlene remarks that he knew her well and that Chin defeated Ebens and Nitz in a face-to-face fight. Because Starlene is presented in the film alongside other witnesses—most of whom are African American—who report being ignored prior to the initial sentencing of Ebens and Nitz, viewers are also positioned to see her statements as a counterpoint to the legal proceedings that the Chin family and community supporters viewed as biased and unjust. What the film fails to acknowledge is that Starlene testified in federal court on behalf of Ebens's defense. Starlene corroborated Ebens's version of the story: that Ebens was sticking up for Starlene and did not care about Chin's race, and that Chin was an aggressor in the altercation. Her testimony was deployed by the defense to support the idea that the conflict was merely the product of a barroom brawl and not a civil rights matter.[33]

In response, the prosecution attacked Starlene's credibility during the first federal trial. The government attorney declared to the jury, "Ms. Starlene is not known for her truthfulness among the circle that she travels in, and the law enforcement agency, her friends and her co-workers. And ladies and gentlemen, her defensive denial that she would never let anyone touch her, let alone have oral sex with her, well, that shows you how much stock she puts in telling the truth here, under oath." As summarized in the appeals court transcript, the government attorney supported this line of attack by producing "testimony from Sharon Fleming, a dancer at the Fancy Pants Lounge, that Ebens had engaged in an act of oral sex with Starlene"—a charge both Ebens and Starlene denied. While recognizing the possible legitimacy of an attempt to portray Starlene as partial to Ebens, the appeals court found the prosecution's actions to be "highly objectionable as tending to demean the witness and also as tending to depict the defendant in a depraved light before the jury." It concluded that the lower court should have upheld Ebens's objection against this testimony.[34]

Ebens must have been pleased to see the court outlaw the prosecution's attacks on Starlene, for it coincided nicely with his version of the story, central to which was that the conflict all began with Ebens defending Starlene against Chin. Michael Moore paraphrased Ebens as saying "he was actually upset at Chin for discriminating against the black dancer." He added with obvious incredulity that Ebens wants the public to believe "that he was acting as a sort of one-man civil rights commission at the Fancy Pants."[35] One need not embrace the prosecution's public shaming of Starlene as a reported sex worker to question the sincerity of Ebens's stance, which at best appears self-serving and at worst exploitative. But given the change of venue, the new arguments allowed, and the prior arguments disallowed, such evidence of Ebens's concern for a black women may have played a role in casting reasonable doubt in jurors' minds that he attacked Chin out of racial motivation.

I have deliberately presented the wide scope of arguments put forward by Ebens and his lawyers for illustrative purposes—to expose and critique the popular discourse on race circulating during the Reagan era, as well as the racial discourse presented by Ebens's defense team and at least in some cases validated by the judicial process. Some of these arguments appeal to societal ignorance or prejudice toward Asian Americans. Some appear easily refuted by contrary evidence. And some just look irrational and necessitate contortions of logic to be understood. However, the Chin case teaches us not to dismiss such "false" forms of consciousness but instead to recognize the power and impact of "common sense" ideology. Analyzing public discourse about Asian Americans consists heavily of breaking down the circulation of ideas guided by ignorance and misinformation. In the Chin case, Ebens's defense lawyers advanced a bricolage of fragmented and inconsistent images of Asian Americans that nonetheless proved effective for their purpose. For instance, they invoked the "model minority" stereotype to discount the notion of anti-Asian discrimination and sever the connection between Asian

Americans' experience and black civil rights. At the same time, Ebens sought to portray Vincent Chin as an aggressor ("looking for trouble") who refused to accept the subordinate status of the "model minority" and thus became the "yellow peril" or a "gook." Moreover, the defense implicitly hoped that the sentencing judge and federal juries would discount the value of Vincent Chin's life.

In closing, the Chin case provides a deep sense of the twisted discourses on race that caused Asian Americans such anguish during the Reagan era. But if we take a step back and put things into a broader and longer-term political perspective, we can see that the patchwork of arguments that worked episodically for Ebens's defense at a particular time and place proved troublesome for the Republican Party's efforts to construct a tent housing both the Reagan Democrats and Asian Americans. During the Reagan/Bush landslides of the 1980s, Asian Americans were generally presumed to have given decisive support to Republican presidential candidates. This carried over into 1992 (the first time publicly reported national exit polling disaggregated Asians), when, even in defeat, George H. W. Bush was reported to have defeated Clinton 55 to 31 percent among Asian Americans. In short, Asian American support for Republicans was marked by a qualified acceptance of the neoconservative image of the "model minority," a libertarian embrace of free enterprise and limited government, and an anti-Communist posture particularly adopted by Southeast Asian refugees.[36]

Two decades ago, it was "common sense" that Asian Americans were somehow conservative (and anti-black) by nature; however, this completely overlooked the fact that new forms of Asian American political consciousness were developing under the radar of the national media—emerging from the social movements of the 1960s but maturing through 1980s campaigns like Justice for Vincent Chin. As the ranks of working-class Asians swelled owing to post-1965 immigration, tens of thousands of them were deftly organized by liberals and progressives, sometimes for direct partisan purposes but more generally through processes of grassroots empowerment. Meanwhile, even professionals and entrepreneurs frustrated by their efforts to breach the "glass ceiling" began to question "model minority" ideology. Almost across the board, Asian Americans concerned by the revival of "yellow peril" and "gook" imagery grew disenchanted with the xenophobic overtones of muscular nationalism and the narrow defense of literal and figurative borders. In California, Republicans directed a series of 1990s campaigns perceived by Latinos and Asians to be anti-immigrant. Conventional observers were also stunned in 1996 when Asian Americans voted by a large margin against the Proposition 209 initiative outlawing affirmative action. Then, during the 2000 primaries, the straight-talking John McCain was so brazen as to repeatedly use the epithet "gook" on the record, then (for a frightening period of time before relenting) refusing to retract it when condemned by Asian American organizations.[37]

The upshot was that the racialized "culture wars," which neoconservatives had once conceived in part as a strategy to drive a wedge between Asian Americans and other communities of color, were being more broadly construed as a backlash against the new discourse and demography of multiculturalism (which Democrats consciously embraced in increasing measure beginning with Clinton/Gore). To be certain, white "middle-class" voters did drift back toward the Democrats in the 1990s. However, the Asian American vote swung much more dramatically to the left and continued to do so. After Dole edged Clinton among Asian Americans in 1996, Gore (2000) and Kerry (2004) carried Asian Americans by double digits. With the multicultural appeal of Barack Obama reaching a new zenith for Democrats, Asian Americans gave Obama at least a 27-point cushion in 2008 and a 47-point cushion in 2012.[38]

The Census now projects that the United States will become a majority nonwhite nation over the next three decades, and in most urban areas that reality has already sunk in. However, with the financial bubble having burst and a new wave of economic hardship sweeping across the nation, growing anxieties about both immigration and US-Asia relations are resurfacing, with China now having eclipsed Japan as the primary source of the American trade imbalance and the principal buyer of American's foreign debt. While sorting out the new politics of race, class, gender, and nation will not be easy, the new lessons we must take away from the narrative of Vincent Chin will prove increasingly salient. What I have attempted to do in this essay in provide an example of the intersectional, multiracial, and transnational analyses we will need to ensure that we rise to the challenge.

NOTES

1. SCOTT KURASHIGE, THE SHIFTING GROUNDS OF RACE: BLACK AND JAPANESE AMERICANS IN THE MAKING OF MULTIETHNIC LOS ANGELES (2008).

2. DON NAKANISHI, IN SEARCH OF A NEW PARADIGM: MINORITIES IN THE CONTEXT OF INTERNATIONAL POLITICS (1975).

3. In repeated tellings of this story, some common errors have been repeated. For instance, Ebens and Nitz are generally described as "two unemployed autoworkers," yet Ebens

was in fact still employed by Chrysler and in the position of foreman, which would distance him from rank-and-file union members and assembly line workers.

4. Yen Le Espiritu, Asian American Panethnicity: Bridging Institutions and Identities (1992) (especially ch. 6); Helen Zia, Asian American Dreams: The Emergence of an American People 91–92 (2000).

5. Zia, *supra* note 4, at 70, 75.

6. Thomas J. Sugrue, The Origins of the Urban Crisis: Race and Inequality in Postwar Detroit (1996). Over the past decade, some Asian Americanists have paid closer to attention to Detroit because of their interest in the centenarian Chinese American philosopher and activist Grace Lee Boggs. *See* Grace Lee Boggs & Scott Kurashige, The Next American Revolution: Sustainable Activism for the Twenty-First Century (2011).

7. For demographic data, see Reynolds Farley et al., Detroit Divided (2000).

8. Some of the most interesting scenes in *Who Killed Vincent Chin?* are of the now extinct Chinatown clinging to its last vestiges of life in the 1980s. One Chinese American elder, who began working at Ford in 1927, interviewed by the filmmakers offers an impassioned plea for justice for Chin. In 2002 I helped launch a volunteer group called the Detroit Chinatown Revitalization Project. This sparked interest in a history project spearheaded by Chelsea Zuzindlak, a Wayne State University graduate student. For more on this project with documents and a historical overview, see smichiee http://www.detroitchinatown.org.

9. All subsequent demographic data, unless specified, is drawn from Joe Darden et al., Detroit: Race and Uneven Development (1987) or the US Census.

10. For more on Oak Park and racial integration, see Darden, *supra* note 9, at ch. 4. Oak Park sits adjacent to Southfield, a larger city with a similar history with regard to first Jewish and later black settlement. Today, both Oak Park and Southfield have slight majorities of African Americans, though neither transitioned as quickly as most middle-class Detroit neighborhoods.

11. See Sugrue, *supra* note 6, especially chs. 8–9; on East Detroit, see http://www.cityofeastpointe.net/history.htm.

12. Det. Free Press, Jan. 14, 1987.

13. See Darden, *supra* note 9, at ch. 2.

14. David Riddle, *HUD and the Open Housing Controversy of 1970 in Warren, Michigan*, 24 Mich. Hist. Rev., no. 2 (Fall 1998), at 1–36.

15. Stanley B. Greenberg, Middle Class Dreams: The Politics and Power of the New American Majority 39 (1996); Ze'ev Chafets, Devil's Night: And Other True Tales of Detroit 136–37 (1990).

16. Michael Moore, *The Wages of Death*, Det. Free Press, Aug. 30, 1987 (Magazine), at 12–20.

17. Kurashige, *supra* note 1. On "differential" and "relational" forms of racialization, see, for example, Laura Pulido, Black, Brown, Yellow, and Left: Radical Activism in Los Angeles (2006); Natalia Molina, Fit to be Citizens? Public Health and Race in Los Angeles, 1879–1939 (2006). For a survey of recent work on transnational Asian American history, see Moon-Ho Jung, *Beyond These Mythical Shores: Asian American History and the Study of Race*, 6 Hist. Compass 627 (2008).

18. Christina Klein, Cold War Orientalism: Asia in the Middlebrow Imagination 1–18 (2003); Mary L. Dudziak: Cold War Civil Rights: Race and the Image of American Democracy (2000); Penny Von Eschen, Satchmo Blows Up the World: Jazz Ambassadors Play the Cold War (2004).

19. Naoko Shibusawa, America's Geisha Ally: Reimagining the Japanese Enemy 3–5 (2006). See also John Dower, War without Mercy: Race and Power in the Pacific War (1986).

20. Robert G. Lee, Orientals: Asian Americans in Popular Culture (1999), esp. ch. 5; Dower, *supra* note 19, epilogue; Dana Frank, Buy American: The Untold Story of Economic Nationalism 160–86 (1999).

21. In addition, after Moore notes that Ebens was "elated" to have finally been acquitted, he quotes a sarcastic Ebens remarking, "About all that's left to charge me with now is rape." Rape would, in his view, be just as obviously bogus a charge as the civil rights violations were. That Ebens would so cavalierly toss around the notion of a false charge of rape further suggests that Moore was quite successful in getting him to open up as if he were just talking with "another guy."

22. Robert S. Chang, *Dreaming in Black and White: Racial-Sexual Policing in* The Birth of a Nation, The Cheat, *and* Who Killed Vincent Chin? 5 Asian L.J. 41, 56, 59 (1998).

23. Both "sneak attack" and "sucker punch" rapidly surfaced within American popular discourse to describe the attacks on September 11, 2001. Bill Bonds, a longtime Detroit newscaster, delivered a jarring and controversial post-9/11 on-air monologue vowing that America would achieve vengeance against Osama Bin Laden for his "sucker punch." A preeminent Cronkite-like figure in the local media, Bonds can be seen in *Who Killed Vincent Chin?* sternly and harshly questioning Judge Kaufman for his light sentence of Ebens and Nitz. By September 2001 he had retired from anchoring the news, so his political monologue was delivered as a commercial for the Gardner-White furniture company. *Bill Bonds Angry Ads Stir Up Emotions*, Det. News, Sept. 18, 2001.

24. Greenberg, *supra* note 15, at 39; Darden, *supra* note 9, at 31.

25. *See* Zia, *supra* note 4, at ch. 3.

26. *Id.* at 68. Part of a family of migrants from Georgia, Sheffield had begun working at Ford in 1934. In short, he epitomized a form of civil rights unionism, becoming a leading figure within the left-leaning UAW Local 600 and helping to found the Trade Union Leadership Council. A brief biography of Sheffield is provided by Wayne State's Detroit African American History Project, http://www.daahp.wayne.edu/biographiesDisplay.php?id=24.

27. United States v. Ebens, 800 F.2d 1422 (6th Cir. 1986).

28. Greenberg, *supra* note 15, at 39; Moore, *supra* note 16.

29. The trial judge in Ebens's trial was Anna Diggs Taylor, a Carter appointee, a veteran of the civil rights movement, and the first African American woman to serve in federal court in the state of Michigan. By contrast, the three-judge panel that overruled her included one Nixon, one Carter, and one Reagan appointee. Taylor's biography is available at http://www.daahp.wayne.edu/biographiesDisplay.php?id=64. The biographies of appeals court judges Engel, Kennedy, and Milburn are available at http://www.ca6.uscourts.gov/.

30. Ebens, 800 F.2d at 1425–26; United States v. Ebens, 654 F. Supp. 144 (E.D. Mich. 1987) (granting change of venue).

31. *See* Ebens, 800 F.2d at 1429; Moore, *supra* note 16.

32. Ebens, 800 F.2d at 1434. Apparently, given Davis's vague testimony, the prosecution even during the initial trial was precluded from informing the jury that Ron Ebens was a regular at the dive bar, that he subsequently owned it for two years, and that Davis lived right near it.

33. *Id.* at 1442.

34. *Id.*

35. Moore, *supra* note 16.

36. For exit poll data on Asian Americans in presidential elections from 1992 to 2008, see *National Exit Poll Table*, N.Y. TIMES, http://elections.nytimes.com/2008/results/presi dent/national-exit-polls.html.

37. A November 7, 1996, *Los Angeles Times* exit poll found 61 percent of Asian Americans voting against the ban on affirmative action in 1996, while polls by Asian American organizations found opposition in the 70–80 percent range for key Asian ethnicities. On McCain in 2000, see, for instance, C. W. Nevius et al., *McCain Criticized for Slur: He Says He'll Keep Using Term for Ex-captors in Vietnam*, S.F. CHRON., Feb. 18, 2000, http://articles.sfgate .com/2000–02–18/news/17638747_1_mccain-s-words-asian-americans-racial-slur. The idea of Asians being immutably opposed to African Americans arose again during the 2008 Democratic presidential primary as a "common sense" rationale for Hillary Clinton's vast Asian American support. See Lisa Takeuchi Cullen, *Does Obama Have an Asian Problem?* TIME, Feb. 18, 2008, http://www.time.com/time/politics/article/0,8599,1714292,00.html.

38. "National Exit Poll Table"; "President Exit Polls," N.Y. TIMES, http://elections.ny times.com/2012/results/president/exit-polls. A number of Asian American organizations and scholars have criticized the national exit polls for undercounting Asians and possibly understating the extent of Asian American Democratic support. What is clear, even if the polls are somewhat off, is the trend of Asian Americans away from the GOP and toward the Democrats in large numbers. A multilingual exit poll of Asian Americans in eleven states found Obama carrying the Asian American vote 76 percent to 23 percent. See Asian American Legal Defense and Education Fund, "The Asian Americans Vote in the 2008 Presidential Election," http://www.aaldef.org/article.php?article_id=403.

6

The Paradox of Reparations
Japanese Americans and African Americans at the Crossroads of Alliance and Conflict

GREG ROBINSON

On August 10, 1988, following almost two decades of political organizing, lawsuits, and lobbying by Japanese Americans and their supporters, the Civil Liberties Act of 1988 was enacted. It granted an official apology and a $20,000 tax-free payment to surviving members of the group of 120,000 Japanese Americans who had been forcibly removed from the West Coast under Executive Order 9066 and confined without charge in government camps during World War II (an event frequently, if imprecisely, termed the Japanese American internment). The 1988 law, along with a parallel settlement for Japanese Canadians signed several weeks later, represents a pioneering instance of monetary compensation awarded for past violations of basic rights. As such, it forms a notable chapter in the growth of civil and human rights activism by minority and racialized populations worldwide. Still, the history of the redress movement was marked by a central paradox: while it began as part of a multiracial movement, as the campaign proceeded it became less universalistic and shifted to more specific and narrow political goals. It thereby grew less attractive and relevant to other minority groups, even as the law it spawned became a useful precedent and rallying point for them.

An investigation of the varied positions of African Americans toward Japanese American redress offers a revealing window on some of these complexities. In theory, blacks should have been the warmest supporters of the redress movement. During World War II, African American citizens, journalists, and activists had been disproportionately visible as critics of the removal policy. The NAACP (although its initial opposition to Executive Order 9066 was quite muted) later joined with the Japanese American Citizens League (JACL) in an important postwar alliance for civil rights before the Supreme

Court. In contrast, during the 1980s African American support for Japanese American redress was generally lukewarm at best.

In order to understand the reaction of African Americans to redress, it is first necessary to review the larger history of connections between the two groups.[1] Until World War II, Japanese Americans and African Americans were geographically distant, apart from pockets of the two populations living in cities such as Los Angeles and New York, and their principal legal problems and concerns were quite distinct. Early Japanese communities, based in rural areas of the West Coast and Hawaii, were dominated by members of the immigrant (Issei) generation. Forbidden by federal statute from becoming American citizens—and ultimately from immigrating at all—the Issei were barred on that basis by state laws from equal rights. The young Nisei, though excluded by social prejudice from housing and employment opportunities, did not generally face state-imposed segregation (apart from laws banning racial intermarriage). Conversely, black communities were concentrated in the South, as well as in northern and midwestern industrial cities. Although almost all black Americans were native-born, the majority who resided in the southern states faced Jim Crow laws as well as official denial of voting rights and equal education, while those in the rest of the country faced unofficial discrimination.

The removal and confinement of Japanese Americans during World War II brought them into large-scale contact with African Americans. First, a substantial number were transported to the South, near black areas. Two government camps, Rohwer and Jerome, were established in Arkansas, and housed a combined population of 20,000 Japanese Americans. In mid-1943, after the famous all-Nisei 442nd "Go For Broke" combat team was formed, volunteers were sent to Fort Shelby, Mississippi, and Fort Livingston, Louisiana, for training. Many Nisei, exposed for the first time to a Jim Crow society, were horrified by the treatment of blacks. Furthermore, tens of thousands of Nisei who left the camps during and after the war became acquainted with African Americans. Beginning in late 1942, Nisei college students and other inmates whom the government adjudged to be "loyal" resettled outside the West Coast, in cities such as New York, Chicago, and Washington, DC. Barred by poverty or racial discrimination from more affluent areas, they moved into or alongside majority black areas and gained African American friends and/or neighbors.

At the same time, during the war years African Americans migrated in waves to the West Coast to work in defense industries. Many of the migrants could find housing only in the "evacuated" Japanese American neighborhoods of the West Coast, such as San Francisco's Japantown and the Little Tokyo area in Los Angeles, which became the black neighborhood of Bronzeville. When Japanese Americans returned to the West Coast at the end of the war, many settled in the prewar Little Tokyos alongside the newer black arrivals, while others found housing in predominantly Latino and African American neighborhoods such as the Watts district of Los Angeles.

The coming together of African Americans and Japanese Americans was spiritual as well as geographical. During the war years, many blacks expressed public sympathy for Japanese Americans and criticized the government's removal policy. Black supporters of "fair play" such as Langston Hughes, Hugh E. Macbeth, and George Schuyler helped by sponsoring civil rights groups, bringing lawsuits, writing newspaper articles, signing petitions, visiting government camps, and/or lobbying officials.

The geographical and spiritual coming together of the groups led to a postwar black-Nisei alliance that expressed itself in diverse forms. Community members formed interracial churches, housing developments, and schools. Nisei in Los Angeles, New York, Toronto, and elsewhere joined black colleagues in interracial organizations such as the Congress of Racial Equality (CORE) and the Fellowship of Reconciliation, and engaged in nonviolent protest actions against discriminating businesses. Activists such as Bayard Rustin, Larry Tajiri, George Yamada, Canada Lee, Sam Hohri, Ina Sugihara, and Pauli Murray contributed to each other's newspapers, addressed social and political group meetings, and/or joined in multigroup activities. Nisei writer Hisaye Yamamoto was hired as a columnist by the African American journal the *Los Angeles Tribune*, while S. I. Hayakawa wrote a column for the *Chicago Defender*.

Most important, the JACL and the NAACP joined in a series of civil rights cases decided by the US Supreme Court. JACL lawyers helped consult with NAACP Legal Defense and Educational Fund counsel on the preparation of cases, and the presence of the Nisei alongside blacks as "friends of the court" sent a powerful symbolic message—especially in the years after their wartime removal—about the harmful results of racial prejudice. The wartime Nisei challenges to removal, plus postwar cases brought by the JACL regarding the rights of Japanese Americans to own property and work on an equal basis, helped lead the Court to form its doctrine of "strict scrutiny" in cases of racial discrimination. Their joint struggle climaxed in the Supreme Court's epochal 1954 *Brown v. Board of Education* decision and its companion case *Bolling v. Sharpe*, which struck down segregated schools and held racial classifications suspect under the Constitution.[2]

Yet by the time the *Brown* and *Bolling* cases were decided, the JACL and the NAACP had largely ceased their collaboration, and contacts between the two groups declined. As prewar and wartime anti-Japanese prejudice waned, a significant fraction of Nisei moved out of inner-city areas to largely white suburbs in search of greater social and economic opportunities, and they increasingly associated (and intermarried) with whites. They left behind their black friends and neighbors, who continued to face housing and school discrimination. Even during the early postwar years, many Nisei had unquestioningly absorbed dominant white social attitudes of black inferiority and inherent criminality. Such attitudes became more common with greater distance.

The nationwide debate over civil rights during the early 1960s revealed grave divisions among Japanese Americans. While scattered Nisei voices, such as Mary (Yuri) Kochiyama, Lloyd Wake, and Taxie Kusunoki, advocated protest against racial injustice, they were largely overshadowed by more hostile remarks. Howard Imazeki, editor of the San Francisco newspaper *Hokubei Mainichi*, published an editorial calling on blacks to do some "soul searching" before seeking equal rights, and challenging members of the black community to make a more concerted effort to better themselves: "They blame society for their womenfolk giving birth to illegitimate children and for living on welfare checks. They blame society for petty thefts and rapes being perpetrated by their manfolks [*sic*] in Nihonmachi. In short, they blame all of their antisocial habits and cultural maladjustment on the 'unjust' community in which they live."[3]

Excerpts from Imazeki's editorial were rapidly distributed via the Associated Press to newspapers throughout the country, and were even cited on the floor of Congress by a segregationist congressman. A number of black writers, as well as Japanese Americans, protested Imazeki's comments.[4]

The controversy inspired by Imazeki's column mirrored a rancorous debate that developed within the JACL after the organization accepted the invitation of Martin Luther King Jr. to send representatives to the March on Washington in August 1963. Numerous local chapter presidents objected, stating that such struggles were not the business of Japanese Americans. While the national board ultimately approved JACL participation, only a few hundred Nisei attended the march.[5] Similarly, the following year Japanese Americans in California became further embroiled in debates over Proposition 14, a ballot initiative to repeal an open housing law and give property owners a constitutional right to discriminate against racial and religious minorities in housing sales and rentals. While the national JACL appropriated

$5,000 to opposing the measure and offered organizational support to the "No on 14" campaign, even opponents of the measure admitted that many Nisei quietly supported it. Journalist Mary Ikuta reported that 49 percent of Japanese Americans surveyed intended to vote for the proposition.[6]

In 1966–1967 the NAACP and the JACL joined together once more as allies in the Supreme Court case of *Loving v. Virginia*, in which the Court struck down laws against interracial marriage.[7] Still, by then even the ambivalent closeness that had grown up between Japanese Americans and black communities following the war had all but worn off. Many older Nisei abandoned even rhetorical support for African Americans. In the wake of the black freedom movement and the development of Black Power, numerous white commentators disseminated conservative images of Asian Americans as a "model minority" who had apparently achieved social and economic parity through the established system without mass protest or government aid. It was tempting for Japanese Americans to buy into such images of themselves and to call on blacks to follow their example.

At the same time, expressions of solidarity toward Nisei among blacks were increasingly rare, while other, more angry expressions of discontent became more frequent. In August 1963 black demonstrators in Fresno, California, picketed two Nisei-owned grocery stores that they alleged had refused them service. In 1965 a group of black ministers in Los Angeles complained that Japanese Americans were fighting the opening of a black-owned funeral home in the multiracial Crenshaw district because "they are now white and don't want Negroes around." Similarly, in early 1967 an anonymous black "ex-GI" scornfully dismissed anti–Vietnam War activism and racial solidarity among nonwhites: "To show the total disregard they have for U.S. Negroes, Orientals who live in this country are quick to discriminate against us. On several occasions, we have had to fight the civil rights battle in Chinese and Japanese restaurants."[8] Even sympathetic blacks deplored the lack of civil rights protest by Nisei, which they attributed to the presence of insular (and immigrant) community social structures. When James Farmer of CORE was asked about the lack of Nisei involvement in civil rights protest, he pointed to a sprinkling of Asian American workers in Mississippi, then commented that "Oriental Americans" had "more tightly-knit structures" that encouraged self-help and deterred outside involvement.[9]

In spite of such friction, African Americans had not forgotten the wartime treatment of Japanese Americans. Indeed, throughout the late 1960s numerous militants referred to the "concentration camps" for Japanese Americans generally as an illustration of American racism and repression of people of color.[10]

Interestingly, at least as early as 1966 the African American press featured discussion of reparations for Japanese Americans. That year, the US Supreme Court took up the Yokohama Specie case, in which prewar bank account holders sued for equitable repayment of funds seized after Pearl Harbor. The *Chicago Defender*, reporting on the Court's upcoming ruling, referred to war-time removal as "[o]ne of the darkest chapters in United States history." While the author was careful to state that "[c]ertainly no award, however equitable, could ever atone for the indignities inflicted on Japanese-American citizens," the article noted that to date "the monetary reparations that have been made amount to just a fraction of the actual loss," and added prophetically that the case might trigger demands for further payment: "The stakes are high for the government, however, in terms of the principle of legal accountability that might accompany a victory for the Japanese American claimants."[11]

Meanwhile, in response to the same case, John Akar, an African visitor to Baltimore, told the local *Afro-American*:

> Many things in your American democratic society baffle, bother and perplex us, the intelligentsia of Africa. We cannot understand or even explain why 75,000 Nisei American citizens of Japanese descent, in one of the most tragic aspects of World War II, were uprooted and incarcerated only because of their Japanese extractions, while [Americans] of German descent went unnoticed. . . . And when time came for compensations to be paid, the Japanese Americans received only 10 cents on the dollar. Is this not a crime against humanity?[12]

In the last years of the 1960s, a new generation of Sansei and Nisei joined together with Chinese American, Filipino American, and Korean American colleagues to forge an Asian American movement (sometimes dubbed "Yellow Power"). As that last phrase suggests, the shock troops of the new awakening were inspired in large measure by the civil rights and Black Power movements, which had reshaped national consciousness regarding the rights of minorities and the costs of assimilation. The new militants called on Asian Americans to take pride in their group culture and history as part of a larger struggle by people of color against white domination. Their movement was determinedly interracial. Activists read works by black and Chicano authors and took part in "Third World peoples" protests, including campaigns for the creation of ethnic studies programs. A few Sansei, among them Richard Aoki and Wendy Yoshimura, plus such Nisei as Paul Takagi and Yuri Kochiyama, centered their organizing work within black communities.[13]

In line with their other efforts, Asian American activists turned considerable attention to studying and commemorating wartime Japanese American confinement—both as a central group historical event and as a showpiece of the harmful impact of white racial domination on racial minorities. Asian Americans for Action, a New York activist group whose leadership included Nisei former inmates such as Kazu Iijima, Minn Matsuda, Aiko Abe (later Aiko Herzig-Yoshinaga), and Yuri Kochiyama, declared, "The economic loss resulting to the Japanese-Americans from [their] internment and forced evacuation was astronomical, and the psychological scars, immeasurable. Yet, in terms of the damage inflicted by means of institutional racism on Native Americans, the Black people, Chicanos, Latinos, Chinese and Pilipino people, the Japanese-American experience is simply one more link to the long chain of racial oppression that pervades the story of this country."[14] Former inmates and their supporters nationwide organized marches, art exhibitions, and Days of Remembrance. In 1969 the Manzanar Committee, a grassroots Los Angeles–based committee led by a former inmate, Sue Kunitomi Embry (herself a onetime leader of the Nisei Progressives in Los Angeles who had supported open housing campaigns for blacks), inaugurated the annual pilgrimages to the site of the War Relocation Authority camp.

In conjunction with the community reappraisal, at the dawn of the 1970s a diverse conglomeration of individuals and groups came together to support reparative justice for Japanese Americans.[15] Part of the initial impetus for community awareness and organization arose through a public campaign to repeal Title II, the section of the Internal Security Act of 1950 that had provided for concentration camps to be held in readiness for arbitrary confinement of suspected subversives by the Executive Branch. Japanese Americans took the lead in fighting for repeal. Drawing on the experience of EO 9066, the activists argued that as a group whose members had suffered arbitrary incarceration, they had a privileged place to denounce arbitrary government repression.[16] The movement to repeal Title II grew to include contributions from major civil rights and political organizations, churches, and labor unions, plus a timely endorsement from retired chief justice Earl Warren, who referenced indirectly his own experience as a leading player in the wartime removal of Japanese Americans. It also appealed to African Americans, who gladly offered rhetorical and logistical support for repeal. Black Power and antiwar groups had suffered from official government harassment, such as the FBI's notorious COINTELPRO program, which featured warrantless raids on offices of movement groups and infiltration by agents provocateurs with the goal of discrediting radical groups. They were well aware that black militants would be the likeliest target for arbitrary arrest and confinement.[17]

Within eighteen months, repeal was enacted by a large majority in Congress. In the wake of this success, Japanese Americans around the country began exploring the question of seeking an apology and restitution from the government for their own incarceration—in the process, the phrase "reparations" was changed to the more palatable "redress."[18] Nisei and Sansei activists in Seattle formed the Evacuation and Redress Committee.[19] Meanwhile, Edison Uno, who had been confined as a teenager in government camps in Granada, Colorado, and Crystal City, Texas, lobbied the JACL to take action. In response to Uno's campaign, the JACL voted resolutions in favor of compensation at its national conventions in 1972, 1974, 1976, and 1978, and formed the National Redress Committee, but did not make the campaign for reparations a priority. JACL leaders realized that seeking financial reparations for past wrongs would be difficult and divisive, especially given the apparent prosperity of the ethnic Japanese population.[20] Community leaders won an initial success in 1976, when President Gerald Ford officially revoked Executive Order 9066 and declared that the wartime removal of Japanese Americans had been "wrong" and a "tragedy." Ford made a ringing statement of regret: "We now know what we should have known then—not only that evacuation was wrong, but Japanese-Americans were and are loyal Americans."[21]

Although Ford's action was not intended to support moves for reparations (indeed, some advisers favored it precisely in order to forestall them), it encouraged redress supporters to redouble their efforts. In 1979 William Hohri, a community activist in Chicago, founded the National Council for Japanese American Redress to lobby for reparations and to raise money for court suits. Meanwhile, a dedicated activist in Washington, DC, Aiko Herzig-Yoshinaga, accumulated and cataloged tens of thousands of documents from the National Archives relating to the confinement of Japanese Americans. In the process of reviewing official files, she uncovered a copy of the censored (and supposedly destroyed) initial version of General DeWitt's Final Report on Evacuation, which stated clearly that the West Coast defense commander had pushed for mass removal because he considered it impossible to trust or determine the loyalty of any Japanese American on racial grounds. This report belied the army's repeated insistence in public statements and Supreme Court briefs that the principal cause of its actions was insufficient time to make individual determinations of loyalty in a wartime emergency, and furnished a "smoking gun" demonstrating official racism and mendacity.

In 1979, in response to the campaign by the National Coalition for Redress/Reparations (NCRR), Seattle congressman Mike Lowry introduced a redress bill in Congress. It granted a $25,000 payment to all inmates or to their heirs. JACL powerbroker Mike Masaoka took the position that Lowry's bill had no chance of passing. Instead, following consultation with Japanese American members of Congress, notably Hawaii senator Daniel Inouye, the JACL and its allies called for the establishment of a government commission to review the history of the wartime events. Hohri and others on the more radical wing of the redress movement opposed the idea, insisting that the facts behind their incarceration were already well known.[22] Nevertheless, the JACL's strategy prevailed, and in 1980 the US Commission on Wartime Relocation and Internment of Civilians (CWRIC) was created by an act of Congress to investigate the wartime removal of Japanese Americans (as well as Aleuts and Pribilof Islanders, included to further broaden support for the measure) and then issue a report and recommendations in regard to potential reparations. President Jimmy Carter appointed Joan Z. Bernstein, a well-regarded attorney, as chair of the CWRIC. Among the other members selected for the commission were one African American member, former Republican US senator Edward Brooke, as well as one Japanese American, federal judge and former JACL general counsel William Marutani.

The CWRIC announced a series of fact-finding hearings in Washington, DC, in which the commissioners examined former army and government officials familiar with the policy, including former Supreme Court justice Abe Fortas, former assistant secretary of war John J. McCloy, and former presidential assistant James Rowe.[23] The commissioners then scheduled outside hearings, which were held in Boston, New York, Chicago, and Alaska, and on the West Coast, during the second half of 1981. During these hearings, dozens of former inmates came to testify.

Following the end of the hearings, the commission named a Washington-based attorney, Angus MacBeth, to prepare a historical study based on the collected documents and testimony. Its report, entitled "Personal Justice Denied," was released in February 1983. On June 16, 1983, the CWRIC issued a separate set of recommendations. The commission agreed that Japanese Americans had suffered a great historical injustice: "In sum, Executive Order 9066 was not justified by military necessity, and the decisions that followed from it—exclusion, detention, then ending of detention and the ending of exclusion—were not founded upon military considerations. The broad historical causes that shaped these decisions were race prejudice, war hysteria and a failure of political leadership."[24] The commission unanimously recommended

the passage of a joint resolution of Congress containing an official apology
and the establishment of a fund for educational and humanitarian purposes.
In addition, the commissioners recommended that an award of $20,000 be
granted to each surviving person—though not their descendants—who had
been covered under Executive Order 9066.[25]

Although both the CWRIC's report and recommendations provided
a strong official endorsement for redress legislation, both were met with
immediate challenges. John McCloy, who considered the redress campaign
a slanderous attack on the record of President Franklin D. Roosevelt and
Secretary of War Henry L. Stimson, used his influence against enactment.
Meanwhile, a former National Security Agency employee, David D. Lowman, publicly charged that the intercepted prewar Japanese diplomatic code
excerpts, code-named MAGIC, revealed large-scale spying by West Coast
Japanese Americans before Pearl Harbor, and concluded that the government
had acted properly in rounding up the entire ethnic Japanese population.
Lawyer/scholar Peter Irons and Col. John A. Herzig, a retired army counterintelligence specialist, offered detailed rebuttals of Lowman's charges in
congressional committee hearings. Redress legislation nonetheless remained
stalled. A number of attempts to bring legislation to the floor of Congress
and to obtain a vote met with defeat.[26]

Meanwhile, a parallel legal proceeding, fueled by the CWRIC's inquiry,
came together. The Supreme Court's decisions in the "Japanese internment" cases of Gordon Hirabayashi, Minoru Yasui, and Fred Korematsu
had weighed heavily on Japanese Americans. These rulings sanctioned the
government's wartime actions with the stamp of constitutionality and thereby
presented a major obstacle to restitution. In 1981, as part of the process of
writing a book on the wartime cases, Peter Irons interviewed the three Nisei
defendants in the wartime cases. Irons suggested to them bringing a *coram
nobis* petition using the historical material that he and Aiko Herzig-Yoshinaga had uncovered. After obtaining the consent of all the former defendants,
Irons recruited a volunteer legal team, directed by Sansei attorneys Dale
Minami, Peggy Nagae, and Kathryn Bannai, to handle the three cases.

On November 10, 1983, following a hearing, Judge Marilyn Hall Patel
summarily granted the *coram nobis* petition, reversing Fred Korematsu's
conviction. In her opinion, Patel found that there was substantial support in
the evidentiary record that the government had deliberately omitted relevant
information and provided misleading information in its papers.[27] The cases
of Minoru Yasui and Gordon Hirabayashi proved more complicated and protracted in their progress through the courts. While Yasui died before his case

could be resolved, in September 1987 a three-judge panel of the US Court of Appeals for the Ninth Circuit ordered Hirabayashi's petition granted, holding that the record demonstrated that racial bias was "the cornerstone of the internment orders" and that official misconduct had materially affected the argument of the case.[28]

Even as the *coram nobis* legal effort had been fueled by the redress movement and the work of the CWRIC, the victories of the former Supreme Court defendants provided fresh impetus for congressional action on redress. At the same time, advocates of redress altered their tactics "from protest to politics" (to paraphrase the words of black activist Bayard Rustin). Rather than presenting the wartime removal of Japanese Americans as part of a larger history of white supremacy, redress activists downplayed the question of endemic racism and narrowed the focus of lobbying to the exceptional wartime violations of constitutional rights of citizens. Lobbyists also underlined the patriotism of Japanese Americans in their efforts, and cleverly gave their bill the number H.R. 442 in honor of the 442nd Regimental Combat Team, the celebrated World War II all-Nisei army unit. In the words of JACL lobbyist Grant Ujifusa, who advised seeking the support of conservatives, the winning strategy was to frame redress as a question of equal opportunity and a "motherhood and apple pie" issue.[29] Phil Tajitsu Nash, hired as a lobbyist by the Seattle-based Washington Coalition on Redress (WCR), later recalled that redress activists made a deliberate choice to distance themselves from blacks:

Once the CWRIC had its hearings, the JACL lobbyists were very conscious of the problem that any reparations for Japanese Americans could be used to argue for "40 acres and a mule" [slavery reparations] by African Americans. Indeed, both JACL and non-JACL activists had been influenced by Yale Law School Professor Boris Bittker's 1973 classic, "The Case for Black Reparations," which gave serious consideration to the legal and political issues raised by righteous demands for reparations.

Thus, myself and everyone I knew of in the lobbying effort were careful to mention the factual differences between the Japanese American and African American grievances, so that fiscal and social conservatives could be assured that we were pushing only for the limited case of redress for Japanese Americans unfairly incarcerated during World War II. Rep. Newt Gingrich and other conservatives supported us because he agreed that property rights of American citizens should not be violated, but his support might have waned if African American property rights had been introduced into the equation.[30]

In summer 1988 H.R. 442 was at last approved by Congress, and was signed by President Reagan in August 1988, in the last months of his presidency. The law established a fund of some $1.2 billion, from which each Japanese American affected by Executive Order 9066 would receive a $20,000 tax-free payment, while the remainder would be awarded for educational and other programs by a new nonprofit body, the Civil Liberties Public Education Fund. Congress did not provide for a speedy allotment of the funds, however, and it was not until the middle years of the administration of President George H. W. Bush that the first redress checks were sent to the former inmates.

During the 1970s, the nascent redress movement attracted powerful support from an important outside constituency—African Americans. There was little direct involvement by black activists in the campaign for reparations during the 1970s, though a few favorable items appeared in the African American press. In 1977 the *Philadelphia Tribune* editorialized in favor of a bill to allow Japanese Americans who had been employed in the camps credit from such work as part of the Federal Civil Service Retirement System. "Nowhere in our short-lived history is there evidence of the kind of barbarism inflicted on a people and sanctioned publicly by the highest officials of government as those acts directed toward Japanese Americans during the great world war." The *Tribune* affirmed that no monetary payment could make up for "many years of imprisonment, suffering and indignities," plus loss of properties and the stigma of false charges of treason. The bill nevertheless deserved "strong support" as it would rectify part of the harm.[31]

Still, the idea of redress swiftly began to attract the support of part of the black political class, mainly those California-based officials who had sizable groups of Nisei constituents. Congressman Augustus Hawkins, who as a state assemblyman in 1942 had denounced the original roundup, lent his full backing. US representative Yvonne Braithwaite Burke was another early convert. Perhaps the most vital black supporter of redress was Rep. Mervyn M. Dymally. Dymally, born in Trinidad of African and East Indian ancestry, was elected lieutenant governor of California in 1974. In 1981 he won a seat in Congress from California's Thirty-First District, which included the heavily Japanese American city of Gardena, and became a leading advocate of redress. In December 1982 Dymally introduced a pair of redress bills drafted by the NCRR. The first, which had provisions similar to the failed Lowry bill, granted individual reparations, while the second offered community-wide aid to restore "social, economic, and cultural well-being" to Japanese communities. As chairman of the Congressional Black Caucus (CBC), Dymally obtained CBC approval for the bills. He meanwhile offered NCRR members the use of his congressional office for lobbying and organizational work.[32]

The CWRIC hearings offered African Americans their first chance to pronounce themselves in large numbers on redress. During their hearings around the country, former senator Brooke and the other commissioners received scattered testimony and letters of support from non-Japanese, including African Americans. For example, in New York, civil rights leader Vernon Jordan, director of the National Urban League, provided a strong endorsement of reparative justice:

> The uprooting and subsequent internment of Japanese Americans during World War II is one of the most shameful chapters in our nation's history. Fear, racism, and hysteria combined to extract a terrible penalty from loyal citizens who had every reason to expect better of their fellow countrymen. Fundamental rights were abridged in the name of national defense and efforts now to right these grievous wrongs, though those wrongs can never really be made right, are entirely appropriate, and should be supported. We should never forget those dark days or the responsibilities we owe to those who were the victims.[33]

Similarly, Basil Paterson, New York's secretary of state, testified that Executive Order 9066 represented "a flagrant violation of civil rights and a shocking violation of human rights," especially as Japanese Americans had not only lost their liberty but been largely despoiled of their property as well. Almost alone among witnesses, Paterson also included the shock and psychological trauma of resettlement in his catalog of damages: "Others will appear before you to recount the horrors and penalties of racial dispersion, forced assimilation, ethnic shame and wounded self-image. Although we in the black community can sympathize with the struggle to preserve cultural roots and family pride under persecution and injustice, I prefer to call your attention to the need for political justice."[34] Another moving statement came from Bay Area congressman Ronald Dellums, who recalled witnessing the removal of West Coast Japanese Americans as a boy and shouting at the soldiers taking away his Nisei friends to let them go.[35]

That same year, the House Judiciary Committee opened hearings on a set of redress bills. Among the witnesses was NAACP leader Clarence Mitchell, a veteran civil rights lobbyist. In his testimony pledging the NAACP in support of Japanese American redress, Mitchell stated that the Nisei, particularly Mike Masaoka of the JACL, had been greatly helpful as supporters of African American civil rights. Mitchell's comments came as a surprise not only to the legislators but also to Nisei militants such as William Hohri, who had always thought of the JACL as a fundamentally conservative organization.

Throughout the 1980s the redress movement retained the support of California's black political class. In 1983 Los Angeles mayor Tom Bradley signed a bill providing compensation to Nisei municipal employees summarily fired from their jobs in 1942. The movement likewise attracted the endorsement of a few visible African American leaders, notably political candidates who sought to court Asian American constituencies. Most notably, in 1988 presidential candidate Jesse Jackson (whose multicultural Rainbow Coalition of activists included Bert Nakano and other Japanese Americans) proclaimed that he favored redress for mass confinement. New York mayoral challenger David Dinkins likewise announced his support for reparations.[36]

In addition, a few outside figures spoke out in support of redress on the basis of universalistic principles and solidarity against racism. For example, in 1982 the group East Coast Japanese Americans for Redress, who had organized testimony at hearings before the CWRIC in New York, received a warm letter of support from Muhammad Ahmad, director of the Southern Institute of Black Studies in Atlanta. Ahmad expressed outrage over "[t]he uprooting of 120,000 Japanese Americans and herding off into concentration camps which resulted in thousands of innocent citizens dying during the incarceration from illnesses or due to inadequate medical care" as well as over their property loss and trauma. He proclaimed that "[a]s an African American who has personally experienced the injustice of illegal detention," he expressed full solidarity with the demands of Japanese Americans.[37] Meanwhile, in 1984 John E. Jacob, president of the National Urban League, made a powerful editorial argument in favor of redress: "A national apology is the least to be expected for such an injustice. And financial compensation for losses is only fair since virtually all who were relocated suffered the loss of homes, businesses, farms and personal goods." He referred as well to the recent murder of Chinese American Vincent Chin. "So ugly racism still lives and is directed against many groups as well as the historical targets of racism—black people. By recognizing past wrongs and present injustices, and by remedying them, we become a stronger, fairer country."[38]

Jacob's article was exceptional, not just in its outspoken support for redress but in placing discrimination toward other nonwhite Americans on a level with that against blacks. In contrast, by the time of his editorial, there had been a shift in the expressed attitudes of African Americans. During the 1980s, the issue of the injustice to Japanese Americans all but dropped out of the discussion. Black writers and speakers who publicly addressed the question of redress focused less on whether Japanese Americans had suffered racist or discriminatory treatment—this was generally admitted—than on the impact of redress legislation. There the collective response was dominated by the question of self-interest: either individuals favored redress because it would promote restitution for slavery, or, on the contrary, they argued that until African Americans received reparations for slavery, Japanese Americans did not deserve redress.

The principle of reparations for slavery was by no means new: there had been sporadic mention of the idea ever since the mythic promise of General William T. Sherman, at the dawn of Reconstruction, to furnish freedmen with "40 acres and a mule." Queen Mother Audley Moore, an ex-Garveyite, had long campaigned for restitution, while Dr. Robert Brock founded the Self-Determination Committee in the early 1960s.[39] The persistence of racial disparities, even after the civil rights movement, and the economic crisis that much of black America faced in the 1980s helped revive widespread interest in the principle of repayment for slavery, which activists claimed was at the root of the continuing economic difficulties blacks experienced. The Japanese American redress movement served as a visible marker of the legitimacy of the principle. Indeed, Robert Brock attempted to bridge the two movements. Brock testified in favor of redress at the Seattle CWRIC hearings, following which he organized meetings in the Los Angeles area to press for reparations for blacks much like those of the Japanese Americans—he argued that if Nisei had a solid case, then blacks had an even stronger one. Brock invited JACL national director Ron Wakabayashi to Self-Determination Committee meetings to speak on the issue of reparations, though Wakabayashi expressed reservations.[40]

Brock was not the only activist to see the potential benefit to blacks of redress. Some months later, after Congressman Dymally introduced his legislation, a review of Vincent Harding's historical work *There Is a River* appeared in the *New York Amsterdam News*. The reviewer noted that Harding's work served an important educational purpose in raising consciousness of the nation's debt to blacks, a cause that paralleled that of the Japanese American redress movement. "The Japanese child [has] joined the march of his parents who are demanding reparations from the United States government because the US uprooted and imprisoned all Pacific Coast residents of Japanese ancestry on February 19, [1942,] two months after the US entered World War II. . . . Unlike the Japanese on the West Coast, African parents and educators are not teaching their children to demand reparations for the 400 million Africans who died during the slave trade."[41] A month later, the *News* reported that the International Tribunal on Reparations for Black People in the U.S. was meeting to demand reparations that would be "[c]onsistent with such historical demands for reparations as those by the Japanese Americans interned during World War II."[42]

However, the hunger by blacks for slavery reparations also led them to see other groups as competitors, and claim priority. In November 1981, at the hearing of the CWRIC in New York, the sole witness to testify against redress for Japanese Americans was Clarence Reynolds, the president of a Chicago-based organization called the Organization for a New Life and Freedom, which advocated the return of 60,000 black Americans to their "homeland" in Africa. Reynolds, who took advantage of almost all of the time allotted him to propagandize on behalf of his own movement, prefaced his statement by explaining that he opposed any payout of money to "the Japanese people." Reynolds admitted that "[w]e know [the Japanese Americans] were mistreated," but stated that blacks had been further mistreated, and were thus more deserving. "We conclude today by reminding the Committee [*sic*] that Japanese Americans received in 1945 38 million dollars in land reparations. Black Americans have never received a dime in reparation for 200 years of enslavement." His prepared statement finished, Reynolds hastened to justify himself by stating that his organization was not a hate group and was not simply opposed to Japanese: not only had he personally made good contacts with people in Japan on business trips there, but he proclaimed that "[d]uring World War II one of my best friends in Chicago was a young man of Japanese origin." His use of the clichéd disclaimer of bias drew derisive laughter from the audience. Commissioner William Marutani, who quipped that the reason for the laughter was that "Some of *our* best friends are Black," responded to Reynolds's comments by expressing his sympathy for the trials of blacks but asking why they should leave a country they had built. When Reynolds proposed that Japanese Americans would also do better to go back to Japan, the audience raised a cry of protest. Marutani retorted that he could not go *to* Japan, where he would be victimized by discrimination as a foreigner.[43]

While Reynolds's position on redress was not heavily publicized, he was not alone. In 1983 the well-regarded *Portland Observer* pondered what reparations would be possible for Japanese Americans. "The equitable payment would be in money—since in this country money is used to pay for injustices. But this will not happen. If the Japanese Americans who were interned and their families were to be paid for their suffering, when will the descendants of the Blacks who were enslaved and the Indians who were murdered and made homeless be compensated?"[44]

Similarly, in 1983 Los Angeles columnist Stanley G. Robertson told at length the story of wartime Japanese removal and deplored the despoiling of Japanese American property and the splitting up of families. He recognized that Japanese Americans had faced discrimination and had been "victimized and taken advantage of, humiliated and denied." Nevertheless, he considered that blacks were even more deserving of reparations for discrimination. As an example, he contrasted the unjust wartime firing of a Nisei civil servant with the more troubling case of all the blacks who remained barred from such civil service positions throughout those decades.[45] Robertson's series drew a good deal of mail, a selection of which he published in a subsequent column. A trio of readers who indicated that they were African American expressed warm support for the idea of reparations for blacks. One woman stated that if Japanese Americans were eligible to receive $20,000 each, then all African Americans should receive $200,000. Two putatively white readers opposed reparations for blacks. One equally opposed redress for Japanese Americans on the grounds that "[n]obody asked the Japanese people to come here" and that "their government" had started the war. Two Japanese Americans also voiced their opinions. A Sansei born after the war supported reparations on the grounds that "the government should somehow try to make amends for abuses which can possibly never really be eradicated." However, a Nisei man who described his experience of being confined as a boy in horse stalls asserted, "I don't think anything Black people have experienced could match it."[46]

In 1987 writer Rozell Leavell placed the issue in the starkest terms. He had no argument with the legal issues in the case, he stated, nor with "the Japanese people" who claimed they were victimized by prejudice and internment. However, he considered that it was egregious favoritism to grant money to such people unless blacks were properly compensated for their longer and harsher suffering than "those recently admitted to citizenship."[47]

The response of black political leaders suggests that such writers as Reynolds and Leavell expressed a popular mindset. Indeed, by the late 1980s *JET* magazine reported that Rep. Dymally faced increasing challenge over his support for redress. "The recent passage of a bill giving $20,000 to each Japanese (or their descendants) held in an internment camp during World War II has created a controversy among Black officials," on the belief that blacks ought to be compensated first for their suffering under slavery. "Dymally's response to critics is that talk without action is all he's heard from Black leaders approaching him about similar legislation for Blacks."[48] According to Nisei congressman Robert Matsui, most members of the CBC, despite their endorsement of the Dymally bills, were slow to warm to the issue of redress on the grounds that African Americans should have priority on reparations.[49]

The support of blacks for redress was further diluted and complicated by the discriminatory statements and actions of officials and businesses in Japan. These rebounded against Japanese Americans who—as during World War II—were unfairly connected with Japan. In 1986 Japanese prime minister Yasuhiro Nakasone asserted in a speech that Japanese educational success was due to Japan's status as a monoracial society, while education levels in the United States were held down by "Blacks, Puerto Ricans and Mexicans." The comments raised a storm of protest, and Japanese Americans proved a handy foil. One critic complained:

> It should be pointed out that it was not Mexicans, Puerto Ricans, or Blacks who were responsible during the Second World War for the illegal and immoral internment of Japanese-Americans under the guise that they were a threat to national security. In fact, blacks in the media, black religious groups, and the National Association for the Advancement of Colored People decried these actions and condemned the United States government for its racist treatment of thousands of Japanese-Americans. Unfortunately, Mr. Nakasone's views are probably shared by too many Americans—the overwhelming majority of whom are not Japanese.[50]

Similarly, Rep. Parren Mitchell (son of NAACP activist Clarence Mitchell) protested the prime minister's remarks on the floor of Congress and said that Nakasone should "remember that it was the Congressional Black Caucus that supported reparations for the Japanese that were treated so badly during World War II." This, he said facetiously, was not evidence of intellectual inferiority![51] Although Mitchell's comments equated Japanese and Japanese Americans, at least implicitly, black press organs did not fail to make the distinction. They approvingly noted that Robert Matsui had immediately associated himself with Mitchell's remarks, even as Japanese American groups called for an immediate apology by the prime minister.[52]

Nakasone ultimately apologized for his words and met with various African American leaders. Still the damage was done, and the sentiment of mistrust was greatly aggravated in July 1988 when Michio Watanabe, a former finance and trade minister (and future deputy prime minister), publicly charged that, unlike Japanese, black Americans were nonchalant about declaring bankruptcy.[53] Such comments, which came in the wake of reports that Japanese firms were making "sambo dolls" and using other stereotyped negative images of blacks in advertising, caused a renewed storm of protest. The CBC leadership called a news conference in which they deplored the Japanese attitude and challenged the Japanese government to act forcefully to curb racial bias against blacks, holding out threats of boycotts. CBC chair Mervyn Dymally was careful to make clear that he did not include Japanese Americans in his strictures against Japan. Rather, he insisted that the CBC members spoke for other members of Congress and people of goodwill across America, including Japanese Americans. Two Nisei representatives, Robert Matsui and Norman Mineta, joined the CBC in denouncing Tokyo's actions, even as Japanese American groups in Los Angeles sponsored a protest at the local Japanese consulate.[54]

Although Japanese prime minister Noburu Takeshita issued a vaguely worded letter of regrets about his minister's offensive remarks, he made no promise of changes in policy, and the incidents continued to rankle.[55] During summer 1988, Japan received a large measure of negative attention in the black press. The *Chicago Defender* and the *Pittsburgh Courier* called for boycotting Japanese products, and added criticism of Japan's ties to South Africa's apartheid regime to protest the official attitudes and stereotyped products. Patricia O'Flynn Thomas, president of the Newspaper Publishers Association, a trade group representing some 200 black newspapers nationwide, issued a statement condemning not only the derogatory comments by Japanese officials but also "the Japanese building many industrial plants in the U.S. that are relatively inaccessible to blacks [plus] Japanese slowness in hiring black labor or in involving black entrepreneurs." Thomas urged the Japanese to undertake an immediate change in policy, on pain of a selective consumer boycott. She added pointedly, "Perhaps the Japanese have forgotten so soon how they were characterized as 'the yellow peril,' that Japanese in America were summarily rounded up in camps and ugly racist jokes proliferated about 'fat japs.' Why this sudden virulent display of venom toward black Americans who despite all have tended to sympathize with the Japanese?"[56]

The press campaign for a Japanese boycott was unleashed in August 1988, just as the Civil Liberties Act was passed by Congress and signed by President

Reagan. No mainstream African American newspapers editorially praised or supported H.R. 442. Instead, they maintained an eerie silence. Only a single writer, Noma LeMoine, chair of the Black Caucus of the California Democratic Party, expressed her joy at celebrating the law with her Nisei friends. Conversely, its enactment catalyzed writer Herbert Dyer Jr. to weigh in strongly against redress. Dyer claimed that the awarding of reparations was a particular "slap in the face" to black Americans in the wake of Japanese officials' criticism of African Americans. Pointing to foreign aid to rebuild Europe and Asia as unfairly prioritized over aid to black Americans, Dyer noted that because of American naval defense of Japan, "for the past 43 years, the Japanese have been able to concentrate their energies almost exclusively in commerce and industry. They have now surpassed even the U.S. in produc- ing goods of high quality and low cost (to themselves)—from cameras to cars. Yet, they have erected virtually insurmountable trade barriers, including high tariffs, which severely restrict entry of American products or disallow them altogether." Redress for Japanese Americans, like other aid to Japan, was undeserved. "True, herding Japanese Americans into concentration camps was wrong. But so was slavery and the theft of Indian lands. The questions become, then, in light of today's realities, who is more deserving to be paid back for past atrocities perpetrated against them—Japanese Americans or Black Americans?"[57]

Dyer's comments seem to have summed up the thinking of many Afri- can Americans, since his column anticipated a number of similar pieces. In 1990 the *Cleveland Call & Post* decried the granting of redress to Japanese Americans when the government had not offered blacks reparations for slavery.[58] It is not clear whether the *Call & Post*'s position was influenced by the renewed fury unleashed among African Americans after Japanese justice minister Seiroku Kajiyama equated blacks with prostitutes as dangerous elements that damaged their surrounding areas. The JACL and the NCRR joined the NAACP in organizing picketing of the Japanese consulate in Los Angeles to protest the racist remarks and to demand apologies.[59]

Meanwhile, the *Atlanta Daily World*, for its part, challenged the basis of redress by recycling discredited rumors of espionage. While its editors agreed grudgingly that Japanese Americans who received redress should be compensated for their suffering, they insisted that the government had acted properly: "There were Japanese American spies on the West Coast. And Japanese-Americans had been intimidated or brainwashed by members of the Japanese consulates in Los Angeles and San Francisco. Internment was an over-reaction. But the sudden treacherous attack on Pearl Harbor shocked and horrified the nation. That sneak attack must be accorded much of the blame for the unjust reaction, derived from fear, that resulted."⁶⁰

The *World* restated its thesis five years later in another editorial, ostensibly condemning the Japanese government's refusal to properly apologize for its actions during World War II and to offer compensation. "While Washington has voted millions to compensate Japanese families and kin for internment in California during the war (there were Japanese American spies there, which did pose a danger, contrary to recent claims), Tokyo is not proposing to compensate victims of Japanese atrocities."⁶¹ The phrase "Japanese families and kin," along with the editorial juxtaposition of the two governments, presented Japanese Americans as foreigners.

Once the initial reaction to redress wore off, there were no further expressions of dissent in the mainstream black press. Rather, over the years that followed, there was silence. In 1991 *Michigan Chronicle* columnist Horace Sheffield offered editorial praise for the apology to Japanese Americans. Sheffield's seems to have remained the sole real positive comment in the black press until late 1998, over a decade after H.R. 442, when several journals reprinted a patriotic address by Federal Communications Commission (FCC) chair William E. Kennard:

> Founded in the spirit of indomitable independence, and guided by principles, of liberty, justice and equality, our nation has been challenged throughout its history to reconcile those lofty notions with some ugly political realities. From the abolition of slavery to women's suffrage, from the civil rights movement to reparations for Japanese-Americans interned during World War II, America has usually managed to find ways to do the right thing—although not always at the right time.⁶²

In the years after 1988, the awarding of redress to Japanese Americans remained African Americans' most powerful argument in favor of slavery reparations, most notably the authoritative pro-reparations manifesto, Randall Robinson's best seller *The Debt*. The redress law provided a new legitimacy to African American claims—to a certain degree it made them thinkable. Even though direct endorsement of redress by African Americans might have been rare, if imitation (or citation) can be considered the sincerest form of flattery, then African American reparations activists paid repeated homage to Japanese Americans in using the grant of redress as an argument in their own favor.⁶³ In January 1988 Dr. Robert Brock, head of the

Self-Determination Committee, Inc., filed a class action suit for relief. The group stated that its claim was based on that for the "interment" of Japanese Americans and the fact that Japanese Americans stood to receive $20,000 for each Japanese who had been "interred" for three years.[64] Queen Mother Audley Moore, by then almost ninety years old, pushed the same comparison in a speech at a public rally: "The Japanese people were just awarded $20,000 each for America's mistreatment of them, for putting them in camps during World War II. When will our elected officials, our people in Congress, begin to demand reparations for the almost irreparable damage that slavery did to our people?" The African-American Summit led by Nation of Islam minister Louis Farrakhan and former Gary, Indiana, mayor Richard Hatcher approved a resolution for emigration costs or for reparations on the model of reparations awarded Japanese Americans.[65]

Official efforts followed. In January 1989 real estate broker Ray C. Jenkins of Michigan proposed legislation for slavery reparations, which was then introduced by First District representative John Conyers. Conyers's bill, H.R. 40, the Commission to Study Reparations Proposals for African Americans Act, was based explicitly on the proposal for a historical commission that gave rise to the CWRIC.[66] In addition, Bill Owens, a black state representative in Massachusetts, introduced a reparations bill in the state assembly to entitle each African American person descended from slaves a fixed amount as compensation for their ancestors' labor. Owens pointed to redress as a precedent: "The Japanese were paid for the loss of work and their loss of housing during the internment. [African Americans] should also be rewarded for being denied fair treatment and decent housing when our ancestors were slaves."[67] The Detroit City Council called on Congress to appropriate money as a reparations fund for educational purposes.[68]

While black activists repeatedly cited redress as a precedent for their own claims for slavery reparations, Japanese American support for reparations for slavery was at best lukewarm. A few prominent activists, most notably Eric Yamamoto, a member of the *coram nobis* legal team, expressed their warm solidarity with black efforts. Yamamoto stated that the support of Japanese Americans for African American reparations and their activism in other efforts "in the repair of other groups' wounds and the mending of tears in society's fabric" would determine the true legacy of Japanese American redress.[69] However, the mass of Japanese Americans did not line up in support of reparations for slavery. While the hostile reaction of the black community to H.R. 442 surely did not encourage them, Japanese Americans were quick to point out the difference between redress, which had been directed at official injustice to living people, and reparations for slavery, which were directed at past injustice perpetrated by individuals. The laws proposed by Conyers and Owens did not provide for payments to the actual victims of conduct, but to their descendants. (The Owens bill, moreover, provided for payment by Massachusetts taxpayers for slavery on a nationwide basis.) Robert Matsui and JACL national director Ron Wakabayashi insisted that since the mass of Japanese Americans who were removed were citizens, unlike enslaved African Americans, their situation was unique and deserved particular remedies.[70]

By 1994 black support for reparations had peaked. The National Coalition of Blacks for Reparations in America (N'COBRA) occupied a visible place in black communities. A number of celebrated African Americans, including Jesse Jackson, Coretta Scott King, the rap group Public Enemy, and the director Spike Lee (who named his production company 40 Acres and a Mule Films in honor of the mythic first reparations proposal), backed the project. However, movement activists were not able to achieve mass support. While Conyers continued to serve as an advocate of reparations, his bill to study the question remained stalled in the House Judiciary Committee.[71] Members of the CBC, though they frequently discussed the question of reparations—including at an annual legislative weekend that explored the background of how the Japanese Americans fared—did not reach any consensus on action. In 1995 a federal appeals court ruled that federal district courts had no jurisdiction to hear lawsuits to obtain damages for slavery.[72]

The Japanese American redress campaign forms part of an ongoing national conversation about "race, rights and reparation" (to cite the title of the law casebook on the Japanese American cases).[73] The artisans of the redress movement of the 1970s forged a powerful weapon for the speaking of truth to power. Long before the advent of government bodies such as the CWRIC (which, again, many activists initially opposed), movement activists sponsored events such as the Days of Remembrance and community oral history projects, as well as memoirs and family conversations, to give victims of confinement space to break the silence of shame and to testify to their experience. The emphasis on "breaking the silence" by former inmates offers an interesting parallel to the existential "coming out" experience that lay at the ideological core of the contemporary lesbian/gay liberation movement.[74]

In judging the redress campaign, it is important not to lose sight of the genuine, if sometimes naively expressed, climate of solidarity against racist oppression that characterized its early stages, or of the role of African American supporters. Much of the earliest and strongest outside backing for reparative justice came from California-based black civil rights and political leaders—Mervyn Dymally, in particular, deserves enormous credit for his unsung leading role as a champion of redress. It is an irony of history that while West Coast black political leaders (apart from Augustus Hawkins) remained fairly inactive in reaching out to Nisei during World War II, they comprised the most prominent faction of the black community in support of redress during the 1970s. Conversely, the national African American press, which had offered disproportionate wartime backing for the rights of Japanese Americans, was largely silent on the issue of redress.

Yet as the redress movement evolved, there was a growing disconnect between Japanese Americans and African Americans. As redress advocates focused their efforts on congressional action, they looked to draw conservatives' votes. In the process, they distanced themselves from the larger antiracist agenda of the original movement. The historian is tempted to ask whether the failure of Japanese American leaders to address the interests of black communities deterred African Americans outside of Congress and national politics from offering greater support for the rights of Japanese Americans.

That said, African American positions toward Japanese Americans and redress were clearly influenced heavily by their attitudes toward Japan, over which Japanese Americans had no control. The simmering resentment that had built up in the black community against Japan rebounded unfairly against Japanese Americans, as black journalists and militants reacted to passage of the 1988 law by a stream of commentary, much of it negative, associating Japanese Americans with Japan as essentially foreign.

In any case, despite the impressive model offered by the redress movement for human rights internationally, on the domestic front the campaign reflected a continuing tension between universalistic principles and solidarity against racism, on the one hand, and patriotic particularism, on the other. The cleavages it produced between blacks and Japanese Americans remained visible, and may have contributed to muting the larger meaning of both the wartime events and their legacy for American society as a whole.

NOTES

1. This section summarizes, with a few important additions, a longer discussion of postwar relations between African Americans and Nisei. *See* GREG ROBINSON, AFTER CAMP: PORTRAITS IN MIDCENTURY JAPANESE AMERICAN LIFE AND POLITICS 217–40 (2012).

2. *See* Greg Robinson and Toni Robinson, Korematsu *and Beyond: Japanese Americans and the Origins of Strict Scrutiny*, 68 L. & Contemp. Probs. 29–55 (Spring 2005)

3. Howard Imazeki, *In Our Voice*, editorial, *Hokubei Mainichi*, June 29, 1963

4. *See, e.g.*, Saburo Kido, *Noted Negro Attorney Who Battled for Civil Rights Answers*, Pac. Citizen, July 19, 1963, at 1–2.

5. Bill Hosokawa, JACL in Quest of Justice 318 (1982).

6. Jerry Enomoto, *By the Board*, Pac. Citizen, Sept. 25, 1964, at 1; Mary Ikuta, *Proposition 14 Spurs Housewife Reaction*, Kashu Mainichi, Nov. 2, 1964, at 1.

7. *See* Phyl Newbeck, Virginia Hasn't Always Been for Lovers: Interracial Marriage Bans and the Case of Richard and Mildred Loving (2004); Susan Koshy, Sexual Naturalization: Asian Americans and Miscegenation (2004).

8. *NAACP Attorney Reveals Store Picketing in Fresno Was Action Not Authorized*, Pac. Citizen, Sept. 6, 1963, at 3; *Negro Weekly Charges Anti-Japanese Sermons Result of $25,000 "Pay-offs,"* N.Y. Nichi Bei, June 17, 1965, at 1; *Readers Express Firsthand Views*, Chi. Defender, Feb. 6, 1967, at 12.

9. James Farmer, *cited in* Taxie Kusanoki, *Color the Nisei Conservative?*, N.Y. Nichi Bei, May 26, 1966, at 1.

10. *Cool It, Dad, Cool It, You Can't Win*, Pitt. Courier, Apr. 30, 1966, at 8B; Ernest Dunbar, *Memo from the Ghetto: The Dispirit of '67*, Look, Sept. 19, 1967; Charles V. Hamilton, *Genocide Is Possible, Says Black Educator*, Chi. Defender, Aug. 3, 1968, at 1.

11. *Justice for Nisei*, Chi. Defender, Nov. 14, 1966, at 13.

12. *We Cannot Understand*, Balt. Afro-Am., Nov. 12, 1966, at 1. *See also* Otis W. Watson, *Congressmen and Flag-Burners*, Norfolk J. & Guide, July 22, 1967, at 7.

13. On the "Yellow Power" movement, see, for example, William Wei, The Asian American Movement (1993); Daryl J. Maeda, Chains of Babylon: The Rise of Asian America (2009). On Yuri Kochiyama, see Diane C. Fujino, Heartbeat of Struggle: The Revolutionary Life of Yuri Kochiyama (2005).

14. Undated statement [1972?], Asian Americans for Action, excerpted in Kazu Iijima, testimony before the CWRIC, New York City, Nov. 23, 1981 (on file with the Tamiment Library, New York University, ECJAR files, Box 6, George Yuzawa Papers).

15. Much of this section summarizes a longer account of redress in Greg Robinson, A Tragedy of Democracy 292–99 (2009).

16. On the movement to repeal Title II, see Masumi Izumi, *Prohibiting "American Concentration Camps": Repeal of the Emergency Detention Act and the Public Historical Memory of the Japanese American Internment*, 74 Pac. Hist. Rev. 165–93 (2005).

17. Augustus Hawkins, *Concentration Camps Violate Constitution*, L.A. Sentinel, Sept. 12, 1971; James Fleming, *Concentration Camps Now and Then*, Balt. Afro-Am., Feb. 19, 1971; David Cunningham, There's Something Happening Here: The New Left, the Klan, and FBI Counterintelligence (2005).

18. On the development of the redress movement, see Mitchell Maki, Harry Kitano, & S. Megan Berthold, Achieving the Impossible Dream: How Japanese Americans Obtained Redress (1999).

19. Robert Sadamu Shimabukuro, Born in Seattle: The Campaign for Japanese American Redress (2003).

20. Mike Masaoka with Bill Hosokawa, They Call Me Moses Masaoka 322 (1987).

21. President Gerald Ford, Proclamation 4417, "Confirming the Termination of the Executive Order Authorizing Japanese-American Internment during World War II," Feb. 19, 1976, https://www.fordlibrarymuseum.gov/library/speeches/760111p.htm.

22. William Hohri, Repairing America: An Account of the Movement for Japanese-American Redress (1988). In addition to lobbying for the Lowry Bill, Hohri instituted a class action suit for damages resulting from the mass confinement of Japanese Americans. The suit, *Hohri v. U.S.*, was filed in 1983 and ultimately dismissed.

23. Kai Bird, The Chairman: John J. McCloy and the Making of the American Establishment 8 (1992).

24. "Recommendations," *reprinted in* U.S. Commission on Wartime Relocation and Internment of Civilians, Personal Justice Denied 459 (1996).

25. *Id.* A single member of the CWRIC, California Republican congressman Dan Lungren, dissented from the final recommendation.

26. U.S. Congress, Japanese American and Aleutian Wartime Relocation Hearings Before the Subcommittee on Administrative Law and Government Relations of the Committee on the Judiciary, House of Representatives, Ninety-Eighth Congress, Second Session on H.R. 3387, H.R. 4110, and H.R. 4322, June 20, 21, 27, and Sept. 12, 1984, (1985); Maki, Kitano, & Berthold, *supra* note 18, at 190

27. Peter Irons, ed., Justice Delayed: The Record of the Japanese American Internment Cases 34 (1989).

28. *Id.*

29. Maki et al., *supra* note 18, at 149.

30. Phil Tajitsu Nash, e-mail to author, May 28, 2012.

31. *A Blemish on the Collective Conscience of the United States*, Phila. Trib., Aug. 13, 1977, at 6. *See also Japanese Should Be Compensated, AFSC Contends*, Phila. Trib., July 17, 1981, at 7.

32. On Dymally and redress, see Miya Iwataki, *Congressman Mervyn M. Dymally— Unsung Hero*, NCRR Archives, http://www.ncrr-la.org/NCRR_archives/dymally/dymally.htm.

33. Statement by Vernon Jordan, National Urban League, for the U.S. Commission on Wartime Relocation and Internment of Civilians Hearings in New York City, Nov. 23, 1981 (on file with the Tamiment Library, New York University, ECJAR files, Box 6, George Yuzawa Papers).

34. Basil Paterson, message to Commission chair [Joan] Bernstein and distinguished members of the U.S. Commission on Wartime Relocation and Internment of Civilians, Nov. 1981, in *id.*

35. Ronald Dellums, *The Total Community*, in Only What We Could Carry: The Japanese American Internment Experience 33–34 (Lawson Fusao Inada, ed., 2000).

36. Simon Anekwe, *Jesse Makes Impressive Showing*, N.Y. Amsterdam News, Feb. 13, 1988, at 1; Naomi Hirahara, L.A. Sentinel, May 19, 1988, at A7; *Asian-Americans for Dinkins Group Formed*, N.Y. Amsterdam News, Apr. 8, 1989, at 6.

37. *Black Spokesman Supports Redress*, N.Y. Nichi Bei, Mar. 11, 1982.

38. John E. Jacob, *Remedying a Wrong*, NORFOLK J. & GUIDE, Sept. 12, 1984, at 4.

39. On the history of the African American reparations movement, see, for example, Joe R. Feagin and Eileen O'Brien, *The Growing Movement for Reparations*, *in* WHEN SORRY ISN'T ENOUGH : THE CONTROVERSY OVER APOLOGIES AND REPARATIONS FOR HUMAN INJUSTICE 341–46 (Roy Brooks, ed., 1990); John Torpey, *Paying for the Past: The Movement for Reparations for African Americans*, 3 J. HUM. RTS. 171–87 (2004).

40. *Black Reparations Meeting Set Sunday*, L.A. SENTINEL, Nov. 19, 1981, at A4; *Black Group Sets Meeting*, L.A. SENTINEL, Jan. 28, 1982, at A13.

41. Yusuf A. Salaam, *Books: The Savage Surf Lashing History's Shores*, N.Y. AMSTERDAM NEWS, Oct. 16, 1982, at 46.

42. Simon Anekwe, *1,000 Expected at Tribunal*, N.Y. AMSTERDAM NEWS, Nov. 13, 1982, at 3.

43. *Back-to-Africa Speaker Opposes Redress*, N.Y. NICHI BEI, Feb. 18, 1982. Reynolds's reference was presumably to the 1948 Japanese Evacuation Claims Act, which awarded token financial compensation (not land) for actual losses provoked by removal. *See* ROBINSON, *supra* note 15, at 276–83.

44. PORTLAND OBSERVER, *cited in Japanese Americans*, PITT. COURIER, Mar. 26, 1983, at 4. Similar sentiments were expressed shortly afterward by renowned sydicated columnist Carl Rowan. Carl Rowan, *Taking Guilt Trips and Making Amends*, PITT. PRESS, June 26, 1983, at 10.

45. Stanley G. Robertson, *LA Confidential: Reparations for Blacks?* (3 parts), L.A. SENTINEL, July 7, 14, and 21, 1983.

46. Stanley G. Robertson, *LA Confidential: Reparations Series Draws Letters*, L.A. SENTINEL, Aug. 4, 1983, at A6.

47. Rozell Leavell, *Due: 40 Acres, Mule*, L.A. SENTINEL, Oct. 1, 1987, at A6.

48. *Dymally Challenges Black Leaders to Seek Reparations Bill Like Japanese Americans*, JET, Aug. 22, 1988, cited in *The Constitution and Black Americans*, N.Y. AMSTERDAM NEWS, Dec. 10, 1988, at 15.

49. MAKI ET AL., *supra* note 18, at 59.

50. Stanley E. Tolliver, *Pity Poor Nakasone*, CLEV. CALL & POST, Oct. 23, 1986, at 8A.

51. *Blacks, Minorities Urged to Boycott Japanese Cars*, PITT. COURIER, Oct. 11, 1986, at 1.

52. *Saying "I'm Sorry" . . . Is Not Enough!*, PHILA. TRIB., Oct. 24, 1986, at 5B.

53. Susan Chira, *The Melting Pot Is a Confusing Idea to the Japanese*, N.Y. TIMES, July 31, 1988, at E9.

54. Robert Shepard, *Blacks Blast Japanese Racism*, PITT. COURIER, Aug. 13, 1988; Simon Anekwe, *Japanese Prime Minister Apologizes for Racist Quips*, N.Y. AMSTERDAM NEWS, Aug. 20, 1988. Rep. Charles Rangel, who also attended the press conference, was insistent that, despite their outrage, black Americans did not wish to become a vehicle for anti-Japanese prejudice in the United States. Charles Baillou, *Japanese Minister's Anti-Black Comments Draw Sharp Criticisms*, N.Y. AMSTERDAM NEWS, Aug. 13, 1988.

55. David E. Sanger, *Japan Apologizes for a Racal Slur*, N.Y. TIMES, Aug. 16, 1988, at A11.

56. *Boycott Japanese Products Now!*, CHI. DEFENDER, Aug. 17, 1988, *reprinted in* PITT. COURIER, Aug. 20, 1988. *See also* Dorothy Gilliam, *Japan: Ignorance or Racism?*, WASH. POST, Aug. 1, 1988, at D3; *Japan in Trouble with Black Press*, PITT. COURIER, Aug. 20, 1988, at 1.

57. Noma LeMoine, *I "Understand" the Rainbow*, L.A. SENTINEL, Sept. 22, 1988, at C1; Herbert Dyer Jr., *Reparations: Another Slap in the Face?*, PITT. COURIER, Sept. 17, 1988.

58. *Distorted Priorities*, CALL & POST, Oct. 11, 1990, at A4.

59. Marsha Mitchell, *Black-, Japanese-Americans Unite; Protest Official's Insult*, L.A. SENTINEL, Oct. 4, 1990, at A1.

60. *1941 & 1989*, ATLA. DAILY WORLD, Sept. 8, 1989, at 6.

61. *No Reparations!*, ATLA. DAILY WORLD, Dec. 15, 1994, at 4.

62. Horace Sheffield, *U.S Admits a Wrong—Finally!*, MICH. CHRON., Jan. 16, 1991, at A7; William E. Kennard, *Lift Every Voice*, PITT. COURIER, Dec. 19, 1998, at 5.

63. Among the dozens of examples of such discourse in the period following enactment of H.R. 442, see *Letters*, N.Y. AMSTERDAM NEWS, Dec. 24, 1988, at 14; Robert E. McTyre, *The Reparations Appeal Is Gaining National Focus*, PITT. COURIER, Mar. 18, 1989, at 3; Constance Burts Jackson, *Why Reparations for African Americans*, COLUMBUS TIMES, Apr. 25, 1989, at B1; Julianne Malveaux, *Paying Reparations to Blacks: Still Waiting for 40 Acres and a Mule*, USA TODAY, May 15, 1989, at 8A; Chester L. Blair, *Case for Black Reparations*, CHI. DEFENDER, Nov. 28, 1989, at 10; Ron Daniels, *A Matter of Unfinished Business*, L.A. TIMES, Oct. 28, 1990, at M7; Parren J. Mitchell, *America Apologizes to Japanese Citizens*, AFRO-AMERICAN RED STAR, Nov. 3, 1990, at A5; RANDALL ROBINSON, THE DEBT: WHAT AMERICA OWES TO BLACKS 36 (2000). For a comparison of the two reparations movements, see Rhoda E. Howard-Hassman, *Getting to Reparations: Japanese American and African Americans*, 83 SOC. FORCES, 823–40 (2004).

64. *The Constitution and Black Americans*, N.Y. AMSTERDAM NEWS, Dec. 10, 1988, at 15. Brock's claim was quickly thrown out of court on jurisdictional grounds.

65. Yusef A-Salaam, *Hundreds Salute Madam Moore*, N.Y. AMSTERDAM NEWS, Aug. 6, 1988, at 22; Yuri Kageyama, *Reparations, Demanded for Slavery*, PHILA. TRIB., Aug. 2, 1994, at 5B; Thomas B. Edsall & Gwen Ifill, *Farrakhan Accuses U.S. of Acting to Hurt Blacks; Reparations Urged for Slaves' Descendants*, WASH. POST, Apr. 24, 1989, at A3.

66. McTyre, *supra* note 63, at 3.

67. Bernard L. Ritter, *Time Is Right*, PITT. COURIER, Mar. 18, 1989, at 1.

68. Mitchell Landsberg, *More and More Blacks Support Idea of Reparations for Slaves' Labor*, L.A. TIMES, July 30, 1989, at 21.

69. *See, e.g.*, Eric K. Yamamoto, *Racial Reparations: Japanese American Redress and African American Claims*, 40 B.C. L. REV. 477 (1998); Eric K. Yamamoto, Susan K. Serrano, & Michelle Natividad Rodriguez, *American Racial Justice on Trial—Again: African American Reparations, Human Rights, and the War on Terror*, 101 MICH. L. REV. 1269 (2003).

70. *Black Group Sets Meeting*, L.A. SENTINEL, Jan. 28, 1982, at A13; Landsberg, *supra* note 68, at 21.

71. THEODORE RUETER, THE POLITICS OF RACE: AFRICAN AMERICANS AND THE POLITICAL SYSTEM 16–18 (1995).

72. Lena Williams, *Blacks Press the Case for Reparations for Slavery*, N.Y. TIMES, July 21, 1994, at B10; Simon Anekwe, *Congressional Weekend to Examine Thorny Issues*, N.Y. AMSTERDAM NEWS, Sept. 16, 1989, at 6; *Oregon Man Sues U.S. for $3 Million for Slavery*, L.A. SENTINEL, Apr. 14, 1994, at A1; Bob Egelko, *Court Rules against Blacks in Suit for Slavery Damages; Appellate Panel Votes 3–0 to Uphold Several Lower Court Rulings*, ST. LOUIS

Post-Dispatch, Dec. 5, 1995, at 11B; James Bolden, *Reparations Debate Heats Up in Courts, Black Communities*, L.A. Sentinel, July 28, 1994, at A1.

73. Eric K. Yamamoto et al., eds., Race, Rights and Reparation: Law of the Japanese American Internment (2001).

74. On the redress movement and the uses of historical memory, see, for example, Alice Yang Murray, Historical Memories of Japanese American Internment and the Struggle for Redress (2008); Karen L. Ishizuka, Lost and Found: Reclaiming the Japanese American Internment (2006). On the uses and evolution of "Internment narratives," see Greg Robinson, "*What I Did in Camp*," 30 Amerasia J. 49–58 (2004).

Part III

CHALLENGES

7

The Birth and Death of Affirmative Action

Is Resurrection Possible?

STEPHEN STEINBERG

This essay provides a historical perspective on both the evolution of affirmative action policy and the discourses that it has engendered. It is not just that historical perspective is good academic protocol. As I argue below, a fatal flaw of much of the popular and academic discourse on affirmative action is that it treats affirmative action as an ahistorical abstraction. Nor is this elision of history politically innocent. Once affirmative action is stripped bare of history, it is easily portrayed as an unsightly wart on the body politic, calling for the surgeon's scalpel.

Only by considering the historical basis of affirmative action policy can we grasp its normative and practical significance. Affirmative action is *about* history: the exclusion of whole groups from entire job sectors for all of American history. This needs to be underscored because so much of affirmative action discourse lapses into facile reductionism: whether individuals should be penalized for crimes that they did not commit; whether it is fair to give preference to the son of a black doctor over the daughter of a white garbage collector; whether affirmative action engenders feelings of inferiority among its recipients; and whether, as Justice Scalia once quipped, we are using the disease as cure. To repeat, when we take up the issue of affirmative action, we are dealing with the exclusion of whole groups from entire job sectors for all of American history, and, as is easily demonstrated, this is a trend that continues down to the present.

Opponents of affirmative action often cite the significant strides that blacks have made during the post–civil rights period. But much of this progress is a direct result of affirmative action programs that pried doors open that have been shut throughout the nation's history. This begins with court decisions in 1971 affirming the constitutionality of the Philadelphia Plan,

and ends with a series of decisions in the late 1980s that essentially gutted affirmative action policy, however much this was masked by a calculated "incrementalism." In July 2003 the cover story of the *Black Commentator* was couched in less prosaic language. The editors called their piece "The Slow and Tortured Death of Affirmative Action." The subtitle was equally blunt: "Redress of Racial Wrongs No Longer Public Policy."[1]

One would have to go back to the discourse over slavery to find such an outpouring of misguided erudition: of philosophical treatises by learned scholars that elide elemental truths or that obscure these truths behind a smokescreen of sophistry and obfuscation.

Given that the political Right has played such a prominent role in the crusade against affirmative action, it would be easy to blame the Right and their intellectual minions for the tantamount death of affirmative action. However, in this essay I contend that much of the culpability rests with liberals and even those farther to the left—those proverbial "friends of the Negro." Not only have they equivocated or defaulted in the struggle to save affirmative action policy, but, as I show below, most of the earliest and most vehement opposition to affirmative action came from the ranks of liberals. Indeed, long before the words "affirmative action" entered the political lexicon, it was liberals—notably, Jewish liberals at *Commentary* magazine—who forged the anti–affirmative action discourse that later was appropriated by conservatives.[2] Not only did conservatives stoke popular antagonism to affirmative action policy, but, as Nancy MacLean has shown, they used this issue to resuscitate conservatism from a long period of senescence and decline and make it into a potent rival for political hegemony.[3]

Misconceptions about the nature, purposes, and evolution of affirmative action policy also abound on the left. Before I get into what affirmative action is, let me say what it is *not*. Affirmative action is not the brainchild of "the multicultural left," as Michael Lind wrote in 1995.[4] Nor does it spring from a newfangled theory of democracy that privileges "group rights" over "individual rights," as Nathan Glazer and Sidney Hook have propounded.[5] Nor is the purpose of affirmative action to "diversify the elite," as Henry Louis Gates Jr. averred in an interview in the *Progressive* in 1998.[6] Nor was affirmative action invented to cheat Stephen Carter of the esteem that he so richly deserves.[7] Nor was affirmative action designed as a political ploy to drive a wedge in the liberal coalition, by fomenting a schism between organized labor, Jews, and blacks, a spurious theory promulgated by Hugh Davis Graham and uncritically accepted by two generations of scholars.[8] Nor, finally, would "racial healing" be served if liberals threw in the towel over affirmative action, as Paul Starr argued in *The American Prospect* and Jeffrey Klein reiterated on the pages of *Mother Jones*.[9]

The extent of bad faith and spineless capitulation within liberal/left circles is not only deplorable, but it has had dire political consequences. Here we can take a lesson from history. As Reconstruction unraveled at the end of the nineteenth century, southern Redemptionists gloated that "all the fire has gone out of the Northern philanthropic fight for the rights of man."[10] I fear that historians will look back on the end of the Second Reconstruction and conclude that liberals were again complicit in the restoration of the status quo ante.

A consistent flaw in the discourse on affirmative action, as Stanley Fish contended in an op-ed in the *New York Times*, is that affirmative action is treated as an abstraction. To quote Fish:

Suppose you were arguing for something but were told that you would have to make your case without the facts that supported it. This is the situation proponents of affirmative action face when they find themselves defending their position in terms of principle rather than policy.

A policy is an attempt to deal with a real-world problem. If that problem is recharacterized in the language of principle—if you stop asking, "What's wrong and how can we fix it?" and ask instead, "Is it fair?"—the real world fades away and is replaced by the arid world of philosophical puzzles.[11]

Fish has a point. Affirmative action is difficult to justify in terms of abstract principle. Affirmative action *does* classify individuals on the basis of race and gender. It *does* conflict with the cardinal principle of the civil rights movement itself: a color-blind society. It *does* institute a system of preferences that evoke distaste and are difficult to justify in terms of democratic theory. In short, affirmative action is a bad *idea*—that is, from the standpoint of abstract theory. We might as well come out and say it: affirmative action is "a necessary evil," made necessary by over three centuries of legal segregation that puts an oppressed minority at an almost insuperable disadvantage.

Does this mean that the disease is being used as cure? Hardly, since affirmative action is not driven by racial animus, and no one proposes to subject whites to permanent injury. On the contrary, the much-maligned racial preferences are designed to override barriers in employment and education that perpetuate racial inequalities and therefore racial stigma as well. A better analogy would be to a vaccine, where weakened cells of the disease are injected to stimulate the body's immune system. Affirmative action is not racist, but, on the contrary, it is an *antidote* to racism. Or as Justice Blackmun famously wrote in the 1978 *Bakke* case, "in order to get beyond racism, we must first take race into account."[12]

So let us heed Fish's admonition: "Those who support affirmative action should give up searching for theoretical consistency—a goal at once impossible and unworthy—and instead seek strategies with the hope of relieving the pain of people who live in the world and not in the never-never land of theory." Let us beware of the trap of addressing real problems in an imperfect world with remedies that pretend that we live in Plato's Republic (which was hardly a racial utopia, for that matter).

A similar note is struck by Charles Mills in *The Racial Contract*. Mills contends that alongside the social contract at the center of Western political thought is an unacknowledged racial contract that provides the framework for the white supremacist state. Like donning a new pair of glasses, recognition of this racial contract casts American political institutions in a wholly different light. As Mills writes:

The "Racial Contract" throws open the doors of orthodox political philosophy's hermetically sealed, stuffy little universe and lets the world rush into its sterile white halls, a world populated not by abstract citizens but by white, black, brown, yellow, red beings, interacting with, pretending not to see, categorizing, judging, negotiating, allying, exploiting, struggling with each other in large measure according to race—the world, in short, in which we all actually live.[13]

To talk about affirmative action, we need to talk about the world in which we actually live: a society riven by race and a system of occupational segregation drawn along racial and gender lines. To repeat, we must confront the reality of whole groups excluded from entire job sectors for all of American history. How else can we rescue American democracy from its own contradictions?

As the title of my essay suggests, the historical trajectory of affirmative action resembles the dramatic arc of a play: of rising action, climax leading to crisis, and tragic denouement. Perhaps this is because life imitates art, perhaps because politics often degenerate into political theater. In any event, this dramaturgical trope is useful for capturing the strange history of affirmative action.

The "rights" phase of the civil rights movement culminated with the passage of the Civil Rights Act of 1964 and the Voting Rights Act of 1965. Today virtually the entire nation celebrates the civil rights struggle as a triumph of democracy. We must remember, however, that the nation's vaunted democratic institutions failed to rectify these civil wrongs until the rise of grassroots insurgency in the South, and even then, not until the entire society was thrown into such crisis that change became a political imperative. Moreover, as important as the 1964 Civil Rights Act and and 1965 Voting Rights Act were, they only restored rights that were supposedly guaranteed by the Reconstruction Amendments a century earlier. These were rights acquired in the decade between 1865 and 1875 only to be lost in the 1890s. The question we must confront is whether the nation is repeating history with the gutting of affirmative action—that is, wiping out in the 1980s and the ensuing decades rights that were won in the 1960s and 1970s. If this is "progress," it is the progress of a people on a historical treadmill.

As is often pointed out, the civil rights revolution was about "liberty," not "equality." It conferred the full rights of citizenship on blacks, but it did nothing to address the deep inequalities that were the legacy of two centuries of slavery and a century of Jim Crow. This idea was given vernacular expression by civil rights leaders who declared that "there is little value in a Negro's obtaining the right to be admitted to hotels and restaurants if he has no cash in his pocket and no job." In 1964 Bayard Rustin wrote: "What is the value of winning access to public accommodations for those who lack money to use them?" That same year Herbert Humphrey commented in congressional debate: "What good does it do a Negro to be able to eat in a fine restaurant if he cannot afford to pay the bill?" In 1968 Martin Luther King Jr. wrote: "What good is it to be allowed to eat in a restaurant if you can't afford a hamburger?" Indeed, the rallying cry for the 1963 March on Washington was "For Jobs and Freedom," with the implication that without jobs, freedom is an empty promise.[14]

The upshot of this conceptual shift from liberty to equality was a demand for "compensatory treatment" in jobs and education. In 1963—a year before passage of the 1964 Civil Rights Act and a decade before "affirmative action" evolved as policy—this idea was debated in no less public a forum than the *New York Times Magazine* under the caption "Should There Be 'Compensation' for Negroes?" Whitney Young argued that the enormous gap in incomes and living standards required some kind of "special effort" to open up job opportunities to blacks. Already on the defensive, he complained that this reasonable demand was being obfuscated with scare phrases like "preferential treatment" that "go against the grain of our native sense of fair play." The "no" side was argued by Kyle Haselden, an editor at *Christian Century* and author of a book entitled *The Racial Problems in Christian Perspective*. Haselden struck the chord that later would emerge as the keynote of anti–affirmative action discourse: "compensation for Negroes is a subtle but pernicious form of racism."[15]

By 1963 the words "compensation," "reparations," and "preference" had already crept into the nation's political discourse. Indeed, this issue rapidly fractured liberals into opposing camps. Some liberals pledged their support. A notable example is Charles Silberman, an editor at *Fortune Magazine* whose book *Crisis in Black and White* appeared on the *New York Times* Best Seller List for ten weeks in 1964. Silberman wrote: "If those who make the decisions in this country are really sincere about closing the gaps, they must go further than fine impartiality. We must have, in fact, special consideration if we are to compensate for the scars left by 300 years of deprivation."[16] However, other white liberals were troubled by this turn of events. In *Why We Can't Wait* King observed: "Whenever this issue of compensatory or preferential treatment for the Negro is raised, some of our friends recoil in horror. The Negro should be granted equality, they agree; but he should ask for nothing more."[17]

This last statement, penned in 1963, was tragically prescient. The underlying message of the crusade against affirmative action, waged over the past half-century, is that the nation has gone as far as it is willing to go by passing landmark civil rights legislation that restored full rights of citizenship to blacks. The renunciation of affirmative action by the nation's highest court means that there will be no further restitution for the descendants of two centuries of slavery and a century of Jim Crow.

As mentioned earlier, initial opposition to the idea of "compensatory treatment" came, not from conservatives, but from liberals, and not from ordinary liberals, but from prominent liberal supporters of the civil rights movement. The brewing discontent among liberals prompted *Commentary*, a preeminent liberal publication of the period, to sponsor a roundtable discussion on "Liberalism and the Negro." The event took place in February 1964 before an overflow audience in New York City's Town Hall. In his introduction, Podhoretz minced no words in describing the split in the liberal camp:

> I think it may be fair to say that American liberals are by now divided into two schools of thought on what is often called the Negro problem. . . . On the one side, we have those liberals whose ultimate perspective on race relations . . . envisages the gradual absorption of deserving Negroes one by one into white society. . . . Over the past two or three years, however, a new school of liberal (or perhaps it should be called radical) thought has been developing which is based on the premise . . . that "the rights and privileges of an individual rest upon the status attained by the group to which he belongs." From this premise certain points follow that are apparently proving repugnant to the traditional liberal mentality.[18]

The other white participants in the roundtable—Nathan Glazer, Sidney Hook, and Gunnar Myrdal—all declared their blanket opposition to any system of racial preference. Glazer touted the success of New York's Fair Employment Practices Law, implying that racial justice could be achieved within the same liberal framework that worked for other groups. Hook argued that, by lowering standards for "Negroes," preference was patronizing and treated blacks as second-class citizens. Myrdal cautioned that preference amounted to tokenism and that what was needed was a program to lift *all* poor people out of poverty.

James Baldwin stood alone, parrying the arguments thrust at him with his usual eloquence and resolve. To the optimistic view that the nation was making progress ("not enough progress, to be sure, but progress neverthe-less"), Baldwin had this to say:

> I'm delighted to know there've been many fewer lynchings in the year
> 1963 than there were in the year 1933, but I also have to bear in mind—
> I have to bear it in mind because my life depends on it—that there are
> a great many ways to lynch a man. The impulse in American society,
> as far as I can tell from my experience in it, has essentially been to
> ignore me when it could, and then when it couldn't, to intimidate me;
> and when that failed, to make concessions.

As the discussion wore on, it became increasingly obvious that a vast differ-ence in worldview separated Baldwin and the others. When Hook gloated over the expansion of ethical principles in American society, Baldwin re-torted:

> What strikes me here is that you are an American talking about
> American society, and I am an American talking about American so-
> ciety—both of us very concerned with it—and yet your version of
> American society is really very difficult for me to recognize. My ex-
> perience in it has simply not been yours.

What better illustration of the clash between the never-never world of theory and the world as it is actually lived, especially by those who must endure its hypocrisies and contradictions.

The meeting only confirmed Podhoretz's foreboding of "a widening split between the Negro movement and the white liberal community." Here in February 1964 was an early sign of the imminent breakup of the liberal coalition that had functioned as a bulwark of the civil rights movement. Even though affirmative action was only in its embryonic stage, the bare mention of "compensatory treatment" was enough to send white liberals fleeing to the exits, leaving blacks to fend for themselves.

Indeed, one could argue that the "crisis in liberalism" that Podhoretz declared in 1964 over black demands for "compensatory treatment" marks the genesis of the neoconservative movement. Most historians of neocon-servatism trace its origins to the 1970s, triggered by reaction to such issues as the rise of the New Left, the antiwar movement, and the strident militancy of Black Power activists that heightened tensions between Jews and blacks. Without doubt, the 1970s was the conjuncture when neoconservatism came to fruition. It is my contention, however, that the seeds were planted a de-cade earlier, precipitated by calls from civil rights leaders for "compensatory programs" in jobs and education.

Affirmative action was never formulated as a coherent policy, but evolved through a series of presidential executive orders, administrative policies, and court rulings, all reflecting shifting political currents.[19] There is general agreement that affirmative action as we know it began with executive orders issued by Presidents Kennedy and Johnson directing government contrac-tors to take affirmative action to end discrimination in hiring. But these orders lacked enforcement power and were generally ineffective. By far the most important initiative in the development of affirmative action was the Philadelphia Plan, initially drawn up by faceless bureaucrats in Johnson's Department of Labor, then shelved. James Sterba offers a fuller explanation for the shelving of the Philadelphia Plan during Johnson's administration: "[T]he Philadelphia Program ran into difficulty with the General Accounting Office for introducing further requirements after contracts were awarded. There was also the worry that the program's affirmative action requirements would run afoul of the Civil Rights Act's prohibition of quotas." The plan was abandoned after Humphrey's defeat in 1968 but was resurrected soon after Richard Nixon took office in 1969.[20] The unsung heroes of affirmative action are Arthur Fletcher, the black assistant secretary of labor who has laid claim to the title of "father of affirmative action"; his boss, Charles Shultz, who provided indispensable support; Attorney General John Mitchell, who successfully defended the revised Philadelphia Plan before the appellate court in 1969; and Nixon himself, who not only backed the plan but also risked a great deal of political capital in rallying congressional Republicans to defeat a move by Democrats to kill the plan before it could be implemented.[21]

Ironically, throughout this period, and particularly during the crucial congressional debate, the Philadelphia Plan received only equivocal sup-port from civil rights leaders, and it faced fierce opposition from labor and liberals. There has been much speculation about why Nixon backed the Philadelphia Plan, and rightly so. After all, Nixon was elected on the basis of a "southern strategy" that appealed to racial backlash, and he promptly nominated two white supremacists to the Supreme Court (both were rejected by the Senate). Some contemporaneous opponents of the Philadelphia Plan, including Bayard Rustin, saw Nixon's action as a cunning ploy to break up the liberal coalition by driving a wedge between the civil rights movement and organized labor and Jews.[22] According to the historian Hugh Davis Graham, author of the influential *The Civil Rights Era*, as Nixon pondered Shultz's proposal to resurrect the Philadelphia Plan, he was swayed by "the delicious prospect of setting organized labor and the civil rights establishment at each other's Democratic throats."[23] Elsewhere Graham has written: "Nixon wanted to drive a wedge between blacks and organized labor—between the Democrats' social activists of the 1960s and the party's traditional economic liberals—that would fragment the New Deal coalition."[24]

This, I submit, is a misreading of history. Indeed, it has been repeated so often that it has assumed the dimensions of a myth, invoked by liberals to justify their default on affirmative action. Let me suggest another explanation for Nixon's support for the Philadelphia Plan.

During the summer of 1969 there was an outbreak of highly publicized protests against discrimination in the construction trades. For documentary evidence, we need look no further than Graham's own book, *The Civil Rights Era*. Graham provides this account:

> In Chicago, job protests launched by a coalition of black neighbor-hood organizations shut down twenty-three South Side construction projects involving $85 million in contracts. . . . The demonstrations in Pittsburgh were more violent than in Chicago, but were similarly organized and focused on job discrimination in construction. One clash in Pittsburgh in late August left 50 black protestors and 12 po-licemen injured. . . . Racial violence over jobs also occurred in Seattle, and black coalitions announced job protest drives for New York, Cleveland, Detroit, Milwaukee, and Boston.[25]

Whatever political calculations led Nixon to back Fletcher's proposal to resurrect the Philadelphia Plan, one thing is clear: without pressure from below, the plan would have remained in the Labor Department's files, where it had been deposited by the outgoing Democratic administration.

As Graham claims, Nixon had little to lose by "sticking it to the Demo-cratic unions." But it is also true that, against the background of the war in Vietnam, Nixon had political reason to defuse black protest, lest he find himself confronted with a second front at home. Consider, too, the larger historical context. Nixon came to power at a juncture when liberalism was in decline and conservatism was ascendant, and he oscillated between these two poles throughout his administration.[26] For example, in the wake of the civil rights revolution and the spiral of "riots" following the 1968 assassination of Martin Luther King Jr., underscored by the Kerner Commission Report with its far-reaching recommendations for national action, Nixon had abundant reason to appease the highly publicized protests emanating from the black community.

At least conceptually, Arthur Fletcher's proposal for a revised Philadelphia Plan was consonant with core tenets of Republican ideology. This may seem implausible, given the heated opposition that eventually developed among conservatives. In 1971, however, the Philadelphia Plan was viewed as a distinctively Republican approach to job discrimination. Consider Fletcher's own account:

> I decided to go ahead with the Philadelphia Plan of putting specifications of minority employment goals in all contracts. I did this because my study and experience had convinced me that such targets were essential if we are to measure results in terms of minority employment. Without such targets, the paper compliance, and the indeterminable ineffectiveness of the government programs would go on. I had not come to Washington to preside over the continuation of the ineffective programs of the past.[27]

The Philadelphia Plan was ideologically congenial to Republicans in that it envisioned no new government programs, no make-work schemes, and no major public expenditures. Instead, it looked to the private economy to lead the nation out of its racial morass. In short, the idea that Nixon revived the Philadelphia Plan in a Machiavellian ploy to fragment the liberal coalition is patent nonsense. Nixon backed Arthur Fletcher's proposal because it allowed him to preempt the liberal agenda on civil rights with a policy predicated on contract compliance.

However—and this is where Graham's theory has some credence—once the Philadelphia Plan was enacted, it triggered fierce opposition from labor and many white liberals, as well as from the "Nixon Democrats" and hardhats who had been instrumental in his election. At this point the Philadelphia Plan became a political liability. What did Nixon do? He did an about-face and attacked the very "quotas" that he had put into place. This was also the context when Daniel Patrick Moynihan, in his capacity as adviser to the president, issued his infamous call for "benign neglect." In 1970 Nixon reached out to the building trades unions to mend fences. As the historian Nancy McLean writes: "Professing agreement with them on the need for 'voluntary' approaches, the administration backpedaled from the Philadelphia Plan and promised no 'undue zeal' in putting it into practice." The Philadelphia Plan was doomed, at least as far as the Nixon administration was concerned. According to McLean, "within a year of its proclamation, word spread that it [the Philadelphia Plan] was to die a quiet death."[28]

Notwithstanding the mounting backlash, affirmative action was destined to live and even flourish before succumbing to a slow and tortured death. The die was cast when John Mitchell's Department of Justice successfully defended the Philadelphia Plan in the federal courts. By 1972 affirmative action was extended to more than 300,000 firms doing business with the government, thus covering approximately half the nonfarm private-sector workforce.[29] This was the inception of affirmative action "as we know it."

No better mechanism has ever existed for influencing employment practices and outcomes on such a large scale. However, one by-product of the extension of affirmative action mandates to all government contractors was that colleges and universities were brought under the umbrella of affirmative action, and subject to contract compliance reviews by the Office of Federal Contract Compliance.

One of the ironies of affirmative action is that it excited far more heated opposition in the university than in the business world. As Skrentny writes: "Businesses, if left alone, do not seem to mind hiring by the numbers, or at least giving the appearance of compliance."[30] Of course, in the business world, where hiring is more concentrated, it is easier to implement goals and timetables, unlike the university, where hiring decisions are decentralized among a score of academic departments. Second, despite its liberal pretensions, the university is notorious as a site of class privilege and snobbery. It is one thing when affirmative action meant hiring blacks as linesmen at AT&T and assembly workers at GM, but another thing when it comes to Yale Law School or Harvard's English Department. It is difficult to escape the conclusion that, just as northern liberals supported integration so long as it meant integrating schools and public accommodations in the South, liberal elites supported affirmative action until it encroached on *their* institutional turf and threatened their entrenched prerogatives.

Thus the application of affirmative action mandates to higher education triggered fierce opposition among a vocal segment of the professoriat, including *Commentary* intellectuals who regarded the university as a sacrosanct refuge for Jews. For them, any semblance of "quotas" was reminiscent of the *numerus clausus*, the quota system in Eastern Europe that restricted Jewish enrollment in higher education. As Jacob Heilbrunn writes in his book on the rise of the neocons, aptly entitled *They Knew They Were Right*: "The demands of black radicals for race-based affirmative action came as a particular shock. The Jews had experienced a Jewish quota; were the blacks now, perversely, to insist on a special quota for themselves? Was merit to be supplanted by skin color?"[31] Thus the idea that students would be admitted to elite universities based on race in accordance with "quotas" was anathema, as was the newfound practice of collecting data on the racial/ethnic identity of faculty or students. Jewish organizations had long fought against the inclusion of ethnicity or religion on the Census, which also evoked dark memories of how official data were used to round up Jews destined for death camps.

Even as neoconservatism took root and extended its purview into broader areas of politics and policy, *Commentary* kept up its attack against affirmative action. The two members of the *Commentary* "family" who participated in the 1964 roundtable at Town Hall—Nathan Glazer and Sidney Hook—emerged as prominent critics during the contentious debates centered on challenges to affirmative action that reached the Supreme Court. In 1975 Glazer published the first book-length tract against affirmative action under the sardonic title *Affirmative Discrimination*. Glazer began with the rosy assessment that the passage of civil rights laws in the 1960s reflected "a national consensus" on race. At long last, color blindness was the law of the land. "Paradoxically," Glazer continues, "we then began an extensive effort to record the race, color, and (some) national origins of just about every student and employee and recipient of government benefits or services in the nation." For some, he allowed, this "monumental restructuring of public policy" was necessary to enforce laws against discrimination, but "others see it as a direct contradiction to the Constitution and the laws, and of the consensus that emerged after long struggle in the middle 1960s." Glazer went so far as to compare affirmative action to the Nuremberg laws: "We have not yet reached the degraded condition of the Nuremberg laws, but undoubtedly we will have to create a new law of personal ethnic and racial status to define just who is eligible for these benefits, to replace the laws we have banned to determine who should be subject to discrimination."[32] Glazer was circumspect in his syntax but he had waved the bloody shirt, and his message surely was not lost on his readers: affirmative action was a throwback to the worst days of persecution and a dire threat to Jewish interests. What Glazer failed to mention was that the Nuremberg laws were themselves inspired by Jim Crow in the United States.

Sidney Hook was an intellectual pugilist par excellence. In his youth, he was a Communist; as an adult he morphed into a fierce critic of the Soviet Union and a champion of American democracy. Like many of the Old Left, he reacted vindictively against the politics of the New Left during the 1960s, especially their politicization of higher education. In retrospect,

Hook's criticism of compensatory programs at the 1964 Town Hall event was only an opening salvo in a torrent of criticism and invective as the affirmative action debate took root in the 1970s and 1980s. Christopher Phelps, Hook's biographer, describes him as "a brigadier general in the academic culture wars of the 1970s and 1980s, condemning university affirmative action programs as 'quotas' and objecting to multicultural reform of the core humanities curriculum at Stanford and elsewhere."[33] Indeed, Hook used his considerable talents as a logician and a polemicist to direct his fire at the politicization of higher education and a putative lowering of academic standards. Like Glazer, he insisted that American democracy was predicated on principles of individual rights, not group rights, and was relentless in his condemnation of "the tyranny of reverse discrimination."[34]

As Benjamin Balint observes in his book *Running Commentary*, "*Commentary* launched a steady barrage on affirmative action through the 1990s, abhorring all the while the spread of affirmative action categories and the sense of 'entitlement' from blacks to other 'underprivileged' groups."[35] To be sure, there were many other sources of opposition to affirmative action, at all ranks of society. What was uniquely significant about the criticism that emanated from *Commentary* is that these erstwhile liberal intellectuals gave the anti–affirmative action crusade an articulation and a legitimacy that it previously lacked. This also marked an ideological shift in the affirmative action debate. Now affirmative action was portrayed as a tug-of-war between merit and preference, and controversy centered almost exclusively on elite colleges and professional schools. Yet as Alan Wolfe observed, "When we debate using racial preferences to admit more blacks and Hispanic students to the nation's best colleges, we are considering the fate of a shockingly small number of people."[36] Furthermore, as the affirmative action debate shifted from employment to education, it obscured the historic impact of affirmative action as an instrument of racial integration in the world of work—not only in the professions and corporate management but also in major blue-collar industries and in the vast public sector where nearly a third of all black workers are found.

The implementation of affirmative action mandates over several decades amounted to the social engineering of the first large black middle class that, unlike the middle class that Franklin Frazier lampooned in *The Black Bourgeoisie*, was anchored in the mainstream of the economy. Not only did this respectable middle class signify racial progress, but it had a transformative effect on the semiotics of blackness, for blacks and whites alike. As Ellen Willis observed, "No longer is whiteness the unquestioned cultural norm."[37]

Conversely, no longer is blackness a badge of inferiority. However, we should not lose sight of the fact that the progress of the black middle class does not signify a deracialization of labor markets, but, on the contrary, the successful implementation of affirmative action mandates for over three decades. Such progress has been stalled by the incremental gutting of affirmative action by the Supreme Court.[38]

Advocates of affirmative action were overjoyed when Justice Powell saved the *Bakke* case from defeat by ruling with the majority that "diversity" was a legitimate goal for a university and therefore could be taken into account in college admissions.[39] In retrospect, the so-called Powell compromise only prolonged the death throes of affirmative action. No longer was affirmative action predicated on the logic of reparations and the moral imperative of remedying past wrongs. Now "diversity" emerged as the governing principle with increasing minority representation in employment and education. As Justice Powell noted, diversity is a long-standing practice in college admissions. Ironically, this practice originated in the 1920s as a subterfuge for limiting Jewish enrollment at elite colleges. It was not until Jewish enrollment at Harvard reached an alarming level of 20 percent that the Board of Overseers discovered the virtues of geographical diversity.[40]

The problem with the "Powell compromise" is that it wiped away the logical underpinning of affirmative action as a remedy for past injustices. As David Hollinger writes, "affirmative action lost an element of clarity it once had when it became entangled with multiculturalism." As preference was extended to recent immigrants from Asia and Latin America, affirmative action drifted far from its original purposes, and it became harder to justify morally and politically. According to Peter Schrag, three-fourths of all legal immigrants qualify for group preferences.[41] By the 1980s what began as a squabble within the liberal coalition emerged as a full-blown anti–affirmative action crusade, now centered in the political Right. What explains this political metamorphosis?

In *Freedom Is Not Enough: The Opening of the American Workplace*, Nancy MacLean reveals how the rhetoric of compensatory treatment and the emerging political battles over affirmative action resurrected the conservative cause from the doldrums of Goldwater's defeat and the Right's inability to find any traction beyond diehard Republicans. By the early 1970s conservative pundits realized they could reap political hay from white resentment over "quotas." Now it was conservative scholars who put their talents as wordsmiths to work, and once again, *Commentary* provided a venue for the attack against affirmative action. As early as April 1973, an article railed against "the equalitarian orthodoxy."[42] It was penned by Richard Herrnstein, who two decades later would collaborate with Charles Murray to write *The Bell Curve*, which resurrected the idea that racial differences in IQ were rooted in biology.[43]

William Buckley, the founding editor of the *National Review*, also found common ground with the *Commentary* crowd. According to MacLean, Buckley "observed the work of the neoconservatives with mounting admiration and excitement as Irving Kristol, for example, argued that conservatives were defending liberal institutions from liberals' own mounting complaints." Affirmative action provided conservatives with an issue that went beyond fighting Communism and championing free enterprise. At the same time, it dispelled suspicions that conservatives were driven by bigotry and harbored a latent anti-Semitism. With this ideological facelift, conservatives could now present themselves, not as the enemy of equality, but as the champion of color blindness. Instead of opposition to blacks and civil rights, they rallied to the defense of white males against "the New Equality," which, according to Robert Nisbet, was "the gravest single threat to liberty and social initiative."[44] Thus, with the help of the neocons, old-line conservatives used the escalating dissension over affirmative action to turn the tables on liberals and to develop an ideological blueprint for the restoration of conservatives to power. Who better to orchestrate this political escapade than the nascent neocons at *Commentary* who, according to Heilbrunn, saw it as "their self-anointed role to serve as the court theologians of the right"?[45]

By the 1980s opposition to affirmative action had grown into a veritable crusade, waged by right-wing pundits and publications, with the indispensable funding of right-wing foundations and think tanks.[46] As in the case of the revolution that the partisans of counterrevolution sought to negate, the shifting political currents reached into the university and the ranks of social science. Charles Murray's 1984 book, *Losing Ground*, argued that the welfare state created the conditions that it purported to remedy: welfare dependency, nonwork, family breakdown, rising crime, moral breakdown.[47] Thomas Sowell, Glenn Loury, and a cadre of black conservatives, lavishly funded by foundations and ensconced in leading universities, put a black face on "white sociology," parrying those who claimed that sociology had sunk into the abyss of racism. Publication of *The Bell Curve* in 1994 marked the apogee of the intellectual backlash, with the reinstatement of the scientific racism that supposedly had been relinquished to the trash heap almost a century earlier. Nor was the backlash only about biology. As Adolph Reed wrote in the *Nation* in 1994: "We can trace Murray's legitimacy directly to the spinelessness, opportunism and racial bad faith of the liberals in the social-policy establishment. . . . Many of those objecting to Herrnstein and Murray's racism embrace positions that are almost indistinguishable, except for the resort to biology."[48]

This was the historical moment when racism receded into code words and circumlocutions that tapped broader ideological currents in the body politic. The electoral success of Republicans during the post–civil rights period was not the result only of a conspicuous racial backlash. It also reflected the inroads that the burnished conservative philosophy had on voters with conservative proclivities who wavered in their loyalty to the Democratic Party.

The anti–affirmative action backlash provided the context and warrant for several reversals of previous Supreme Court decisions that sanctioned affirmative action policy. Nor was there much support from President Clinton, notwithstanding his nebulous "mend it, don't end it" slogan. As Joe Klein shrewdly observed in a column in *Newsweek*, Clinton's doublespeak provided a rhetorical facade for the quiet dismantling of affirmative action policy, which always depended on vigorous enforcement by the Office of Federal Contract Compliance and the Department of Justice. In effect, affirmative action has been allowed to die the quiet death that Nixon's operatives had pronounced as early as 1970. By 1995 the obituary for affirmative action was emblazoned on the cover of *Newsweek*, proclaiming "The End to Affirmative Action."[49] A year later, another nail in the coffin of affirmative action was delivered by an appellate court in *Hopwood v. Texas* (1996), which stipulated that a college could implement affirmative action only as a remedy for past discrimination at that very institution, thus rejecting the goal of educational diversity as a general principle. In response, the Texas state legislature passed a "10 percent plan," requiring the major state universities to admit all undergraduate applicants who graduated in the top 10 percent of their high school class. However, a year after the *Hopwood* decision, the percentage of blacks entering the University of Texas Law School dropped precipitously—from 5.8 percent (twenty-nine students) in 1996 to 0.9 percent (six students) in 1997. The number of Latino students also declined, though not as sharply: from 9.2 percent (forty-six students) in 1996 to 6.7 percent (thirty-one students) in 1997.[50]

Thanks to Justice Kennedy's concurrence in the 2003 case of *Grutter v. Bollinger*, the Court affirmed the University of Michigan's method for achieving diversity in its student body, offering another reprieve from the Grim Reaper. In reaction, Ward Connerly launched the so-called Michigan Civil

Rights Initiative, which proscribes the use of preferences based on race or gender. It passed by a margin of 58 to 42 percent in the 2006 election, though in 2011 it was overturned by the Sixth Circuit Court, offering yet another reprieve while the decision was under appeal.

The conclusion is inescapable: affirmative action is all but dead, eviscerated by a relentless campaign waged over four decades. To continue the metaphor, there were desperate attempts to resuscitate the patient. I refer here to the transmutation of affirmative action that began with the "Powell compromise" in the 1978 *Bakke* case and was reaffirmed in the 2003 ruling in *Gratz v. Bollinger*. These rulings made it illegal to target affirmative action to particular minorities, on the grounds that this amounted to a system of "reverse discrimination" in violation of the Fourteenth Amendment. However, it was held that promoting "diversity" was a legitimate goal, whether in employment policy or college admissions. This was the saving remnant that allowed advocates of affirmative action to breathe a sigh of relief, on the assumption that African Americans and other protected minorities would fit under the expanded umbrella of "diversity."

However, as affirmative action morphed into diversity, it lost its credibility. Instead of advancing the cause of racial justice, corporations came to recognize the uses of "diversity" both in the domestic consumer economy and the global market. This is documented in an incisive paper by Sharon Collins under the title "Diversity in the Post Affirmative Action Labor Market: A Proxy for Racial Progress?" Collins cites a 1995 survey of the fifty largest US industrial firms, 78 percent of whom either had a formal diversity management program or were developing one. Another survey in 1998 found that 75 percent of *Fortune* 500 companies had instituted programs to promote diversity.[51]

A similar trend has emerged in higher education as affirmative action transitioned from "minority" to "diversity," as Peter Schmidt showed in a 2005 article in the *Chronicle of Higher Education*:

Over the last three years, mainly in response to two landmark U.S. Supreme Court rulings in June 2003 that defined the limits of affirmative action, colleges across the country have been concluding that they are in legal jeopardy if they continue to offer some services or benefits solely to minority students. As a result, the institutions have been abandoning the use of race-exclusive eligibility criteria in determining who can be awarded scholarships and fellowships or can participate in recruitment, orientation, and academic enrichment programs.[52]

Schmidt documents the abandonment of "minority" programs at colleges across the nation over the protest of the NAACP Legal Defense and Education Fund, which contended that the Supreme Court rulings did not "address, much less prohibit, considerations of race outside the admissions context."[53] That went unheeded, as philanthropies and some federal agencies withdrew their support for college programs with race-exclusive criteria. It is difficult to escape the conclusion that affirmative action "as we knew it" is dead in American higher education.

To be sure, "diversity" is a legitimate and unassailable principle in college admissions. Not only does it reflect changing demographics of the student population, but diversity has also spawned whole new fields of inquiry and challenged orthodoxies in established disciplines. My objection is not to "diversity" as such, but to the *substitution* of the diversity principle for affirmative action as a remedy for apartheid in employment and education. Not only do few African Americans receive benefits under this revised formula, but affirmative action is shorn of the compelling moral and political reasoning that previously conferred it with legitimacy.

From a historical perspective, the gutting of affirmative action signifies the end of the Second Reconstruction and a return to the status quo ante: the period before affirmative action when there were laws on the books that were ineffectual in combating institutionalized racism in employment and education.

In 1993 James E. Jones, a legal scholar at the University of Wisconsin, published a paper entitled "The Rise and Fall of Affirmative Action," which traces the unraveling of affirmative action policy by a series of Supreme Court rulings. Jones could not conceal his exasperation that the policy that he did so much to spawn had been severely eviscerated by the courts. Jones has a deep personal investment in this issue since he is one of those faceless bureaucrats who played a key role in the genesis of affirmative action policy. Upon graduating from the University of Wisconsin Law School in 1956, he went to work in the US Department of Labor. There he had a hand in the implementation of President Kennedy's famous 1961 Executive Order calling for "affirmative action" in employment, and under President Nixon he helped to craft the revised Philadelphia Plan so that it would pass muster with a skeptical controller general who held that the plan violated procurement law by restricting the employment practices of government contractors.[54] Nevertheless, on a strained note of optimism, he writes, "I shall endeavor to convey my conviction that, like the mythical Phoenix, affirmative action shall rise again."[55]

This is precisely the question before us: Is this a case of wishful thinking, or is there a realistic possibility that affirmative action will rise again from its ashes?

The proverbial phoenix was given a boost with the election of Barack Obama in 2008, leading to the appointment of Sonia Sotomayor in 2009 and Elena Kagan in 2010 to the Supreme Court. This meant that one tantalizing vote could change the balance on the Court. There is an obstacle, however, as Erwin Chemerinsky has shown. In 2012 the ages of the five conservative judges were: Scalia, seventy-six; Kennedy, seventy-five; Thomas, sixty-four; Alito, sixty-two; and Roberts, fifty-seven. Chemerinsky's conclusion: "absent unforeseen events, the five conservative judges are likely to remain another decade."[56]

Even if a Democrat were to be elected to the presidency and even if a vacancy were to occur among the conservative judges, there is still reason to doubt that a jurist sympathetic to affirmative action would be nominated and confirmed, or that a majority on the Court would act to reverse previous decisions and bring back affirmative action. Again, some historical perspective may provide a lens on the future.

Conservatives cemented a majority on the Supreme Court with three appointments by President Reagan (O'Connor in 1981; Scalia in 1986; and Kennedy in 1988). Affirmative action was already a hot-button political issue throughout the 1980s, furiously debated in the media as well as in academic discourses. The new majority on the Court wasted no time in delivering three devastating setbacks to affirmative action:

- *Wygant v. Jackson Board of Education* (1986) stipulated that any institution seeking to compensate for past discrimination must be shown to have committed discriminatory acts in the past.
- *City of Richmond v. J. A. Croson Co.* (1989) reversed the 1980 decision in *Fullilove v. Klutznick*, thus all but killing affirmative action in contracting.
- *Wards Cove Packing Company v. Atonio* (1989) reversed the 1971 decision in *Griggs v. Duke Power Company* by stipulating that "disparate impact" must be shown to have discriminatory *intent*.

What is startling here is the alacrity with which the Court reversed decisions that had been laid down only nine years earlier in the case of *Croson*, and eighteen years earlier in the case of *Wards Cove*. In short, stare decisis went out the window with Reagan's appointment of three conservative jurists.[57]

The end result was the abrogation of policies that had only recently passed constitutional muster, and a virtual death knell to affirmative action policy.

The question before us is whether this scenario might repeat itself in reverse if liberals became a majority on the Court. Probably not. In a recent article in the *Washington Monthly*, Dahlia Lithwick asks the key question: "Why have the Republicans been so much more effective at dragging the judicial branch rightward than Democrats have been in yanking it back?" Lithwick continues: "Imagine a Democratic presidential nominee running on promises to reshape, remake, make over, hog-tie, or even just refinishing the federal bench. It doesn't happen."[58] In other words, it cannot be assumed that a liberal majority on the Court would vote to review, much less reverse, decisions on affirmative action made by the Rehnquist and Roberts courts.

Let us put this in larger political context. The movement to kill affirmative action began with a white backlash and political realignment of the South, which led to Republican victories in seven of the ten presidential elections between 1968 and 2004. Nixon appointed Burger, Blackmun, Powell, and Rehnquist to the Supreme Court—stalwart conservatives all. However, it soon became apparent that in the eyes of the emergent legal movement, it was not enough to appoint conservative judges who did not go beyond opposing liberal programs and policies. As Pat Buchanan observed, this was "the counter-revolution that wasn't."[59]

In *The Rise of the Conservative Legal Movement*, Steven Teles offers an incisive account of the role that the Federalist Society played in this emergent legal movement that sought nothing less than the overhaul of jurisprudence in the United States.[60] The Federalist Society began with a symposium on federalism at Yale Law School in 1982, and gradually burgeoned into a national movement. By 2006 it had 40,000 members and chapters on all 180 law school campuses, not to mention seventy more chapters for lawyers and judges.[61] Indeed, this was an epochal story of successful organizing from the bottom-up.

Nor was the emergent legal movement an instant success. As Teles shows, it "went through a very long period of almost complete organizational failure." Key to its success was the steadfast support of conservative foundations, including Olin, Koch, Bradley, and Smith Richardson. According to Teles, "they invested in the Federalist Society, despite the fact that the organization's main outputs, such as networks and idea development, were difficult to measure or trace back to their source and would only bear fruit decades later, when generations of law students matured into senior, practicing lawyers and law professors."[62]

To be sure, the success of the Federalist Society coincided with a conservative backlash in the society at large and the ascendancy of the Republican Party to national power. Yet, as Teles shows, during its early stages the Federalist Society was removed from electoral politics. It came to fruition through an extensive network of conservative students who, step by step, countered liberal domination of the nation's legal institutions. This included the development of a distinctively conservative theory and praxis of American jurisprudence. In the end, conservatives even developed their own version of public interest law.

This fledgling movement eventually flowered into an activist network of conservative legal institutions, think tanks, and advocacy groups who vied for influence and power that previously were the domain of legal liberals. By the time that Reagan came to power, there was in place an entrenched cadre of legal talent, backed up with intellectual capital and activist discourses. This movement gradually gained influence in Republican administrations that extended to appointments to the federal courts, including the Supreme Court. It is precisely because more was involved than counting conservative votes that George W. Bush's appointment of Harriet Miers to the Supreme Court evoked such fury among legal conservatives. The movement got what it wanted when it prevailed upon Bush to withdraw Miers's nomination, and instead nominate Samuel Alito, a member of the Federalist Society—as were Clarence Thomas, Antonin Scalia, and John Roberts.[63]

Teles is careful not to exaggerate the success and current influence of the conservative legal movement. Liberals still outnumber conservatives on the faculties of law schools, and liberal advocacy groups have not gone away. The point is liberals are no longer hegemonic, and a new brand of conservatives now vies for power and influence throughout the world of law.

To restate the question before us: What would the impact of this new political standoff be on the Supreme Court if liberals should secure a five-to-four majority? Here we must consider the influence of the political Zeitgeist on the Court. When the Supreme Court issued its long series of rulings on race, beginning with *Brown* in 1954 and extending through *Griggs* in 1971 and *Fullilove* in 1980, liberals enjoyed a hegemonic position in the nation's legal institutions. Not only that, but they were also buttressed and empowered by momentous political developments—the eruption of black insurgency in the South, a grassroots civil rights movement that triggered a constitutional crisis, the rise of black militancy punctuated with a series of urban revolts that escalated after the assassination of Martin Luther King Jr. in 1968, and finally a heightened sense of racial crisis that gave voice to minority and radical viewpoints long cast to the sidelines of academic and public discourses. Indeed, the entire society was thrown into crisis, the reverberations of which eventually reached inside the legal profession and even the cloistered chambers of the nation's highest court.

This is a far cry from the situation today. The racial mobilization of the 1960s and 1970s has been blunted, and has faded in memory and impact. It is not only the fabled liberal coalition that is split on affirmative action. Many on the left regard the struggle against racism as a political dead-end and a deflection from the larger project of class transformation.[64] For them, affirmative action is at best a reform that replaces blacks for whites, but does little or nothing to alter the hierarchies of power, much less the political and economic institutions in which these hierarchies are anchored. Thus, for many on the left, affirmative action only provides capitalism with a multi-cultural face.[65]

Twenty years have passed since *Newsweek* expressed in its cover story the idea that that "Affirmative Action Is Dead." At least by outward appearances, even black civil rights organizations seem resigned to the fact that affirmative action has been irrevocably lost. Hence, there is no significant political constituency demanding the restoration of affirmative action. Given this, even if Democrats have an opportunity to appoint a justice to the Supreme Court, it is doubtful they would go on the offensive and risk political capital by reigniting the contentious debates over affirmative action.

So here we are, one last nail from the end of the Second Reconstruction. It is difficult to avoid the conclusion that the gutting of affirmative action is a fait accompli, only waiting for the coup de grace by the Roberts court. Just as the First Reconstruction ended with the abrogation of laws intended to provide restitution to emancipated slaves, the Second Reconstruction is ending with the gutting of affirmative action. Think what this means: we are left with the preposterous outcome that an entire people can be subjugated on the basis of race for centuries, but pious principles of jurisprudence are invoked to obscure the difference between a racial classification whose intention is to oppress a people and a racial classification whose purpose is to provide remedy—and meager remedy at that—for the ravages of that oppression.[66]

Only one caveat can rescue us from total pessimism. Perhaps the very success of the anti–affirmative action crusade will plant the seeds for its comeback. With the gutting of affirmative action, racial inequalities will grow larger and more dangerous, exacerbating the condition that gave rise to affirmative action in the first place. This is copiously documented by a recent study, *Documenting Desegregation*, based on records collected by the Equal

Employment Opportunities Commission on over five million workplaces between 1966 and 2005. Kevin Stainback and Donald Tomaskovic-Devey found that equal opportunity progress halted abruptly for blacks after 1980 and for white women after 2000.[67] In short, with the weakening of affirmative action mandates, we have returned to the old ways of doing business. This should come as no surprise. In justifying the Philadelphia Plan, Secretary of Labor George Shultz told a historian that in the construction industry, "We found a quota system" for black workers. "It was there. It was zero."[68]

In a 2012 op-ed in the *New York Times*, Thomas Espenshade, a sociologist at Princeton University, estimates that between 10,000 and 15,000 blacks and Hispanic students enroll in selective colleges every year through race-conscious policies. This raises the possibility that as the devastating consequences of the rollback of affirmative action become manifest, it may engender pressures for its reclamation, especially if the balance on the Court swings in favor of Democrats. We can take comfort in knowing that if or when pressures mount for change, insurgent groups will have the memory and the precedent of a robust affirmative action policy that, in its short life, passed muster with the Supreme Court and succeeded in driving a wedge into the wall of occupational apartheid that had its origin in slavery. James Jones is dead, but history marches on. It may be unlikely, but it is within the realm of possibility that his undying hope will be realized and, "like the mythical Phoenix, affirmative action shall rise again."

NOTES

This essay is dedicated to Derrick Bell, who neither surrendered to false optimism nor allowed pessimism to diminish his struggle against white supremacy. Early sections of it borrow from my previous work on the history and politics of affirmative action: STEPHEN STEINBERG, TURNING BACK: THE RETREAT FROM RACIAL JUSTICE IN AMERICAN THOUGHT AND POLICY (2001); *L'Essor et le Déclin de l'Affirmative Action Aux États-Unis*, in MARCO MARTINIELLO & ANDREA REA, DISCRIMINATIONS ETHNIQUES, ACTIONS POSITIVES: DES POLITIQUES ET DES PRATIQUES EN DÉBAT (2003).

1. THE BLACK COMMENTATOR 49 (2003), http://www.blackcommentator.com/49/49_cartoons.html. It is noteworthy how many authors, including myself, have invoked the trope of "death" in relation to affirmative action. To mention a few: FAYE J. CROSBY, AFFIRMATIVE ACTION IS DEAD: LONG LIVE AFFIRMATIVE ACTION (2004); Manning Marable, *The Death of Affirmative Action*, ZNET, http://www.zcommunications.org/the-death-of-affirmative-action-by-manning-marable-1; Sam Fulwood, *The Death of Affirmative Action*, ALTERNET (Apr. 10, 2012), http://www.alternet.org/education/154933/the_death_of_affirmative_action;

Michele Goodwin, *The Death of Affirmative Action*, CHRON. HIGHER EDUC., Part I (Mar. 15, 2012), Part II (Mar. 21, 2012).

2. Stephen Steinberg, *Nathan Glazer and the Assassination of Affirmative Action*, 35 N. POL. (Summer 2003), http://nova.wpunj.edu/newpolitics/issue35/Steinberg35.htm; JACOB HEILBRUNN, THEY KNEW THEY WERE RIGHT: THE RISE OF THE NEOCONS (2008).

3. NANCY MACLEAN, FREEDOM IS NOT ENOUGH (2006), chs. 6–7.

4. Michael Lind, *Symposium on Affirmative Action*, DISSENT 470 (1995).

5. NATHAN GLAZER, AFFIRMATIVE DISCRIMINATION: ETHNIC INEQUALITY AND PUBLIC POLICY (1975). Sidney Hook railed against affirmative action with op-ed pieces in the *New York Times* and other public media. Sidney Hook, *Discrimination against the Qualified?* Op-ed, N.Y. TIMES, Nov. 5, 1971, and *A Quota Is a Quota Is a Quota*, Op-ed, N.Y. TIMES, Nov. 12, 1974; Sidney Hook & Miro Todorovich, *The Tyranny of Reverse Discrimination*, 7 CHANGE 42–43 (Winter 1975/76).

6. Henry Louis Gates Jr., *Interview with Jane Slaughter*, 62 PROGRESSIVE 30 (January 1998).

7. STEPHEN L. CARTER, REFLECTIONS OF AN AFFIRMATIVE ACTION BABY (1991).

8. HUGH DAVIS GRAHAM, THE CIVIL RIGHTS ERA 325 (1990).

9. Paul Starr, *Civic Reconstruction: What to Do without Affirmative Action*, AM. PROSPECT 7–14 (Winter 1992); Jeffrey Klein, *The Race Course*, MOTHER JONES, Oct. 1997, at 3. Michael Walzer also frets about the real political costs of affirmative action. Editor's Page, DISSENT 435 (Fall 1995).

10. NEIL R. MCMILLEN, DARK JOURNEY: BLACK MISSISSIPPIANS IN THE AGE OF JIM CROW 7 (1990).

11. Stanley Fish, *When Principles Get in the Way*, N.Y. TIMES, Dec. 26, 1996, at 27.

12. *Quoted in* Vikram Amar, *Knowing When Race Matters*, Op-ed, N.Y. TIMES, Feb. 22, 2012, at 24.

13. CHARLES W. MILLS, THE RACIAL CONTRACT 130–31 (1997).

14. WHITNEY M. YOUNG JR., TO BE EQUAL 54 (1963); Bayard Rustin, *From Protest to Politics: The Future of the Civil Rights Movement*, 39 COMMENTARY 25 (Feb. 1964); Hubert Humphrey, *quoted in* RICHARD A. EPSTEIN, FORBIDDEN GROUNDS: THE CASE AGAINST EMPLOYMENT DISCRIMINATION LAWS 400 (1992); Martin Luther King Jr., *Showdown for Non-Violence*, LOOK, Apr. 16, 1968, at 24.

15. *Should There Be "Compensation" for Negroes?*, N.Y. TIMES MAG., Oct. 6, 1963, at 43ff.

16. CHARLES SILBERMAN, CRISIS IN BLACK AND WHITE 237 (1964). The back cover contained a long blurb from Malcolm X, including this plaudit: "Mr. Silberman's swordlike pen scientifically vindicates the innocent, while indicting only the guilty who refuse to face up to the facts and atone while there is still time."

17. MARTIN LUTHER KING JR., WHY WE CAN'T WAIT 147 (1963).

18. The proceedings were published as *Liberalism and the Negro: A Round-Table Discussion*, 25 COMMENTARY 25–42 (Mar. 1961), along with Letters from Readers in the August issue. Note that Podhoretz was already embroiled in controversy from an article, published a year earlier—"My Negro Problem—and Ours"—in which he describes his "feelings of fear, envy and hatred" toward the blacks he encountered growing up in

Brooklyn. Podhoretz envisions a future that erases racial stigma via amalgamation. Norman Podhoretz, *My Negro Problem—and Ours*, 35 COMMENTARY 93–101 (FEB. 1963).

19. JOHN DAVID SKRENTNY, THE IRONIES OF AFFIRMATIVE ACTION (1996); GRAHAM *supra* note 8, chs. 11–13.

20. JAMES P. STERBA, AFFIRMATIVE ACTION FOR THE FUTURE 17 (2009).

21. Joe Holley, *Affirmative Action Pioneer Advised GOP Presidents*, WASH. POST, JULY 13, 2005, at 13. Dean J. Kotlowski writes that "even if Nixon often shunned his offspring, he still must be acknowledged as the sire of affirmative action." DEAN J. KOTLOWSKI, NIXON'S CIVIL RIGHTS 124 (2001).

22. SKRENTNY *supra* note 19, at 208, 221, 285.

23. GRAHAM, *supra* note 8, at 325.

24. Hugh Davis Graham, *Race, History, and Policy: African Americans and Civil Rights since 1964*, 6 J. POL'Y HIST. 23 (1994).

25. GRAHAM, *supra* note 8, at 334–35.

26. TERRY H. ANDERSON, THE PURSUIT OF FAIRNESS: A HISTORY OF AFFIRMATIVE ACTION 119 (2004).

27. ARTHUR FLETCHER, THE SILENT SELL-OUT 65 (1974).

28. MACLEAN, *supra* note 3, at 100–101.

29. Graham, *supra* note 24, at 19–20.

30. SKRENTNY, *supra* note 19, at 141. *See also* Roberta Downing et al., *Affirmative Action in Employment and Higher Education*, 10 DIVERSITY FACTOR 13 (Winter 2002).

31. HEILBRUNN, *supra* note 2, at 88.

32. GLAZER, *supra* note 5, at 44, 201.

33. CHRISTOPHER PHELPS, YOUNG SIDNEY HOOK 3 (1997).

34. Hook & Todorovich, *supra* note 5.

35. BENJAMIN BALINT, RUNNING COMMENTARY 138 (2012). In an endnote Balint lists thirteen articles during the 1990s and beyond that railed against affirmative action.

36. HERMAN BELZ, EQUALITY TRANSFORMED: A QUARTER-CENTURY OF AFFIRMATIVE ACTION (1991); Epstein, *supra* note 14; Alan Wolfe, *Affirmative Action: The Fact Gap*, N.Y. Times Book Rev., Oct. 25, 1998, at 15.

37. ELLEN WILLIS, DON'T THINK, SMILE! 91–113 (1999).

38. I am indebted to University of Illinois Chicago sociologist Sharon Collins for this insight.

39. It is worth noting that Powell was a corporate lawyer who "laid the groundwork for a right-wing rise in all areas of public life, including law firms, think tanks, campus organizations and media outlets." Katrina vanden Heuvel, "The Supreme Court Works for Corporate Power," NATION, Sept. 17, 2012, at 5.

40. STEPHEN STEINBERG, THE ETHNIC MYTH 238–46 (1989). *See also* JEROME KARABEL, THE CHOSEN: THE HIDDEN HISTORY OF ADMISSION AND EXCLUSION AT HARVARD, YALE, AND PRINCETON (2006).

41. David A. Hollinger, *Group Preferences, Cultural Diversity, and Social Democracy: Notes toward a Theory of Affirmative Action*, in RACE AND REPRESENTATION: AFFIRMATIVE ACTION 99 (Robert Post & Michael Rogin, eds., 1998); Peter Schrag, *So You Want to Be Color-Blind: Alternative Principles for Affirmative Action*, AM. PROSPECT 45 (Summer 1995).

42. MacLean, *supra* note 3, at 227 *passim*.

43. Richard Hernnstein & Charles Murray, The Bell Curve: Intelligence and Class Structure in American Life (1996).

44. MacLean, *supra* note 3, at 230, 235.

45. Heilbrunn, *supra* note 2, at 165.

46. Jean Stefancic & Richard Delgado, No Mercy: How Social Conservatives and Think Tanks Changed America's Social Agenda (1996).

47. Charles Murray, Losing Ground: American Social Policy, 1950–1980 (10th Anniversary Ed. 1995).

48. Adolph Reed Jr., *Looking Backward*, Nation, Nov. 28, 1994, at 661–62.

49. Joe Klein, *The End of Affirmative Action*, Newsweek, Feb. 13, 1995, at 137.

50. Sterba, *supra* note 20, at 21–22.

51. Sharon M. Collins, *Diversity in the Post Affirmative Action Labor Market: A Proxy for Racial Progress?*, 37 Crit. Soc. 524 (2001).

52. Peter Schmidt, *"From "Minority" to "Diversity,"* Chron. Higher Educ., Feb. 3, 2006, at 1.

53. *Id.* at 7.

54. For an informative biographical sketch, see Vicki Schultz, *A Tribute Honoring James E. Jones, Jr.*, 8 Emp. Rts. & Empl. Pol'y J. 525 (2005). *See also* James E. Jones Jr., *The Origins of Affirmative Action*, 21 U.C. Davis L. Rev. 383 (1988); James E. Jones Jr., Hattie's Boy: The Autobiography of James E. Jones, Jr. 449–61 (2006).

55. James E. Jones Jr., *The Rise and Fall of Affirmative Action*, in Race in America: The Struggle for Equality 346 (Herbert Hill & James E. Jones, eds., 1993).

56. Erwin Chemerinsky, The Conservative Assault on the Constitution 29 (2010). Since this essay was written, the death of Justice Antonin Scalia in 2016 has left the future left-right balance of the Supreme Court in doubt.

57. Although he had been an adviser to Reagan, Arthur Fletcher called Reagan "the worst president for civil rights in this century." Holley, *supra* note 21. Another factor was the dogged opposition of Assistant Attorney General William Reynolds.

58. Dahlia Lithwick, *The Courts: The Conservative Takeover Will Be Complete*, Wash. Monthly, Jan./Feb. 2012, at 4

59. Vincent Blasi, The Burger Court: The Counter-Revolution That Wasn't (1980).

60. Steven Teles, The Rise of the Conservative Legal Movement (2010).

61. David Montgomery, *No Secrets Here: Federalist Society Plots In the Open*, Wash. Post, Nov. 18, 2006, at 23.

62. Teles, *supra* note 60.

63. Montgomery, *supra* note 61.

64. Adolph Reed Jr., *The Limits of Anti-Racism*, 121 Left Observer (Sept. 2009), http://leftbusinessobserver.com/Antiracism.html.

65. Walter Benn Michaels, The Trouble with Diversity: How We Learned to Love Identity and Ignore Diversity (2006); Jodi Melamed, *The Spirit of Neoliberalism: From Racial Liberalism to Neoliberal Multiculturalism*, 24 Soc. Text 89 (2006); Adolph

Reed Jr. & Merlin Chowkwanyun, *Race, Class, Crisis: The Discourse of Racial Disparity and Its Analytical Discontents*, 46 SOCIALIST REG. 149–75 (2012)

66. Leland Ware, *Turning Back the Clock: The Assault on Affirmative Action*, 54 WASH. U. J. URB. & CONTEMP. L. 3 (1998).

67. KEVIN STAINBACK & DONALD TOMASKOVIC-DEVEY, DOCUMENTING DE-SEGREGATION: RACIAL AND GENDER SEGREGATION IN PRIVATE-SECTOR EMPLOYMENT SINCE THE CIVIL RIGHTS ACT (2012).

68. ANDERSON, *supra* note 26, at 118.

Segregated Together
Latino-Black Interethnic Conflict

TANYA KATERÍ HERNÁNDEZ

For the last several years news agencies have been riveted by the issue of racial strife between Latinos and African Americans in various urban locations across the country. In the summer of 2010 Staten Island, New York, became the focal point. Of particular interest was the surprising vision of a historically white borough subject to black-on-Mexican crimes. How could this occur in what has been the least diverse borough in New York City? As a result, news agencies devoted much of their accounts to the growing diversity of the area. Indeed, according to Census data, since 1990 the Latino population has increased by 77 percent, and the Mexican population in particular has increased by 428 percent, much more than in any other borough. Between 2000 and 2008, the number of Latinos living in Staten Island grew roughly 40 percent, according to Census Bureau statistics analyzed by the City University of New York's Latino Data Project. Much of that growth has come from Mexican migrants. Of the eleven assaults on Mexicans in the Port Richmond area of Staten Island since April 2010, ten have involved blacks attacking Mexicans. For many commentators, that statistic alone has been sufficient to presume that interethnic economic competition and anti-immigrant resentment have ignited the violence, despite yearly Gallup polls that consistently show that the majority of blacks and Latinos report that relations between the two groups are good.[1] Indeed, the Gallup polls show that it is non-Hispanic whites who often report the view that relations between Latinos and blacks are bad rather than Latinos or blacks themselves. Furthermore, actual empirical research of black-Latino relations suggests that a variety of factors contribute to what are very context specific interactions that can vary by region of the country.[2]

Missing from the typical media account is a nuanced presentation of the racial context that can more fully explain the complexity of the interethnic violence. This chapter focuses upon how black-Latino relations in the United States are structurally shaped by residential segregation. For instance, while it is true that Staten Island is an area with increasing diversity, that diversity is geographically segmented in ways that preserve traditional white/nonwhite segregation. Specifically, the primary areas of Staten Island that have been transformed by Latin American immigration have been its historically black working-class neighborhoods.

In contrast, Staten Island's general population is still overwhelmingly white, at a rate of 63.7 percent, according to the 2010 Census. The growing population of Latinos, reported in the 2010 Census as 17.6 percent, has primarily settled in the few areas in which blacks are allowed to reside. For instance, in Port Richmond, the site of much of the violence, the 2000 Census reported blacks as 24 percent of the population, Latinos as 24 percent, and non-Hispanic whites as 45 percent, while in Staten Island as a whole blacks were only 9 percent of the population, Latinos 12 percent, and non-Hispanic whites 71 percent. In the neighborhoods of Arlington and Mariners Harbor in which blacks are the most numerous, making up 34.13 percent of the 2010 Census population, Latinos were 37.9 percent of the local population, while non-Hispanic whites were only 13.36 percent. In short, the growing diversity of Staten Island has been a highly segregated affair—and that fact is key to understanding the current racial dynamics that exist in Staten Island and other communities.

The simultaneous existence of stark white segregation from nonwhites and segregated proximity of nonwhites with one another in Staten Island means that opportunistic crimes like robbery by nonwhite perpetrators are more likely to affect nonwhite victims. The question then arises as to whether the victimization of Staten Island Latinos by Staten Island African Americans should even be considered racially motivated. Yet the great disparity of the black-on-Latino crime rate in Staten Island suggests that racial considerations may have had some influence in how victims were chosen and/or how so many robberies escalated into violence.

As such, the racial context of Staten Island warrants closer examination. However, it should be noted that this chapter's examination does not purport to present the dynamic of black-Latino violence as the predominant interaction between blacks and Latinos, nor as the primary source of violence in communities of color. Indeed, it still continues to be the case that the greatest source of violence in communities of color is intraracial.[3] Nevertheless, even though the interethnic violence may be a statistically small occurrence, it is still a troubling state of affairs that civil rights organizations state merits analysis and one day a resolution. Most commentators agree that it is important to understand the historical context and structural conditions that shape interethnic violence.[4] This chapter offers an in-depth analysis that compares black versus Latino violence in an East Coast setting with Latino versus black violence in a West Coast setting. Though there are many factors that contribute to the context for these violent eruptions, one key is the creation and maintenance of segregated nonwhite spaces/neighborhoods. Part of understanding possible solutions requires understanding law and its limits in addressing segregation. In the end, though, only a renewed societal focus on combating the institutional forces of poverty and racism, along with segregation, can address interethnic relations nationwide.

The black presence on Staten Island dates back to the formation of the nation. In fact, Staten Island's hangman during the Revolutionary War was black prizefighter Bill Richmond. The first record of a free black person purchasing land in Staten Island is in 1828 (one year after New York State abolished slavery). Free blacks came to Staten Island decades before the Civil War to work as vegetable farmers and oystermen. Furthermore, the first black churches in New York were formed in Staten Island. The Sandy Ground neighborhood of Rossville, Staten Island, was an early North American settlement established by free blacks, and according to local historians, it is the oldest continuously held settlement. Of the New York City free black settlements, Sandy Ground also has the largest number of direct descendants of its first residents still living in the neighborhood. Yet today less than 1 percent of that historic neighborhood's population is black. Instead, the black population has traditionally been located in Port Richmond and a few other limited areas, and is otherwise known not to be welcome in the "white" areas of the island (as so clearly communicated in November 2008, when, on Election Night, four white men, including a white Latino,[5] sought "revenge" for President Obama's victory by randomly beating blacks on the island).

Thus blacks are effectively limited to particular geographic spaces on Staten Island, and those same areas have seen the greatest influx of Latino migrants. While the distance between Anglo white and nonwhite Staten Island neighborhoods ranges between four and fourteen miles, the distance between black and Latino Staten Island neighborhoods is the much smaller range of two to five miles.[6] Sociologists suggest that such a demographic pattern of new mass entries into established communities is the primary condition under which racially motivated crime occurs. In a study of individual incident reports to the Bias Crime Unit of the New York Police Department over an eight-year period, sociologists found that racially motivated crime stemmed not from economic resentment but instead from an exclusionary impulse on the part of residents defending what they perceived to be their territory in the face of large-scale demographic change.[7] Where a racial group has long been the predominant community in an area, racially motivated crime becomes more severe with in-migration of other racial groups.

While economic grievances may be infused in the rhetoric of bias crime perpetrators, the sociological data discounts the actual role of macroeconomic conditions in instigating racially motivated crimes. For instance, no relationship has been found between the fluctuation in the rates of unemployment and rates of racially motivated crime. Thus, despite the economic recession, New York State and much of the nation saw a decrease in the number of reported hate crimes. New York as a whole experienced a 7.8 percent decline in reported hate crimes in 2008 according to a study conducted by the California State University Center for the Study of Hate and Extremism. In contrast, in Staten Island, hate crimes have doubled between 2009 and 2010 according to the Staten Island District Attorney's Office.

The contrast between the New York State hate crime reduction (amid a greater population of blacks and Latinos) and the Staten Island hate crime increase suggests that it is where a racially homogenous group wishes to preserve their residential homogeneity that racially motivated crime will be deployed as a "turf defense." The social-psychological dynamic of turf defense in turn helps explain how socially excluded young black men in Staten Island can be involved in anti-Latino immigrant crimes despite the fact that surveys of African Americans in the United States show that African Americans disproportionately have positive social attitudes about Latino immigrants. The Pew Charitable Trusts public opinion poll of 2006 found that a large majority of African Americans feel that immigrants are hard-working and have strong family values.[8] In addition, African Americans were more than twice as likely as Anglo whites to support public benefits for undocumented immigrants, and were also more prone than Anglo whites to support a policy permitting undocumented immigrants to attend public schools.

Yet when institutionalized racism limits the socioeconomic mobility of black youths in underresourced public schools and erects network barriers to promising employment opportunities that thereby entrap them in very limited geographic spaces that symbolize their socially derided status, it is not so surprising that youthful social frustration might unfortunately be misdirected to desperately trying to maintain racial dominance over the limited physical space accorded to blacks by treating Mexican migrants as interlopers who do not belong and thus can be easily victimized. Indeed, all nine of the persons arrested in the recent Staten Island bias crimes have been eighteen or younger, and very much reflect the criminal law understanding that crime is often a "consequence and marker of societal stratification and disadvantage across population subgroups."[9] In short, the racial isolation of blacks in Staten Island, in combination with their perception of losing ground within the physical space of their racial containment, heightens the turf defense of the least socially mobile young black men and their pattern of opportunistically targeting politically vulnerable Latino immigrants as victims of violent robberies.

Unfortunately, the government response has solely been to deploy additional foot and mounted patrols, and a command post. While police vehicles periodically sit on Port Richmond streets and police officers on horseback have patrolled the main street, the deeper issues of institutionalized racism and segregated racialized spaces have gone unaddressed and public attention averted from the more prevalent forms of white versus nonwhite racism. This poorly serves the Mexican victims of interethnic violence and the African American victims of institutionalized racism in New York City.

Still, it should be noted that there has been some contention as to whether the Staten Island interethnic violence and other incidents like them should be properly characterized as hate crimes. For instance, the grand juries in a number of the Staten Island incidents declined to include hate crime charges in the criminal indictments because the African American perpetrators were seemingly more motivated by an intent to rob, which later escalated with violence.[10] This is quite distinctive from the "pure" hate crime example of the group of white Long Island, New York, teenagers (including one Puerto Rican) who pleaded guilty to an ongoing campaign to simply attack Mexicans, which culminated in the murder of Marcelo Lucero in 2008—the Long Island teens admitted to walking around town with the purpose of "hitting beaners" (a derogatory term for Mexicans).[11] Again, this is a marked contrast to the Staten Island pattern of African American perpetrators seeking out Hispanic victims to rob because of their presumed undocumented status in work-for-cash employment that makes them easier prey for robbery without reprisals. It is a pattern that has also been documented in Baltimore; Durham, North Carolina; and San Antonio, Texas.[12]

One study suggests that, on a national level, Latino migration to urban areas increases black crime rates, due in part to the displacement of blacks from the low-skill job market, in much the same way that Latino migration to rural areas increases the non-Hispanic white rate of crime for whites displaced from low-skill jobs in rural areas.[13] While there are conflicting reports as to the actual displacement effects of immigration upon US citizen employment, many scholars do agree that the public anti-immigrant rhetoric alone can create the perception of labor market displacement that in turn erodes interethnic relations.[14] More important, the segregated proximity of Latinos to African Americans makes Latinos easier targets in much the same way that African Americans are the disproportionate victims of African American criminals with whom they live in closer proximity. California presents a distinctive racial pattern but one just as mired in the legacy of residential segregation.

In California, interethnic violence is centered upon the targeting of African American residents by Latino street gangs operating with the explicitly stated goal of eradicating African Americans from "Latino" spaces. This is clearly demonstrated by the evidence brought forth in a number of criminal cases and the police and FBI investigations that precipitated them. For instance, in June 2011 a federal grand jury in California issued a twenty-four-count indictment charging fifty-one Latino defendants for conspiring to murder African Americans in Azusa, California.[15] Detective Robert Landeros of the Azusa police department noted, "This has been a 20 year (1992–May 2010) conspiracy to violate the civil rights of African Americans in the city."[16]

Azusa is a bedroom community thirty minutes northeast of Los Angeles in which 67.57 percent of the inhabitants, according to the 2010 Census, are Latino, 3 percent African American, 19.3 percent Anglo white, and 8.7 percent Asian. The indictment was the culmination of a three-year criminal investigation of the Varrio Azusa 13 gang, a Latino gang attempting to racially cleanse Azusa of African Americans during a two-decade crime spree of harassment and attacks. Particularly relevant to the issue of interethnic violence is that the attacks were not against rival gang members. Rather, the conspiracy was characterized by its animus against civilian African American homeowners and students whom Azusa 13 wanted to push out of the city or prevent from moving there. All fifty-one gang members were convicted of various charges, including a conspiracy to cleanse Azusa of its black residents. At the sentencing of the guilty parties, the judge emphatically stated that the gang leader "was a proponent of the racial cleansing of the city of Azusa."[17]

The very same charges were lodged in the 2009 criminal indictment against 147 members of the Varrio Hawaiian Gardens Latino gang, one that followed the largest gang sweep in US history, for engaging in a conspiracy to systematically rid Hawaiian Gardens of all African Americans. The accused

gang leaders were convicted and received lengthy prison sentences for their
"conspiracy against African American community members, solely due to
their race" after boasting about being racist and referring to themselves as a
"hate gang."[18]

Like the murder on December 15, 2006, of Cheryl Green, a fourteen-
year-old eighth grader who was gunned down in broad daylight as she
perched near her scooter chatting with friends in her Harbor Gateway
neighborhood of Los Angeles, the Azusa 13 case is yet another Latino gang
attack on African Americans with no gang affiliations themselves. In the
case of Cheryl Green, members of the Latino 204 Street Gang were tried
and found guilty of murder and a hate crime. A 2007 investigation into the
Los Angeles–area Latino anti-black violence noted that the predominant
pattern was one of Latino gang members assaulting black passersby while
either yelling racial expletives such as "Fuck niggers. This is T-Flats [Varrio
Tortilla Flats gang area]," and "What the fuck are you niggers doing here? . . .
monkeys," or posting racially exclusionary graffiti by the murder sites such
as "Mayates [niggers] get out" and "187 Niggers [California Penal Code 187
for murder]."[19] At the same time, the involvement of gangs in Los Angeles
has induced many to deny the racial import of the violence. Indeed, Denisse
Rodarte and Sean Wright, two dynamic Los Angelenos filming a documentary about the black-Latino violence in Los Angeles,[20] have expressed
frustration with the vast numbers of residents who deny there is a racial
problem and refuse to talk about it.

Yet the Los Angeles County Commission on Human Relations notes
that Latino street gangs have been the most violent perpetrators of hate
crimes in the region, primarily against African Americans. Furthermore,
longitudinal studies of hate crimes in Los Angeles County demonstrate a
very clear racial aspect. When Karen Umemoto conducted a statistical study
of Los Angeles County law enforcement data over a five-year period in the
1990s, she uncovered a number of disturbing patterns. First, there was a
disproportionate rate of increase in the victimization of African Americans
as compared with other groups. The number of African American victims
increased by 70 percent, while the number of Asian American and Pacific
Islander victims increased 21 percent, the number of white victims increased
by 6 percent, and the number of Latino victims decreased by 8.4 percent. In
contrast to the victimization trends, there was a slight decline in the number
of reported African American perpetrators, while there was an increase with
all other groups. Latino perpetrators had the sharpest rise in number with
a 59.2 percent increase. Most disturbing, though, was the study's discovery

that Latinos were disproportionately the perpetrators of bias crimes against African Americans with no known gang affiliations.

While it is true that general crime statistics very likely undercount the number of incidents where Latino immigrants are victims of crime given their reticence to call any attention to their undocumented status when reporting a crime, it is also true that the number of incidents where African Americans are the victims of Latino crime may also suffer an undercount from the manner in which many criminal databases code Latino offenders as white.[21] Furthermore, the more specific context of hate crime *murders* is not one where victim reporting is necessary for criminal investigation. And it is within this context of hate crime fatalities that Latinos have been documented as the disproportionate aggressors against African Americans rather than being the victims of African American violence.

This is an unfortunate trend that civil rights organizations have noted and find alarming. An event similar to the 2006 Cheryl Green murder conviction and the 2011 Azusa hate crime convictions is the August 2006 conviction of The Avenues Latino gang members for a six-year conspiracy to assault and murder African Americans in Highland Park, Los Angeles.[22] Thus, while intraracial violence makes up the majority of violent incidents in Los Angeles and elsewhere, the overt racist motivations of these emerging interethnic conflicts has justifiably created a public concern. During the 2006 trial of The Avenues gang members, prosecutors demonstrated that African American residents (with no gang ties at all) were being terrorized in an effort to force them out of a neighborhood now perceived as Latino, in a manner suggestive of ethnic cleansing. For example, one African American victim in the case was murdered as he looked for a parking space near his Highland Park home, and another African American victim was shot simply for waiting at a bus stop in Highland Park. Debra Wong Yang, the US Attorney for the Central District of California, stated that the men "were killed by the defendants simply because they were African Americans who chose to live in a particular neighborhood. As this case demonstrates, we will aggressively pursue hate crimes such as this and convict those responsible for such reprehensible acts." In another case, a woman was knocked off her bicycle and her husband was threatened with a box cutter by one of the defendants who said, "You niggers have been here long enough."[23]

In the vast majority of the cases, links to prison criminal syndicates could be found whereby Latino prison gang leaders would issue the orders for racial cleansing of African Americans from "Latino spaces."[24] Nevertheless, the connection to prison criminal syndicates does not explain away the interethnic violence as simply a nonracial "criminal matter" for the simple reason that the targets have not been gang members themselves or in any way related to gang competition over drug trade and vengeance. Blacks have been singled out for the racial violence in ways that make the issue of racism inescapable. Indeed, the court convictions detailed in this chapter demonstrate that labeling the violence as racially motivated is not the mere result of sensation-seeking media outlets that describe it as such, but, more important, a reflection of the careful presentation of evidence with the exacting criminal law standard of "guilt beyond a reasonable doubt."

At first blush, it may be mystifying why such animosity exists between two ethnic groups that share so many of the same socioeconomic deprivations. Over the years, the hostility has been explained as a natural reaction to competition for blue-collar jobs in a tight labor market, or as the result of turf battles and cultural disputes in changing neighborhoods. Others have suggested that perhaps Latinos have simply become adept at learning the US lesson of anti-black racism, or that perhaps black Americans are resentful at having the benefits of the civil rights movement extended to Latinos. Although there may be a degree of truth to some or all of these explanations depending upon context, they are insufficient to explain the extremity of the ethnic violence and its explicitly stated racial agenda of black removal exemplified in the Latino versus black California criminal convictions and jury trial findings.

The fact is that racism—and anti-black racism in particular—is a pervasive and historically entrenched reality in Latin America and the Caribbean. More than 90 percent of the approximately ten million enslaved Africans brought to the Americas were taken to Latin America and the Caribbean (by the British, French, and Spanish, primarily), whereas only 4.6 percent were brought to the United States. For instance, by 1793 colonial Mexico had a population of 370,000 Africans (and descendants of Africans)—the largest concentration in all of Spanish America.[25]

The legacy of the slave period in Latin America and the Caribbean is similar to that in the United States: having lighter skin and European features increases the chances of socioeconomic opportunity, while having darker skin and African features severely limits social mobility. White supremacy is deeply ingrained in Latin America and continues into the present. In Mexico, for instance, citizens of African descent, estimated to make up 1 percent of the population, report that they regularly experience racial harassment at the hands of local and state police.[26] The ethnographer Christina Sue also demonstrates how skin-color discrimination adversely affects Mexicans of

African descent whether or not they racially identify as Afro-Mexicans.[27] Furthermore, the maintenance of transnational ties between immigrants and those remaining in the home country facilitates Mexicans' engagement with US racial ideologies prior to migration.

Anti-black sentiment also manifests itself in Mexican politics. During the 2001 elections, for instance, Lázaro Cárdenas Batel, a candidate for governor of the state of Michoacan, is believed to have lost substantial support among voters for having an Afro-Cuban wife. Even though Cardenas had great name recognition (as the grandson of Lázaro Cárdenas del Río, Mexico's most popular president from 1934 to 1940), he only won by 5 percentage points—largely because of the anti-black platform of his opponent, Alfredo Anaya, who said that "there is a great feeling that we want to be governed by our own race, by our own people."[28]

Given this, it should not be surprising that migrants from Mexico and other areas of Latin America and the Caribbean arrive in the United States carrying the baggage of racism, or that this facet of Latino culture is in turn transmitted, to some degree, to younger generations along with all other manifestations of the culture. Studies of social distance among US racial groups bear this out.

The sociological concept of "social distance" measures the unease one ethnic or racial group has for interacting with another. Social science studies of Latino racial attitudes often indicate a preference for maintaining social distance from African Americans. And although the social distance level is largest for recent immigrants, more established communities of Latinos in the United States also show a marked social distance from African Americans. For instance, in sociologist Tatcho Mindiola's 2002 survey of 600 Latinos in Houston (two-thirds of whom were Mexican, the remainder Salvadoran and Colombian) and 600 African Americans, the African Americans had substantially more positive views of Latinos than the Latinos had of African Americans. Although a slim majority of the US-born Latinos used positive identifiers when describing African Americans, only a minority of the foreign-born Latinos did so. One typical foreign-born Latino respondent stated: "I just don't trust them. . . . The men, especially, all use drugs, and they all carry guns." This same study found that 46 percent of Latino immigrants who lived in residential neighborhoods with African Americans reported almost no interaction with them.[29]

The social distance of Latinos from African Americans is consistently reflected in Latino responses to survey questions. In a 2000 study of residential segregation, the sociologist Camille Zubrinsky Charles found that

Latinos were more likely to reject African Americans as neighbors than they were to reject members of other racial groups.[30] In addition, in the 1999–2000 Lilly Survey of American Attitudes and Friendships, Latinos identified African Americans as their least desirable marriage partners, whereas African Americans proved to be more accepting of intermarriage with Latinos. More recently, a qualitative study of young adult children of Latino immigrants in Los Angeles suggests that immigrant parents send strong racialized messages about African Americans that deter their US-born Latino children from dating African Americans. Ironically, African Americans, who are often depicted as being averse to coalition building with Latinos, have repeatedly demonstrated in their survey responses that they feel less hostility toward Latinos than Latinos feel toward them. Although some commentators have attributed the Latino hostility to African Americans to the stress of competition in the job market, a sociological study of racial group competition suggests otherwise. In a study of 477 Latinos from the 1992 Los Angeles County Social Survey, Lawrence Bobo and Vincent Hutchings found that underlying prejudices and existing animosities contribute to the perception that African Americans pose an economic threat—not the other way around. Moreover, the 2006 Latino National Survey indicates that Latinos in Los Angeles identify other Latinos as economic competitors rather than blacks, suggesting that the black-Latino competition narrative is overstated.[31]

It is certainly true that the acrimony between African Americans and Latinos cannot be resolved until both sides address their own unconscious biases about one another. But it would be a mistake to ignore the Latino side of the equation as some observers have done—particularly now, when the violence in Los Angeles and California has involved Latinos targeting peaceful African American citizens. In fact, no other multiracial city has reported this level of anti-black Latino violence. How did the Los Angeles metropolitan area come to such a state of affairs despite the cautionary legacy of the 1992 unrest? To begin to understand the Los Angeles context, it is centrally important to first disaggregate the position of Latino immigrants from that of US-born Latinos.

While Latino immigrants have been documented to express negative views of African Americans and demonstrate a preference for segregation from African Americans, the violence in Los Angeles has been perpetuated in large measure by US-born Latinos.[32] US-born Latinos, in becoming "Americanized," experience themselves as socially undesirable raced subjects. Those who are not wealthy enough or light enough to be permitted the social access of assimilation are seemingly locked into the urban poverty quagmire of underfinanced schools, inadequate health care, and scarcity of employment opportunities.

At the same time that employers actively seek Latino immigrant labor for low-wage positions, low-skill labor US-born Latinos are excluded as a "less malleable" worker population. Indeed, the Americanization process provides English-speaking US-born Latinos with greater information and assertiveness about worker rights. Moreover, US-born Latinos have a sense of enhanced status as US-educated applicants, and this, in combination with their repeated exposure to rampant US consumerism, disinclines them to seek the same low-wage jobs as Latino immigrants. This results in a high rate of jobless US-born Latino men on the street searching for status and meaning. This is a context ripe for gang culture violence that exploits the tensions of residential segregation.

Living in segregated proximity to African Americans who are derided in Latin America as well as in the United States facilitates the notion that US Latino status depends upon a clear separation from and removal of African Americans from "Latino spaces." Like African American youth in Staten Island, Latino gang members in California are employing turf defense. Segregated out of Anglo white spaces and fighting for status in limited "colored" spaces, turf defense explodes into interethnic violence as a continuing legacy of white segregation. Indeed, in each of the California locations in which the federal government has investigated and prosecuted Latino gang members for what is tantamount to ethnic cleansing campaigns, African Americans have made up a very small percentage of the neighborhood statistically dominated by Latinos, where both groups are clearly segregated from Anglo whites.[33]

Demographic rates of segregation (from an "Index of Dissimilarity") indicate that Latinos are generally segregated from African Americans but are even more segregated from Anglo whites, while other measures suggest that in some locations Latinos are more segregated from African Americans than they are from Anglo whites. Nevertheless, recent trends indicate that Latinos and African Americans are increasingly likely to be neighbors. Moreover, in a recent study that examines Census data and arrest data from New York and California, a correlation was found between racial segregation and black and Latino homicide. Specifically, the study noted that the racial segregation of Latinos and blacks from non-Hispanic whites seemingly contributes to the commission of homicides by Latinos and blacks who are jointly excluded from white spaces.[34]

Nonetheless, the actual rate of segregation is less important to facilitating turf defense than the social meaning of the space. As Elise Boddie notes, geographic spaces can have a racial identity and meaning based on socially engrained biases regarding the people who inhabit, frequent, or are associated with particular places and racialized cultural norms of spatial belonging and exclusion. Once those social meanings are developed, residents may become inclined to enforce spatial separation as a means to perpetuate racial hierarchy. Moreover, the construction of social meaning adapts with the changing demography of a location. This then helps to explain how the historically black area of Compton, Los Angeles, has also witnessed Latino anti-black hate crimes against nongang affiliated residents since its shift to becoming 65 percent Latino and only 33 percent black as of the 2010 Census.[35]

Boddie calls it "racial territoriality" when people of color are excluded from public spaces that are identified as "white" and treated as being only for white people. Extending Boddie's useful concept of racial territoriality to the exclusionary actions of people of color themselves helps to elucidate the turf defense dynamic observed within the interethnic violence among African Americans and Latinos. This is well exemplified by a Pomona [California] 12th Street Gang member who, during his murder trial for participation in the "Nigger Killers" set, stated that it would be "humiliating" to 12th Street gangsters to allow African Americans to live in their neighborhood.[36]

In short, a significant factor in the interethnic violence between Latinos and African Americans can be attributed to the nation's long-standing spatial racial containment of nonwhites, the social exclusion and educational abandonment of Latinos and African Americans, and the operation of racial prejudice. Thus the conflict cannot be sloughed off as simply another generation of ethnic group competition in the United States (like the historically familiar rivalries between Irish, Italians, and Jews in the early part of the last century). Nor should it be disregarded as simply a matter for nonwhites to resolve themselves. The white investment in segregation has everything to do with the complicated dynamic of interethnic violence, and thus white maintenance of racial segregation and racial hierarchy must also be addressed. As Robert Chang and Neil Gotanda remind us, it is important to engage "in careful multigroup analysis that keeps an eye on White supremacy [to] help us see beyond binaries, real and false."[37] A brief review of the existing legal avenues for addressing residential segregation will help to further elucidate the challenges that exist for resolving the segregation problem that facilitates multiracial intergroup conflict as has on occasion occurred between Latinos and African Americans.

This section focuses upon residential racial segregation as a propulsive feature of racial subordination inasmuch as segregation influences the dedication of governmental financial resources, creation of jobs, and adequate education. In other words, the concern with residential segregation is embedded in the reality that the investment in infrastructure and services that facilitate upward mobility has historically been related to the number of whites in a community, giving force to the old adage "green follows white." Hence the call to address residential segregation is connected to all the resources that are tied to communities with non-Hispanic white residents. Moreover, insofar as the ethnic conflict discussed above is connected to "turf wars" over the remaining constricted nonwhite segregated spaces, it is important to understand the power of law, as well as its limits, in addressing this problem.

Official government concern with remedying residential segregation can be traced to the enactment of the Fair Housing Act (FHA) in 1968, which is commonly referred to as the "last plank of the civil rights movement." Congress passed the FHA in response to the race riots of the 1960s that many attributed in part to the poor living conditions wrought by residential segregation and the racialization of poverty. However, by the time the government attempted to step in, it might be said that the die had already been cast. The government had to counter decades of its previous active involvement and complicity in maintaining segregated neighborhoods, decades that had resulted in highly segregated neighborhoods.[38]

Nevertheless, the FHA's purpose was to further "the goal of open, integrated residential housing patterns and to prevent the increase of segregation." In order to accomplish this, Sections 3604 and 3605 of the act make it unlawful to discriminate against a person in a residential real estate transaction based on his or her inclusion in a protected class. The act provides for three ways of enforcing its provisions: administrative enforcement by the US Department of Housing and Urban Development (HUD), federal litigation, and private litigation. Furthermore, courts have expanded the ability of the FHA to provide for causes of action for some of the most common examples of indirect discrimination that contribute to residential segregation. These include "mortgage redlining, insurance redlining, racial steering, exclusionary zoning decisions, and other actions by individuals or government units which directly affect the availability of housing to minorities."[39]

While the FHA was designed to eliminate residential segregation and promote integration, a number of shortcomings have undermined its effective enforcement. These shortcomings surface in how the FHA deals with steering by real estate brokerage firms, redlining by mortgage lenders, discriminatory zoning by government entities, the phenomenon of "white flight," and the difficulties of bringing suit under the FHA. While many of these housing law issues may appear discontinuous from the racial discord between black and Latino communities, they all contribute to the racialized housing context that fosters conflict. For that reason it is important to acknowledge all facets of how residential segregation is sustained and our current legal enforcement insufficient.

"Racial steering" can be defined as a practice by which a real estate broker directs buyers toward or away from particular houses or neighborhoods according to the buyer's race. This practice is a factor that contributes to racial residential segregation. Prior to the passage of the FHA in 1968, "[r]acial discrimination was institutionalized in the real estate industry . . . and . . . [d]iscriminatory behavior was open and widespread among real estate agents at least until" that point. While it became rare to "outright refus[e] to rent or sell" to minority groups such as blacks after 1968 due to the threat of prosecution, a number of less obvious methods of racial steering were still available to real estate agents. These include: "(1) advising customers to purchase homes in particular neighborhoods on the basis of race; and (2) failing, on the basis of race, to show, or to inform buyers of, homes that meet their specifications." While the FHA was successful in dealing with more overt versions of racial steering, its shortcomings lay in how it dealt with the more subtle forms of steering that remained open to real estate agents. Because the discrimination was "unobservable, . . . the only way to confirm whether it has occurred" was by means of a housing audit.[40]

A housing audit matches paired teams of a white individual and one from a minority group. Each pair is supposed to be as similar as possible in all characteristics relevant to a real estate agent, such as their family and economic traits. Because the pair's only major difference is race, a housing audit can isolate discrimination based on race by observing how each individual of the pair is treated by real estate agents compared to the other. Yet to be effective, audit studies require a commitment of resources and time that has unfortunately been absent on the part of the government.[41]

Moreover, the FHA coverage of racial steering deals only with the practice as initiated by real estate agents without a customer's or client's consent. However, much of racial steering today occurs at the behest of real estate agents' clients, through the practice of "self-steering." If a home seeker actively wants a segregated community, some courts have held that a real estate agent who steers the client to such a location because of the client's preference is

justified. The court in *Dwivedi* noted that the FHA "does not require a broker
to endeavor to make his customers better people by withholding information that they request about the racial composition of the communities in
which the broker sells houses."[42] Statistical data regarding the prevalence of
self-steering is not available. Yet the recent surveys demonstrating that only
a minority of whites, Latinos, and Asians indicate a willingness to consider
moving into neighborhoods that are largely black, and that they find black
neighborhoods the least desirable of any racial makeup, suggest that self-
steering is a significant problem.[43]

Mortgage redlining and reverse redlining are other segregatory practices
that the FHA seeks to contain. "Redlining" is defined as "mortgage credit
discrimination based on the characteristics of the neighborhood surrounding the would-be borrower's dwelling." It was practiced by both the federal
government and the lending industry as a whole prior to the FHA's enactment in 1968 and was a contributing factor in racial residential segregation.
While courts have held that the FHA prohibits redlining in home financing,[44]
the shortcomings of the FHA in dealing with residential segregation can be
observed in the burdens imposed on plaintiffs looking to establish a cause
of action under the FHA.

To prove a case of redlining, the plaintiff must provide evidence of discriminatory intent. Requiring a showing of discriminatory intent is problematic in the realm of mortgage loans because it is "easily hidden among the
maze of variables an applicant must navigate to obtain a mortgage loan."[45]
Indeed, courts have noted that "an intent requirement would strip the statute
of all impact on de facto segregation."[46] To address this, some courts have
developed redlining analyses that do not require a plaintiff to show discriminatory intent, but instead show discriminatory impact. Yet, where disparate
impact is used, "the test required remains muddled, and the trend seems to
be toward a strict test that demands a great deal from any potential housing discrimination plaintiff."[47] While the Supreme Court's recent decision
upholding the ability to bring disparate impact claims under the FHA is a
welcome harbinger for enforcing the law, the Court refrained from articulating what legal standards and burdens of proof should apply in disparate
impact claims, thereby delegating to trial courts an excess of discretion that
may continue to overburden plaintiffs.[48]

The development of additional judicial tools was not the only approach
to shoring up the FHA's goal of combating residential segregation. The Home
Mortgage Disclosure Act (HMDA) of 1975 required mortgage lenders in
metropolitan areas to disclose information to the public about the mortgages

they approved within Census tracts. It was later amended to also require additional information, the most significant of which was the approval rates of mortgages by race.[49] Opening such information to the public has two effects on racial segregation. First, it helps combat segregation by providing awareness to the public about which institutions practice redlining on "[t]he theory ... that many city residents would not deposit their savings in institutions found to practice redlining." Second, it serves as a tool to identify where discriminatory practices such as redlining are occurring.[50]

The practice of redlining denies minorities access to capital used to further home ownership. While courts have interpreted the FHA to disallow redlining, the FHA was not originally equipped to deal with new tools of discrimination. One such tool is "reverse redlining." If racial redlining is the practice of denying loans to areas due to the racial makeup of those areas, then "[r]everse redlining is the practice of extending credit on unfair terms to those same communities."[51] The "bias in home lending has shifted from the outright denial of mortgages to individuals and neighborhoods on the basis of race, to a pattern of predatory lending whereby poor minorities received less favorable loan terms and are channeled into problematic forms of housing."[52]

On the surface, redlining and reverse redlining appear to have little in common as far as prohibition under the FHA is concerned. Whereas redlining is designed to exclude loans to minorities, reverse redlining actively targets them for loans. However, "[w]hen borrowers' loan options are limited due to historical discrimination in ... redlining, purposeful exploitation of these conditions should be, in itself, actionable discrimination."[53] Courts that have encountered reverse redlining cases have agreed with this and held that this practice violates the FHA. In order to deal with the differences between showing a prima facie case of redlining discrimination versus reverse redlining, courts have turned to an "exploitation theory" in order to show liability. This theory establishes liability on the part of a lender by showing that "(1) as a result of racial segregation, dual housing markets exist, and (2) defendant[s] ... took advantage of this situation by demanding prices and terms unreasonably in excess of prices and terms available to white citizens for comparable housing."[54]

Similar to how courts have interpreted the FHA in establishing a prima facie case for mortgage discrimination, courts that have addressed cases dealing with residential segregation due to government zoning have found that a showing of discriminatory effect on a protected class is sufficient to establish a prima facie case brought under the FHA. The elimination of an intent requirement was thought to further the integration goal of the FHA by removing a burden that plaintiff would be hard-pressed to prove. "Effect, and not motivation, is the touchstone, in part because clever men may easily conceal their motivations."[55] State courts that have dealt with cases challenging the validity of government zoning ordinances have also favored the elimination of inquiries into a defendant's intent in order to make a plaintiff's prima facie case. Instead, a prima facie case for zoning discrimination was established if a plaintiff could show such rules would have a discriminatory effect on a protected class. Once this is shown, the burden then shifts to the government to show this was necessary in order to further a compelling governmental interest.[56]

The aforementioned legal restrictions on exclusionary zoning are inadequate when conventional land use devices, such as minimum lot sizes, minimum floor space requirements, costly building code requirements, height limitations, and the restriction of apartments, multifamily dwellings, and manufactured home districts, are often viewed by courts as legitimate mechanisms for promoting compelling government interests in public health and environmental soundness despite how the restrictions work as direct class-based exclusions and indirect racial exclusions. While the fair housing doctrine permits plaintiffs to challenge the discriminatory effects of land use regulations without demanding proof of a specific discriminatory intent, courts have generally tended to find nothing inherently improper in density restrictions and other regulations that favor the construction and maintenance of exclusive suburban areas.

All the same, it is consistently the case that racial segregation is strongly affected by density zoning. Specifically, from 1980 to 2000, metropolitan areas that allowed higher density development had higher rates of racial integration than those areas with strict density limitations. Demographers who have noted the correlation between class-based density regulations and racial segregation have recommended that the legal system prohibit the most severe density restrictions outright because current fair housing doctrine inadequately attends to the societal harms of seemingly race-neutral density restrictions.[57]

The legal restrictions on exclusionary zoning are also inadequate for resolving the preference of private developers to create housing solely for the wealthy and those with easier access to credit. Operating against the disproportionate number of nonwhites living in poverty, the private developer economic preference for moneyed residents results in the construction of racially exclusive developments without the use of zoning. In response, local governments have used "inclusionary zoning." Inclusionary zoning is where an ordinance is enacted that can either mandate or encourage builders of new housing developments to make some specified percentage of their new housing units available to low- and moderate-income residents. The nonmandatory version of this "usually contain[s] incentives for . . . developers to build affordable housing, such as tax abatements, waivers of fees, expedited permitting, or subsidies for required infrastructure, or waivers of zoning requirements or concessions such as density bonuses." The mandatory version of this is a "statute, ordinance, or permit . . . that requires a residential developer to set aside a specified percentage of new units for low- or moderate-income housing or to maintain a low rental price on a percentage of the units for a significant period of time."[58]

New Jersey's *Mount Laurel* series of cases provide a prime example of legal devices that its courts have created to combat exclusionary zoning practices, which end up being a form of judicially imposed inclusionary zoning. In *Southern Burlington County N.A.A.C.P. v. Twp. of Mount Laurel*, the New Jersey Supreme Court found that a township ordinance was invalid because its effect was to exclude low- and moderate-income residents by limiting residential units to single-family dwellings, allocating unnecessarily large amounts of land to industrial use, and other construction restrictions. This ordinance was invalid because such a zoning ordinance was a land use regulation, which "is encompassed within the state's police power." Because "a zoning regulation, like any police power enactment, must promote public health, safety, morals or the general welfare[,] . . . a zoning enactment which is contrary to the general welfare is invalid." As housing is a basic need, "[t]he question of whether a citizenry has adequate and sufficient housing is certainly one of the prime considerations in assessing the general . . . welfare of that body." The court further noted that "the universal and constant need for . . . housing is so important and of such broad public interest that the general welfare which developing municipalities like Mount Laurel must consider extends beyond their boundaries and cannot be parochially confined to the claimed good of the particular municipality."[59]

In other words, New Jersey municipalities have an obligation to consider the housing needs of a broad class of people outside their boundaries, not just those of the people within. This "obligation arises for each such municipality affirmatively to plan and provide, by its land use regulations, the reasonable opportunity for an appropriate variety and choice of housing, to meet the needs, desires and resources of all categories of people who may desire to live within its boundaries[, and thus] may not adopt regulations or policies which thwart or preclude that opportunity." In order to satisfy this obligation, the New Jersey Supreme Court held that municipalities were required to provide people with a realistic opportunity to obtain low- and moderate-income housing. This obligation "extends at least to the municipality's fair share of the present and prospective regional need" of low- and moderate-income housing.[60] Therefore zoning ordinances that are exclusionary and do not meet this obligation are held invalid.

While some states like New Jersey use inclusionary zoning to mandate integration, many more prefer to restrict themselves to using voluntary financial incentives for developers in order to further socioeconomic integration that can simultaneously provide racial integration. One of the major federal incentives for promoting integrated housing along socioeconomic lines is the Low-Income Housing Tax Credit (LIHTC), which was created under the Tax Reform Act of 1986. The LIHTC was designed to incentivize private investment into creating affordable housing for low-income residents by providing tax credits to developers who build affordable rental housing. These tax credits are allocated by state agencies, and the "LIHTC is currently the largest federal subsidy for the construction of new low-income rental housing."[61]

New York City provides an example of the LIHTC in action and the kinds of incentives that are offered to developers in order to encourage the creation of integrated low-income housing. Among the more prominent examples are several programs offered by the New York City Department of Housing Preservation and Development (HPD) and the New York State Housing Finance Agency (HFA): the 421-a/421-g Affordable Housing Programs (AHPs) and the Inclusionary Housing Program. The 421-a AHP offers tax abatements to developers in exchange for those same developers to set aside at least 20 percent of their new construction project to affordable housing. The 421-g program acts similarly, except it applies to projects that convert nonresidential buildings into residential ones.[62] The Inclusionary Housing Program (IHP) is another incentive for developers to build affordable housing. However, the incentive differs from that offered by the AHP in that what developers receive in exchange is to qualify their project for a zoning bonus. This bonus allows developers to exceed the density normally allowed—in other words, it gives them allowance to build a larger building. The quid pro quo is that developers can earn greater profits by building a larger building (especially in an expensive real estate market like Manhattan), and these additional profits will subsidize the reduced rents from the affordable housing units.[63]

Nevertheless, LIHTC incentive programs have long been criticized for disproportionately allocating the tax credits to minority-concentrated underresourced neighborhoods of poverty, thereby reinforcing racial segregation. Moreover, all these LIHTC incentives focus upon the creation of new housing, which is vulnerable to economic downturns, and leaves completely unaddressed the plethora of existing housing stock that is highly segregated by class and race. Furthermore, the inclusionary zoning attempts exemplified by New Jersey's *Mount Laurel* fair share doctrine have led to modest results given the resistance of municipalities and state elected officials to the doctrine. While more affordable housing units have been developed in New Jersey over the years, much of the housing stock is still firmly entrenched in racial segregation.[64] A significant factor in the maintenance of racial segregation in New Jersey and elsewhere has been the dynamic of "white flight"—the phenomenon where whites flee residential areas that contain an increasing number of minorities.

An issue that the FHA has failed to address is the voluntary exodus of whites from neighborhoods that begin to achieve racial integration. It has been consistently documented that "White prejudice is such that when Black entry into a neighborhood is achieved, that area becomes unattractive to further White settlement and Whites begin departing at an accelerated pace." Indeed, the noted sociologist and demographer Douglas Massey posits that blacks tend to prefer a higher proportion of racial mixing with whites. This leads to a disparity in housing demand for racially integrated communities, therefore leading to situations where an increase in the presence of black families in a neighborhood results in both white families trying to move out and practically no white families trying to move in.[65]

Yet attempts to address white flight have themselves encountered concerns with racial discrimination. For instance, in *U.S. v. Starrett City Associates*, a developer of a housing project that received government subsidies in the form of a tax abatement in exchange for assuring that the project was intended to be a racially integrated community then encountered legal challenges to the developr's crude attempts to deal with white flight. Starrett sought to maintain a specific racial distribution by maintaining tenant quotas for each type of minority group. It was thought that such quotas were "necessary [in order] to prevent the loss of White tenants, which would transform Starrett City into a predominantly minority complex." In order to maintain racial integration and prevent white flight from occurring, Starrett unfortunately also discriminated against black applicants for housing because of their race and in violation of the FHA.[66]

The court held that while race was not always an inappropriate consideration in trying to promote integrated housing, Starrett's use of racial quotas that restricted minorities from renting in Starrett City in furthering this goal violated the FHA. However, the court in *Starrett* distinguished between ceiling quotas and access quotas in adjudicating the claim. An access quota pursues integration by setting a minimum floor amount of racial minority participation but places no maximum limit on the amount. In contrast, a ceiling quota seeks to maintain integration by setting a maximum limit on minority participation so as to minimize white flight. One commentator notes that "measures designed to increase or ensure minority participation, such as 'access' quotas, have generally been upheld . . . while programs designed to maintain integration by limiting minority participation, such as ceiling quotas, are of doubtful validity."[67]

Given these legal limitations on addressing white flight directly, it is even more important that the existing avenues for challenging segregation be fully enforced. Under the FHA, the primary responsibility for enforcing the FHA's residential integration and nondiscrimination provisions fell on HUD. However, from the inception of the FHA, the funds Congress allocated to HUD were far less then what the HUD secretary at the time requested. With such inadequate funding, it was feared that HUD would not have the staff available to enforce the FHA's provisions. This fear was realized by the early 1970s, when a HUD staff of only forty-two people was required to handle FHA complaints that numbered in the thousands each year. HUD funding continued to operate at a decreased level during the 1970s and 1980s until it was increased during the late 1990s.[68]

Nevertheless, the 2008 Report of the National Commission on Fair Housing and Equal Opportunity indicates that fair housing enforcement at HUD is still under great strain. HUD's shortcomings include: not pursuing enough discrimination cases, delayed and deficient discrimination investigations, underutilization of system investigations (where HUD "examine[s] whole agencies or industries for widespread entrenched discrimination practices[] such as real estate steering"), lack of sufficiently trained personnel to enforce fair housing, and having too much on its plate due to the responsibility of enforcing laws other than the FHA. Pro Publica's 2012 investigative report illustrated that this continues to be the case.[69] In addition, HUD's multiple responsibilities may put it in a position where its "fair housing mandate . . . take[s] a backseat to other interests." For example, one of HUD's non-FHA obligations is "to support urban economic and housing development . . . [by] working collaboratively with major housing and mortgage lending institutions," which can conflict with its affirmative duty to enforce fair housing.[70]

In order to deal with HUD's fair housing enforcement shortcomings, the Report of the National Commission on Fair Housing and Equal Opportunity recommends "the establishment of an independent fair housing enforcement agency that can provide the country with a powerful force that supports fairness and fair housing choice in a unified and systemic way." This agency would have three main components: employ staff with fair housing experience and competence; have an advisory commission representative of industry, advocates, and enforcers; and possess sufficient resources to enforce fair housing.[71] Such interventions are strongly recommended because the current status quo of effectively relegating the enforcement of the FHA to the private litigation efforts of the victims of segregation who have few resources to combat the systemic problem results in a devastating underenforcement of the law. Margalynne Armstrong observes that "[u]sing private litigation to address residential segregation results in treating the problem as one of individual access rather than as illegal activity aimed at a segment of society" and is therefore ineffective in checking group-oriented behavior that results in a larger social problem.[72]

For instance, the individual litigation model would have been ill-equipped to uncover the recent discriminatory practice of one Ohio housing development that HUD's specially trained testers discovered was purposely denying rental opportunities to African Americans in favor of Latinos. On January 27, 2012, an Ohio court entered a consent decree requiring the defendant to pay monetary damages and comply with a mandate to refrain from further discrimination pursuant to an injunction order.[73] The discrimination found in this case is a troubling dynamic that can only facilitate greater turf defense conflicts between blacks and Latinos.

While *Cincinnati Capital Partners* is the only documented HUD case that has raised the issue of Latino versus black segregation practices, a greater commitment of resources to HUD enforcement might reveal more, given the empirical finding that contemporary integrated "global neighborhoods" are only feasible when Latinos and Asians are the pioneer integrators of previously all-white zones.[74] Specifically, white flight is mitigated (or "buffered") when Latinos and Asians slowly integrate a neighborhood in limited numbers. Once this occurs, blacks are then able to enter this neighborhood, albeit in small numbers. Only the incremental introduction of blacks that follows the settlement of Latinos and Asians averts an onslaught of white flight. In contrast, the initial entry of blacks alone continues to trigger a direct white flight effect. Such findings underscore the need to more amply fund a revitalized legal enforcement of Anglo white segregation practices.

Despite the fact that this chapter's review of fair housing law indicates that the law has been historically limited in its challenge to racial segregation, there is cause for a renewed attention to fair housing law. The Supreme Court's recent reaffirmation of the federal obligation to advance integration issues a call to action for advocates to use the law to help "achieve our historic commitment to creating an integrated society." Moreover, the Court specifically noted that Congress enacted the FHA "to resolve the social unrest in the inner cities" because of the Kerner Commission Report, which "identified residential segregation and unequal housing and economic conditions in the inner cities as significant, underlying causes . . . of social unrest." Furthermore, just two weeks after the Supreme Court issued its opinion, President Obama announced a new requirement that cities and localities account for how they will use federal housing funds to reduce racial disparities, or face penalties if they fail.[75] The new administrative rules are part of President Obama's attempt to address the racial violence in cities like Ferguson, Missouri, and Baltimore, where hypersegregation has contributed to violent clashes with police officers reminiscent of 1960s racial unrest. While the executive and judicially reinvigorated support for the enforcement of fair housing law emanates from a concern with the legacy of historic black-white segregation, this same kind of reasoning should apply equally to the interethnic racial violence facilitated by white versus nonwhite segregation discussed in this chapter. It is thus a propitious moment for those concerned with interethnic violence to prioritize fair housing law enforcement as part of the panoply of issues around which to organize.

In short, only a renewed societal focus on combating the institutional forces of segregation along with racism and poverty can address interethnic relations nationwide. When that is done, Latino and African American communities will be better positioned to diminish the violence and build coalitions. Past experience has shown that these two groups can work together. There are a number of notable examples. In the 1960s the Young Lords' alliance with the Black Panthers provided an example of Chicago black and Latino communities coming together to pursue programs of direct action to bring their neighborhoods services, such as day care, free breakfasts, and vocational training.[76] In New York, the Young Lords Party also participated in movements for Black Power and African American civil rights.[77]

Within the context of electoral politics, black-Latino cooperation is exemplified by the example of the 1983 Chicago mayoral election campaign of Harold Washington, the city's first black candidate for mayor.[78] Latino communities in Chicago voted in huge numbers for Washington. Of the 48,000 votes that separated Washington from his Republican rival, close to 28,000 of them were cast from Latino communities.

More recently, there has been a growth of interethnic community-based advocacy organizations and worker-based coalitions. For instance, in Los Angeles, the Community Coalition was founded in 1989 as an African American and Latino organization with the goal of transforming beleaguered South Los Angeles neighborhoods through public safety campaigns, gang reduction efforts, and many other programs.[79]

The formation of the Bay Area's Black Alliance for Just Immigration (BAJI) provides an example of black-Latino cooperation in response to the growing societal anti-immigrant animus.[80] The BAJI is an education and advocacy group comprised of African Americans and black immigrants from Africa, Latin America, and the Caribbean who together oppose repressive immigration bills. The BAJI also brings together African Americans and black immigrants from Africa, Latin America, and the Caribbean to dialogue about the myths and stereotypes as well as the cultural, social, and political issues that divide those communities. Moreover, the BAJI provides the African American community with a progressive analysis and framework on immigration that links the interests of African Americans with those of immigrants of color. The BAJI's analysis emphasizes the impact of racism and economic globalization on African American and immigrant communities as a basis for forging alliances across these communities.

Similarly, the Encuentro Diaspora Afro in Boston was founded in response to the growing racial tensions from increased Latino immigration to the city. The organization acts as an ambassador of Afro-Latino culture to African American community advocacy and political events, and also designs community seminars and programs to improve cross-ethnic relations. Notably, participants have been quick to identify Boston's intense residential racial segregation as a key factor in racial hostilities.[81]

What this small sampling of black-Latino coalition efforts suggests is that there are hospitable venues for furthering more frequent, extensive, and lasting collaborations that can honestly confront all the sources of interethnic conflict. This chapter proposes that issues of residential segregation should also be made part of each organization's list of priorities. Including residential segregation legal reform as part of racial coalition work enhances the potential for reducing violent interactions and building peaceful multiracial societies.

NOTES

1. Lydia Saad, *Whites May Exaggerate Black-Hispanic Tensions*, GALLUP, July 17 2008, http://www.gallup.com/poll/108868/Whites-may-exaggerate-Blackhispanic-tensions.aspx.

2. JOHN D. MARQUEZ, BLACK-BROWN SOLIDARITY: RACIAL POLITICS IN THE NEW GULF SOUTH 12 (2013); EDWARD TELLES, MARK Q. SAWYER, & GASPAR RIVERA-SALGADO, EDS., JUST NEIGHBORS? RESEARCH ON AFRICAN AMERICAN AND LATINO RELATIONS IN THE UNITED STATES 3 (2011).

3. Darrel Steffensmeier et al., *Reassessing Trends in Black Violent Crime, 1980–2008*, 49 CRIMINOLOGY 197 (2011).

4. JOSH KUN & LAURA PULIDO, EDS., BLACK AND BROWN IN LOS ANGELES: BEYOND CONFLICT AND COALITION 1 (2014).

5. While it is not known how the Latino assailant personally identified along racial lines, his white appearance is salient to the analysis inasmuch as he was permitted to police the racial boundaries of white-identified Staten Island. Indeed, while media accounts make much of the notion that Latinos are racially mixed, it remains the case that many Latinos are unambiguously identifiable as predominantly either of black, white, Asian, or Indigenous ancestry. Moreover, Latino socioeconomic status has been shown to be affected by Latinos' racial appearance separate and apart from their Latino ethnic origin. John R. Logan, *How Race Counts for Hispanic Americans*, Lewis Center for Comparative Urban and Regional Research Report, July 14, 2003, at 8. In particular, Latinos of visible African ancestry have a socioeconomic profile that is much worse than that of Latinos of predominant white ancestry. *Id.* at 9.

6. CUNY Center for Urban Research, Staten Island, Urban Research Maps, 2010, at 1.

7. Donald P. Green et al., *Defended Neighborhoods, Integration, and Racially Motivated Crime*, 104 AM. J. SOC. 372 (1998).

8. http://www.pewresearch.org/2006/04/25/attitudes-toward-immigration-in-black-and-white/.

9. Sam Quinones, *L.A. County Hate Crimes Drop to 21-Year Low*, L.A. TIMES, Nov. 19, 2011, http://articles.latimes.com/2011/nov/19/local/la-me-hate-crimes-20111119.

10. People v. Goodman et al., Indictment No. 112/2010 (Supreme Court of the State of New York Criminal Term Apr. 5, 2010); Richmond County District Attorney Press Release, 2010, at 1.

11; Frank Eltman, *Four Teens Sentences in NY Hate Crime Stabbing*, BOST. GLOBE, Aug. 25, 2010, http://www.boston.com/news/nation/articles/2010/08/25/4_teens_sentenced_in_ny_hate_crime_stabbing/.

12. Nick Madigan and Peter Hermann, *Latinos Fear Increasing Crime against Community*, BALT. SUN, Aug. 24, 2010, at 1; John McCann, *Officer: Black, Latino Gang Violence to Grow*, HERALD SUN, Jan. 25, 2011, at 1; Jeffrey M. Cancino, *The Impact of Neighborhood Context on Intragroup and Intergroup Robbery: The San Antonio Experience*, 623 ANNALS AM. ACAD. POL. & SOC. SCI. 12 (2009).

13. Edward S. Shihadeh & Raymond E. Barranco, *Latino Employment and Black Violence: The Unintended Consequences of U.S. Immigration Policy*, 88 SOC. FORCES 1393 (2010).

14. Telles et al., *supra* note 2, at 14.

15. U.S. v. Rios et al., Docket No. 2:11-cr-00492 (C.D. Cal. June 1, 2011).

16. Christina Ng, *Latino Gang Charged with Racial Cleansing Attacks in California Town*, ABC NEWS.COM, June 9, 2011, http://abcnews.go.com/US/latino-gang-charged-racial -cleansing-california-town/story?id=13794815#.UHuGJ4bF271.

17. Earl Ofari Hutchinson, *Will Latino Gang Arrests Deepen Black-Brown Divide?*, THE GRIO, MSNBC.COM, June 8, 2011, http://thegrio.com/2011/06/08/will-latino-gang -arrests-deepen-black-brown-divide/; Sam Quinones, *Azusa 13 Street Gang Leader, Son Sentenced to Prison*, L.A. TIMES, Jan. 15, 2013, http://articles.latimes.com/2013/jan/15/local /la-me-0115-gang-sentence-20130115.

18. U.S. v. Flores et al., Docket No. 2:09-cr-00445 (C.D. Cal., May 6, 2009); U.S. Attorney's Central District of California Office Press Release, 2009; Jason F. Cunningham & Sharon R. Kimball, *Gangs, Guns, Drugs and Money*, 62 UNITED STATES ATTORNEYS' BULLETIN: GANG PROSECUTIONS 16 (2014); Scott Glover & Richard Winton, *Dozens Arrested in Crackdown of Latino Gang Accuse of Targeting Blacks*, L.A. TIMES, May 22, 2009, http://articles.latimes .com/2009/may/22/local/me-gang-sweep22.

19. Sam Quinones, *Two Reputed Latino Gang Members Are Charged in Fatal Shooting of Black Girl*, L.A. TIMES, Dec. 27, 2009, http://articles.latimes.com/2006/dec/27/local/me -charged27; People v. Alcarez et al., Docket No. NA072796 (L.A. C'ty Sup. Ct., Jan. 1, 2007); TONY RAFAEL, THE MEXICAN MAFIA, 216 (2007)

20. www.myspace.com/Blackandbrownproject.

21. Robert C. Davis & Edna Erez, *Immigrant Populations as Victims: Toward a Multicultural Criminal Justice System*, NATIONAL INSTITUTE OF JUSTICE RESEARCH IN BRIEF (1998), at 1.

22. U.S. v. Cazares, 788 F.3d 956 (9th Cir. 2015).

23. U.S. Dep't of Justice Central District of California Attorney General Press Release, *Gang Members Convicted of Federal Hate Crimes for Murders, Assaults of African Americans* (regarding U.S. v. Martinez, CR 04–415[b] [D. Ca. Aug. 1, 2006]), www.usdoj.gov/usao/cac /pr2006/102.html, at 1.; Andrew Murr, *A Gang War with a Twist: Gangbangers in L.A. on Trial for Deadly Hate Crimes*, NEWSWEEK, July 17, 2006.

24. Sam Quinones, *Race, Real Estate, and the Mexican Mafia: A Report from the Black and Latino Killing Fields, in* Kun & Pulido, *supra* note 4, at 261.

25. TANYA KATERÍ HERNÁNDEZ, RACIAL SUBORDINATION IN LATIN AMERICA: THE ROLE OF THE STATE, CUSTOMARY LAW AND THE NEW CIVIL RIGHTS RESPONSE 73 (2013); MIRIAM JIMENEZ ROMÁN & JUAN FLORES, THE AFRO-LATIN@ READER: HISTORY AND CULTURE IN THE UNITED STATES 8 (2010); Ben Vinson III, *The Racial Profile of a Rural Mexican Province in the "Costa Chica": Igualapa in 1791*, 62 THE AMERICAS 269 (2000).

26. EDWARD TELLES, PIGMENTOCRACIES: ETHNICITY, RACE AND COLOR IN LATIN AMERICA 3 (2014); Alexis Okeowo, *Blacks in Mexico: A Forgotten Minority*, TIME, Sept. 15, 2009, http://www.time.com/time/world/article/0,8599,1922192,00.html; SAGRARIO CRUZ-CARRETERO, THE AFRICAN PRESENCE IN MEXICO: FROM YANGA TO THE PRESENT 1 (2006).

27. CHRISTINA A. SUE, LAND OF THE COSMIC RACE: RACE MIXTURE, RACISM AND BLACKNESS IN MEXICO 114 (2013).

28. Yvette Cabrera, *Exposing Latinos' Third Root*, ORANGE COUNTY REG., Mar. 1, 2002, at 1; Ginger Thompson, *Race Strains a Mexican Campaign*, N.Y. TIMES, Nov. 11, 2001, http://www.nytimes.com/2001/11/11/international/americas/11MEXI.html.

29. GEORGE YANCEY, WHO IS WHITE? LATINOS, ASIANS, AND THE NEW BLACK/NONBLACK DIVIDE 69, 70–71 (2003); TATCHO MINIDOLA JR. ET AL., BLACK-BROWN RELATIONS AND STEREOTYPES 25–26 (2002).

30. Camille Zubrinksky Charles, *Neighborhood Racial-Composition Preferences: Evidence from a Multiethnic Metropolis*, 47 SOC. PROBS. 379 (2000).

31. YANCEY, *supra* note 29, at 70–71; Erica Morales, *Parental Messages Concerning Latino/Black Interracial Dating: An Exploratory Study among Latina/o Young Adults*, 10 LATINO STUD. 314 (2012); Lawrence Bobo & Vincent L. Hutchings, *Perceptions of Racial Group Competition: Extending Blumer's Theory of Group Position to a Multiracial Social Context*, 61 AM. SOC. REV. 63–64 (1996); Matt. A. Barreto et al., *Rainbow Coalition in the Golden State? Exposing Myths, Uncovering New Realities in Latino Attitudes toward Blacks*, *in* Kun & Pulido, *supra* note 4, at 203.

32. Seth Adam Meinero, *La Vida Loca Nationwide: Prosecuting Sureno Gangs Beyond Los Angeles*, 62 U.S. ATTORNEYS' BULLETIN: GANG PROSECUTIONS 27 (2014).

33. Data from the 2010 Census reports the racial demographic statistics for each of the following California neighborhoods as:

Azusa: 3% African American, 67.57% Hispanic, 19.3% white persons not Hispanic;

Harbor Gateway: 9.63% African American, 48.48% Hispanic, 28.66% white persons not Hispanic;

Hawaiian Gardens: 3.83% African American, 77.24 Hispanic, 7.32% white persons not Hispanic;

Highland Park: 2.13% African American, 71.69% Hispanic, 13.16% white persons not Hispanic.

http://quickfacts.census.gov/qfd/states/06/0632506.html.

34. Logan, *supra* note 5, at 1; Domenico Parisi et al., *Multi-Scale Residential Segregation: Black Exceptionalism and America's Changing Color Line*, 89 SOC. FORCES 838 (2011); Telles et al., *supra* note 2, at 1.; B. Feldmeyer, *The Effects of Racial/Ethnic Segregation on Latino and Black Homicide*, 51 SOC. Q. 600 (2010).

35. Elise C. Boddie, *Racial Territoriality*, 58 UCLA L. REV. 401 (2010); Dep't of Justice Press Release, 2013.

36. JEANNINE BELL, HATE THY NEIGHBOR: MOVE-IN VIOLENCE AND THE PERSISTENCE OF RACIAL SEGREGATION IN AMERICAN HOUSING 162–63 (2013); Rafael, *supra* note 19, at 216.

37. Robert S. Chang & Neil Gotanda, *The Race Question in LatCrit Theory and Asian American Jurisprudence*, 7 NEV. L. REV. 1028 (2007).

38. Brian Patrick Larkin, *The Forty-Year "First Step": The Fair Housing Act as an Incomplete Tool for Suburban Integration*, 107 COLUM. L. REV. 1617 (2007); STEPHEN GRANT MEYER, AS LONG AS THEY DON'T MOVE NEXT DOOR: SEGREGATION AND RACIAL CONFLICT IN AMERICAN NEIGHBORHOODS 197–222 (2000).

39. Otero v. N.Y.C. Hous. Auth., 484 F.2d 1122, 1134 (2d Cir. 1973); 42 U.S.C.A. §§ 3604–05; 42 U.S.C.A. §§ 3612–14; Southend Neighborhood Imp. Ass'n v. St. Clair County, 743 F.2d 1207, 1209 (7th Cir. 1984) (quotations omitted).

40. *Racial Steering: The Real Estate Broker and Title VIII*, 85 YALE L.J. 808, 809 (1976); Douglas S. Massey *America's Apartheid and the Urban Underclass: The Social Service Review Lecture*, 68 SOC. SERV. REV. 471 (1994).

41. John Yinger, *Measuring Racial Discrimination with Fair Housing Audits: Caught in the Act*, 76 AM. ECON. REV. 881 (1986); Douglas Massey, *The Past & Future of Am. Civil Rights* 2 DAEDALUS 37–54 (Spring 2011) .

42. Larkin, *supra* note 38, at 1624.; Village of Bellwood v. Dwivedi, 895 F.2d 1521, 1531 (7th Cir. 1990).

43. James Robert Breymaier, *The Need to Prioritize the Affirmative Furthering of Fair Housing: A Case Statement*, 57 CLEV. ST. L. REV. 245 (2009).

44. Town of Springfield, Vt. v. McCarren, 549 F. Supp. 1134, 1142 (D. Vt. 1982); Massey, *supra* note 40, at 478; Laufman v. Oakley Bldg. & Loan Co., 408 F. Supp. 489, 493 (S.D. Ohio 1976).

45. Charles L. Nier III, *Perpetuation of Segregation: Toward a New Historical and Legal Interpretation of Redlining Under the Fair Housing Act*, 32 J. MARSHALL L. REV. 617, 641–46 (1999); Benjamin Howell, *Exploiting Race and Space: Concentrated Subprime Lending as Housing Discrimination*, 94 CAL. L. REV. 101, 132–33 (2006).

46. Huntington Branch, N.A.A.C.P. v. Town of Huntington, 844 F.2d 926, 934 (2nd Cir. 1988).

47. *Id.*; Nier, *supra* note 45, at 648; Howell, *supra* note 45, at 134–35; Peter E. Mahoney, *The End(s) of Disparate Impact: Doctrinal Reconstruction, Fair Housing and Lending Law, and the Antidiscrimination Principle*, 47 EMORY L.J., 409 (1998).

48. Texas Dep't of Housing and Community Affairs v. Inclusive Communities Project, 135 S. Ct. 2507 (2015).

49. 12 U.S.C. § 2803 (2011); 12 U.S.C. § 2801.

50. Laufman v. Oakley Bldg. & Loan Co., 408 F. Supp. 489, 498 (S.D. Ohio 1976). *See also* 12 U.S.C. § 2801(b); Nier, *supra* note 45, at 632–33 (noting that such information can alert authorities to potential cases of mortgage lending discrimination).

51. Laufman, 408 F. Supp. at 489; Honorable v. Easy Life Real Estate System, 100 F. Supp. 2d 885, 892 (N.D. Ill. 2000).

52. Douglas S. Massey, *Racial Discrimination in Housing: A Moving Target*, 52 SOC. PROBS. 148 (2005) (quotations omitted).

53. Howell, *supra* note 45, at 131.

54. *See* Honorable, 100 F. Supp. 2d at 887, 892; *see also* Hargraves v. Capital City Mortg. Corp., 140 F. Supp. 2d 7, 20 (D. D.C. 2000).

55. U.S. v. City of Black Jack, Missouri, 508 F.2d 1179, 1184–85 (8th Cir. 1974); *see also* Huntington Branch, N.A.A.C.P. v. Town of Huntington, 844 F.2d 926, 935 (2nd Cir. 1988).

56. *Id. See also* Southern Burlington County N.A.A.C.P. v. Mount Laurel Tp., 92 N.J. 158, 220–21 (1983) (the court notes that inquiries into a municipality's "bona fide efforts" in order to avoid denying housing to lower-income individuals were too vague to be useful to courts or municipalities).

57. Jonathan Rothwell & Douglas S. Massey, *The Effect of Density Zoning on Racial Segregation in U.S. Urban Areas*, 44 URB. AFF. REV. 779, 801–2 (2009).

58. Jay M. Zitter, *Validity, Construction, and Application of Inclusionary Zoning Ordinances and Programs*, 22 A.L.R. 6th 295 at 5 (2007).

59. Southern Burlington County N.A.A.C.P. v. Twp. of Mount Laurel, 67 N.J. 151, 162–65, 174, 175, 178–9 (1975).

60. *Id.* at 179–81, 188–89.

61. 26 U.S.C. § 42 (2009); U.S. Dep't of Housing and Urban Development, 2010 at 5; Manhattan Community Board 1 Affordable Housing Task Force, Affordable Housing in Lower Manhattan, http://www.nyc.gov/html/mancb1/downloads/pdf/About_District /AH_REPORT.pdf, at 15.

62. 421-a Affordable Housing Program, http://www.nyc.gov/html/hpd/html/devel opers/ahp.shtml (last visited July 8, 2012); 421-g; http://www.nyc.gov/html/hpd/html /developers/421g.shtml.

63. Inclusionary Housing, http://www.nyc.gov/html/hpd/html/developers/inclusion ary.shtml.

64. Florence Wagman Roisman, *Mandates Unsatisfied: The Low Income Housing Tax Credit Program and the Civil Rights Laws*, 52 U. MIAMI L. REV. 1011 (1998); Mary Jo Patterson, *Towns Racing to Meet Affordable Housing Deadline*, N.Y. TIMES, Dec. 5, 2008, http://www .nytimes.com/2008/12/07/nyregion/new-jersey/07affordablenj.html?pagewanted=all.

65. DOUGLAS S. MASSEY & NANCY A. DENTON, AMERICAN APARTHEID: SEGREGATION AND THE MAKING OF THE UNDERCLASS 114 (1993); Massey, *supra* note 40, at 474–75.

66. U.S. v. Starrett City Associates, 840 F.2d 1096, 1098, 1099 (2nd Cir. 1988).

67. Michael F. Potter, *Racial Diversity in Residential Communities: Societal Housing Patterns and a Proposal for a "Racial Inclusionary Ordinance,"* 63 S. CAL. L. REV. 1151, 1230 (1990).

68. MEYER, *supra* note 38, at 197, 214; John Goering & Gregory Squires. *Guest Editor's Introduction*, 4:3 CITYSCAPE: A JOURNAL OF POLICY DEVELOPMENT & RESEARCH 1, 10 (1999).

69. Nat'l Commission on Fair Housing and Equal Opportunity, *The Future of Fair Housing: Report of the National Commission on Fair Housing and Equal Opportunity*, at 13–18 (2008); NIKOLE JONES, LIVING APART: HOW THE GOVERNMENT BETRAYED A LANDMARK CIVIL RIGHTS LAW (2012).

70. Goering & Squires, *supra* note 68, at 11.

71. Nat'l Commission on Fair Housing and Equal Opportunity, *supra* note 69, at 19.

72. Margalynne Armstrong, *Desegregation through Private Litigation: Using Equitable Remedies to Achieve the Purposes of the Fair Housing Act*, 64 TEMP. L. REV. 912 (1991).

73. U.S. Dep't of Housing and Urban Development Press Release No. 11–154, HUD Charges Owner and Manager of Cincinnati Apartment Complex with Race Discrimination, July 21, 2011; U.S. v. Cincinnati Capital Partners (S.D. Ohio Civ. Action No. 00617, Jan. 27, 2012).

74. John R Logan & Charles Zhang. *Global Neighborhoods: New Pathways to Diversity and Separation*, 15 AM. J. SOC. 37 (2010).

75. Texas Dep't of Housing and Community Affairs v. Inclusive Communities Project, 135 S. Ct. at 2516, 2525; 24 C.F.R. § 570.601 (2015).

76. GEOFFREY FOX, HISPANIC NATION 132–33 (1996).

77. ROMAN & FLORES, *supra* note 25, at 9.

78. LANI GUINIER & GERALD TORRES, THE MINER'S CANARY: ENLISTING RACE, RESISTING POWER, TRANSFORMING DEMOCRACY 232–33 (2002).

79. Ricardo Millet, *Case Study of Black-Brown Bridging: A Study Commissioned by the Marguerite Casey Foundation*, unpublished manuscript (2010) at 30–35; Jennifer Gordon & Robin A. Lenhardt, *Rethinking Work and Citizenship*, 55 UCLA L. REV. 1231 (2008); http://cocosouthla.org/civic-power/.

80. Andrew Grant-Thomas, Yusuf Sarfati, & Cheryl Staats, *Natural Allies or Irreconcilable Foes? Reflections on African American/Immigrant Relations*, 19 POVERTY & RACE RESEARCH ACTION COUNCIL 12 (2010).

81. Millet, *supra* note 79, at 30–35.

9

A Modest Proposal
Rethinking Black History, 1865–1965

CLARENCE WALKER

Although the title of my essay is borrowed from Jonathan Swift, I will not suggest in this essay that the Irish eat their children. What I will propose is a new conceptual framework or narrative strategy for black American history from 1865 to 1965. As it is currently written, the history of black people during this period of political, social, cultural, and economic change remains largely exceptional, treated as different from the history of Chinese, Mexican, and Japanese Americans during the last third of the nineteenth century and the first six decades of the twentieth century. I base this observation on my reading of black history textbooks being used in college courses today. These include *From Slavery to Freedom* (first published in 1947 by John Hope Franklin and extensively revised by Evelyn Brooks Higginbotham in 2010) and two more recent books: Darlene Clark Hine, William Hine, and Stanley Harrold's *The African-American Odyssey* and Thomas Holt's *Children of Fire.*[1] The authors of these books are all accomplished historians who have made important contributions to the field of black American history, and their books tell us a great deal about the current strengths and weaknesses of the field. These books are important because they are used in classrooms throughout the country and influence how students, regardless of their color, understand the history of black people in the United States. The story they tell is of the triumph of blacks over adversity. But I wonder what the efficacy of this Whiggish paradigm, exclusively focused as it is on black and white interactions, will be in the twenty-first century, as the "American Dilemma" is redefined.

When Gunnar Myrdal wrote his important book *An American Dilemma: The Negro Problem and Modern Democracy* sixty-eight years ago, black people were the focus of American race relations. Today this is no longer the case, as blacks have been displaced by Hispanics as the largest racial minority in the United States.[2] Globalization and immigration have transformed and complicated race in America; this is apparent on the ten campuses of the University of California, where black students have become a minority within minorities. I no longer assume that the majority of the students in my black history classes will be black, as was the case when I began lecturing thirty-nine years ago at Wesleyan University.

Currently I am a professor at the University of California, Davis, where for the past several years I have taught a course called "Race in America" that compares the racial formation of Asian, black, Mexican, and Native Americans, and others, from 1450 to the present. As the constituency of my classroom has changed, I have read more broadly so that I can answer questions about the effects of what I call in this essay a "regime of differential citizenship" during the last third of the nineteenth century and the first sixty-five years of the twentieth.[3] My Japanese, Chinese, and Mexican American pupils continue to be interested in black history, but they also want to know how their own ancestors became citizens and whether they were sharecroppers, or were victims of lynching, or could marry whites. These issues are not addressed in the texts mentioned above, and maybe they should not be in books devoted to the history of blacks. But in this essay I want to argue that they require attention, for both historical and political reasons. Readers of Franklin and Higginbotham, Holt, and Hine et al. will find that these authors do not break out of the racial binary of black and white. How could it be otherwise, given the history of black history?

Born in the eighteenth century, the discipline of black American history was part of a defense mounted "against an omnipresent 'white supremacist social order.'" Its principal components, "identity and inspiration," were intended to counter a white image of blacks as simply being hewers of wood and drawers of water.[4] In many ways current black historiography is still influenced by the tropes of "identity and inspiration," and thus needs to be rethought. Book titles such as *Children of Fire*, *The African-American Odyssey*, and *From Slavery to Freedom* simultaneously contest and reinscribe the white master narrative of American history, with its triumph of a people over adverse circumstances. If the Puritans and western pioneers subdued the wilderness and Native Americans to create the United States, black people have similarly created a world of their own.

To be sure, the black world was not a simulacrum of that created by whites, but a place with its own institutions and culture. Franklin and Higginbotham, Holt, and Hine et al. do an excellent job of documenting the space blacks created after the Civil War in the face of white hostility, op-position, and violence. In their histories the black past is teleological, in the sense that it builds up to a victorious conclusion embodied in the civil rights movement. But this mythic story obscures more than it reveals, because it ignores the fact that those of Chinese, Japanese, and Mexican origin living in this country at the same time were also struggling for political, social, and economic equality: maybe not in the same way that blacks were, but contesting white racism nonetheless.

Black history, as it is imagined in these textbooks, is endowed with a unique or singular quality that obscures the fact that the history of blacks in the years from 1865 to 1965 was part of a larger racialized historical process. I take 1865 as the starting point of this process because that date marks the end of the Civil War and the beginning of the movement toward the late nineteenth-century disfranchisement of blacks in the South. Its end point, the Voting Rights Act of 1965, signaled the conclusion of the work begun during the Civil War and Reconstruction and was a major step forward in the creation of an interracial democracy in this country.

The United States in the period framed by these dates is best understood as what I am calling a "regime of differential citizenship." In other words, this was a nation where black and brown people's citizenship differed from that of whites, and where for a time Asians were denied it altogether. Although legally defined as white after they were admitted to citizenship in ceded territories at the end of the Mexican-American War, Mexican Americans were nevertheless widely discriminated against because of their skin color. They also posed a problem for the American Imperium because they, like the Chinese and the Japanese, were seen as being different from white Americans in terms of not only racial but also national identity. Chinese, Japanese, and Mexicans, like Jews in Europe in the nineteenth century, were perceived as "enzymes of decomposition." [5] Not being phenotypically white, these groups endangered the racial homogeneity and stability of the United States. The triple signification of the Chinese, Japanese, and Mexicans in some ways distinguished their condition from that of blacks, who became citizens in 1868 in recognition of their service in the Civil War. By contrast, Chinese and Japanese immigrants in the United States were long denied citizen-ship altogether, and Chinese families were sundered when immigration was prohibited for decades. And although Mexican Americans were classified as white for legal purposes, they were not otherwise accepted as such.

Despite the distinctions we can make among these various groups, the important point here is that within this racial state the term "American" was understood, as Toni Morrison has written, to mean "white." Defining the nation in this way created what Benedict Anderson has called "a deep, horizontal comradeship" between all whites, regardless of their class and ethnicity.[6] During the last part of the nineteenth century and the first two-thirds of the twentieth century, white people were "white" first and only secondarily Anglo-Saxon, German, Irish, and so on. In making this generalization, I understand that the "WASPs" and "ethnics" did not get along and sometimes hated each other; were divided by national origin and religion; and fought over jobs and neighborhoods. Still, when confronted with blacks, Chinese, Japanese, or Mexicans, all of them were white together.

Regardless of their class or educational attainments, white people believed that "Radical Reconstruction had flown in the face of history and science," and that as a white man's country, the United States had been founded on the idea "that multiracial democracy was an impossibility." This was the lesson whites drew from the collapse of Reconstruction. James Bryce, Viscount Bryce, a professor of civil law at Oxford University, noted in 1888 the unsuitability of blacks exercising the franchise when he wrote that "[r]ights which the agricultural labourers of England did not obtain until 1885 were in 1867 thrust upon these children of nature, whose highest form of pleasure had hitherto been to caper to the strains of a banjo."[7]

Viewed from this perspective, the Civil War and Reconstruction constituted only a momentary hiatus in the history of American white supremacy. The cultural attitudes that had defined black people as denizens and slaves before the Civil War did not disappear after five years of internecine conflict and a twelve-year struggle devoted to creating interracial democracy in the South. "Emancipation's theoretical effect," in the words of Robin Wiegman, was to create a "social sameness" between black and white men; a space where supposedly black and white males were equal under the law. In reality, this was more fiction than fact. A former slave, George King, captured the problematic nature of this assumption about black freedom when he observed, "The master he says we are all free, but it don't mean we is white. And it don't mean we is equal."[8] King's skepticism about his and other blacks' freedom can be extended to the post–Civil War and Reconstruction histories of Chinese, Japanese, and Mexican Americans because all of these people wore what University of Chicago sociologist Robert Park once called the "racial uniform": they were not white.

In the period between 1865 and 1965, black people constituted one of the nation's "excepted populations"—that is, people who occupied excepted spaces outside the public sphere—but Chinese, Japanese, and Mexican

Americans were "excepted populations" too.[9] Membership in these groups meant exclusion from what Herbert Croly called "the promise of American life" in his 1909 book by that name. I think black history textbooks should take note of this fact by also foregrounding the history of the Chinese, Japanese, and Mexicans in this country. As such books currently present this material, one would think that only black people, for example, were denied citizenship, were victims of extralegal violence such as lynching, worked as sharecroppers, were prohibited from marrying whites, and had to fight for their civil rights.

Blacks became citizens in 1868 after the ratification of the Fourteenth Amendment. The struggle to make the former slaves citizens also involved a discussion of whether Chinese immigrants living on the West Coast should be included in this legislation. This debate centered on the suitability of Chinese in the Pacific states to become citizens of the United States. Even before the issue of black citizenship was discussed in the 1860s, the Chinese had become conflated in the American mind with blacks and were imagined as possessing a Negroid phenotype. "In thickness of lips, flattened noses and extended nostrils, [the Chinese] bear a considerable resemblance to the Negro," a reporter for the popular American magazine *Harper's Weekly* wrote in 1858. He also claimed that Chinese women from Hong Kong had "baboon-like faces,"[10] a construction that reiterated the seventeenth-century English charge that Africans resembled apes. The perception of the Chinese as black/apes suggests that what Frantz Fanon once called the "pit of niggerhood" encompassed more than the South and blacks.[11]

Chinese immigrants were denied American citizenship on the grounds that they were aliens and therefore did not satisfy the requirement of *jus soli*—that is, they were not born in the United States. Although blacks were permitted to naturalize beginning in 1870, the Chinese and most "other nonwhites" had to wait until the 1940s and 1950s for the right to naturalize. Even the citizenship status of Chinese who were born in this country to immigrants was unclear until the Supreme Court's ruling in *United States v. Wong Kim Ark* in 1898.[12] The Chinese occupied a different position in the white racial imagination from either blacks or Mexicans, in part because they were pagans and were perceived as unassimilable culturally and politically. One US senator, in arguing against enfranchising the Chinese under the Fifteenth Amendment, railed against their "political filth and moral pollution" and claimed that the Chinese population in this country constituted "an imperium in imperio—China in the United States."[13]

For their part, Mexicans were white legally, but not socially. Elite Mexicans were defined as white because of their Spanish blood, but Mexicans who were phenotypically Indian were not. Mexican racial identity was thus ambiguous, and this status, as the legal scholar Laura E. Gómez observes, "positioned them to play roles as an intermediate group between whites and nonwhite groups like blacks and Indians. Mexicans' status as a racially mixed group both made it possible for some Mexicans to occupy an 'off-white' position and for the group overall to be classified as an inferior 'mongrel' race." Constructed as half-breeds, Mexicans, like blacks, were incorporated into a nation where the very definition of republican liberties "and the color of liberty" were white.[14] This conception of the nation requires a more cautious reading of the Fourteenth Amendment than is offered by current black history textbooks.

According to Holt, the amendment was part of a cluster of reforms that granted "male citizens . . . of whatever race, color, or previous condition" the same constitutional protections as whites. Higginbotham echoes this observation when she writes that "the Fourteenth Amendment . . . guaranteed the citizenship of 'all persons born or naturalized in the United States.'" Hine and her coauthors state that the Fourteenth Amendment "fundamentally changed the Constitution by compelling states to accept their residents as citizens and to guarantee that their rights as citizens would be safeguarded."[15] None of the preceding is false or inaccurate in terms of the letter of the law. Like these textbook authors, I think the passage of the Fourteenth Amendment was an important milestone in the black struggle for racial equality. Nevertheless, they overstate the transformative power of this legislation as an agent of racial progress. The ambiguous status of both Chinese Americans and Mexican Americans under this legislation raises important questions about the interpretation of the Fourteenth Amendment that are not addressed in their texts. None of these authors examines the implications of the "two classes" interpretation of the Fourteenth Amendment, according to which the amendment was construed to apply only to two racially defined classes of people, blacks and whites, and held not to be concerned with nationality groups. This interpretation allowed for de facto segregation and discrimination against Mexican Americans, on the pretext that because they were white, they were not "being discriminated against as a separate class of people." Whiteness under the law did not confer on Mexican Americans a badge of uncontested privilege, as it did for Anglos in the age of segregation. The status of American-born children of Chinese immigrants was also left ambiguous under the Fourteenth Amendment, with opponents arguing that birthright citizenship did not extend to those whose parents were nonnaturalized foreigners—as Chinese immigrants by statute and legal precedent were.[16]

Following the precedent established by the traditional master narrative of American history, Franklin and Higginbotham, Holt, and Hine et al. have constructed a black history that obscures more than it reveals about the United States as a racial state. Nowhere in their books, for example, is there a discussion of Chinese, Japanese, and Mexican laborers in the postbellum Union. After the Civil War, black sharecropping and tenant farming was not an isolated institution, but part of a larger system of coerced labor within the continental United States and Hawaii. In the 1870s, for instance, planters in Louisiana imported Chinese "coolies" to work on their plantations. The Asian immigrants, it was thought, were more industrious than blacks and could be paid less. Furthermore, as a nineteenth-century version of a "model minority," the Chinese, unlike blacks, were not expected to challenge white supremacy. According to one southern newspaper, the Chinese would side with "the Conservative white vote of the South or, more likely, prefer their own institutions, refuse to have anything to do with politics, or take interest in them." The Union general and Arkansas governor (1868–1871) Powell Clayton observed that "[u]ndoubtedly the underlying motive for this effort to bring in Chinese laborers was to punish the negro for having abandoned the control of his old master, and to regulate the conditions of his employment and the scale of wages to be paid him."[17] Both of these comments address what Critical Race theorists call "differential racialization."[18] In this case, the Chinese were differentiated from blacks for political and economic reasons. Unfortunately for the planters, their efforts to replace the former slaves with Chinese labor did not work. The Chinese proved to be as troublesome as black labor had been after the Civil War. Commenting on this state of affairs, the historian John Rodrigue has written, "Nor were the Chinese more amenable to working in a slavelike manner than had been freedmen, and they resented the planters' efforts to lower wages and impose discipline."[19] Ultimately, the plantation owners returned to what they knew: that is, black people. "Accustomed to black labor in the fields, white planters and farmers could not contemplate any other way of life."[20] In noting the attempt of white southern land owners to replace their former bondspeople with a different workforce, I am not trying to erase the importance of sharecropping in black history. On the contrary, awareness of this fact complicates but also enriches our understanding of sharecropping by indicating that there was nothing inevitable about it, just as there was nothing foreordained about slavery.

Labor is not the only place where the history of the Chinese and blacks in America intersects. The Chinese, like blacks, were also excluded or segregated in the public sphere of the late nineteenth and early twentieth centuries. The anti-Chinese campaign in California was coterminous with the rise of Jim Crow in the South. If blacks, both men and women, were hypersexualized, described as unclean, and perceived as a threat to civilization, so were the Chinese. Indeed, constructed as menaces to society, the Chinese, blacks, and Mexicans were all victims of extralegal violence. Although blacks were the main victims of lynching during the last quarter of the nineteenth century and first decades of the twentieth, this type of violence was not confined to blacks alone. White mobs also lynched Chinese and Mexicans. When viewed from this perspective, the violation of black civil rights was part of a national project of white terror directed at other races.[21] Lynching, as the literary critic Jacqueline Goldsby writes, should not be understood as either "regional" or "aberrant." Because this crime against humanity "lays bare the neuroses shaping the ideologies of white supremacy against the humanism of democratic liberalism ... the lynching murders of Mexicans and Chinese in the West, Southwest, and far North ought to be a first clue that we need to develop sustained analyses that posit lynching to evince more than the South's economic provincialism or its perverse will to racial dominance."[22] In suggesting that lynching was something that only happened to black people, black history textbooks perpetuate a historiographical tradition that needs to be revised. The problems that black people faced were situated in a multiracial nation. Because of this, we cannot continue to write about American racism in an exceptionalist fashion, identifying blacks as the nation's sole "excepted population."

The time is past when black history could be imagined as an isolated experience in American history, because how we currently understand the racial history of the United States has changed. One aspect of this reimagined racial past must involve a reconsideration of the civil rights movement. Although the three books discussed in this essay present a panoramic analysis of the post–World War II black quest for political, economic, and social equality, their focus is solely on black people and sheds no light on the Asian American and Mexican American civil rights movements. Their discussions of civil rights after 1945 is curiously silent about the fact that there were "numerous civil rights movements ... [t]hroughout the United States involving African Americans, Mexican Americans, Native Americans ... and in many cases combinations of a variety of these groups."[23] When viewed from this perspective, the black civil rights movement, although important, was part of a larger process to overthrow white supremacy.[24] Indeed, its significance is lost if it is not placed in this wider context.

All of these groups thought that access to quality education, good jobs, and the right to vote were necessary to realize the American Dream. In pursuit of this goal, other minorities sometimes worked along with blacks. Eight years before *Brown v. Board of Education*, for example, Mexican American parents in Orange County, California, filed a lawsuit challenging segregation in the county's public schools, *Mendez v. Westminster*.[25] Along with a number of other groups, the NAACP filed an amicus brief challenging the doctrine of separate but equal. Unfortunately, because the three books discussed in this essay do not mention this case, the result is a history constructed around the erasure of others. Black history needs to move beyond this mode of analysis.

First, although the books under discussion here are well researched and written, they reveal a high degree of specialization in which expertise has run amok to produce a self-contained narrative that suggests blacks were the only people victimized by white supremacy between 1865 and 1965. Writing history in this fashion not only makes other groups less important; it is also dangerous politically because it may result in a history that speaks only to black people.

Second, broadening the focus of the narrative found in these black history texts is easy and has already been accomplished by a scholar working in another field. Nineteen years ago, the late Ronald Takaki published *A Different Mirror: A History of Multicultural America*. This book is a model for anyone working in black history or any field of ethnic studies.[26] It weaves together the history of America's "excepted populations" in a way that is both accessible and illuminating for undergraduates. This magisterial study of multiracial America was followed by Tomás Almaguer's *Racial Fault Lines* and Evelyn Nakano Glenn's *Unequal Freedom*. Together, these three books present insightful and comparative treatments of racial formation in America by moving the story beyond the binary of black and white.[27]

Such scholarship provides a comparative framework for understanding what I have called a "regime of differential citizenship." For example, while Higginbotham uses the term "Empire of Color" to describe US expansion abroad in the last decade of the nineteenth century,[28] I would argue that the nation was an "Empire of Color" before it expanded abroad. The Mexican-American War, Chinese exclusion, and Jim Crow all created imperial racial subjects who were "identified by an indelible mark of color."[29] Thus the United States constituted itself as a white imperial racial space long before the 1890s. And currently, despite the twaddle about being a postracial society, the election of a black president has reignited in some white Americans a political feeling that I call "political whiteness," a term coined by the political scientist Daniel Martinez HoSang to describe a "political subjectivity rooted in white racial identity."[30]

Currently, this sense of identitarianism expresses itself in a belief that whites have lost their country, a sense of loss most clearly seen in the white Right's anxiety about the writing and teaching of American history. The comfortable, reassuring, yet faulty narrative that focused on George Washington, Thomas Jefferson, and the other founders has been replaced by a story that decenters white men and whiteness. Blacks, Native Americans, and women have become agents rather than ciphers in the colonial history of the United States, for example. Most important, this revised national history does not ignore the dispossession and genocidal destruction of Indians, the central place of American Negro slavery in the economic development of the nation, and the oppression of women irrespective of their class and color. Unfortunately, such recasting of national history with a focus on gender and nonwhite people has produced a political backlash. In Arizona, for example, the state legislature has passed a law that includes among its provisions the prohibition of instruction that "[promotes] resentment toward a race or class of people," where the phrase "race or class of people" is a euphemism for white people.[31] A critical reading of this section of the statute reveals that the law prevents teachers from teaching that the war with Mexico (1846–1848) was a war of colonial conquest. Children in the Arizona schools are to be taught a past in which "Manifest Destiny" is stripped of its racial content. Placed in a broader context, the Arizona law is a southwestern version of the neo-Confederate reading of Southern secession in which states' rights and not slavery caused the Civil War. White Arizonans, like their southern peers, want to imagine a history of the United States as a homogeneous place/space in which blacks and Mexican Americans are once again reduced to secondary roles. Arizona's efforts to rewrite the American past is not an isolated event. In Tennessee, the Tea Party has called for the elimination of references to slavery in textbooks that note that some of the founding fathers owned slaves.[32] These examples clearly debunk the notion that the United States is a postracial society, a reactionary idea that is not supported by the day-to-day lives of a number of people of color in the nation. Calling the United States postracial is like imagining France or Saudi Arabia to be post-anti-Semitic or postgender.

The election of a black president has not ushered in a racial nirvana in which race as a category of ascription has disappeared. Race may have a changing significance, but it has not gone away. How does postracialism explain a federal judge sending a racist e-mail about the chief executive's parentage? Or another e-mail issued by a right-wing think tank that makes fun of the president's sexuality and shows him eating a bucket of fried chicken?[33] Both stereotypes deployed in the second e-mail draw on classic racist images of black men, who were constructed in the postbellum South as being sexually promiscuous and given to stealing chickens. What these caricatures of the president indicate is that although American society has made a great deal of racial progress, it still has a way to go before it is free of the virus of racial hatred. This hatred is not directed exclusively at black people today, any more than it was directed exclusively at black people in the past. There is, for example, the recent case of the Connecticut mayor whose response to a scandal involving his police force's alleged mistreatment of Latinos was to quip that he might help their community by eating tacos. (The racism inherent in the mayor's remark was compounded by his ignorance of the fact that the majority of Latinos in his city are Ecuadorians, for whom tacos are not a traditional food.) Or the fact that ESPN, referring to the end of a New York Knicks winning streak spurred by Taiwanese American Jeremy Lin, used the headline "Chink in the Armor."[34] History, and black history in particular, has played an important role in helping the nation rethink the place of race in its past and so has the history of Asians and Mexicans in America, but there is more work to be done.

I realize that these groups have not always had amicable relations politically, socially, and intellectually, but at this particular moment in American history, it may be time for black historians to create a multiracial history of the United States that explores historical intersections and divergences, inclusive not only of Asian Americans and Mexican Americans, but of others who are targets of "political whiteness," including certain classes of white people. History, as the philosopher Reinhart Koselleck says, "always performs a political function." It is more than facts and dates. Furthermore it is never neutral, as Keith Jenkins has noted: "[h]istory is never for itself; it is always for someone."[35] Believing as I do that history has a function beyond the glorification of the nation-state, I hope that re-visioning the history of black Americans in the context of the Asian American and Mexican American experiences will be understood as part of larger historical and political processes and thus will usher in a new understanding of the American past.

NOTES

1. John Hope Franklin & Evelyn Brooks Higginbotham, From Slavery To Freedom: A History of African Americans (9th ed., 2011); Darlene Clarke Hine et al., The African-American Odyssey (2011); Thomas C. Holt, Children of Fire: A History of African Americans (2011).

2. Gunnar Myrdal, An American Dilemma: The Negro Problem and Modern Democracy (1944; rpt. 1972); http://www.census.gov/prod/cen2010/briefs/c2010br-04.pdf. I use the term "Hispanic" here because it is the Census Bureau's term of choice.

3. I want to thank my colleague Edward Dickinson for talking about this problem with me and for suggesting a framework for discussing Asian, black, and Mexican American history. I have not included a discussion of Native American history in the present essay because I think the Native Americans' history of genocide and dispossession differs from that of America's other racialized subjects. I have also chosen to focus here on Chinese, Japanese, and Mexican Americans. This approach both reflects the background of my own students and avoids confusing matters by trying to treat the experiences of all nonblack minority groups as identical. My analysis, in other words, is intended to offer a model for moving beyond the black-white binary rather than to be an all-inclusive survey.

4. Clarence E. Walker, Deromanticizing Black History: Critical Essays And Reappraisals 87 (1991); Eugene D. Genovese, In Red and Black 201 (1984).

5. Quoted in James Davidson, The Greeks and Greek Love 203 (2009).

6. Toni Morrison, Playing in the Dark 47 (1992); Benedict Anderson, Imagined Communities 16 (1983).

7. Marilyn Lake & Henry Reynolds, Drawing the Global Colour Line 6, 65, 69 (2008).

8. Quoted in Linda Frost, Never One Nation 38 (2005); quoted in Leon Litwack, Been in the Storm So Long 224 (1979).

9. Ann Laura Stoler, On Degrees of Imperial Sovereignty, 18 Public Culture 1141 (2006).

10. Quoted in Najia Aarim-Heriot, Chinese Immigrants, African Americans, and Racial Anxiety in the United States, 1848–82, 60–61 (2003).

11. Winthrop D. Jordan, White Over Black 30–32 (1968); Frantz Fanon, Black Skin, White Masks 47 (1967).

12. Ian Haney López, White by Law 32 (2006); United States v. Wong Kim Ark, 169 U.S. 649 (1898).

13. Aarim-Heriot, supra note 10, at 93.

14. Laura E. Gómez, Manifest Destinies: The Making of the Mexican American Race 83 (2007); Stoler, supra note 9, at 133.

15. Hine et al., supra note 1, at 314.

16. The language of the Fourteenth Amendment is controversial even today, playing a prominent role in debates over whether birthright citizenship extends to the children of immigrants who are in this country illegally: http://www.nytimes.com/2011/01/06/us/06immig.html?_r=1&ref=fourteenthamendment; Mario García, Mexican Americans 50 (1989). See also Brian Behnken, Their Own Battles (2011).

17. Moon-Ho Jung, Coolies and Cane 108 (2006); Ronald Takaki, Strangers from a Different Shore 100 (1989).

18. For this concept, see Richard Delgado & Jean Stefancic, Critical Race Theory: An Introduction 8 (2001).

19. John C. Rodrigue, Reconstruction in the Cane Fields 137 (2001).

20. Leon Litwack, Trouble in Mind 118 (1998).

21. Alexander Saxton, The Indispensable Enemy (1995). See the discussions or descriptions of lynching in Franklin & Higginbotham, *supra* note 1, at 282–86; Hine et al., *supra* note 1, at 362–64; Holt, *supra* note 1, at 189. *See also* Victor Jew, *"Chinese Demons": The Violent Articulation of Chinese Otherness and Interracial Sexuality in the Midwest, 1885–1889*, 37 J. Soc. Hist. 390–409 (2003); William D. Carrigan & Clive Webb, *The Lynching of Persons of Mexican Origin or Descent in the United States, 1848–1928*, 37 J. Soc. Hist. 411–37 (2003). Lynching in the New South is examined in Fitzhugh Brundage, Lynching in the New South: Georgia and Virginia, 1830–1930 (1988). For the lynching of blacks in both the South and the country at large, see Phillip Dray, At the Hands of Persons Unknown (2002). The fine collection of photographs in James Allen, ed., Without Sanctuary: Lynching Photography in America (2000) is essential for anyone interested in this subject.

22. Jacqueline Goldsby, A Spectacular Secret: Lynching in American Life and Literature 21 (2006).

23. Brian D. Behnken, The Struggle in Black and Brown 5 (2011). For the discussions of civil rights, see Franklin & Higginbotham, *supra* note 1, at 510–79; Hine et al., *supra* note 1, at 568–640; Holt, *supra* note 1, at 285–331.

24. For Chinese American and Japanese American struggles with Jim Crow, see Roger Daniels, Asian America *passim* (1988); Takaki, *supra* note 17, *passim*. For the Mexican American quest for equality, see Brian D. Behnken, Fighting Their Own Battles (2011); Neil Foley, Quest for Equality (2010); Philippa Strum, *Mendez v. Westminister* (2010).

25. Foley, *supra* note 24, at 102–7; Strum, *supra* note 24, *passim*.

26. Ronald Takaki, A Different Mirror (1993).

27. Tomás Almaguer, Racial Fault Lines (1994); Evelyn Nakano Glenn, Unequal Freedom (2002).

28. Franklin & Higginbotham, *supra* note 1, at 275.

29. Stephen Steinberg, Race Relations 112 (2007).

30. Daniel Martinez HoSang, Racial Propositions 20 (2010). On this point, see also Clarence E. Walker, *"We're Losing Our Country": Barack Obama, Race & the Tea Party*, 140 Daedalus 125–30 (Winter 2011).

31. Nicole Santa Cruz, *Arizona Bill Targeting Ethnic Studies Signed into Law*, L.A. Times, May 10, 2010, http://articles.latimes.com/2010/may/12/nation/la-na-ethnic-studies-20100512.

32. *Tea Party Groups in Tennessee Demand Textbooks Overlook US Founder's Slave-Owning History*, Huffington Post, Jan. 23, 2012, http://www.huffingtonpost.com/2012/01/23/tea-party-tennessee-textbooks-slavery_n_1224157.html.

33. Kirk Johnson, *Montana Judge Sends Racist Joke about Obama*, N.Y. Times, Mar. 2, 2012, http://www.nytimes.com/2012/03/02/us/montana-judge-sends-racist-joke-about-obama

.html; *Obama Photo Illustration on Blog Brings Apology from John Locke Foundation,* WINSTON-SALEM J., Mar. 23, 2012, http://www2.journalnow.com/news/2012/mar/23 /wsmain01-obama-photo-illustration-on-blog-brings-a-ar-2077352/.

34. Peter Applebome, *After Charges of Latino Abuse, Focus Shifts to Major for His "Taco" Remark,* N.Y. TIMES, Jan. 25, 2012, http://www.nytimes.com/2012/01/26/nyregion/on-lati no-abuse-mayor-says-i-might-have-tacos.html; Chris Greenberg, *ESPN Racist Jeremy Lin Headline: Network Apologizes for Insensitive Headline for Knicks Loss,* HUFFINGTON POST, Feb. 18, 2012, http://www.huffingtonpost.com/2012/02/18/espn-racist-jeremy-lin-headline -mobile-apology_n_1286277.html.

35. Quoted in ELIZABETH A. CLARK, HISTORY, THEORY, TEXT 22 (2004).

10

Gay Is the New White (Gay Is the New Straight)

DEVON W. CARBADO

An ongoing question about coalitional politics concerns the political inter-actions between LGBT communities and African American communities. Note already how that articulation posits these groups as mutually exclusive, as if there are no African Americans who are also members of LGBT com-munities. Yet civil rights advocacy effectuates this disaggregation all the time. That is to say, advocacy on the part of LGBT communities continues to marginalize the experiences of African Americans who are LGBT, and advocacy on the part of African Americans continues to marginalize the experiences of LGBT people who are African American. This essay focuses on the former problem—that is to say, pro–gay rights advocacy. The central claim I advance is that, historically, pro–gay rights advocacy has reflected a racial ideology that invokes and trades on black civil rights symbols, political victories, and legal reforms, on the one hand, and elides contemporary black disadvantage and social inequality, on the other. I refer to this ideology as gay rights color blindness. I do so because the ideology relegates racial inequality to the domain of history, stages a gay civil rights agenda that obscures the existence of black LGBT communities, and conceptualizes racial equality in formalistic terms. Put another way, gay rights color blindness deploys African American identity and civil rights history to advance a gay rights agenda in which black LGBT people are nowhere to be found and blackness, more generally, is marked as an identity whose civil rights aspirations have already been fulfilled.

I focus my comments on how gay rights color blindness figured in LGBT challenges to the "Don't Ask, Don't Tell" policy. I do so because the color-blind strategy that gay rights advocates employed in the context of "Don't Ask, Don't Tell" created a precedent for more recent LGBT challenges to state-sanctioned homophobia. In a recently published article, the legal scholar Rus-sell Robinson interrogates the ways in which LGBT advocacy for marriage privileged the experiences of white gay men in particular and obscured the racial disadvantages of African Americans across gender and sexual identity. He refers to this advocacy as an instance of "marriage equality post-racialism" and illustrates the way it was manifested in media campaigns, legal briefs, and political discourse.[1] As I show, the practice of foregrounding white gay male experiences and displacing or marginalizing black experiences has an earlier manifestation in gay rights advocacy—gay rights challenges to "Don't Ask, Don't Tell."

To challenge "Don't Ask, Don't Tell," some gay rights proponents analogized the rhetoric the military deployed to exclude (out) gays and lesbians from the military service to the rhetoric the military deployed to exclude African Americans in the past. They reasoned that because we repudiated the latter, we should also repudiate the former. This analogizing of rhetoric was the predicate for a formal equality analogy about discrimination— namely, the exclusion of African Americans from the military is like the exclusion of (out) gays and lesbians. The analogy sets up an equivalency between race-based and sexual orientation–based military exclusion. Buttressed by color-blind intersectionality, the analogy obscured important civil rights history, elided the existence of black gays and lesbians, normalized whiteness as the natural but unarticulated racial default for the expression of gay identity, and produced a civil rights discourse that traded on white normative masculinity.[2]

According to David Smith, the spokesperson for the gay and lesbian coalition group Campaign for Military Service, the language the military employed to exclude blacks from military service is like the language the military employed to exclude (out) gays and lesbians. Smith's argument has additional force if we examine two texts: a Department of Defense (DoD) directive justifying the military's discrimination against (out) gays and lesbians, and a 1942 statement from the secretary of the navy supporting racial segregation in the armed forces. The DoD directive reads, in part:

> The presence in the military environment of persons who engage in homosexual conduct or who, by their statements, demonstrate a propensity to engage in homosexual conduct, seriously impairs the accomplishment of the military mission. The presence of such members adversely affects the ability of the armed forces to maintain discipline, good order and morale; to foster mutual trust and confidence among service members; to insure the integrity of the system of rank and command; to facilitate assignment and worldwide deployment of

service members who frequently must live and work in close conditions affording minimal privacy; to recruit and retain members of the
armed forces; to maintain the public acceptability of military service.[3]

Now consider the navy's statement, which, in relevant part, reads:

> Men onboard ships live in particularly close association; in their
> messes, one man sits beside another; their hammocks or bunks are
> close together; in their tasks such as those of gun crew, they form a
> closely knit, highly coordinated team. How many white men would
> choose, of their own accord, that their closest associates in sleeping
> quarters, at mess, and in gun crews should be of another race?[4]

These texts suggest that at different historical moments in America, the
armed forces have employed military-necessity arguments to justify both
racial segregation and the exclusion of (out) gays and lesbians from the military. Blackness and homosexuality threaten military discipline, organization,
morale, and readiness. Fair enough? Maybe. But this discursive analogy then
became the basis for a comparison about discrimination: gay exclusion from
the military is like black exclusion from the military. Part of the problem
here is that this claim of formal inequality obscures the history of Jim Crow
and the ways in which that history was sexualized. Rather than employing
the politics of Jim Crow to discuss how racial regimes regulate sexuality
(and how sexuality is often a technology for policing racial boundaries), gay
rights proponents imposed a gay gaze—or sexual orientation qua sexual
orientation frame—onto the racial exclusion of blacks from the military.
As George Chauncey puts it in a related context, "claiming the two experiences have been the same does no justice to history and no service to the
gay cause."[5]

To appreciate the importance of historical contextualization here, consider
again the following language from the navy's statement: "Men onboard ships
live in particularly close association; in their messes, one man sits beside
another; their hammocks or bunks are close together."[6] On its face, and read
outside of its historical context, this language seems to be more about (homo)
sexual anxiety, racially unmodified, than an intersectional racial anxiety that
was, to borrow from Kendall Thomas, "sexuated."[7] The language invites us
to think about "cruising" or the "gay gaze." The notion would be that heterosexual military men are worried about being the object of gay desire, for
such objectification threatens their notion of manhood. Read outside of its

political and historical context, the language from the navy's statement can be interpreted to be solely (and presumably unracially) about the relationship among homosexual orientation, manhood, and military social norms—the extent to which homosexual presence threatens heterosexual manhood and heterosexist military culture.[8]

But the statement also explicitly speaks of "white men" and men "of another race," querying, rhetorically, whether the former "would choose, of their own accord" to share sleeping quarters with the latter. We know the answer. This explicit invocation of race in the navy document invites an engagement of the specific historical context in which the navy produced the statement. Gay rights proponents did not perform that engagement. Their strategy was to replace the racial signifiers in 1940s military documents with sexual orientation signifiers. Under this approach, the text in the navy's 1942 statement that reads "How many *white* men would choose, of their own accord, that their closest associates in sleeping quarters, at mess, and in gun crews should be of another *race*?" becomes "How many *heterosexual* men would choose, of their own accord, that their closest associates in sleeping quarters, at mess, and in gun crews should be of another *sexual orientation*?"[9]

This strategy of replacing race with sexual orientation displaced black civil rights' history and the opportunity to explore how that history was sexualized, even as gay rights proponents were drawing on black civil rights for moral authority. Replacing race with sexual orientation, in other words, obscures that the navy's statement was written in the context of Jim Crow. The pro-segregation military officials who promulgated this document might have been worried about black (presumptively heterosexual) men cruising white (presumptively heterosexual) men. But heterosexuality was so thoroughly embedded in military culture, so naturalized a default, that the concern likely was not consciously about the gay gaze as such or gay bodies as such, though bodies and sexuality as they intersected with race certainly mattered, a point to which I will return presently.

Instead, the navy's statement reflects the then-pervasive notion of the black body as contaminated and contaminating and the perception of black men as inferior and failed men in two contradictory senses. On the one hand, the notion was that black men were infantile, happy-go-lucky, and effeminate; they were men for whom "boy" was a more appropriate designation. On the other, black men were perceived to be hypermasculine and sexually aggressive, men for whom "buck" was a more appropriate designation. In this respect, rather than reading the navy's statement abstractly, we should read it against the backdrop of this boy/buck racial dialectic. Constituted by an "imputed combination of masculine lack and masculine excess,"[10] this racial dialectic places black men both between and beyond the borders of male and man, effectively rendering them impossible subjects of masculinity.

This is not to say that sexual orientation, and sexuality more generally, is irrelevant to this analysis. Under the logic of the boy/buck racial dialectic, black men threatened to "turn" or de-masculinize white military men in at least two ways: effeminization (via sexual violence or engendering in white men an infantilized man-boyhood) or sexual corruption (via same sex intimacy or other acts of perceived sexual immorality). Thus, for example, when Georgia congressman Stephen Pace argued, in a letter to the secretary of the navy, against the racial integration of the armed forces on the ground that "white boys [would be] forced to sleep with . . . negroes,"[11] it is not enough—indeed it is misleading—to say simply that Pace's statement reflects a homophobic panic (as distinct from a racial panic).

Nor is it enough to assert that the military's concern about racial integration is just like the military's concern about sexual orientation integration. Framing the analogy along either of the preceding lines disaggregates race from sexuality and dehistoricizes the context in which Congressman Pace articulated his anti-black racial phobia. More fundamentally, such analogizing obscures that laws barring blacks from military service were crucial sites, not merely for regulating racial access, but for constituting race and racial power. That is, the exclusion of blacks from the military further constituted blacks and whites as oppositional social categories within a regime of racial hierarchy.

The navy's statement and Pace's concerns about "white boys [and] negroes" should be understood contextually with reference to the racial dynamics I set out above. Those dynamics were unequivocally invested with sexuality. The navy's statement and Pace's comments were deeply bound up with and reflected profound anxieties about a quintessential and racially sexualized Jim Crow boundary—the "amalgamation of the races." Concerns about this boundary were not exhausted by the perceived effects that black male presence in, or racial penetration of, the military would have on white men in terms of either sexual intimacy or infantalization. The exclusion of black men shored up the racially masculinist Jim Crow order. Vesting any power in black men—including the power to (tres)pass across a white masculine color line (the military)—undermined the anti–racial amalgamation imperative that underwrote the entire Jim Crow edifice.

Motivating this imperative was the sense that racial amalgamation always already portended one of the most transgressive acts of racial integration:

heterosexual intimacy between black men and white women. A black man could become "strange fruit"—the victim of a lynch mob—upon the mere allegation that he crossed that gendered color line. In the context of Jim Crow, white women constituted a rigorously policed racial and gendered territory. Excluding black men from military service helped to preserve the integrity of a woman's borders and at the same time kept both black men and white women in their respective racial and gendered places. Understood in this way, racial segregation in the armed forces helped to manage a racially inflected heterosexualized panic that was an important part of the broader disciplinary apparatus of Jim Crow. It is precisely this panic that explains the overpolicing of consensual black male heterosexuality across the color line (and the historical punishment of these associations as rape) and the underpolicing of nonconsensual white male heterosexuality (and the historical failure to punish this sexual violence as rape). Simply comparing language in military documents and substituting identity categories in order to advance a formal inequality argument erases this history.[12]

And yet it would be inaccurate to say that gay rights proponents completely ignored black civil rights history. In fact, they traded on the moral authority of the civil rights movement. But they did so without actually engaging the racial conditions under which African Americans were fighting for reform. The gay rights advocacy against "Don't Ask, Don't Tell" selectively incorporated African American history—and African Americans—to compare sexual orientation per se (read: presumptively white gays and lesbians of today) with race per se (read: presumptively black heterosexuals of the Jim Crow era). Underwriting the advocacy was the notion that, in a historical sense, gays are like African Americans; in a contemporary sense, gays are just like everybody else (white normative heterosexuals).

This strategy should disturb us. It exploits and displaces black civil rights history, trades on white privilege, and renders whiteness an invisible particularity of gay identity. Like the *Jespersen* litigation, gay rights advocacy against "Don't Ask, Don't Tell" reflected intersectional color blindness. Throughout the gay rights campaign against "Don't Ask, Don't Tell," gay identity is (almost entirely) intersectionally constituted as white. Naming this as an intersectional activity is crucial not only to articulating color blindness as a racial preference for whites but also to highlight gay identity as a repository for the expression of that preference. In the context of the gay rights challenges to "Don't Ask, Don't Tell," whiteness anchors the intelligibility of gay identity and blackness as a heterosexualized social category whose disadvantages and civil rights aspirations reside in the domain of history.

The intersectional color blindness of gay rights advocacy helps to explain why black gay men were largely invisible as victims of "Don't Ask, Don't Tell" and why normatively masculine white men were visible. The "just like everybody else" refrain created a discursive field from which the "but for" gay male victim could grow. This figure is just like other white normatively masculine men, but for the fact of his sexual orientation. A mimic of a copy,[13] this gay male icon is gay like a white heterosexual man.

Black men could not perform this "gay like a white heterosexual man" role. They lack the homonormative conventionality that this imperative demanded. This might not be obvious. One could surmise that the perceived masculinity surplus of black identity would cure the perceived masculinity deficit of gay identity. However, the excesses of black masculinity complicate that possibility. Black men are perceived to be too masculine to be authentically gay in the first place.

As Russell Robinson has argued, discourses about black men reify this inauthenticity. While black men are presumed to be on the down low (DL), which implies a desire to live a straight life while secretly and pathologically having sex with men, white men are presumed to be in the closet, which implies being forced to claim straightness against the desire for open and normal relationships with other men.[14] The DL engenders condemnation; the closet, sympathy. Whereas DL men are perceived to be villains, closeted men are constructed as victims. The DL phenomenon is pathologized and thus described as an unnatural part of the gay experience. The closet, in contrast, is normalized and thus described as a comparatively natural part of being gay. DL men are described as physically hypermasculine (essentially bucks). Closeted men are described as straight acting (essentially normative). All of this situates black men outside of white gay normativity and thus outside the "gay like a white heterosexual man" frame.

There is another racial explanation for the absence of black men in the "gay like a white heterosexual man" role—the image of the "wishy-washy" effeminate black gay man, an image that trades on the boy (effeminacy) side of the boy/buck racial dialectic. Marlon Riggs wrote compellingly about this "wishy-washy" iconography. "Snap-swish-and-dish divas have truly arrived," wrote Riggs, "giving Beauty Shop drama at center stage, performing the read-and-snap two-step as they sashay across the movie screen, entertaining us in the castles of our homes." Riggs's point is that images of black effeminate gay men have been commodified and voyeuristically included in our culture, but always as a sign of nonnormativity. To put the point the way Riggs does, "Negro faggotry is the rage! Black gay men are not."[15]

The intersection of race, masculinity, and sexuality helps to explain why gay rights advocates focused on the white casualties of "Don't Ask, Don't Tell" despite the fact that African Americans have been disproportionately affected by the policy. Too masculine to be gay and too feminine to be men, black gay men cannot be gay like a white heterosexual man. Thus, while Perry Watkins, a black army sergeant, established an important milestone when he became the first openly gay serviceman to successfully challenge "Don't Ask, Don't Tell," gay rights advocates largely marginalized him in their campaign.[16] As Tom Stoddard, the important gay activist lawyer who directed the Campaign for Military Service, said, "[T]here was a public relations problem with Perry Watkins." Watkins often performed in drag at recreational centers, social clubs, and other official and unofficial military gatherings. Notwithstanding that the military sometimes specifically requested these performances, they were at odds with the boy-next-door representative gay man around whom gay rights advocates sought to structure their advocacy. Watkins was very aware that this representative gay man was racialized. According to Watkins, gay right proponents preferred "poster children," many of whom had "lied" about their sexual orientation, over "a black man who had to live the struggle nearly every day of his life."[17] From Watkins's perspective, much of the public gay rights advocacy against "Don't Ask, Don't Tell" rendered him invisibly out.

Enter Keith Meinhold. A white navy petty officer who revealed that he was gay on *ABC World News Tonight*, Meinhold became the poster child for the gay rights campaign. He appeared on the cover of the February 1, 1993, issue of *Newsweek* magazine, in full navy uniform, performing the role of the all-American boy. The headline accompanying his image asks: "How Far Will Clinton Go?"[18] On the one hand, one could say that this cover invites the reader to conclude that Clinton would have to go very far. On the other hand, one could argue that after reading Meinhold's story, the American public would come to see him as an ordinary man, but for his sexual orientation, and conclude that Clinton would not be going too far if he admitted men like Meinhold—men who were gay like white heterosexual men—into the military.

Joseph Steffan, a former midshipman who was expelled from the US Naval Academy a few weeks before graduation, made a similar public appearance. Consider the following account:

The host is interviewing Joseph Steffan. . . . Raised in the Midwest, Catholic, a choirboy in his local church, Steffan was the kid next door.

Clean-cut, an excellent student, exceptional in track, he took as his date for the senior prom the high school's homecoming queen. From his small town in Minnesota, Joe Steffan entered Annapolis. At the Academy he was ranked in the top ten in his class, became battalion commander his senior year, and received the unique honor of twice singing, solo, the national anthem at the Army-Navy game.

The TV monitor shifts to a film of Joe Steffan, standing on a platform as the Army-Navy game is about to begin, bearing erect, singing the anthem against the red, white, and blue backdrop of the American flag waving in the stadium breeze. The television studio camera again trains its lens on Joe Steffan's face, his sincere gaze, his serious eyes. . . . Joseph Steffan . . . is now "out" to the USA.[19]

Significantly, it is not just Steffan who is "out" here. For, in this context, Steffan, like Meinhold, functions as a representative gay man. He is respectable. He is accomplished. He is an athlete. He is American. He is white. He is normatively masculine. And he is also gay. I employ "and" and not "but" here because the theater invites us to conceptualize Steffan's gay identity as incidental or beside the point with respect to his military manhood. Steffan's normative masculinity, which his whiteness helped to intersectionally constitute, rendered him gay like a white heterosexual man.

To the extent that "Don't Ask, Don't Tell" is now a dead letter, one can query whether it makes sense to interrogate how gay rights contestations of this policy managed questions of race. Why should we care about that now? Surely gay rights advocacy today is more intersectionally nuanced? With respect to gay rights advocacy for marriage equality, the answer is "no."[20] A slogan that circulated in pro–gay rights discourses about marriage equality is that "gay is the new black."[21] This slogan relegated racial inequality to the domain of history, staged a gay civil rights' agenda that treated race as largely irrelevant, obscured the existence of black LGBT communities, and conceptualized racial equality in formalistic terms. In short, more than five years after the formal repudiation of the "Don't Ask, Don't Tell" policy, at least some gay rights advocacy continues to frame African Americans as a group whose civil rights aspirations have already been fulfilled.

NOTES

1. Russell K. Robinson, *Marriage Equality Postracialism*, 61 UCLA L. Rev. 1010 (2014).

2. This white normative masculinity excluded not only black men but also black women. Because I am interested in interrogating maleness and masculinity as intersectional subjectivities, my focus is on the former.

3. RANDY SHILTS, CONDUCT UNBECOMING: LESBIANS AND GAYS IN THE U.S. MILITARY: VIETNAM TO THE PERSIAN GULF 378–79 (1993).

4. John Sibley Butler, *Homosexuals and the Military Establishment*, 31 SOCIETY 13, 16–17 (1993).

5. GEORGE CHAUNCEY, WHY MARRIAGE? THE HISTORY SHAPING TODAY'S DEBATE OVER GAY EQUALITY 161 (2005).

6. Butler, *supra* note 4, at 16.

7. Kendall Thomas, *"Ain't Nothin' Like the Real Thing": Black Masculinity, Gay Sexuality, and the Jargon of Authenticity*, in REPRESENTING BLACK MEN 55 (Marcellus Blount and George P. Cunningham, eds., 1996).

8. Kenneth L. Karst, *The Pursuit of Manhood and the Desegregation of the Armed Forces*, 38 UCLA L. Rev. 499 (1991); SHILTS, *supra* note 3; Garry L. Rolison & Thomas K. Nakayama, *Defensive Discourse: Blacks and Gays in the Military*, in GAYS AND LESBIANS IN THE MILITARY: ISSUES, CONCERNS, AND CONTRASTS 121–34 (Wilbur J. Scott & Sandra Carson Stanley, eds., 1994).

9. H. G. Reza, *Blacks' Battle in the Military Likened to Gays'*, L.A. TIMES, June 14, 1993, at A3.

10. Christopher Looby, *"As Thoroughly Black as the Most Faithful Philanthropist Could Desire": Erotics of Race in Higginson's Army Life in a Black Regiment*, in RACE AND THE SUBJECT OF MASCULINITIES 71 (Harry Stecopoulos & Michael Uebel, eds., 1997).

11. David Ari Bianco, *Echoes of Prejudice: The Debates over Race and Sexuality in the Armed Forces*, in GAY RIGHTS, MILITARY WRONGS: POLITICAL PERSPECTIVES ON LESBIANS AND GAYS IN THE MILITARY 47, 61 (Craig A. Rimmerman, ed., 1996).

12. For arguments that gay rights analogizing often elides important historical nuances, see Chandan Reddy, *Time for Rights? Loving, Gay Marriage, and the Limits of Legal Justice*, 76 FORDHAM L. REV. 2849 (2008); CHAUNCEY, *supra* note 5; Randall Kennedy, *Marriage and the Struggle for Gay, Lesbian, and Black Liberation*, UTAH L. REV. 781, 788 (2005).

13. JUDITH BUTLER, GENDER TROUBLE: FEMINISM AND THE SUBVERSION OF IDENTITY (1990).

14. Russell K. Robinson, *Racing the Closet*, 61 STAN. L. REV. 1463 (2009).

15. Marlon Riggs, *Black Macho Revisited: Reflections of a SNAP! Queen*, in BLACK MEN ON RACE GENDER, AND SEXUALITY: A CRITICAL READER 306–7 (Devon W. Carbado, ed., 1999).

16. Watkins v. U.S. Army, 875 F. 2d 699 (9th Cir. 1989); Josh Rosenthall & Christopher Contreras, *Piling One Prejudice onto Another*, Feb. 23, 2010 (Center for American Progress), http://www.americanprogress.org/issues/2010/02/prejudice_another.html.

17. Keith Boykin, One More River to Cross: Black and Gay in America 218–20 (1996).

18. Newsweek, Feb. 1, 1993.

19. Mary Fainsod Katzenstein, *The Spectacle of Life and Death: Feminist and Lesbian/Gay Politics in the Military*, in Gay Rights, Military Wrongs: Political Perspectives on Lesbians and Gays in the Military 229, 233–34 (Craig A. Rimmerman, ed., 1996).

20. For an indication of how marriage equality proponents have mobilized race in the context of litigation, see Russell K. Robinson, "Marriage, Equality, and Post-racialism," paper presented at the Social Justice and Public Service conference Race, Sexuality, and Social Justice, Santa Clara, CA, Apr. 13, 2012. For a critique of how gay rights proponents have employed *Loving v. Virginia*, the case that rendered antimiscegenation laws unconstitutional, in their advocacy, see Reddy, *supra* note 13. Significantly, and as I have argued elsewhere, I am not arguing that race/sexual orientation analogies should never be employed. *See* Devon W. Carbado, *Black Rights, Gay Rights, Civil Rights*, 47 UCLA L. Rev. 1467 (2000). Robin Lenhardt's work, for example, provides a sense of how one might engage in this kind of comparative project. *See* R. A. Lenhardt, *Forgotten Lessons on Race, Law, and Marriage: The Story of* Perez v. Sharp, in Race Law Stories 343 (Rachel F. Moran & Devon W. Carbado, eds., 2007); R. A. Lenhardt, *Beyond Analogy:* Perez v. Sharp, *Antimiscegenation Law, and the Fight for Same-Sex Marriage*, 96 Cal. L. Rev. 839 (2008).

21. This slogan appeared on the December 2008 cover of the *Advocate* magazine and has circulated more broadly in gay rights discourses about marriage equality. For an indication of the extent to which this is so, see Robinson, *supra* note 20.

ABOUT THE CONTRIBUTORS

Greg Robinson is professor of history at l'Université du Québec À Montréal. He is a specialist in North American ethnic studies and US political history, and teaches courses on African American history, twentieth-century US foreign policy, and American immigration history. He is the author of *By Order of the President* and *After Camp*.

Robert S. Chang is a professor of law at Seattle University School of Law. He writes primarily in the area of race and interethnic relations and is the executive director of the Fred T. Korematsu Center for Law and Equality. He is the author of *Disoriented: Asian Americans, Law, and the Nation-State*.

Taunya Lovell Banks is the Jacob A. France Professor of Equality Jurisprudence at the University of Maryland School of Law. She writes about the continuing impact of gender, race, racial formation, and racial hierarchies on the quest for social equality. She is a coeditor of *Screening Justice—The Cinema of Law: Significant Films of Law, Order and Social Justice*.

Devon W. Carbado, is a professor of law at the UCLA School of Law and recently served as the vice dean of the faculty. He writes in the areas of critical race theory, employment discrimination, criminal procedure, constitutional law, and identity. He is the author of *Acting White? Rethinking Race in Post-Racial America* (with Mitu Gulati) and editor of *Black Men on Race, Gender and Sexuality: A Critical Reader*.

Cheryl Greenberg is the Paul E. Raether Distinguished Professor of History Trinity College. Her areas of expertise include African American history, race and ethnicity in the United States, twentieth-century US history, and civil rights. She is the author of *"Or Does It Explode?" Black Harlem in the Great Depression* and *Troubling the Waters: Black-Jewish Relations in the American Century*.

Tanya Katerí Hernández is a professor of law at Fordham University School of Law. Her primary areas of interest include comparative civil rights, employment discrimination, critical race theory, Latin American studies, Latino studies, ethnic studies, trusts and estates, and comparative inheritance law. She is the author of *Racial Subordination in Latin America: The Role of the State, Customary Law, and the New Civil Rights Response.*

Scott Kurashige is a professor in the School of Interdisciplinary Arts and Sciences at the University of Washington Bothell. He is the author of *The Shifting Grounds of Race: Black and Japanese Americans in the Making of Multiethnic Los Angeles* and coauthor, with Grace Lee Boggs, of *The Next American Revolution: Sustainable Activism for the Twenty-First Century.*

Stephen Steinberg is a Distinguished Professor at the City University of New York's Urban Studies Department. He is an internationally renowned authority on race and ethnicity in the United States. He is the author of *Race Relations: A Critique* and *The Ethnic Myth: Race, Ethnicity, and Class in America.*

Clarence Walker is a professor of history at the University of California, Davis. His research interests include black American history: 1450–present; nineteenth-century social and political history of the United States; history of sexuality, film, and popular culture. He is the author of *The Preacher and the Politician: Jeremiah Wright, Barack Obama, and Race in America* (with Gregory D. Smithers) and *We Can't Go Home Again: An Argument About Afrocentrism.*

Eric K. Yamamoto is the Fred T. Korematsu Professor of Law and Social Justice at the University of Hawaii William S. Richardson School of Law. He is known for his legal work and scholarship on civil rights and racial justice, with an emphasis on redress for historic injustice. He is the author of *Interracial Justice: Conflict and Reconciliation in Post–Civil Rights America* and *Race, Rights, and Reparation: Law and the Japanese American Internment* (with Margaret Chon, Carol Izumi, Jerry Kang, and Frank Wu). His chapter is coauthored with **Amanda O. Jennsen**, a 2014 graduate of the University of Hawaii School of Law and a progressive family law practitioner with Hartley and McGehee in Hawaii.

INDEX

www.ingramcontent.com/pod-product-compliance
Lightning Source LLC
Chambersburg PA
CBHW031411270326
41929CB00010BA/1406